Culture and Critique

Culture and Critique

An Introduction to the Critical Discourses of Cultural Studies

Jere Paul Surber

The University of Denver

WestviewPress

A Division of HarperCollins*Publishers*

Figure 4.1 is reprinted from *New Introductory Lectures on Psycho-Analysis* by Sigmund Freud, translated by James Strachey, translation copyright © 1965, 1964 by James Strachey. Reprinted by permission of W.W. Norton & Company, Inc. We also acknowledge Sigmund Freud © copyrights, The Institute of Psycho-Analysis and the Hogarth Press, for permission to quote from *The Standard Edition of the Complete Psychological Works of Sigmund Freud,* translated and edited by James Strachey.

Figure 6.8 is reprinted from *Structural Anthropology, Volume 1,* by Claude Levi-Strauss. English translation copyright © 1993 by Basic Books. Reprinted by permission of Basic Books, a division of HarperCollins Publishers, Inc.

Figure 8.1 is reprinted from Richard Johnson, "What Is Cultural Studies Anyway?" *Social Text* 16 (vol. 6, no. 1, Winter 1986/87), p. 47. Copyright © Duke University Press. Reprinted with permission.

Published in 1998 in the United States of America by Westview Press, 5500 Central Avenue, Boulder, Colorado 80301-2877, and in the United Kingdom by Westview Press, 12 Hid's Copse Road, Cumnor Hill, Oxford OX2 9JJ

Library of Congress Cataloging-in-Publication Data
Surber, Jere Paul.
   Culture and critique : an introduction to the critical discourses
of cultural studies / Jere Paul Serber.
      p. cm.
   Includes bibliographical references and index.
   ISBN 0-8133-2046-1.—ISBN 0-8133-2047-X (pbk.)
   1. Culture—Study and teaching.   2. Culture—Philosophy.
3. Critical theory.   4. Discourse analysis.   5. Social sciences—
Philosophy.   I. Title.
HM101.S947   1998
306'.071—dc21   97-29379
                                                                        CIP

The paper used in this publication meets the requirements of the American National Standard for Permanence of Paper for Printed Library Materials Z39.48-1984.

10   9   8   7   6   5   4   3   2   1

Contents

Acknowledgments

This work is a genuinely collective project, involving not only my own study and thought but that of the many students and colleagues in dialogue with whom I learned what now appears between its covers. I thank them one and all for their patience, generosity, and support. Most of all, however, I am grateful for their continually "holding my feet to the fire," for reminding me that the enterprise of cultural critique must remain constantly in touch with the joys, sufferings, and hopes of real human beings who are trying to navigate their diverse ways through the labyrinth of everyday life in the contemporary world—and for never letting me forget that it can still be changed for the better. If I did not learn your lessons well enough, be assured that I'm still trying.

Several notes of special thanks are also in order. My colleagues in the department of philosophy at the University of Denver have, over many years, provided a warm home for me—someone who in most places would have been regarded as an intellectual transient or worse. Professor M. E. Warlick of the department of art and art history has been one of the fixed stars in my intellectual firmament for these many years, and I thank her for sharing in so many of my academic and intellectual adventures at the "margins of the modern mind." If Sophia has a face, it is hers. I should also like to express my appreciation for the staff at Westview Press, especially my text editors, Melanie Stafford and Rebecca Ritke, whose thoughtful and perceptive suggestions have managed to remove much of the detritus of a Roman Catholic and later German education from my often Teutonic writing style.

Most of all, I want to thank my "partner" (in many more senses than I could enumerate), Karen C. Smith. She, more than anyone, provided the energy and support that allowed me to bring this project to a conclusion. And I have to thank my son Guy not only for the space to work but for keeping me at the cutting edges of popular culture as only an early teen can. He is certainly the most exacting and critical semiotician that I know.

Jere Surber
Denver, Colorado

Introduction:
Theorizing Culture,
Practicing Criticism

It is difficult to imagine a time at which human beings were entirely satisfied with the conditions of their lives. It is equally hard, if not impossible, to conceive of a state of affairs either natural or cultural to which every person or group would give its unqualified assent. In fact, the most archaic narratives we have, from mythologies to founding religious texts, to the earliest histories of world civilizations, are full of conflict, opposition, and revolt against established order. Since the beginnings of documented human association, human culture and its implicit critique seem to have developed hand in hand.

However, the subject of this book is not an implied, vague dissatisfaction with a particular policy, institution, or order of things; it is rather the various explicit and particular critical conceptions of and articulations about culture that have influenced our common understanding of ourselves and our societies. These conceptions can be grouped into certain categories. Each type or style of cultural critique is founded on certain assumptions, proceeds more or less methodically from that foundation, and implies definite judgments about the nature, values, and ends of what is being criticized.

In the European tradition, such an articulated critical enterprise can be regarded as commencing with the interrogations of **Socrates** (470–399 B.C.), the Athenian gadfly usually credited with founding the discipline of philosophy. Socrates, who apparently wrote nothing of note himself, is known primarily through the various Dialogues of **Plato** (427–347 B.C.), in which he appears as the central figure. It is virtually impossible to disentangle the views of Socrates from those of his student-chronicler, but Socrates appears to have been instrumental in bringing to prominence several conceptual distinctions that are important for understanding the development of our views of culture and its critique.

Even before Socrates the Greeks had come to a critical differentiation between natural and human phenomena. As early as the seventh or eighth century B.C.— as evidenced by the *Iliad* and the *Odyssey*—it had become customary to distinguish those objects in the surrounding world that appeared to remain always and everywhere the same—plants, animals, the seasons, the stars, and so forth—from

1

others that seemed to vary from time to time and place to place, such as languages, customs, laws, political institutions, and so on. The Greeks came to refer to the former sorts of things collectively as *physis*, or what we would roughly translate as nature, and to the latter as *nomos*, or, approximately, custom or perhaps even culture. The crucial point of this distinction was that while nature, *physis*, provided the fixed context to which human beings could do nothing else but adjust their lives, human-made things and institutions, *nomoi* (plural of nomos), could, at least in principle, be changed by human activity.

There was, however, a crucial problem in this distinction, as Socrates seems to have recognized. As he went about Athens talking with his fellow citizens, he noticed that most persons tended unthinkingly to hold firm opinions about existing values, practices, and institutions that made these *nomoi* appear to be as stable and unchangeable as the natural phenomena of *physis*. Many of the Platonic dialogues, such as the *Euthyphro*, portray encounters between Socrates and another Athenian in which Socrates attempts to shake his interlocutor's complacency by questioning his received opinions about the existing cultural world. Often the opinions of Plato's interlocutors reflected what might be called the common sense prevailing in that particular society at that time. In this respect, Socrates can be fairly regarded as the first cultural critic (in the sense indicated above), since his task was to call into question the commonsensical conviction of the truth of widely held opinions—opinions that on further discussion turned out to be as unstable and variable as the cultural phenomena that they concerned.

Socrates's manner of questioning widely held but unvalidated opinions naturally led him to take another important step. In examining the network of opinions that make up what we call common sense, he found not only that many opinions turned out to be inconsistent with one another, but also that some opinions seemed to stand the scrutiny of his questioning better than others. In a case where his interlocutor came to contradict himself, Socrates concluded that the other's opinion *(doxa)* on a given topic could not amount to knowledge *(epistēmē)*, since to maintain, at the same time, both that something is a certain way and also that it is not, is self-canceling and amounts to saying nothing at all. On the other hand, some commonsensical opinions, even on sustained questioning, at least failed to result in contradiction. In such cases, Socrates tended to regard them as meeting at least the minimal conditions for qualifying as "true belief," subject, of course, to further investigation. Thus, while Socrates stopped short of claiming that these latter opinions, or *doxai*, should straightaway be counted as knowledge or *epistēmē*, he did take their withstanding critical scrutiny while others did not as indicating an important distinction between those things that we can legitimately claim to know and those that we either cannot consistently assert or can merely believe without any real evidence in their favor.

Even if he had stopped at this point, Socrates would already have established a rudimentary basis for a critical approach to culture. For beginning with the distinction between *physis* and *nomos*, the natural and the human or cultural, his questioning established that especially in the sphere of the latter, what persons believed on the basis of common sense or tradition was often either an arbitrary expression of personal or societal prejudice or downright inconsistent and ultimately unintelligible. And of those beliefs that survived at least initial interrogation, he intimated that there might be a method of proceeding that would allow us to discriminate between what could be fairly regarded as knowledge backed by sound reason and argument and what must remain, at best, likely stories.

Of course, it is probable that Socrates went on to take the step into philosophy proper by developing the first widely influential doctrine about the ultimate grounds of truth: the famous Theory of Forms or Ideas. This theory held that beyond the observable, mutable things of the world presented to the senses, whether natural or cultural, there must be another realm of stable and unchangeable entities, that of forms or ideas apprehended not by the senses but by the soul or mind and on the sole basis of which the mutable things of the world of appearance could be known.

Whether such a theory (or something like it) is required by a critique of culture has remained controversial throughout subsequent European history, but it did lead to another distinction, made most forcibly by Plato's one-time disciple **Aristotle** (384–322 B.C.), which is crucial for the critique of culture. This is the distinction between **theory** *(theoria)* and **practice** *(praxis)*. According to Aristotle, *theoria* and *praxis* were the two most important forms of human activity, the former involving the intellect's coming to apprehend, categorize, and articulate what is constant, unchanging, and intelligible, and the latter having to do with voluntary human activity in altering what can be changed about ourselves, the world around us, and our relationships to it. Aristotle acknowledged the importance of theoretical contemplation of such apparently eternal things as mathematics, the ultimate forms of motion, and the "fixed stars." He also seemed to suggest that such human phenomena as politics and ethics might likewise obey certain stable laws that appropriate theoretical activity could apprehend and articulate. Further, it was especially the theoretical consideration of these human cultural spheres that could provide the knowledge necessary for voluntary human action aimed at changing them, hopefully for the better. In turn, such *praxis* might provide further evidence for theory to consider in determining what actions might be most effective or what results might be most desirable.

While the discourse of philosophy and that of cultural critique have not always been identical throughout European history, the two traditions nonetheless can be traced to a common set of fundamental concerns. They also share certain important assumptions and terminological distinctions, and they have borrowed insights, concepts, and methods from one another. Especially at the level of methodology and operative concepts, the two have always intersected in certain areas, at times to a greater or lesser degree depending on the specific approaches in question and the particular historical period being considered. Most of all, however, for neither philosophy nor cultural critique can the received views of common sense or general opinion be taken at face value: No culture can be regarded as self-justifying in the face of theoretical inquiry and no human institution can be considered immune to change through further human activity.

What Is Culture?

History has left us no generally consensual definition of culture, nor could any completely satisfactory definition be given. We have already seen that culture, understood in a very general sense approximating the Greek *nomos,* can be contrasted with nature, or *physis.* This contrast assumes that one can distinguish between what is naturally produced and hence inalterable by human volition, and what is humanly produced and thus subject, at least in principle, to voluntary human intervention. But problems immediately arise. On the one hand, as Plato and Aristotle had already suggested, human beings are themselves part of nature and possess their own human nature subject to principles that are to some extent inalterable. If this is true, then human cultural products, institutions, and even history itself may be subject to natural laws that are just as binding as those governing nature's lower orders. On the other hand, what at one time might have been regarded as immutable laws of nature might well turn out to be alterable by deliberate human actions and policies, as modern research into ecosystems and genetics well illustrates. So even a basic attempt to define culture by contrasting it with nature is unsettled by ambiguities, imprecisions, and uncertainties.

However, we should not conclude from all this that culture is a meaningless or vacuous concept. If we were to attempt to avoid using this difficult concept altogether, we would have to invent another no less problematic to do its semantic work. Rather, in the present work, we will view *culture* as a term that is context-specific—that is, one that takes its meaning from the particular context, both historical and conceptual, in which it is being used. For the purposes of our discussion of various types of cultural critique, the most important point to remember is that *the operative definition of culture is inseparable from the type of critique being pursued, as the two constantly interact with and influence one another.* On the one hand, each way of regarding the task of critique implies a specific conception of culture to which it applies itself or over which it ranges. Every notion of critique presupposes or projects a certain field of cultural phenomena, an extensional definition of culture, to which it is applicable. Conversely, already implicit in every definition of culture with which we might begin is a particular understanding of critique that would be appropriate to it. One of my major aims in authoring this text is to enable readers to understand the most historically influential and important ways in which culture and its critique have influenced and defined one another.

It will make our task somewhat easier if we begin by making a few distinctions between the various sorts of contexts within which the term *culture* functions. For our purposes, the most important contexts are those of **disciplines, theories,** and **discourses.**

For various historical reasons, we are all probably most familiar with those contexts provided by the existing academic disciplines. Since the beginning of modern university studies in the eighteenth century, the general realm of theoretical inquiry has tended toward segmentation into various **disciplines,** each concerned with a particular field of objects or phenomena encountered in human experience. Typically, this division of theoretical disciplines has been reflected in the organization of the university into various administrative departments, in the proliferation of various professional organizations, in the founding of scholarly journals, and so forth. Particularly in the nineteenth century, with the rise of the various social or human sciences, some of these disciplines have taken culture (or some aspect of it) as their particular area of investigation. Thus, for example, in most contemporary universities, we find departments of anthropology (or ethnography), linguistics, sociology, social psychology, political science, history, literature, art history, and so on. Each of these disciplines is concerned with culture or one of its aspects.

Once this division of theoretical inquiry occurred, each of these disciplines tended for some time to follow its own course of development in relative autonomy from the others. The result was that the theoretical concept of culture came to imply quite different things, depending on the way in which it functioned and the methods by which it was studied by practitioners of the various disciplines. For example, British anthropologist Edward Burnett Tylor, writing in 1871, defined culture in a very broad sense as "that complex whole which includes knowledge, belief, art, morals, custom and any other capabilities and habits acquired by man as a member of society." By contrast, the literary critic Matthew Arnold, at about the same time, defined culture in an equally broad but very different way as the "disinterested pursuit of perfection . . . simply trying to see things as they are, in order to seize on the best and make it prevail." Neither definition can be judged right or wrong; rather, each serves to delineate a broad area of inquiry appropriate to the interests and methods of the discipline within which it is taken to function.

The task of determining the meaning of *culture* within any particular discipline is made even more complex by the fact that each discipline tends to develop through competition among various general **theories** about the phenomena with which the discipline is concerned. For example, although anthropologists might accept Tylor's general characterization of culture as the concept more or less defining the field of their discipline, they might disagree over the proper way to explain the phenomena cited in the original definition. One anthropologist might choose to focus on the symbolic or communicative character of such phenomena while another emphasizes the role of culture in furthering the adaptation of a group to its physical environment. Each theory thus implies a somewhat different understanding of the basic notion of culture, although enough agreement remains among the various theories to permit all practitioners of cultural analysis to regard themselves as anthropologists.

However, over time, the list and configuration of the various disciplines and the theories maintained within any one of them have altered. There are many reasons for this. For our purposes, the most important reason is that, in a sense broader than that of the various disciplines, the meaning of what constitutes a theoretical inquiry has itself altered. In particular, whereas most of the recognized modern disciplines originally assumed that the procedures of the natural sciences served to set the procedural rules and define what a theoretical inquiry should be, this assumption began to be questioned on a broad scale quite early in the nineteenth century. This was especially true of those disciplines broadly concerned with the field of culture. As a result, questions about the very nature of the sort of inquiry the disciplines were pursuing began to emerge both within and across the established disciplines. Unlike competing theories within a discipline, which must share some common core of basic assumptions, such questions concerning the very meaning of theoretical inquiry gave rise to rival **paradigms,** or general styles of **discourse,** that cut across the boundaries of existing disciplines. By the first decades of the twentieth century, several paradigms, or discourses, had begun to emerge in competition with one another but allied in opposition to models derived from the natural sciences. Among them were Schleiermacher's and Dilthey's hermeneutics, Marx's dialectical materialism, Freud's psychoanalysis, and Husserl's phenomenology. The emergence of new discourses in the terms of which theoretical inquiry might be conducted has continued into our own time.

This emergence of new discursive frameworks for theoretical inquiry has had far-ranging effects both on the existing disciplines and on their subordinate theories. While most of the disciplines established in the past two centuries have, for various political and administrative reasons, continued to exist, their practitioners have become increasingly divided over which available paradigm or discourse is most appropriate to their field of inquiry. Today, for example, one is as likely to find a hermeneutic, semiotic, or Marxist researcher in the field of anthropology as in art history, literature, or religious studies.

To a considerable extent, these various discourses, operating within a single discipline, have tended to become identified with its most important competing theories. However, since such discourses transcend the limits of any particular discipline, concerned as they are with the nature of theoretical inquiry itself, they also tend to encourage theoretical formations from one discipline to link up with those of others that share the same discursive assumptions and vocabulary. Thus, by their very nature, such discourses or paradigms tend to encourage interaction and mutual enrichment across established disciplines, allowing problems to be posed that can be addressed only by drawing on the insights of various established disciplines. These mutual affinities in some cases have even given rise to new interdisciplinary entities within the academy, such as American studies, women's studies, gay/lesbian/bisexual studies, cultural studies, and so forth. Of course, all of this has important implications both for the meaning of culture and for its critique.

Approaches to Culture and Cultural Studies

Perhaps the most significant implication of these developments for the understanding of culture is that the meaning of the term has come to be increasingly discourse-specific rather than discipline- or theory-specific. It is probably now more informative to know in what discursive practice (or practices, since many hybrids are possible) a given author or researcher is engaged than to ask with what discipline they are involved, of which academic department they are a member, or what particular subject matter interests them. This makes sense because, as we have seen, the term *culture*, like *paradigm* or *discourse*, tends to be employed across disciplines.

As used in this book, *cultural studies* has both a general meaning and a more specialized one. In its broad and more theoretical sense, it indicates the range of modern discourses that go beyond disciplines and their particular theories, employing the notion of culture in a distinctive way and specifying certain critical practices as appropriate for analyzing given cultural activities, products, and institutions. In its narrower sense, it indicates a recently developed sort of discourse that first appeared in several British universities in the 1950s. While eclectically drawing on certain theoretical aspects of earlier forms of critical cultural discourse, cultural studies is oriented toward the analysis and practical critique of concrete, contemporary cultural distinctions that are based on and that propagate differentials in economic and political power.

This book is an introduction to cultural studies in both of these senses, and in fact, we could not discuss one without dealing with the other. On the one hand, understanding almost any text in recent cultural studies requires a detailed knowledge of the theoretical terms and critical strategies that it has deliberately "poached" from other discourses; this involves an acquaintance with the discursive traditions within which these terms and strategies first came to prominence. On the other hand, contemporary cultural studies is only one form of critical discourse that must take its place, both theoretical and historical, alongside other still vital and viable traditions, with which it often also contends. For this reason, contemporary cultural studies in the narrower sense itself must be subjected to a broader historical critique based on a sound understanding of other discourses and their paths of historical development.

Varieties of Critical Discourse About Culture: A Historical and Conceptual Overview

This book is organized according to historical chronology as well as conceptual development in cultural criticism. The sequence in which the various critical discourses are discussed is roughly chronological, based on the historical order in which the most important, founding texts of the discourse first appeared. However, as each discourse has undergone its own course of development up to the present and each chapter traces a particular line of development, there is necessarily a good deal of historical overlap among the various sections. Since a fairly clear course of conceptual development can be discerned within the historical sequence, a brief overview of this progressively unfolding "argument" among various schools of thought can serve as a convenient synopsis of the different ways in which culture and critique have been and are still being defined.

The Liberal Humanism of the Enlightenment Era

The beginning of the modern era is usually associated with the period of European history known as the Enlightenment, which commenced sometime toward the end of the sixteenth century and lasted until the French Revolution in 1789. While a great number of ideas are typically associated with the Enlightenment—the ascendance of the secular over the sacred, the rise of modern science, the belief in unlimited progress, and the modern conception of democracy, to name some of the most often cited—perhaps the single most important feature of the Enlightenment was its self-consciously critical stance. If the thinkers of the Enlightenment agreed on any single point, it was that all received beliefs, whether religious, ethical, philosophical, historical, or commonsensical, must be subjected without exception to the most thoroughgoing critique. Enlightenment thought emerged as a critical reaction, a protest on behalf of reason against what were regarded as the prevailing superstitions, prejudices, and outright falsehoods inherited from the medieval period, which was considered a "dark age." The critical undertakings of the Enlightenment, however, faced serious opposition from the prevailing cultural authorities: the church and the aristocracy, in conjunction with absolute monarchy. Enlightenment thinkers tended to speak of culture interchangeably with civilization, which implied barbarism as its opposite. For them, no term was more apt than *barbarism* to characterize the superstitions and prejudices inherited from the medieval period. Thus, philosophical critique during the Enlightenment was not directed at culture but rather launched against the barbarism of religious and secular authority on behalf of culture, or civilization. Since culture, or civilization, was directly bound up with the values (such as those mentioned above) that Enlightenment figures wished to promote, their critical practice usually took the form of asserting these values against practices and institutions that tended to suppress or undermine them.

Enlightenment thinkers most often invoked the human capacity to reason—loosely understood as a spirit of free and open inquiry directed against the blind acceptance of dogma backed by authority—to validate their critical pronouncements. They tended to view culture or civilization as a product of the advance of reason, and they threw the weight of their talents on reason's side against the still very powerful authoritarian forces that opposed it.

As this tradition continued, the notion of reason came gradually to be joined with an ideal of what human beings could be and accomplish in a civilized society, free of the prejudices of the past. Thus, the critique was aimed not only at producing a civilized social condition in which rational human nature could flourish but also at creating rational human beings capable of fulfilling their roles in such an order. This tradition has often been called **liberal humanism:** liberal by virtue of its opposition to artificial constraints, especially of church and state, on human achievement; humanist because of its focus on the realization of human potential as the highest aspiration of both nature and history.

The Romantic Reaction Against the Enlightenment: Hermeneutics

Even before the French Revolution, doubts about this ideology of the Enlightenment had already begun circulating among writers such as Jean-Jacques Rousseau and the young Johann Wolfgang von Goethe. Their doubts were amply confirmed for many by the bloody and seemingly futile outcome of the French Revolution. Particularly in German-speaking countries, close observers of the revolution were troubled by the Enlightenment concepts of abstract reason, history as material progress, and the individual as its focal point. Beginning with such thinkers as Herder, Kant, Fichte, and the early Romantics, all admirers of Rousseau, the logical and mechanistic notion of reason that had developed during the Enlightenment was either altered in favor of a more ethical or practical conception or else rejected in favor of imagination as the central human faculty. In place of the Enlightenment's tendency to view genuine history as commencing with the critique of medieval superstition and prejudice and moving ever forward through scientific and technological progress, history increasingly was viewed not as a bold charge into the future but as a reverent recovery of the past and its traditions. The individual increasingly came to be seen not as the final result of nature and culture viewed mechanistically, but as part of a larger and more complex natural organism that embraced human beings both individually and collectively.

All this prepared the way for a new critical discourse, that of **hermeneutics**, which began to emerge at the turn of the nineteenth century. First in the German theological seminaries and later in such fields as literature and history, this new discourse insisted that the primary human relation to the world was not that of description and explanation, of objective observer to observed object, but of communication and interpretation, of reader to text. Within the discourse of hermeneutics, culture was viewed as the sum of human productions, all regarded as **texts** to be read and interpreted. From this perspective, reading was not so much a matter of rational argumentation as it was a creative or re-creative act, a process whereby the meanings contained in cultural texts were reconstructed in the imagination of the reader. The idea of progress through scientific and technological innovation, so important in the Enlightenment, was replaced by a sense of belonging to a tradition that enabled the reader to understand its texts even as it was further developed in the reader's imaginative appropriation of those texts in new ways. While the liberal humanism of the Enlightenment was not entirely abandoned, the individual human being came to be viewed more as a limited circuit or conduit in a broader process of the production of cultural meaning than as an end in itself.

However, the notion of critique, which had been so confident and robust in the Enlightenment, became more tentative and ambiguous in hermeneutics. Certainly there was an important critical strain in hermeneutic discourse, especially with regard to texts that were held to be divinely inspired. Indeed, modern hermeneutic discourse originated, to a great extent, among Biblical scholars who sought to apply to sacred texts the same historical and critical methods of reading and interpretation that other scholars had been applying to secular texts. To the extent that hermeneutic discourse undermined any presumed authoritativeness of certain types of texts and subjected them to principles and procedures of interpretation rooted in the imagination of the reader, it fostered a generally critical attitude. But the very move by which hermeneutics turned all human cultural productions into texts of roughly equal standing and subjected them to the interpretation of the individual reader deprived it of any solid ground for making critical judgments about either the contents of the texts or the actual historical or political forces that gave rise to their production.

Demystifying Romantic Attitudes: Materialist Critique

For thinkers of a more radical critical persuasion, the discourse of hermeneutics seemed to mystify a good deal more than it demystified. Beginning in the 1830s and 1840s, such young radicals as Ludwig Feuerbach and Karl Marx firmly rejected the hermeneutic textualization of all cultural production, its operative model of reading ultimately guided by the subjective imagination, and its backward-looking view of history. All of this, together with hermeneutics' intellectual ties to liberal Protestantism, struck them not only as idealistic constructions out of touch with the real driving forces of culture and history but as conduits by which all the old religious and political superstitions attacked by the Enlightenment might be reintroduced. Hermeneutic discourse, they asserted, was unable to provide a genuine critique of culture precisely because it ultimately reduced such an enterprise to the "subjective imagination" of the individual reader.

To the subjective idealism of hermeneutic discourse, the radical critics opposed **materialism**, a strand that had already appeared in the Enlightenment critical project but that was totally ignored by the hermeneutic stance. As early as the eighteenth century, such scientist-theoreticians as the Baron d'Holbach and Julien de LaMettrie had begun to oppose the mainstream liberal humanist tradition of the Enlightenment. They asserted that any approach to nature, society, or human beings that did not adopt the rigorously deterministic, mathematical, and materialist assumptions of the natural sciences was merely another form of superstitious mystification and hence no real advance over the preceding "dark ages." Another eighteenth-century development, less rigorously materialistic yet equally significant, was the beginning of modern political economy in the writings of such figures as Adam Smith. The classical political economists sought the principles underlying modern politics, culture, and human motivation in the material processes by which human beings and nation-states satisfied basic human needs, accumulated wealth, and devised systems by which goods and their monetary tokens circulated through market economies. Finally, although he was not a materialist, the French philosopher and literary figure Jean-Jacques Rousseau must be mentioned as the most forceful and widely read eighteenth-century critic of the liberal humanist commitment to the idea that scientific and technological progress was the most important index of civilization's advance. Rousseau's advocacy of a radical socialist view of democracy influenced both the materialist and the liberal humanist traditions of critical discourse.

Around the middle of the nineteenth century, Karl Marx and his frequent coauthor Friedrich Engels began drawing on certain "dialectical" methods for interpreting history, developed by the German Idealist philosophers, especially G.W.F. Hegel, in order to synthesize these earlier materialist and critical strands of the late Enlightenment into a new type of materialist critical discourse variously called **dialectical materialism, historical materialism,** or **scientific socialism.** According to Marx and Engels, the notion of culture was obscured and mystified if it was regarded as equivalent either to some set of presupposed values defining civilization or to a totality of tradition-bearing texts. Rather, culture must be regarded as a secondary phenomenon, a mere reflection of more fundamental historical forces, the explanation of which was ultimately to be sought in material economic processes. In Engel's famous phrase, just as the hand plow gave rise to the culture of feudalism, so the steam engine produced the cultural formations of industrial capitalism. To understand culture at any given point in history, one must look to the underlying material processes of economic production that gave rise to that culture. Culture was merely the reflection of those processes in the realm of human psychology and society.

It should be noted that Marxist materialism, like the liberal humanism of the Enlightenment but even more explicitly, was guided by a deep-seated practical and critical impulse. As the young Marx himself wrote, "The philosophers have only *interpreted* the world, in various ways; the point, however, is to *change* it." True to this dictum, instead of beginning with a particular view of culture as setting the agenda for critique, Marx tended throughout his long career as a theorist and activist to adapt his thinking about culture to his primary critical and practical aim. Ultimately, this aim was to overthrow the prevailing capitalist economic system, which he regarded as intrinsically alienating to human existence, irrationally self-limiting of its own productive potential, and destructive of individual and social human development and creativity. Marx's critique of culture was merely a preliminary strategy preparing the way for concrete political action.

Even so, cultural critique was indispensable to Marx's practical project. For in Marx's view, even though culture was but a psychological and social reflection of the more fundamental economic realities of industrial capitalism, culture did serve to stabilize and reinforce the status quo. Culture, understood as civilization, not only rendered oppressive economic realities palatable and even attractive, as Rousseau earlier had suggested. It also insulated contemporary economic and social arrangements from fundamental change by making them appear natural and inevitable, and it operated through its legal and political aspects to enforce the existing social and political configuration against those who would challenge it. Thus, the task of Marxist cultural critique was to begin dismantling the dominant capitalist system by unmasking the various cultural forms in which the system perpetuated itself in the minds, practices, institutions, and lives of its subjects.

One of the central operating assumptions of Marx, Engels, and their followers was that the scientific study of social and historical phenomena, the critique of culture, and revolutionary political practice were inseparable. However, many who were concerned with similar issues did not accept these assumed connections as either obvious or axiomatic. Throughout most of the nineteenth century, Marxian discourse represented a decidedly marginal and radical alternative both to the discourse of mainstream social science, the methods of which were borrowed by and large from the mechanistic models of the Enlightenment, and to hermeneutic discourse, which by midcentury had begun to stake a claim as the proper "method" for understanding human social and cultural phenomena. In the works of such theorists of the social sciences as Wilhelm Dilthey and Max Weber, these two strands became intertwined, though sometimes uneasily, in significant ways. Leaving aside objections to the radical political implications bound up with materialist discourse, such thinkers viewed even Marx's sophisticated version of materialist cultural critique as ultimately reductionistic, an attempt to explain the irreducible and unique features of human social and cultural interaction at the cost of jettisoning their most distinctive and important characteristics, thus explaining little. However, many viewed the mechanistic and hermeneutic alternatives as either equally reductionistic in their own ways or as too dispersed in their seemingly interminable methodological disputes—or both.

From Society to Psyche: The New "Science" of Psychoanalysis

Thus, by the turn of the century, new paradigms of critical discourse began to emerge. The most immediately influential of these was the new "science" of **psychoanalysis** developed by Sigmund Freud. Freud, trained as a medical doctor in the field of neurology, had arrived at the conclusion, even before the turn of the century, that a significant number of the symptoms of his neurological patients could not be explained or treated on the basis of prevailing physiological models. However, neither could more humanistic paradigms based on rational self-control be brought to bear in the cases of patients who were clearly unable to understand, resist, or alleviate their symptoms, despite their declared wishes to do so. In the face of this dilemma, Freud took the novel step of postulating the existence of the **unconscious**, a part or layer of the human psyche that he situated between biological needs and impulses and that part of the psyche that was conscious, or self-aware, and in immediate touch with its environment. In attempting to understand this unconscious, Freud became convinced that it was formed out of desires, rooted in biology, that were denied access to the conscious part of the mind but remained operative in the unconscious psyche as repressed materials. This postulate provided Freud the key to an allegedly scientific exploration of a whole realm of human experience and behavior that until then had been the province mainly of creative artists, sages, and (to a limited extent) philosophers. Such phenomena as dreams, various forms of insanity, human sexual practices, mystical experience, artistic creativity, and even jokes and slips of the tongue could now be explained on the basis of unconscious processes linking physiological constitution with conscious awareness.

As his discoveries unfolded, Freud quite naturally expanded his research into the arena of human culture and society. Freud's own general approach to cultural and social issues was to view them, as Plato had in his *Republic*, as the "soul writ large," that is, as collective projections of processes and conflicts rooted in the psychodynamics of every human being. Against liberal humanism's concepts of self and culture, psychoanalysis asserted not only that individuals were generally unaware of the true wellsprings of their actions but also that culture could never be adequately understood or criticized purely in terms of conscious, rational standards. While Freud did develop a general theory of interpretation, he regarded it as scientifically grounded in the actual dynamics of the human psyche, unlike hermeneutic theory. And even though Freud accorded an important role to the material processes of human biology and physiology, he also believed, unlike materialist critics, that the proper direction of explanation and critique led from the individual psyche to society and culture rather than the other way around.

While Freud himself was concerned with cultural critique only in a limited way, his ideas were soon taken up by others who attempted to make psychoanalysis the basis for a comprehensive critique of culture. Taking the lead from some of Freud's later writings, some arrived at the conclusion that the principal problem facing modern society was the needlessly high degree of repression that its increasingly complex structures and institutions demanded of the individual. The Freudian psychoanalysis of the individual was thus expanded and put to work in the interests of a therapeutic critique of existing society and culture, culminating in various proposals and experiments designed to produce not only psychologically "healthy" individuals and social institutions but also the conditions that would promote and support them. However, psychoanalysis soon underwent attack both as a clinical practice and as a cultural theory—partly because of the bad press generated by the "crackpot" nature of certain schemes associated with it, partly due to critical disagreements about the validity of psychoanalysis's basic concepts and theories, and partly because of various uncritical biases that observers from other disciplines noticed in the general orientation of the new "science." Nonetheless, the explanatory and interpretive power of psychoanalysis was sufficient to allow it to enjoy a number of subsequent revivals, albeit often in heavily revised forms.

Semiological and Structural Critique: The New Science of Signs in Society

The other important discourse that arose around the turn of the century and began to exert an influence, though somewhat later than psychoanalysis, was **semiology** (also called **semiotics**). A few decades later, semiology gave rise to a **structuralist** development. As elaborated by Charles Sanders Peirce, and particularly by Ferdinand de Saussure in the first decades of the twentieth century, semiology was deliberately projected as a new "science that studies the life of signs within society." While Saussure's semiology took human linguistic communication as its point of departure and its central paradigm, it was by no means limited to the field of linguistics, which Saussure always regarded as a subfield within a much broader project. Rather, Saussure's semiology was to be a sort of "master science" that would elucidate the structural laws of signification governing all forms of human cultural production, interaction, and communication. Thus, semiology was conceived of as a discourse about culture that would, on the one hand, be comprehensive enough to embrace all recognized cultural phenomena, but on the other, would be free of the perceived reductionistic tendencies of the various versions of nineteenth-century social science.

Saussure's semiology was based on three assumptions. First, all distinctly human activity involves the use of signs, understood in the broadest sense as any arbitrary relation between a signifier and some mental concept with which it is customarily associated. Second, because the relation constituting the sign is not natural but arbitrary and variable, the meaning of a sign cannot consist in any intrinsic feature of the sign itself but can only be determined by the place it occupies in the entire system of signs to which it is related and from which it specifically differs. Third, although a sign—that is, the relation between a signified (an image or concept) and its signifier (the object, word, or gesture that provokes the image or concept)—is completely arbitrary, specific signs can have a determinate meaning by virtue of the stable structural features of the entire semiological system to which they belong.

From the point of view of cultural critique, semiology had two important implications. First, it permitted culture in general to be viewed as a total system of signification, operating independently of the individual psychologies of its participants. In this way it reversed the emphasis on subjective interpretation that was implicit in hermeneutic and psychoanalytic discourse. Second, however, it contained an implicit critical dimension in its insistence on the arbitrariness, that is, the nonnatural character, of all signs. Since no cultural formation or phenomenon can be viewed as natural and hence inalterable, semiology provided a critical vehicle for denaturalizing and relativizing any cultural configuration that had come to appear to its engaged participant as wholly natural, obvious, and unquestionable. This dimension of the semiological approach allowed it not only to counteract the materialist emphasis in cultural critique but also to appear to offer a much more sophisticated and nonreductive procedure for analyzing specific cultural activities and institutions than was available in materialist and other types of discourse.

Still, many who were familiar with the principal ideas of earlier, nineteenth-century forms of cultural critique found it difficult to accept semiology. The major difficulties with Saussure's semiology (and its offshoots) as a critical discourse lay in the extremity of its emphasis on **synchronic** as opposed to **diachronic** analysis and in its privileging of systematic structures to the almost total neglect of their effects on individual psychological functioning. Although Saussure realized that significational structures evolve over time (diachrony), such an investigation always remained for him secondary to the explication of structures functioning at a given cross-section of time (synchrony). Further, while he admitted that psychology could study the effects of various significational structures on the individual, it was the overall structure of a given sign system, viewed independently of the various idiomatic inflections given it by individuals, with which semiology was principally concerned. Put simply, then, in the name of the new science of semiology, Saussure and his structuralist offspring seemed to many critics to have rejected the relevance of both history and psychology to critical discourse.

Cultural Critique Between the World Wars: The Frankfurt School of Critical Theory

During the period between the world wars, cultural critics found the limitations of semiology and structuralism especially troubling. In Germany, in particular, the failure of the republican Weimar government and the rise of national socialism posed complex and novel problems with which neither the older Marxist materialist tradition nor the more recent semiological and structuralist discourse was prepared to deal. On the one hand, the victory of nationalist and fascist mass movements over their communist rivals called into serious question the Marxist theory of history on which the latter were based. On the other, the ultraright's successes in using modern mass communications media and organizational techniques to manipulate the populace opened up new prospects for political coercion unforeseen in any of the earlier critical paradigms.

The Institute for Social Research (often called the **Frankfurt School** because of its original location) was founded in 1923 as a response to such developments. The overall task of the **critical theory of society,** which is associated with this group, was twofold. First, while most members of the Frankfurt School rejected as simplistic and totalitarian the dominance of materialist discourse by what had become a Marxist orthodoxy (particularly of the Soviet or Leninist cast), they nevertheless remained committed to the general principles of materialist critique. However, they believed that Marx's historical materialism was in need of thorough reconstruction before it would be applicable to the drastic changes in cultural circumstances. Absent such a reconstruction, Marxists could not avoid the totalitarian abuses toward which they were heading in the Soviet system. Second, while their attitudes toward the traditional social sciences and Freudian psychoanalytic theory tended to be guarded, they nonetheless believed that both, with some revision, could be incorporated into a broader critical framework aimed at understanding the effects of modern mass media and social organization on the thought and behavior of individuals and social groups.

A further, more general aspect of the critical theory of the Frankfurt School was its attitude toward the overall critical project of the Enlightenment. Critical theorists of the Frankfurt School shared the reservations expressed in the critical discourse of the nineteenth century concerning the liberal humanist tendency to derive certain substantive human values from an abstract notion of rationality. Still, they agreed with the Enlightenment's affirmation that reason, suitably redefined and applied, was the privileged, indeed the only vehicle through which the genuine enlightenment and liberation of humanity could be accomplished. For the Frankfurt School of critical theory, the major importance of liberal humanism was to have commenced a historical project of human emancipation that had been temporarily derailed by the totalizing philosophical systems of German Idealism, from which Marx's materialist critique had taken its methodological cues. As the members of the Frankfurt School saw it, the Enlightenment project of liberation from dogmatic authoritarianism remained incomplete, and it was their aim to develop a critical discourse that would fulfill it. However, to accomplish this, such a discourse would itself have to avoid any dogmatic or theoretically aloof stance of its own, remaining actively engaged with culture as it concretely exists, altering along with changes in social structure and function, and most of all, practicing an ongoing and open-ended self-criticism of its own developed theories.

New Attacks on Liberal Humanism: Poststructuralist and Postmodernist Critiques

It was this reaffirmation of the liberal humanist strand of the Enlightenment, albeit in a heavily revised and self-critical form, that began to appear problematic in the period following World War II. German existentialist philosopher Martin Heidegger's famous "Letter on Humanism," which appeared in 1947, can be regarded as the opening salvo against the entire tradition of liberal humanist thought, including its modern critical forms. In this letter, Heidegger, drawing on his extensive writings beginning in the 1920s, charged that all European thought since Plato had been guided by a specifically metaphysical conception of Being. Heidegger's novel explanation of this most fundamental idea of all later European thought implied that this intellectual tradition would always pursue scientific knowledge and technical control of nature and culture at the expense of more direct and intimate experiences of them through art, interpersonal relationships, and even meditation. In the metaphysical definition of Being, human beings were viewed merely as one among many different kinds of things, albeit a type with its own specific essence. Heidegger claimed that this conception of a human being as a particular kind of thing with its own essential values lay at the basis of any humanism, including the modern, Enlightenment version. However, even as it provided a grounding for the human sciences and many modern cultural institutions, the concept of humanism ultimately obscured any more fundamental questioning about Being and our participatory engagement with it. Worse yet, in asserting a notion of rationality derived from the Enlightenment as an essential feature of human being, humanism served, even if inadvertently, to further the very technological attitudes that Heidegger believed should be criticized.

Heidegger's "antihumanism" (as his view was somewhat misleadingly characterized) became an important point of departure for the generation of post–World War II French intellectuals, most of whom had already been influenced by the Marxist existentialism of Jean-Paul Sartre and the structuralism of anthropologist Claude Lévi-Strauss, which sprang from Saussure's semiology during the 1930s and 1940s. Such figures as psychoanalyst Jacques Lacan, cultural historian Michel Foucault, and philosopher and literary critic Jacques Derrida came to be collectively referred to as **poststructuralists,** since despite many differences in their critical orientation and approach, they shared in common a rejection of structuralism as a viable critical discourse, at least in part under the influence of the antihumanist ideas of Heidegger and of Friedrich Nietzsche (who earlier had influenced Heidegger's own views).

Any general characterization of poststructuralism runs the risk of imposing an overarching structure on a group of thinkers whose critical tenets included the rejection of any such amalgamating or "totalizing" procedure. Nonetheless, one may with justification indicate several points of convergence among them with regard to their attitudes toward cultural critique.

First, their common rejection of semiological or structuralist methods was based on a shared conviction that if all structures, whether psychological, social, or cultural, were comprised of a set of specific differences among their basic elements, then the play of these differences must be more basic or fundamental than the structures to which they give rise. Just as semiology had revealed the arbitrary and nonnatural character of any specific cultural structuring of meaning, so the poststructuralists sought various interpretive strategies that would destabilize the structures themselves, showing that even such apparently well-regulated structures as language were actually products of an often chaotic and transgressive play of differences. Second, radicalizing the hermeneutic claim that meaning was nothing more than a product of the encounter between a reader and the open possibilities presented by a cultural text, they came to question the hermeneutic assumption that the consciousness of the reader could be a sufficiently stable site in which meaning could be produced. Taking their lead from Heidegger's critique of humanism and Lacan's revisions of psychoanalysis, they held that the notion of the subject as a fixed locus where meaning was somehow produced must itself be **deconstructed**—that is, shown to be a sort of idealist fiction that was itself constructed out of the play of language and its texts. Finally, when brought to bear against the historical materialism of Marxists and critical theorists of the Frankfurt School, the poststructuralist deconstruction of the unitary and meaning-producing subject implied that history could no longer be conceived of as a unitary narrative of rational, conscious, or collective human action. Further, materialism itself came to be viewed as just one of many types of metaphysical theory, all produced out of the play of the linguistic and conceptual differences constituting the structure of certain European texts. In the end, then, poststructuralism represented the most extreme intensification of the skeptical tendencies of the Enlightenment, shorn of any of its more constructive moral or political projects.

Though some have seen poststructuralism as a recent and sophisticated form of Nietzsche's nihilism and Heidegger's antihumanism, at least one important aspect of poststructuralist discourse suggests a somewhat different interpretation. Explicitly in Nietzsche and Foucault and at least implicitly in Derrida, the various differences presupposed, fixed, and maintained by the texts of existing cultural structures ultimately raise questions of power at the very concrete levels of language and signification, where such questions were formerly most difficult to confront. The liberal humanism of the Enlightenment, Marxian materialism, and in a more sophisticated way, the critical theory of the Frankfurt School all viewed differences in the distribution of power, whether among individuals or social groups, as questions of economic, social, and political structures that could, at least in principle, be altered by large-scale historical changes in the structures themselves. By contrast, the poststructuralists, well aware of the concrete historical failures of such projects of large-scale structural change, especially in the twentieth century, began to suggest a radically different approach to cultural criticism. First, they believed, we must stop thinking about power through metaphors borrowed from the physical sciences, which lead us to suppose that power is some quantitative feature of entities or aggregates that obey laws such as reciprocity, conservation, and so on. Indeed, in Foucault's view, power is not so much a function of political institutions and their ability to physically coerce in some external sense as it is a qualitative feature of the various sorts of cultural discourses, including those of the sciences, that have historically developed as ways in which we define ourselves, locate ourselves in a world, and act within it. And if we trace power to the forms in which it is most elementary and difficult to access, we will find that it functions in the realm of differences by which the very languages we speak, the metaphors we rely on, and the cultural texts we read and write unconsciously hierarchize and privilege one term over another—active/passive, light/dark, male/female, normal/abnormal, civilized/primitive, Western/Oriental, and so on in an endless and mutually reinforcing chain that privileges one term while marginalizing the other. It could thus be argued that it was the common critical task of the Lacanian decentered subject, Foucaultian genealogy, and Derridean deconstruction to trace the most basic operations of power to the cultural discourses and institutions that we most take for granted and hence are least likely to suspect of promoting political domination. Employing such strategies, we should thus be able to identify the subtle, hierarchized differences operative in cultural texts and initiate a process of subversion whereby what has been historically and textually subordinated and marginalized returns to disrupt the discourses that originally produced and maintained their marginality.

Cultural Studies: Contemporary Anglo-American Cultural Critique

At about the same time that poststructuralism was developing as a new critical discourse in Europe and attracting a growing audience in North America, another critical tradition was emerging at several British universities. Marxist and other materialist styles of critique had a long history in Great Britain, where Marx himself had lived during the last decades of his life and where he had written his magnum opus, *Das Kapital*. But for rather obvious reasons, this radical tradition had lain dormant during World War II. However, as Great Britain began to recover from the war, this critical tradition reemerged in a new and vital form that was closely attuned to cultural conflicts rooted in the long-standing class stratification of British society, which seemed increasingly oppressive and outdated in the postwar era. With the founding of the Centre for Contemporary Cultural Studies at the University of Birmingham in the 1950s, a number of various critical approaches began to coalesce into what has become a new critical discourse, that of **cultural studies**.

Like continental poststructuralism, cultural studies does not refer to a single doctrinal position but to a more loosely related set of attitudes and approaches toward cultural criticism. While some varieties of contemporary cultural studies have come to borrow heavily from the arsenal of critical tools developed by poststructuralism, their paths of development have been quite different and sometimes opposed.

Cultural studies is heavily indebted to the work, beginning in the 1950s, of the British literary critic, cultural historian, and social activist Raymond Williams; and its distinctive style, practical orientation, and general theoretical framework continue to bear traces of his influence. First, one important source of the basic ideas of cultural studies was the dissatisfaction of some literary scholars, best expressed in the early works of Williams, with the elitist character of British literary studies, based on a canon of "great works" that had virtually defined its field of inquiry for the previous century. Williams rejected the narrow, essentially humanist conception of culture as paradigmatically encountered in a canon of great works, and he sought to expand it not only to include but to emphasize popular or mass culture, a tendency already evident in the critical theory of the Frankfurt School. Second, in contrast to a view of cultural texts as finished products awaiting interpretation, cultural studies emphasizes the processes by which various cultural texts are produced, the various ways in which they are consumed, and the manner in which they maintain and contest existing social differences. Third, in ways often more explicit than in poststructuralism, cultural studies tends to view concrete power differentials, closely related to but never reducible to material features of existing society, as lying at the heart of cultural criticism. In articulating this idea, many working within this discourse have drawn on the earlier revisionist Marxist theories of Louis Althusser and Antonio Gramsci. Finally, cultural studies has tended to emphasize concrete analyses of specific forms of cultural domination—issues involving class, gender, race, ethnicity, sexual orientation, and so forth—at the expense of "higher-order" theorizing. For example, it has often focused on how the various forms of popular culture—film, television, rock music, youth fashion, and so on—not only entertain but also, at a more subtle level, promote and reinforce various racial, ethnic, and gender stereotypes. This gives cultural studies a distinctively activist and practical orientation in comparison with continental poststructuralism, which to practitioners of cultural studies has often seemed too abstract, remote, and jargon laden.

As the most recently developed critical discourse, cultural studies has both drawn on and furthered three significant developments in the current intellectual landscape. After more than a century of intense debate about appropriate methods of cultural critique, cultural studies has shared in the shift of emphasis away from further theorizing and toward more substantive analyses of concrete modes and sites where issues of power and dominance are contested in contemporary society. In doing so, its attitude toward methodological issues has been very open. Rather than defining itself in terms of one or another methodological orientation, cultural studies has very explicitly "poached" on other traditions of critical discourse, borrowing such analytical and critical tools from one or another as seem most appropriate and useful for the subject matter under consideration. Finally, given the broad notion of culture which this discourse assumes, its various topics cut across the more traditional fields of inquiry, making it necessarily cross- and interdisciplinary. It is a matter of heated debate, both within cultural studies circles and academic institutions at large, whether this critical discourse will or even should take its place alongside other recognized disciplines or whether it should remain a sort of "parapraxis" operating at the margins of other disciplines.

Recurrent Questions

As we discuss in much greater detail the various critical discourses that form the background of contemporary cultural critique, several crucial but difficult questions will continue to surface. It will be helpful to call explicit attention to them before we proceed any further. In a sense, they are philosophical questions about the nature of cultural critique itself. While each discourse, and even particular variants of a given discourse, will imply certain distinctive ways of responding to these questions, it should not be assumed that there is any single or final answer to them. Rather, these questions should be taken as a sort of broad grid or map allowing us to begin placing the various discourses in relation to each other. Most importantly, however, it is hoped that they will lead the reader to discover some of the intrinsic advantages and disadvantages of the various discourses and to formulate her or his own informed critical perspective on culture.

Locating the Critic in Relation to Culture

While critical discourses must initially be described by employing the more or less abstract framework of concepts, arguments, and strategies, they "live" at the concrete level where an actual critic employs them in the analysis of concrete cultural practices and institutions. This immediately raises a rather complex set of questions regarding the position of the critic with respect to the cultural formations that she or he is addressing. Three closely related issues are involved in analyzing any critical stance.

The first concerns the question of whether the critic's position is **immanent** or **transcendent**. For the purposes of cultural studies in the broad sense, the critic will almost always also be a participant in at least some of the practices and institutions that she or he sets out to analyze and critique. Indeed, some have even argued that any critical project presupposes an understanding based on some such engagement. Granting this, we can still ask what entitles a critic to claim that she or he can, in a sense, see or know something about a cultural formation that others similarly situated do not.

One response would maintain that any critical project presupposes that the critic has attained some sort of transcendent position from which vantage point she or he can see cultural practices as a whole and offer an analysis from the outside. Certain sorts of critical discourse in fact present themselves as precisely such "transcultural platforms." At the other extreme, it also has been held that there can be no truly transcendent position and that any critique is entirely immanent to the practices and institutions that it addresses. Both options are problematic. A transcendent notion of criticism runs the risk of simply imposing a set of theoretical prejudices on cultural formations, ultimately rendering itself irrelevant to the real problems involved. By contrast, a completely immanent notion suggests that the critic is actually only reproducing the very prejudices that she or he might have set out to dispel.

It seems clear that any viable critical discourse must presuppose some degree of cultural engagement on the part of the critic yet present a way by which the critic can achieve enough distance from the relevant cultural practices in order to be able to critique them without merely reproducing their operative prejudices. Exactly how these demands are met will vary with each (and within each) critical discourse, but it is important in every case to consider exactly what a given discourse assumes.

The second dimension of the broader issue concerns whether a given application of critical discourse should be regarded as **objective** or **subjective**. Most critical discourses are located between these extremes, since for reasons similar to those discussed above, it is probably impossible to make much sense of a purely objective or purely subjective stance. However, assuming that the physical sciences provide the closest approximation to an objective attitude, we should note to what degree a critical discourse seems to invoke or be based on scientific theories or methods. We will find that certain critical discourses, such as that of materialism, hew more closely to scientific tenets and thus claim an objective status for themselves, while others, like hermeneutics, tend to ally themselves more closely with more "subjective" practices, such as literary interpretation.

Finally, the scope asserted on behalf of a critical discourse should be kept in mind. Certain critical discourses aim at a *general* critique of cultural practices and institutions taken as a totality. Marx's historical materialist theory of capitalism tends in this direction. Others, like contemporary cultural studies, regard themselves as much more modest in scope, attacking particular *local* practices or institutions without pretending to offer any more general or comprehensive theory regarding culture as a whole. About the former, we must ask how effectively a general theory allows us to critique particular practices and institutions, about the latter whether more general theoretical assumptions are covertly being made in the practice of local critique.

Cultural Critique and the Problem of Values

Closely connected with the position of the critic in relation to culture is the question of the assumed values on which criticism rests. Again, the question seems to pose a dilemma. On the one hand, were there no sense on the part of the critic that at least some existing cultural practices were not as they should be and that, based on analysis and critique, they might be changed for the better, there would be no point in engaging in the difficult process of cultural critique at all. The very practice of cultural criticism presupposes that the critic must invoke certain values against prevailing cultural practices. On the other hand, doing so immediately opens the critic to the question of why her or his values, or the altered cultural practices that those values dictate, should be regarded as preferable to the values that she or he is challenging. Thus, if the critic (or a critical discourse) claims to be value-free, it is difficult to see what point there is to the enterprise of critique at all; if the critic assumes or asserts certain values as the basis for her or his critical practice, then the seemingly interminable process of justifying those values tends to postpone the initiation of critical practice indefinitely, or if the values remain unjustified, vitiates the practical conclusions of the critique.

Again, this is an open-ended question to which no final answer is forthcoming. However, it should alert us to the fact that every critical discourse makes certain value-laden assumptions that we should attempt to clarify as we come to understand the terms of the discourse. Perhaps we will find, as Socrates did long ago, that while we (or any critical discourse) might not be able to give some final justification for the values that we assume, we might be able to distinguish between values that are incoherent or self-defeating and those that appear worthy of further reflection and discussion.

The Practice of Self-Critique

To varying degrees, most if not all of the critical discourses that we will discuss have attempted to address the preceding two questions by including within their critical practice the notion of *self-critique*. While the immediate object of critical practice is, of course, existing cultural formations, including discourses and texts, any critical practice, once it has been articulated or acted on, must take its own place as a new element within the cultural formation with which it deals. The question then arises whether or to what degree this new configuration can be subjected to the same form of critique. For example, one might ask whether the establishment of a department of Marxist philosophy (as occurred at the University of Berlin in the 1950s) can be explained and critiqued on the basis of the sort of historical materialism that originally demanded its own institutionalization. Or, as is currently being done, practitioners of cultural studies can concern themselves with the effects on their own critical discourse and political commitments of becoming housed in academic departments or institutes.

Clearly, self-critique can never assume the form of a closed, seamless, and self-justifying circle, since self-critique, like the cultural critique in which it was originally engaged, is also directed toward practical change. Self-critique will always involve alterations and adjustments in the attitudes and assumptions of the critic, and this in turn will alter the stance of the critic toward other cultural configurations. However, one way of evaluating the various cultural discourses in relation to one another is to assess the degree to which they have practiced or are capable of practicing self-critique. How we view a given critical discourse should be determined in part by whether it allows for a significant dimension of self-critique and, if so, whether its critical approach to other cultural formations still seems adequate when applied to its own stance in relation to them.

Critique as Theory and Practice

From all that has been said so far, two things should be clear: First, any critical discourse will involve certain distinctive theoretical claims about the meaning and functions of culture; second, it will be directed toward practically altering that culture in certain ways specified by its theoretical commitments. Nonetheless, the degree of emphasis on theory or practice as well as the tightness of the fit held to obtain between them will vary from discourse to discourse. Critical discourses function between the extremes of purely theoretical investigations that often characterize the empirical social sciences and certain types of academic philosophy, and mere political rhetoric designed simply to persuade others, without further justification, to think or act as the speaker wishes. This suggests that the various critical discourses are positioned in a continuum, from those more concerned with theory construction and more willing to let the practical consequences take care of themselves, to those with a decidedly practical emphasis, which concern themselves with theory only insofar as it provides stratagems toward an end. Our historical survey suggests that the various discourses have tended to swing back and forth from one emphasis to another, both in relation to one another and in their own internal developments. Still, in assessing the merit of various discourses, it is important to be aware of specific characteristics such as these, as well as to take into account what the various discourses originally set out to accomplish.

1
The Critical Discourse
of Liberal Humanism

The first modern critical discourse arose during the Enlightenment. In fact, one might say that the defining characteristic of Enlightenment thought was a new, self-consciously critical attitude toward prevailing cultural practices and institutions. Although the broadly liberal humanist basis for the Enlightenment's cultural criticism has itself been attacked by virtually every subsequent critical discourse, we should not overlook its crucial role in initiating a project that has continued into our own time.

As we will see, the critical discourse that commenced in the Enlightenment involved several different strands. Still, the cultural critics of the Enlightenment all shared a number of important convictions; these permit us to refer to their collective orientation, despite their other differences, as that of liberal humanism. The first and most pervasive characteristic was a common opposition to any claim to truth or knowledge based solely on authority. At the beginning of the modern era, there were three major sources of authority of particular concern to Enlightenment thinkers: the church, the state, and Greco-Roman antiquity.

During the Middle Ages, the Roman Catholic church was the most important, pervasive, and powerful cultural institution. Although the universality of its influence had been seriously challenged in the early sixteenth century during the Reformation, the subsequent fragmentation of the Catholic church into various competing religious groups often resulted in an overall intensification rather than a waning of the influence of religious beliefs, practices, and institutions on culture. The bigotry, intolerance, and violence frequently resulting from adherence to opposed religious creeds provoked critical responses from early Enlightenment thinkers, who increasingly came to regard the institutionalized religions' demands of faith on the part of their followers as diametrically opposed to reason, to the human being's natural ability to adjudicate claims to truth for itself.

The Reformation was closely connected with the historical emergence of the modern nation-state, a geographical area with fixed boundaries under a single, centralized political authority. In many places in Europe, the nation-state first took the form of absolute monarchy, based on a theory of the divine right of kings, itself supported by the authority of religious doctrine. Again, while their concrete political views ranged over a wide spectrum, almost all Enlightenment critics agreed that the legitimate exercise of political authority was a secular question rather than a religious one and that in some form, the consent of the governed should play an important role in such considerations. Against the absolutist state as the primary locus of political right, the proponents of the Enlightenment came to assert the primacy of the individual as the ultimate bearer of political rights and the liberty of the individual as at least one of the aims of any legitimate state.

Both church and state often invoked the authority of antiquity to bolster their claims, especially in cases where scriptural authority was ambiguous or silent. Most influential were the Platonic doctrine of a natural political hierarchy and the Aristotelian view of a static cosmos articulated into eternally fixed genera and species. Enlightenment thinkers did not hesitate to cite antiquity for their own purposes, but they tended to shift emphasis from the more "primitive" Greeks to the more "civilized," practical, and (to their minds) republican Romans as their historical and intellectual forebears. The undermining of Aristotelian natural philosophy by the new mathematical sciences and the growing sense of the political order as dynamic and subject to purposive human intervention combined to produce a new sense of history as constituting a field of open-ended and indefinite human progress.

Thus, the Enlightenment's cultural critics tended to view their basic task as that of opposing one notion of culture—theocentric, authoritarian, and static—with the vision of another—anthropocentric, liberal, and progressive—which through their own intellectual and practical efforts should gradually replace the former. The strategies of cultural critique developed by the party of Enlightenment were, in turn, determined by this ubiquitous contrast between a barbaric culture of superstition, ignorance, and repression and the newly emergent civilized culture of well-grounded knowledge, individual liberty, and historical progress, the latter position fairly summed up in the phrase liberal humanism. The proponents of liberal humanism often tended to view themselves as a beleaguered band of civilized philosophes who firmly and optimistically believed that by spreading their gospel of Enlightenment primarily through their literary activities, they could gradually come to displace "medieval barbarism" with their own "modern civilization."

Like some later critical discourses, that of liberal humanism involved a number of distinguishable strategies of cultural critique that, intertwined in various configurations, remain influential today.

Skepticism and the Origins of Modern Critique

Probably the earliest and most straightforward type of cultural critique was that of skepticism, which involved both a general critical attitude toward all claims to knowledge on the basis of authority and a more specific process of challenging particular claims case by case. Socrates practiced a form of skepticism in his insistent interrogation of the opinions of his interlocutors and his unwillingness to make any final claims on his own part. A bit later, during Hellenistic times, a recognized school of skeptical post-Platonic philosophy emerged, carrying forward this strand of Socratic-Platonic thought. However, most ancient forms of skepticism were relatively ad hoc and piecemeal. Modern skepticism differs from them in its attempt to provide a systematic framework for identifying the various ways of knowing or types of knowledge claims and the specific sorts of arguments or considerations that can be brought against each.

One of the first and most enduring presentations of skepticism can be found in the *Novum Organum* (1620) of **Francis Bacon** (1561–1626), which was part of his comprehensive attempt to replace the old *Organon* of Aristotle with a new configuration of human knowledge conducive to the emergence of the "new science." However, Bacon's Theory of the Idols (the name he gave to his particular form of skeptical critique) was more than just a set of challenges to particular prevailing ideas or a narrow treatise on epistemological themes. Rather, it must be read as a genuine document of modern cultural critique, oriented as it is toward examining the various sources of human delusion and the manners in which they are institutionalized in culture.

Bacon identified four main sources of human error and delusion, which he referred to as idols, deliberately suggesting the distinction between barbarism and civilization discussed above. Also characteristic of Bacon's modern approach is his insistence that although the human capacity for self-delusion is natural, it must be seen as intimately connected with and reinforced by its institutionalization in cultural forms, which tend both to exaggerate and to perpetuate it. In his theory of the idols, Bacon offered an early example of what later thinkers would refer to as "ideological critique."

The first major source of human error Bacon identified as the idols of the tribe. Such errors and delusions arise from the general manner in which the human understanding operates. On the one hand, we must rely on sensory data to know the world around us, but such data are imprecise and give us no idea of the real physical mechanisms at work in the substances with which we are acquainted. On the other, we tend to organize and filter our sensations through abstract concepts, which take us even further from the real material causes underlying the data of the senses. We are thus naturally led to take for reality what is actually a highly selective and abstracted picture of our own making.

Second, Bacon called our attention to what he referred to as idols of the cave. This phrase, of course, recalls Plato's famous allegory in the sixth book of the *Republic*. As a natural development from the first idol, individuals will tend to favor one or another abstract picture of the world depending on their own peculiar abilities, prejudices, and propensities. Some individuals will excel at detailed analysis, others at broad synthesis, and each will favor a view of the world or a particular discipline that best fits those abilities and yields the greatest personal satisfaction. Our own individual idiosyncrasies thus will tend to be projected on the world and taken as an accurate picture of it.

Bacon noted that "the most troublesome of all" are the idols of the market-place, which arise from "the alliances of words and names." Bacon thus accorded language a pivotal place in the practice of cultural critique, arguing that language, while natural and indispensable to human cultural intercourse, nonetheless harbors the capacity for the greatest delusion. In particular, we must especially be on our guard in using language not only because the mere existence of a word can lead us to believe that something in reality corresponds to it, but also because language, being imprecise, leads us to the false assurance that the mere making of a distinction has captured the nature of the thing itself. Bacon thus identified language as the primary mechanism of an "ideological effect," whereby a fictional but socially shared set of beliefs and prejudices is established and propagated.

Finally, Bacon referred to idols of the theater, roughly his equivalent for philosophical systems. These idols, in contrast to the others, are not innate in the human constitution and social existence but are deliberately circulated as total accounts of knowledge in the various intellectual and academic disciplines and their debates. Here, Bacon was particularly interested in the dominance that a particular conception of method can exercise over a whole field of human knowledge, and he calls to our attention, in an almost contemporary way, the importance of adopting a critical perspective with respect to any allegedly exclusive or privileged form of methodology.

How, then, are these idols to be overcome? The first step, of course, is to become and remain critically aware of their types, their sources, and the scope of their influence. Although Bacon's skeptical doctrine of the idols provided a broad framework for cultural critique that has rarely been surpassed, like most Enlightenment thinkers he was not a thoroughgoing skeptic but ultimately invoked the empirical procedures of the new science as a general antidote to the reign of the idols, especially those drawn from antiquity and its appropriation by Christianity.

Bacon's skepticism was, therefore, not an end in itself but only a starting point for a much broader project whereby the development of the sciences would come to replace the superstitions of the past with more accurate, scientific knowledge. Bacon was probably the first modern thinker to realize that knowledge is power, that from scientific knowledge followed the ability to control nature rather than merely adapt passively to it. However, he remained well within the ambit of Enlightenment thought, both in regarding skepticism as a merely preliminary stance and in stopping short of considering what might be the results of an application of the new science to the control of human affairs. Bacon was followed by others in a line running from **René Descartes** (1596–1650) through **Pierre Bayle** (1647–1706) and **Voltaire** (1694–1778), to the logical positivists of the twentieth century.

A new sort of skepticism that pointed beyond the Enlightenment emerged in the writings of the Scottish philosopher and historian **David Hume** (1711–1776). Hume expanded the skeptical critique of the Enlightenment to include the sciences as well. According to Hume, the ultimate aim of scientific knowledge is to discover necessary and inalterable relations of cause and effect among observed natural events. However, all our ideas, whether scientific or not, have their origins in the welter of impressions provided us by the senses; if we wish to determine the actual meaning of an idea, we must trace it back to the impressions in which it originated. In the case of ideas of cause and effect, Hume argued, try as we might, we will never discover any discrete impression corresponding to either. Rather, the idea of causality is based simply on the past observation of one type of impression being followed by another, reinforced by the natural habit of expecting to see the same sequence of impressions repeated in the future. Of course, as Hume was quick to point out, there is no guarantee that our future expectations will be fulfilled, that future impressions will manifest the same patterns that past ones have.

The skeptical result, which directly challenged the faith in scientific reason of such enlighteners as Bacon and Descartes, was that science itself had no more right to claim the privilege of truth for its view of the world than did other areas of human endeavor. Hume was well aware of the practical advantages in precision, explanation, and prediction to which the sciences could fairly lay claim. However, what the sciences had no ground to claim, Hume's critique indicated, was that their theoretical descriptions of the world amounted to any privileged or true picture of the world as it really is. And if this allegedly preeminent form of knowledge was open to skeptical objection, then any of the less rigorous forms of cultural discourse and practice would be all the more open to question.

Like Bacon's views, Hume's more radical skepticism generated its own tradition, which in the twentieth century led to views suspicious of existing cultural practices but equally critical of any allegedly scientific explanation of them. Repercussions of Hume's skepticism can be seen in American pragmatism; in British ordinary language philosophy, which was derived from the later views of **Ludwig Wittgenstein** (1889–1951); and in various subsequent critiques of scientific claims to provide some privileged way of describing and explaining the world.

Moral Critique: Reason and Moral Sense

A second critical strategy employed in the discourse of liberal humanism, and one that proved in the long term more characteristic of it than skepticism, involved attempts to establish some natural basis for individual moral judgment regarding existing practices and institutions. The ancients had tended, with Aristotle, to see individual morality as an extension of political practice, and the Middle Ages had generally subordinated individual moral judgment to theological doctrine. Skeptical of both tendencies, Enlightenment thinkers looked to the individual as the only possible source from which a critique of existing cultural practices might emerge. Enlightenment thinkers relied on the natural capacity of the individual to see through corrupt institutions and call them to account. Whereas skeptical strategies tended to return to questions regarding the status of human knowledge, which many believed could be satisfactorily addressed by the sciences, strategies of moral critique were based on the affirmation of a capacity for moral judgment that must somehow reside in human nature itself. The critical discourse of liberal humanism traded heavily in moral condemnations of existing cultural practices, offering several justifications in support of such judgments.

The first justification, the notion of natural law, became prevalent in the seventeenth century. It emerged in its secularized form out of ancient and medieval thought, and its earliest variants held that natural law was derived from the will of a deity that had created both the natural and human orders and had endowed human beings with reason. Reason was defined in the natural law tradition as the innate human capacity to discover the inalterable laws of nature and to apprehend and institute other laws that could become equally binding on human affairs. Of course, as the English philosopher **John Locke** (1632–1704) observed toward the end of the century, this conception of natural law was beset in practice by numerous "inconveniences," not the least of which was the fact that the putative laws governing human affairs were not nearly so clearly legible in the nature of things as were those governing material nature. The legitimacy of government based on the consent of the governed, for example, was clearly not of the same order as that of the universal law of gravitation, or it would not have been so highly contested and so rarely practiced throughout history.

More important to the subsequent fate of the natural law approach, however, was the emergence, also during the seventeenth century, of a new conception of reason, totally opposed to that of the ancient and medieval traditions. **Thomas Hobbes** (1588–1679), in what is often regarded as the first treatise of modern political science, *Leviathan* (1651), presented a purely instrumental conception of reason. There he argued that like any other science, the science of politics must deal, first and foremost, with basic material forces. In the case of political science, which concerned relations among human beings, these were the elemental passions of attraction and repulsion. Rather than viewing reason as some deity-conferred human faculty that directly connected human beings with a natural law, Hobbes asserted that reason was merely an instrument of the passions. Our passions, that is, our basic desires, established the ends to be achieved by our actions and our reason functioned merely to help us discover the most efficient means of satisfying them. Reason, however, contained no natural ends in itself, and no moral law could be extracted from a capacity that was wholly subservient to natural passions.

While Hobbes's critique of reason as a source of moral judgment did not immediately win the day, it did force a wide-ranging reconsideration of the connection between reason and moral judgment. Two lines of response to Hobbes's views soon arose. One was that of John Locke, who attempted to grant the instrumental function of reason noted by Hobbes without restricting its operation solely to this function. Locke thus hoped to salvage a moral dimension for reason while stopping short of invoking some divinely decreed social order. According to Locke in his "Second Treatise on Government" (1690), human reason cannot be regarded merely as the slave of the passions because it is always capable of balancing short-term satisfaction against potential long-term effects. More specifically, "the natural light of human reason" informs us that if in satisfying our desires we harm or violate the person or property of other human beings, they will be inclined to do the same to us. Thus, human reason itself informs us of the advisability of exercising self-restraint in our dealings with others, on the basis of **enlightened self-interest**. According to Locke, the latter was sufficient to establish minimal moral principles for human action, which he went on to employ as the basis for his broader critique of political and cultural institutions.

A second response to Hobbes's instrumental critique of reason was developed in the first half of the eighteenth century by the third **Earl of Shaftesbury** (1671–1713) and **Francis Hutcheson** (1694–1746). Whereas Locke attempted to expand Hobbes's notion of instrumental reason to include rationally self-interested moral constraints, these thinkers took the opposite path by asserting that among our passions (or "sentiments," as they would say) there was one called the **moral sense**. Besides the passions of attraction and repulsion recognized by Hobbes, there was innate in human nature itself an irreducible feeling of pleasure attached to virtuous actions and of pain connected with vicious ones. Indeed, they went so far as to claim that under certain conditions and thanks to their moral sense, human beings were fully capable of recognizing the just claims of others and acting benevolently on their behalf, independently of the sort of self-interest required by Locke's view.

Either the enlightened self-interest of Locke or the moral sense theory of Shaftesbury and Hutcheson could and did provide a platform from which a moral critique of cultural and political institutions could be launched. For the former could condemn a given practice or institution as irrational by arguing that it violated certain basic conditions of social existence recognized by all human beings, while the latter could invoke its repugnance to the moral sensibilities of civilized human beings. However, Humean skepticism marked the limit of the moral strategy of liberal humanism. In Hume's analysis, there was no rational connection between what is and what ought to be (as Locke's argument required), nor was there any evidence for a separate faculty of moral sense that would invariably attach feelings of pleasure or pain to specific practices as the "moral sense" theorists claimed. However, despite Hume's critique of the bases for strategies of moral critique developed during the Enlightenment, liberal humanism has continued into our own time with at least the general conviction that somehow the moral judgment of individuals is an important starting point for cultural criticism.

Liberty and Human Rights

Probably the most characteristic critical strategy developed within the discourse of liberal humanism was that centered on the notions of liberty and human rights. This strategy still dominates the cultural and political discourses of Europe and the United States, whose basic political principles are almost without exception stated in these terms. To begin with, we should note that while, historically, moral critique and the present strategy are closely intertwined and sometimes indistinguishable from one another (especially in a thinker like Locke), as critical strategies each can be and sometimes is employed without the other. The reason for this is that while a moral critique ultimately depends on certain convictions of the individual that can be asserted even if not widely shared by others, invoking the language of liberty and rights presupposes, to be effective, a more generally shared set of attitudes regarding general social constraints and political aims. That is, moral strategies tend to assert principles that should be operative but in fact are not, while strategies invoking rights (or allegations of the violation of liberty) presuppose certain accepted operative principles that are claimed to have failed in a given instance.

In the discourse of liberal humanism, the terms *right* and *liberty* are somewhat ambiguous. To understand why, we must consider the patterns of argument within which they were developed. In the broadest sense, there were two distinguishable, although often interacting, contexts in which they were presented. The first, which we have already met, might be called the **naturalist, or essentialist,** theory. In this view, the very nature, essence, or definition of human beings includes the capacity to express themselves in their own freely chosen actions. *Liberty* thus can be defined as Hobbes defined it, as the freedom from external constraint on individual choice and action. *Rights* then will be those natural dimensions of human expression and practice that are violated whenever external constraint is illegitimately brought to bear on the individual. In an essentialist view of human nature, the problem turns on determining which actions can be *legitimately* constrained and by whom, and who is to decide what is a legitimate constraint and what is not. The other view is sometimes called the **contractarian.** Such a view, probably the dominant one in the Enlightenment, holds that, while the human being possesses no rights by nature, rights are brought into being by a free agreement whereby each individual promises to acknowledge certain rights of others if those others will reciprocally acknowledge the same rights in her or his own case. The crucial difference between the essentialist and the contractarian views of rights is that in the former, liberty and rights are defined as natural and essential attributes of human beings, while in the latter, they are neither natural nor essential but are founded on some prior agreement that presumably can be rescinded by the mutual consent of both parties.

Beyond the philosophical problem of adequately defining the nature of human beings, there were strong historical reasons why the founders of liberal humanism tended to prefer the contractarian view of rights and liberty. Rejecting any notion of a particular political configuration, especially the divine right of kings, as part of the natural order, they wanted to insist that the political sovereign was, in effect, a product of human artifice and that it could be legitimated only if viewed as called into existence by the mutual agreement of those who were governed. Once the state was created, they tended to think of it as a party to the agreement and wanted to be able to hold it to terms agreed on between itself and its citizenship. Based on this patent fiction, such thinkers as Locke wished to claim a "right of rebellion," whereby the governed could legitimately absolve themselves of their duties toward the state in cases where the state violated the original terms of the contract that had called it into being.

Ingenious as this was as a critical strategy, the opposition between the essentialist and the contractarian views of rights and liberty opened a rift in the heart of liberal humanism that has yet to be fully mended, if such is even possible. It is particularly important to understand these problems because liberal humanism ultimately became the dominant form of European and American critical discourse, and the recognition of its shortcomings and inconsistencies eventually led to the development of alternative critical discourses. Three areas of difficulty, which can be stated in the form of dilemmas, have often been cited as especially problematic.

First, although the essentialist and the contractarian approaches to rights and liberty make assumptions that are logically opposed to one another, it seems that liberal humanism can eliminate neither set of assumptions in favor of the other. On the one hand, most Enlightenment thinkers were firmly and genuinely committed to a universalist notion of rights and liberty as extending to all humans, simply by virtue of their being sentient, rational beings. The most immediate and forceful way of asserting this commitment was by attributing such features to the essence or definition of what it means to be human. In this sense, having rights or exercising freedom required no prior agreement. On the other hand, as critics of contemporary culture, they were equally concerned to develop a strategy by which the aura of legitimacy could be stripped from the existing institutions under which they lived and by which their own right to rebel against those institutions could be vindicated. This favored a critical discourse based on the fiction of a contract that when violated by one party would justify the other in reneging on it as well. The problem was that this device made rights and liberty creatures of an agreement to which some persons were parties while others were excluded. The issue of the status of slaves under the U.S. Constitution was one of the most vivid historical examples of this dilemma. Much later, in the twentieth century, this problem was reformulated in terms of human and civil rights, but the conflicting claims posed even by this reformulation were by no means resolved, any more than were an essentialist as opposed to a contractarian or nonessentialist notion of rights, liberty, and human nature.

Second, the concept of liberty in particular became even more problematic if one attended carefully to the contractarian argument. For while the essentialist view simply posited freedom or liberty as a natural feature of human beings without further argument, the contractarian approach implied a contrast between a "natural" freedom sufficient at least to permit deliberate entry into an agreement and an "artificial" liberty that resulted from the agreement. As **Jean-Jacques Rousseau** (1712–1778) clearly saw, the price demanded by deciding against the "natural freedom" outside the bounds of social constraint and in favor of the "artificial liberty" based on contractual civil society might well be regarded by many as too high. While attempting to justify living under laws democratically agreed on and enforced by a "general will," Rousseau himself remained ambivalent about whether the liberty of the citizen or the freedom of the natural and nonpolitical individual was preferable. Perhaps the most eloquent advocate for subordinating oneself to collectively determined law was also one of the most forceful spokespersons for the natural freedom of a presocial condition. Again, this issue continues today in any conflict where the natural freedom of an individual's conscientious resistance to laws perceived as unjust is pitted against the artificial liberty made possible by an existing legal system.

Third, the status of rights has remained problematic throughout the discourse of liberal humanism. The problem is that the term *right* often functions in a purely abstract manner. In this discourse, one can be said to possess a right even though the actual conditions by which one could actually exercise the right are absent. For example, a person can be regarded as having a right to equal employment without possessing the training or qualifications necessary to enter the workforce. The difficulty lies in the fact that in the discourse of liberal humanism, rights tend to be treated as potentialities that an individual need not, but in many cases cannot, realize in actuality. Liberal humanism has been divided throughout its history on the issue of whether the legal or moral recognition of certain rights entails as well the creation of the actual conditions under which, in a given case, they could in fact be exercised. This ambiguity in the concept of rights, as well as the tendency to arbitrarily restrict their expression in the political sphere by such notions as suffrage, made possible a new level of critique, well illustrated in such writings as *A Vindication of the Rights of Woman* (1792) by **Mary Wollstonecraft** (1759–1797). Probably the first, and still one of the most influential articulations of what would later be called feminist critique, Wollstonecraft's *Vindication* powerfully argued that any consistent notion of rights or liberty must apply equally to women and men—an idea that was absent from the discussion among such thinkers as Locke and Rousseau.

Historical Critique

Although its heyday was the nineteenth century, historical critique first appeared as a distinctive critical strategy during the Enlightenment, when it was decidedly less prominent than the skeptical, moral, or rights-based styles of critique. The hesitation of many Enlightenment thinkers in embracing historical critique probably stemmed from the fact that Christianity was based on a comprehensive interpretation of history as a work of divine grace, thus tainting the historical approach to cultural criticism. Another factor contributing to their hesitation was that such early apologists for the natural sciences as Galileo, Bacon, and Descartes often contrasted the methods and results of the new science with the superstitions, inaccuracies, and falsehoods propagated by historians. Finally, as yet relatively little historical documentation was readily available, apart from religious texts and their biased interpretations. Even so, historiography did make notable advances during the Enlightenment, especially in such works as Hume's multivolume *History of England* (1752–1762) and Edward Gibbon's *The Decline and Fall of the Roman Empire* (1776–1788).

Giambattista Vico

While historians like Hume and Gibbon were admitted skeptics and generally employed the writing of history as another vehicle to extend their skeptical style of critique, the Italian philosopher and social theorist **Giambattista Vico** (1668–1744) developed a distinctively modern theory concerning the writing of history, the general principles governing history, and its status as a discipline. In so doing, Vico laid the foundations of a new critical strategy, which Hegel and Marx would use later in developing a new form of critical discourse.

Vico entitled his major historical work *The New Science,* the first edition of which was published in 1725, followed by a second in 1730 and a third underway at his death in 1744. His choice of title was a calculated polemical reference to the other "new science" of his day, that developed by such proponents of the natural sciences as Galileo and Descartes, with whose works Vico was well acquainted. Amid the excitement surrounding the application of mathematics to unlock the secrets of nature, Vico asserted a principle that not only implied an interpretation of the natural sciences radically different from Galileo's and Descartes's but that also established the possibility of a science of human affairs, based on history, that could be ranked alongside the natural sciences in its potential for increasing the stock of human knowledge. This principle was summed up in the Latin phrase *verum ipsum factum:* What is true *(verum)* is the same *(ipsum)* as what is created *(factum).*

For the science of nature, this principle implied that scientists were not, as they themselves tended to think, actually discovering the eternal mathematical laws of nature but rather developing mathematical constructs (or as we might say today, models) by which nature could be understood. As the German philosopher Immanuel Kant would claim more than a century later, natural scientists could never know nature as it was in itself because they had not created it. Rather, what we are able to know of nature is what we have constructed for ourselves and, as it were, "read back into it." Although Vico's reinterpretation of natural science did not evidence the skepticism of Hume, it did work to constrain the claims made in behalf of a scientific view of the world. It also implied that the theories and activities of natural scientists might be subjected to historical critique, since their constructs of nature were not eternal but had gradually evolved.

For Vico, however, the main force of his principle was to affirm that since history is the account of human practical activity, that is, since history is preeminently created by human beings, then we are, in a sense, capable of understanding historical phenomena even better than we understand natural ones. While the hidden springs of nature will always continue to elude us because nature was made by God, the underlying principles of human history can be brought to light because they result solely from the productive activities of human beings.

However, Vico was decidedly **antiessentialist** in his approach to history. He firmly rejected any ahistorical view of a fixed human nature that might lead us to imagine, as he thought someone like Hobbes mistakenly did, that human beings in past ages thought or acted just as we do, or were motivated by the same forces as we are. Rather than understanding past ages in terms of our present outlook, values, and cultural practices, Vico insisted, we should understand our own condition as the outcome of a process of development that preceded us. Neither moral conviction nor a modern doctrine of rights and liberty but only a scientific grasp of our current cultural state as emergent from its historical past could provide a basis for critical discourse.

The word *culture* does not appear as a central term in Vico's texts; but it is nonetheless abundantly clear that Vico believed the principal focus of history should not be on mere events and their chronology but on language, myths, and other forms by means of which past tradition is communicated to the present. This idea was without precedent in Vico's day. Prefiguring the next major critical discourse to emerge, Vico saw the main task of the historian as one of *interpretation* of past cultural forms rather than mere compilation of historical "facts." Furthermore, he emphasized that what we might at present regard as fables, myths, or metaphors were, for earlier periods, the very vehicles by which a previous culture constructed and made sense of its world. As historians, we should resist the tendency to reduce earlier cultural products to our own conceptual terms; rather, we should strive to understand how they formed a distinctive, organically connected, and wholly viable worldview.

Particularly important for some later critical discourses are two features of Vico's theory of the general principles underlying historical development. First, Vico saw various types of economic and political organization as intimately connected with other cultural forms such as art, literature, rhetoric, law, and philosophy. Indeed, a good part of Vico's *New Science* is devoted to demonstrating how the various aspects of culture fit together and mutually reinforce one another in specific social and economic conditions at a given point of historical development. Anticipating Marx by some two centuries, Vico even suggested that class conflict was an essential factor in large-scale economic and cultural transformations. Second, Vico believed that particular human societies pass through a predictable sequence of stages, driven by social reconfigurations resulting from disturbances in kinship and economic relations. While Vico stopped short of presenting a universal history in which the present age could be inserted and its fate predicted, and contented himself with tracing the cycles of history within particular societies, one might easily infer that he regarded his contemporary culture as already having entered the final stage of a "barbarism of reflection" and class conflict that would ultimately lead to its collapse and to the beginning of a new cycle. While many features of Vico's thought about culture were generally consistent with and eventually came to influence the discourse of liberal humanism, particularly through the historical writings of **Johann Gottfried Herder** (1744–1803), his implicit pessimism about current conditions, based on his cyclical view of history, seems more characteristic of the nineteenth than of the seventeenth century. Nonetheless, Vico must be credited with developing yet another critical strategy that, with revision, came to be widely employed within the discourse of liberal humanism.

The Marquis de Condorcet

A view of historical critique much more consistent with the mainline assumptions of liberal humanism was developed by the **Marquis de Condorcet** (1743–1794). Like Vico, Condorcet rejected the idea that the study of human culture and history should be seen as less precise, reliable, or important than the investigation of nature. However, unlike Vico he believed that in a suitably developed form, the mathematical methods employed by the natural sciences could be equally well applied to the study of human social and historical phenomena. In his pioneering work on the **mathematical theory of probability**, still the basis for much research in the modern social sciences, Condorcet brought the Enlightenment's general enthusiasm for and confidence in the methods of the natural sciences together with its concern for effecting concrete change in existing social conditions. According to Condorcet, the mathematical theory of probability not only helps clarify issues involved in the dynamics of collective decisionmaking, thus providing a scientific basis for the emerging notion of procedural democracy, but it also could help guide individual and collective decision-making processes by permitting the outcomes of various competing policies to be quantitatively specified and accurately evaluated. Thus, Condorcet's theory of probability laid the foundations for a new line of critique that would link the mathematically precise methods of the sciences directly to the solution of concrete human problems. At least in principle, the inherent problems of moral and rights-based critiques could finally be resolved through a quantitative analysis and comparison of the effects of human choice among various alternatives. In spirit if not in detail, such an approach lay at the basis of what was to become one of the dominant social theories of the nineteenth and twentieth centuries, a view associated with **Jeremy Bentham** (1748–1832) and **John Stuart Mill** (1806–1873). This theory, called **utilitarianism**, held that in any given case, the morally best action or policy was the one that would produce "the greatest good for the greatest number." Utilitarianism, or some variant thereof, remains the basis for most contemporary social planning. It has often been used by historians as well to evaluate the effectiveness of past decisions or policies.

Even more directly relevant to the liberal humanist tradition was Condorcet's theory of historical progress. In his *Sketch for a Historical Picture of the Progress of the Human Mind* (1794), Condorcet offered a broad reading of history that aimed to finally vindicate all the other critical attitudes and strategies of liberal humanism. His *Sketch* was based on two assumptions. First, Condorcet believed, as would many theorists who came after him, that the structure of individual development closely paralleled that of cultural or historical development. The individual began life in a state totally dependent on its environment and provided with nothing but a welter of seemingly random sensations. Gradually, however, one achieved mastery of one's surroundings by forming ideas, connecting them into larger bodies of knowledge, and applying the knowledge gained to harnessing forces formerly beyond its control. Likewise, the human race began in a sort of primitive chaos but became progressively more organized, developing political institutions, technologies, and cultural formations, and finally reaching a point where it was able to control nature and direct it toward human ends.

The second assumption was that this overall trajectory of progress was not wholly seamless and continuous but must pass through various stages, each of which posed distinctive obstacles to development that had to be overcome before the next stage could be entered. Condorcet divided human history into ten such stages. Not surprisingly, some of the major obstacles to be overcome were such traditional enemies of liberal humanism as ignorance, superstition, dogmatic religion, and political tyranny. Condorcet regarded himself as living at the point of transition from the ninth to the tenth and final stage of human history. Significantly, he regarded the ninth epoch as beginning with Descartes's *Discourse on Method* and ending with the fall of the Bastille in 1789. Its task had been to abolish the obstacles to human progress posed, on the one hand, by the political tyranny of absolute monarchy and, on the other, by the continued intellectual reliance on external authority rather than on humankind's own rational capacities, which were manifested in the highest sense in the new sciences. This accomplished, Condorcet optimistically believed that there was no further limit to the degree to which the human race could perfect itself in the tenth and final phase of history. Democratic institutions promoting scientific and technological advance and expanding this enlightened culture through universal education would ultimately lead—and soon, he believed—to the final eradication of all the traditional sources of human misery: poverty, war, disease, bigotry, and so on. Furthermore, he saw no natural limits to such progress and he believed that cultural advances would go hand in hand with the increasing moral perfection of human nature.

As a critical strategy, Condorcet's account of history as a gradual evolution from dependence, ignorance, and superstition to power, knowledge, and enlightenment provided him with a broad basis on which to identify certain cultural institutions as counter-progressive remnants of past epochs and to call for their removal as obstacles to the course of human progress that all history affirms. In Condorcet more than in any other Enlightenment thinker, liberal humanism assumed a form intimately linked to the notion of **modernization**, the process by which scientific and technological development brings about cultural transformations in which traditional practices and institutions are eliminated and continually replaced by new cultural configurations.

Although Condorcet regarded modernization as both historically inevitable and morally desirable, his assessment was not shared by all Enlightenment thinkers or by all later representatives of the liberal humanist tradition. Rousseau, always regarded by Condorcet as a principal antagonist, had already presented a scathing critique of modernization in his *Discourse on the Sciences and Arts* (1750), where he argued exactly the opposite point, that historical progress in these areas entailed a gradual corruption of human nature from its originally free and healthy state. In his famous phrase, the modern sciences and arts "spread garlands of flowers over the iron chains with which men are burdened, stifle in them the sense of that original liberty for which they seem to have been born, make them love their slavery, and turn them into what is called civilized peoples." Of course, Rousseau himself could never be regarded as a spokesperson for the liberal humanist position, but his reservations concerning modernization did strike an ever more responsive chord in the later development of this movement. Indeed, as we will see, the difficulties that later liberal humanism experienced in attempting to reconcile its modern political liberalism with a more traditionalist idea of humanist culture played an important role in the emergence of later critical discourses.

Kant's Systematic Restatement: Liberal Humanism as Critical Rationalism

We have seen that, as the Enlightenment unfolded, several quite different critical strategies appeared. Liberal humanism thus assumed a number of different inflections, not always entirely harmonious with one another. However, most mainstream Enlightenment figures were suspicious of too much logical subtlety or overly panoramic metaphysical visions, since these smacked of the sort of medieval scholasticism to which they were ideologically opposed. As a result, their liberal humanist convictions tended to operate as a sort of broadly assumed intellectual context within which more specific points could be debated and battles with the common enemy joined. As a result, there were few general or comprehensive attempts to spell out in detail what the overall position involved, thus allowing considerable latitude for views that would have appeared flatly contradictory if they had been clearly articulated. Hume began to probe this soft underbelly of the liberal humanist stance, but his skepticism was so radical that it threatened to undermine the whole Enlightenment project.

Still, Humean skepticism succeeded in forcing the issue, and German philosopher **Immanuel Kant** (1724–1804) was thereby moved to undertake the difficult task of systematically reconstructing the position of liberal humanism in his **Critical Philosophy**. It is important to understand at least the general contours of Kant's philosophy, not only because it is the most comprehensive and explicit statement of liberal humanism, but because it came to serve as a historical reference point for the subsequent development of liberal humanism as well as for most other later critical discourses. In particular, it was in Kant's Critical Philosophy that liberal humanism's various concepts and strategies were brought together and given a proper place within a more comprehensive and clearly articulated critical project.

As we have seen, the entire project of the Enlightenment was thoroughly critical in its attitudes toward the "barbarian" culture inherited from the premodern period. Through various critical strategies, it tended to pit its "civilizing" influences and convictions against prevailing cultural practices based on a general and mostly unquestioned faith in human reason. However, it was not until Hume that a serious critique was aimed at the notion of reason itself. Prior to that, reason had assumed a number of quite different and often inconsistent guises: a source of innate mathematical ideas in Descartes, an instrument of the passions in Hobbes, a "natural light" dictating basic moral constraints in Locke, and so forth. Against all of these, the radical upshot of Hume's skepticism was that reason, however decked out, could provide no reliable basis for either human knowledge or practical action.

Kant believed that it was at this fundamental level that the issue must be joined if the Enlightenment project was to be salvaged. For Kant, this involved nothing less than radicalizing the disparate critical tendencies of the Enlightenment into a comprehensive critique of pure reason, which was in fact the title of his first major critical work (1781, 1st ed.; 1787, 2d ed.). Kant believed that if reason were to be vindicated against skeptical attacks such as those launched by Hume, there was no alternative but to look to reason itself to provide the response. Thus, as he explained it, the critique of pure reason was not only a critique directed *at* reason but one carried out *by* reason. In other words, for Kant the root of all critique was ultimately *self-critique*. Any critique of other views, practices, or institutions could be effective only if one's own entitlement to a critical stance could be legitimated in the first place; and this result was precisely that sought by Kant in his *Critique of Pure Reason*.

Kant began by distinguishing three senses in which the term *reason* appeared in the critical discourse of the Enlightenment. First, in the broadest sense, which embraced all the others, reason was nothing but the capacity to think in an orderly and consistent manner. The principles governing this had been well-known since the time of Aristotle: They were simply the basic laws of logic, which if violated, resulted in fallacy, confusion, and ultimately absurdity. This capacity Kant called **pure reason**, since it was completely formal, lacking any specific content of its own but universally applicable to any and all content. The second sense of reason was that involved with the production of knowledge and manifested, in its highest instance, in the natural sciences. This Kant called **theoretical reason**. While the theoretical reason employed by the sciences and other disciplines must obey the logical laws inherent in pure reason, as any meaningful discourse must, it also re-

quired a specific content, which was derived from the sensory observation of nature. Finally, a third sense of reason as employed in the Enlightenment concerned
human action and the moral principles that ought to govern it. Kant called this
practical reason. Like theoretical reason, practical reason was also governed by
the laws of logic, and it too required a particular content. But where the content
of theoretical reason was supplied by our sensory awareness of nature, that of
practical reason involved certain morally relevant features of human nature. This
threefold distinction, then, provided the conceptual matrix within which Kant's
critical project was developed.

The first step in Kant's critical reconstruction of liberal humanism was to
clearly demarcate what human beings merely think from what they can legitimately claim to know. It was here that Kant sought to give the skeptical strategy
its due while stopping short of Hume's challenge to the natural sciences themselves. Through a complicated series of arguments, Kant concluded that whereas
pure reason could generate any ideas whatsoever as long as they did not violate
the basic laws of logic, theoretical reason, and therefore human knowledge, was
strictly limited to those spatial and temporal objects which can be observed and
causally linked through the mathematical laws of the sciences. Further, agreeing
with Vico, Kant held that mathematics was precisely that construct of the human
mind that permitted the accurate description of natural phenomena. Thus, Bacon, Hume, and other skeptics had every right to challenge ideas of pure reason—
superstitions, religious dogma, the naive views of antiquity, even extravagant
metaphysical claims—for which no concrete experience provided solid evidence.
Nonetheless, the natural sciences, because they were rooted in the productive
abilities of the human mind, could always be relied on to yield reliable and coherent knowledge of nature, so long as they remained within the limits of what could
be observed in space and time.

Kant's critique of pure reason, that is, of the human ability to *think* anything
that is not self-contradictory, clearly distinguished pure reason from theoretical
reason, which provides humans with the ability to *know* whatever is based on empirical evidence. Thus, Kant's critique validated the methods of the natural sciences. It also had another important result: It implied that while pure reason can
pose questions to us for which we will never be in a position to know the answers—questions about whether God exists, whether human beings have immortal souls, whether human action is free or determined, like the rest of nature, by
mathematical laws—theoretical reason has nothing to contribute to the resolution of such issues. The theoretical reason of the sciences, limited as it is to observations of spatial and temporal objects, can never assist us in either proving or
disproving what lies in the realm of the supernatural. Thus, there is nothing to
prevent us from *believing* that God exists, that we have immortal souls, and that
we are by nature free, even if we cannot prove it. In other words, Kant's critique
leaves room for "rational faith," even as it certifies natural science when limited to
its proper sphere.

This last consideration led naturally to Kant's *Critique of Practical Reason* (1788). In this work Kant provides a basis for the moral and rights-based strategies mentioned earlier in this chapter. According to Kant, both of these strategies inevitably presuppose that human beings are free to choose among alternatives and to act on their choices. To morally judge a human action or cultural practice assumes that the action or practice could be otherwise and thus that it makes sense to hold a person or society responsible for what it does—something we would never do in the case of a rock, a tree, a table, or an animal. And to critique an institution implies that it is possible for our critique to have some effect on it; for if it were otherwise, there would be no possible motivation for criticizing the institution.

Now, we cannot prove and hence cannot finally know that we are free so long as we regard ourselves as purely natural beings, as physical objects in space and time. But while this is one way in which we can view ourselves and other human beings, it is by no means the only one. Kant's humanism is most evident at this point, for he asserts that we all possess a distinctly free and moral nature that transcends anything we can observe about one another as merely physical organisms. (For this reason and others, Kant's philosophy is sometimes referred to as **transcendentalism.**) Viewed from the perspective of theoretical reason, we are all natural beings that, like any other natural phenomenon, can be the objects of study by the sciences; but viewed from the perspective of practical reason, we are also free, moral beings, and to this moral view of human nature the sciences can offer no challenge.

Kant, however, insists that this moral view of human nature is not just a matter of feeling or sentiment. Rather, practical reason is as much an application of pure reason as is the theoretical reason employed by the sciences. Thus, the moral view of human nature has its own laws and human freedom its own rational principle. Kant calls this ultimate principle the **categorical imperative,** a command (imperative) that our reason issues to us as moral beings without exception (categorically). Much like the Christian golden rule, it states, "Act only on that principle which you could also will to be a principle for all rational (human) beings." In other words, moral action involves the recognition that I cannot consistently require of another what I would be unwilling to require of myself; likewise, I cannot morally do to another what I would be unwilling to allow the other to do to me.

Here, then, is the rational basis for liberal humanism's moral strategy: Any cultural practice or institution that involves the manipulation, degradation, or exploitation of another human being is one to which neither I nor any other rational being can reasonably consent. Such a practice or institution is wrong, not because it violates the terms of a contract or because some moral sentiment makes it seem painful to me, but because I would be irrational and thus fundamentally inhuman if I were to countenance such a thing in the case of others while rejecting it in my own case. The same judgment, of course, could also be applied to others who would except themselves from practices or institutions that they would nonetheless permit in the case of individuals other than themselves.

From here it is easy to see how Kant developed his rights-based strategy. For Kant, rights are simply the political expression of the moral constraints just outlined. When we say that human beings have rights, we are not referring to some contingent, natural human feature like eyes or ears but to the transcendent quality of being free and rational agents, capable of recognizing moral principles and acting on them. To claim that a cultural practice or political institution violates a person's rights is not just to assert that it has transgressed the terms of some prior agreement or that it merely acted arbitrarily, but that it has violated the moral dimension of human nature itself. And since this transcendent moral dimension of human nature necessarily presupposes the freedom to express itself in action, then any specific infringement of a right must be understood as a particular instance of a violation of human freedom itself. Thus, Kant's humanism necessarily implies a liberal stance in relation to political institutions. Of all the thinkers in the secular tradition of liberal humanism, Kant offers the strongest justification for conscientious objection to policies and actions of authority that are in violation of human rights.

While the historical strategy of critique was not one that Kant regarded as central to his philosophical argument (nor has it been for most liberal humanists), he did offer a sketch of what it would involve in his remarkable essay, "Idea for a Universal History with Cosmopolitan Intent" (1784). Adopting a broad, synoptic perspective, Kant considers history in this essay as the site of interaction between the natural order dealt with by theoretical reason and the moral order of practical reason. The questions he poses are whether the historical development of the human species can be legitimately regarded as tending toward a natural end, and if so, what that end might be. As we have already seen, it is central to Kant's view that any discussion of natural ends must include human nature as a part of it, and that human nature implies the expression of reason in the form of free moral activity. This being the case, history must be viewed as the gradual unfolding of conditions under which human freedom can be realized within the constraints placed on it by physical nature. According to Kant, "[t]he latest problem for mankind, the solution of which nature forces him to seek, is the achievement of a civil society which administers law generally." In other words, Kant saw the major accomplishment of the Enlightenment as the emergence of states based on *reasonable and consistently applied laws* that were designed to establish and promote the free activity of their citizens.

However, beyond this Kant notes that the internal freedom established by individual states will not be secure so long as they remain in constant antagonism and warfare with one another. Thus, Kant argues for the necessity of an international or **cosmopolitan** order, whereby states would come to respect and act toward one another according to the same rational principles by which individual moral action ought to be governed. Thus, Kant's historical strategy provided a basis for political critique whereby institutions could be judged by the degrees to which they have instituted internal rule by law and are pursuing stable and peaceful relations among themselves.

We can conclude this discussion of Kant's synoptic reconstruction of liberal humanism by noting the meaning and significance he assigned to culture in his essay "Idea for a Universal History with Cosmopolitan Intent." There, Kant wrote: "[C]ulture actually consists in the social value of man. All man's talents are gradually unfolded, taste is developed. Through continuous enlightenment the basis is laid for a frame of mind which, in the course of time, transforms the raw natural faculty of moral discrimination into definite practical principles."

Three aspects of Kant's view of culture should be especially kept in mind as we follow the further development of liberal humanism. First, Kant used the term *culture* as a virtual synonym of *civilization*, the expression of "the social value of man," and viewed it, like his Enlightenment predecessors, as the overcoming of barbarism. Second, culture for Kant was intrinsically moral in its import. Its principal function was to heighten consciousness to the point of establishing "definite practical principles." Finally, Kant regarded the role of culture as central for promoting the formation of individual tastes and the unfolding of individual talents and abilities. As we will soon see, from the point of view of critical discourse, serious problems arise when culture is viewed in this way.

Post-Enlightenment Liberal Humanism: Matthew Arnold's "Culture of Criticism" and Its Successors

I suggested at the beginning of this chapter that the Enlightenment was driven by a modern secular spirit of criticism directed against the authority of church, state, and antiquity and aimed at effecting significant change in existing practices and institutions. While it would be inaccurate to regard Enlightenment philosophers as revolutionaries in the same sense in which we use the term today, it is nonetheless true that over a period of about 200 years, their critical efforts did contribute to fundamental social and cultural changes. As examples one can cite the development of the enlightened monarchy in Frederick the Great's Prussia, the founding of the United States, the French Revolution, and the series of British reforms begun in the last decade of the eighteenth century. In viewing liberal humanism as a critical discourse from our present perspective, it is easy to forget that during most of that 200-year period, the advocates of Enlightenment were a distinct minority. Many among them, such as Galileo, Descartes, Voltaire, and even Kant, were actively suppressed or persecuted by the authorities. However, by the beginning of the nineteenth century, if liberal humanism had not entirely triumphed, it had certainly begun the process of transformation from an oppositional discourse critical of the status quo to the basis for a set of newly emergent practices and institutions. As time went on, liberal humanism itself became the dominant ideology of the most powerful countries of Europe and the Americas, as it remains, for the most part, today.

This transformation significantly altered the notions of both critique and culture that were operative within liberal humanism. Certainly by the middle of the nineteenth century, many who regarded themselves as legitimate heirs to this tradition were forced to dramatically reformulate their position and project as cultural critics. Perhaps the most forceful and influential of these reformulations was that of the British poet, literary critic, and educator **Matthew Arnold** (1822–1888). His essays "The Function of Criticism at the Present Time" (1865) and "Culture and Anarchy" (1869) remain classic statements of liberal humanism in the post-Enlightenment era.

In his essay "On Translating Homer" (1861), Arnold had already come to think of himself as continuing the Enlightenment tradition of liberal humanism. There, he wrote, "Of the literature of France and Germany, as of the intellect of Europe in general, the main effort, for now many years, has been a critical effort; the endeavour, in all branches of knowledge, theology, philosophy, history, art, science, to see the object as in itself it really is."

Arnold used similar terms to describe his own critical undertakings. But in his explanations of what is involved in this sort of criticism, it becomes clear that his critical stance differs from that of most cultural critics during the Enlightenment. For Arnold, the appropriate stance for a critic is **disinterestedness** rather than the advocacy practiced by Enlightenment critics. This stance is adopted "[b]y keeping aloof from what is called 'the practical view of things'; by resolutely following the law of its own nature, which is to be a free play of the mind on all subjects which it touches." Indeed, Arnold believed that the sort of criticism he was advocating was corrupted whenever it concerned itself with any practical polemics or controversies.

What, then, was the object of Arnold's critical practice? In both of the essays mentioned above, he defined genuine criticism as "the idea of a disinterested endeavour to learn and propagate the best that is known and thought in the world, and thus to establish a current of fresh and true ideas." In "Culture and Anarchy," he went on to claim that this was what constituted genuine "Culture," which he called "a study in perfection." Here the implied distinction is between what has often been called high culture ("Culture with a capital C," as it has sometimes been called) and the culture of the existing order or the masses. Only the former was "true Culture" for Arnold, and an appropriate object of criticism. The latter type of culture was merely the product of delusion, debasement, and self-aggrandizement: ultimately, it was **anarchy**. Any attempt to critique it would enmesh the true critic in practical affairs, which would signal the death of the critical stance of disinterestedness that Arnold advocated.

Further developing this line of thought, Arnold asserted in his characteristic rhetorical fashion that true Culture was "sweetness and light," and its criticism the disinterested pursuit of the beauty and knowledge implied by that descriptive phrase. But where could a true critic be found who could disinterestedly pursue such lofty aims? Arnold used the terms *barbarians, philistines,* and *populace* to indicate the aristocratic, commercial, and working classes of the England of his day, charging each with distinctive faults that made them unsuitable for the pursuit of cultural perfection. Nonetheless, he argued that from every class a few enlightened individuals could emerge (he classified himself in this category) who were capable of transcending the limits of their own social station and functioning as intellectual and moral guardians of the sweetness and light of genuine Culture.

Thus, there are significant differences between the liberal humanism of the Enlightenment and that of the post-Enlightenment period as represented by Arnold. Of course, the critical discourse of the Enlightenment did counterpose itself to an entire culture that it regarded as barbarian, as did Arnold to his own; but it also called into question all authority but the right of the individual to decide for itself on the basis of innate human reason. Arnold, by contrast, sought to establish a new sort of authority based on "the best that has been thought and known in the world," which he seemed to regard as contained preeminently in a **canon,** or a list of great literary works of the past, including the ancient Greek poets and dramatists, Shakespeare, and Goethe. Arnold's brand of humanism was no longer that of rational human beings in general but of the humanities as great works of literature and art. Further, his liberalism was not that of universal human rights and political mechanisms for ensuring them but more that of the liberal arts. He was suspicious of any such cultural or political machinery, maintaining that the Enlightenment had been too much concerned with freedom "worshipped in itself" and too little with "the ends for which freedom is to be desired." This is not to say that later liberal humanists like Arnold were all antidemocratic; but there was an elitist dimension to their point of view, in that they tended to regard themselves as possessing the appropriately disinterested and classless stance from which to evaluate what the "true ends of freedom" might be. Arnold, in particular, went so far as to advocate a more robust state, to which the anarchy of individual competition and caprice could be subordinated, and he suggested that poetry might come to replace religion as the force that could bind the individual to the broader social whole.

The influence of Arnold and like-minded critics has extended to the present. It can be traced through literary critics such as **T. S. Eliot** (1888–1965) to **Lionel Trilling** ((1905–1975) and **F. R. Leavis** (1895–1978), in reaction to whom modern British cultural studies emerged. Today one continues to encounter ambiguity in the terms *culture* (is that popular culture, or high culture?) and *criticism* (literary or social?). Such ambiguities are a result of the transformation of liberal humanism most notably wrought by Arnold, wherein the earlier Enlightenment notion of the humanist critique of culture on behalf of the rights of the individual became a culture of criticism practiced by specialists housed in various academic departments of modern universities.

Liberal Humanism Today

Liberal humanist critical discourse is now almost 400 years old. Its current inflections are shaped by several important factors. Its earlier Enlightenment version continued on beyond and alongside the new form given it by such figures as Arnold. Often the two have been in uneasy tension with one another, particularly over the issue of the more populist tendencies of the former versus the elitism of the latter. Many educational institutions have become deeply divided over questions of teaching only a classical canon or incorporating elements of popular culture into the curriculum.

Further, the fact that liberal humanism became the dominant ideology of most European and American governments has appeared to many to have compromised its original critical stance. Rather than being a progressive force, liberal humanism has increasingly come to be viewed as part of the problem and a major target for other critical discourses. Especially since World War II, broader philosophical objections have emerged not only to the humanism that is operative in the modern era but to its very beginnings in ancient Greece. Poststructuralism, in particular, has tended to reject any critical stance that depends on the human being or reason as its central notion.

Closely related to these developments is the sense that liberal humanism is a distinctively Eurocentric point of view and that it has served to maintain colonialist patterns of cultural dominance based on a conviction of moral superiority. The present "culture wars" over such areas as educational curricula often involve charges and countercharges about the extent to which liberal humanism privileges Euro-American views.

It is safe to say that at very least, liberal humanism as a critical discourse can no longer count on the general acceptance it once enjoyed. It has been forced, in recent years, to justify itself or reformulate its basic position in the face of intensified criticism. Such works as John Rawls's *A Theory of Justice*, Robert Nozick's *Anarchy, State, and Utopia*, E. D. Hirsch's *Cultural Literacy*, and Allan Bloom's *The Closing of the American Mind* (all published in the 1960s, 1970s, and 1980s) represent in various ways the continued attempt to assert and defend liberal humanism against its detractors. Although beleaguered, liberal humanism remains for now the dominant cultural discourse and often the critical starting point for other critical discourses. It is therefore essential that its main contours be understood by anyone wishing to approach the contemporary study of culture.

Bibliographic Essay

All of the primary texts cited in Chapter 1 are readily available in numerous editions and most also appear in various anthologies, so the reader should have no problem locating them. Probably the best chosen and most extensive collection of Enlightenment selections (including many by authors discussed in this chapter) is *The Enlightenment: A Comprehensive Anthology*, edited by Peter Gay (New York: Simon & Schuster, 1973). The final edition of Vico's major work, *Principi di una Scienza Nuova*, is available in English translation under the title *The New Science of Giambattista Vico*, tr. Thomas Bergin and Max Fisch (Ithaca: Cornell University Press, 1984). The relevant works of Matthew Arnold can be found in *Poetry and Criticism of Matthew Arnold*, ed. A. Dwight Culler (Boston: Houghton Mifflin, 1961).

One of the classic accounts of the modern liberal humanist tradition, itself written from a decidedly liberal humanist perspective, is *The Making of the Modern Mind*, by John Herman Randall, Jr. (New York: Columbia University Press, 1926). Still the best introduction to the political philosophy of Enlightenment liberal humanism is *French Liberal Thought in the Eighteenth Century*, by Kingsley Martin (New York: Harper & Row, 1963). Also highly recommended and somewhat more revisionist in its interpretation than the former, although perhaps too detailed for an introduction to the subject, is Peter Gay's *The Enlightenment: An Interpretation* (New York: Knopf, 1966).

On Kant's defense of the Enlightenment conception of reason and its liberal humanist implications, see Frederick Beiser's *The Fate of Reason: German Philosophy from Kant to Fichte* (Cambridge, Mass.: Harvard University Press, 1987), as well as his *Enlightenment, Revolution, and Romanticism* (Cambridge, Mass.: Harvard University Press, 1992).

Lionel Trilling's *Matthew Arnold* (New York: W. W. Norton, 1939) was an important though not entirely uncritical conduit of Arnoldian ideas into contemporary discussions. A more recent assessment is that of Joseph Carroll, *The Cultural Theory of Matthew Arnold* (Berkeley: University of California Press, 1982). For an extremely important discussion, seminal for the emergence of British cultural studies, of a number of writers in the post-Enlightenment tradition of liberal humanism including Arnold, consult Raymond Williams, *Culture & Society: 1780–1950* (New York: Columbia University Press, 1958). His very brief essay entitled "A Hundred Years of Culture and Anarchy" in *Problems in Materialism and Culture* (London: Verso, 1980) also presents a trenchant critique of Arnold and his influence, from the perspective of the founder of British cultural studies.

2

Hermeneutics:
Interpretation and Critique

The French Revolution signaled the beginning of a period of tremendous political and cultural upheaval and transformation. In the wake of the Napoleonic Wars and the conservative retrenchment that followed France's defeat in 1815, nineteenth-century Europe witnessed three other major periods of political revolution (1830, 1848, and 1870) and many more local outbreaks of resistance. Because the discourse of liberal humanism was gradually transformed from a stance of opposition to one of dominance, new critical discourses that would reconceptualize the operative notion of culture and establish new critical stances seemed necessary.

The first new critical discourse to emerge in the nineteenth century was that of **hermeneutics**. The term was derived from the Greek verb *hermēneuein* (to interpret or understand), which was based on the name of the priest of the Delphic oracle, who was in turn named for the messenger-god Hermes. Aristotle's *Organon* on logic included a treatise entitled *Peri hermēneias*, thus according this area a long-standing intellectual pedigree; but Aristotle's enterprise was simply to put forward general principles for formulating statements that can be evaluated as true or false. It was not until the eighteenth century that hermeneutics attained the much broader and more complex meaning that would permit it to be classified as a modern critical discourse.

In the seventeenth and eighteenth centuries, the forerunners of modern hermeneutics were principally concerned with issues of biblical exegesis and interpretation, especially as practiced within the Protestant tradition. However, the development of modern philology and historiography came to exert important influences on biblical hermeneutics, so that the interpretation of sacred texts gradually became subject to some of the same critical methods and constraints applied to texts generally. For example, as early as 1761, J. A. Ernesti had already argued that the only criteria governing the correctness of the interpretation of any text were the uses of words, their historical circumstances, and the intention of the author in using them.

By the end of the eighteenth century, under the influence of Enlightenment rationalism, the link between interpretation and critique had already been forged. The so-called **lower criticism** of biblical writings involved the use of external and internal evidence to establish a preferred and corrected version of specific original documents. **Higher criticism** employed broader contextual factors such as historical and archaeological evidence, literary stylistics, comparison of sources, and so on in assisting with determining the meaning of biblical texts. Of course, both of these were applications of interpretive procedures already in use in relation to secular texts, but their employment in relation to religious texts implied a certain skeptical and critical attitude toward the latter.

However, although the roots of hermeneutics were planted in the soil of the Enlightenment, it did not achieve its form as a modern critical discourse until the Romantic period, following the French Revolution, in the work of German philologist and theologian **Friedrich Schleiermacher** (1768–1834). Schleiermacher can be viewed as reformulating and radicalizing four ideas that were already present in the hermeneutic approaches that preceded him. These basic ideas provided the transition from the critical standpoint of the Enlightenment to that of later hermeneutics. They also have proved crucial to many other later critical discourses.

The first of these ideas was that the primary form in which culture existed and developed was that of the **text**, which displaced practices and institutions as the focal point of critical discourse. In its earliest manifestations, especially in Enlightenment biblical hermeneutics, this term was used quite literally to refer to written documents, these being viewed as a privileged medium through which other, nontextual cultural phenomena, whether past or present, were accessible. Gradually, however, the term *text* came to be metaphorically extended to include, first, other cultural products of a broadly artistic nature beyond the specifically literary (examples of the visual arts, music, and the like), and later, all products of human historical and cultural activity whatsoever (that is, cultural practices and institutions themselves).

Second, the most important function of a text was to communicate meaning. In the critical discourse of the Enlightenment, existing cultural practices and institutions generally were viewed as facts on which critical value judgments were brought to bear. The practitioners of emergent modern hermeneutic discourse, however, realized that they were dealing not so much with facts as with much more complex objects. The meaning of a text was not just a fact to be described or explained but was itself a manifestation of an already complex set of perspectives, orientations, and judgments made by its "author" that required as well the active complicity of a "reader." Thus, the cultural engagement of the Enlightenment critic with practices and institutions that she or he wished to alter gave way to the interpretive engagement of a "reader" with a "text" that was to be illuminated or revised in the interpretive process.

Third, in focusing on the meanings of texts, hermeneutics came to stress as its primary aim **understanding** rather than **explanation**. Even practitioners of Enlightenment hermeneutics were aware that a different attitude from that of the natural sciences was called for in dealing with complex cultural productions. While later hermeneutics sometimes aspired to develop its own distinctive methodology, it remained insistent that its aims and methods differ from those of the natural sciences.

Finally, language itself played a fundamental role in the critical discourse of hermeneutics. If the primary goal of hermeneutics was to understand the meanings of texts, then language must appear central to its enterprise at several different levels. To speak of texts was immediately to suggest that they were specific constructions utilizing language as their medium. This, in turn, implied that the stance of the cultural critic was more appropriately described as that of a reader and author of texts rather than of an observer and judge of events—in other words, the role more of a philologist or literary critic than of a scientist or political activist. Further, as the operative notion of language followed that of text in metaphorical extension, hermeneutics could come to speak of the languages of the visual arts, music, and ultimately any cultural practice or institution. However, since the primary sense of language remained that of spoken and written human expression, it was natural to apply insights gained from the study of such language, often drawn from the historically concurrent development of linguistics, to the understanding of texts in their more extended signification. The entire cultural world could thus be viewed as a linguistic text and its principles of operation sought within a linguistic paradigm. From the beginning, then, hermeneutics involved a linguistic emphasis that was to remain central to its project throughout its development as a critical discourse.

Friedrich Schleiermacher: Romantic Hermeneutics and Human Understanding

As mentioned earlier, Schleiermacher can be regarded as the originator of hermeneutics as a modern critical discourse. Before we can evaluate Schleiermacher's contributions, however, we must understand his connections with Romanticism and hence his differences with the liberal humanism of the Enlightenment. In so doing, we should remember that as in the relationships among most of the various critical discourses, the differences concern, in the first instance, choices among general problematics, vocabularies, and strategies, and should not be understood as necessarily implying, in any direct sense, controversies over the evaluation of specific practices, institutions, or political configurations (although, of course, these often occurred).

Schleiermacher employed the term *culture* in a much more deliberate and self-conscious sense than did most Enlightenment figures, in whose thought it tended to become absorbed into considerations of civil or political society. Schleiermacher treated culture as a distinctive sphere of inquiry in its own right and located it, in a way reminiscent of Kant's essay on history, at the point where human practical reason, intersecting natural events in space and time, produces history. However, the Enlightenment tended to equate practical reason with individuals as abstract bearers of rights and to view history as the gradual process by which individual rights came to be recognized within the political sphere. For his part, Schleiermacher, in step with the new Romantic outlook, preferred a more organic perspective: On the one hand, the abstract individual was transformed into a unique, living **subject** that inwardly and self-consciously distinguished itself from all others while acknowledging that others did the same in their own cases. On the other hand, he stressed that individual uniqueness could be expressed and maintained only in the context of various **communities** such as the family, the nation, the church, and so on. Culture was thus the outcome of this reciprocal interaction between irreducible subjects self-consciously aware of their own uniqueness and the various communities in which their personalities could find expression. Just as the contents of the inner life of the individual were drawn from the communities in which it participated, so communities were nurtured and developed through the expression of the unique subjectivities of their members. Subject and community thus lived in and through one another and culture was the organic, living result of the historical unfolding of this reciprocal interaction.

Schleiermacher's idea of hermeneutics followed quite directly from these assumptions. During the Enlightenment, various **specialized hermeneutics** had been developed that dealt with the interpretation of philological, theological, and legal texts. Schleiermacher, however, envisioned a **general hermeneutics,** an "art of understanding" that would apply to any and all possible texts. For him, Understanding replaced Enlightenment philosophers' Reason as the preeminent human activity. However, because Schleiermacher like most Romantics was intensely concerned with the individuality and uniqueness of cultural agents and their products, he was suspicious of any universalistic philosophical pronouncements. In place of philosophical system building, Schleiermacher pursued a broad theory of the operation of human understanding at its most basic level—a theory that reached its fruition in the twentieth century, in the **philosophical hermeneutics** of Heidegger and Gadamer.

Schleiermacher's general hermeneutics was based on a specific conception of the relationship between thought (or experience), language, and the nature of human communication. According to Schleiermacher, thought always involves the use of an existing language in an internal discourse: In thinking, we in effect are talking to ourselves. Communication of our internal thoughts occurs when we externalize our thoughts in texts (which can be either spoken or written). Interpretation, for Schleiermacher, was a paradigmatic example of the fundamental operation of human understanding. It was the process by which an interpreter or reader who is familiar with the language that an author or speaker has employed gains access to the internal thoughts of the author or speaker by **reconstructing** in her or his own mind the author's thought processes or experiences. Hermeneutic understanding therefore involves the process of interpretation, all interpretation aims at reexperiencing the thought of another as it is expressed in texts, and language is the medium by virtue of which this sharing of thoughts or experiences through texts can occur.

Following from this train of thought was Schleiermacher's invocation of **dialogue** as the most adequate description of the interpretive process. By this he meant that the aim of interpretation is to establish a **reciprocity** between an author and a reader through the medium of the text. As opposed to explanation, which is merely a one-sided consideration of objects on the part of the explainer, interpretation involves a two-way process whereby the living thoughts of one person are recreated in those of another, creating (at least in principle) the possibility of further mutual engagement in the context of an interpretive community.

Schleiermacher maintained that language played a dual role in this process, thus giving rise to two different aspects or dimensions of the enterprise of general hermeneutics. Every instance of the use of language refers, on the one hand, to the entirety of the language that it employs, and on the other, to the mind of the speaker or author, with its specific characteristics and intentions. A reader attending to the meanings of the words and linguistic constructions on the basis of her or his knowledge of the language is involved in **grammatical interpretation**. By contrast, **psychological** (or, as Schleiermacher sometimes called it, **technical**) **interpretation** concerns the specific and individual ways in which a given author uses the language to express her or his own distinctive thoughts or experiences. This, of course, may involve the reader in drawing on additional historical, cultural, and biographical factors which go well beyond the merely grammatical.

According to Schleiermacher, all interpretation will involve both grammatical and psychological or technical factors, though one or the other might predominate in a given case. That is, as readers we must always attempt to understand both what is being said in any text and how what is being said conveys the author's individual meaning or intention to us. It is only these taken together that permit us to reconstruct in our own minds the meaning or intention of the author, which is the ultimate aim of all interpretation. If skillfully practiced, Schleiermacher claimed, a full interpretation might eventually come "to understand the discourse just as well and even better than its creator," since interpretation will have made conscious and explicit many factors of which the author was unaware at the time of producing the text.

As a schematic overview, this notion of general hermeneutics seems fairly straightforward. However, a crucial problem, which Schleiermacher is usually credited with being the first to see, arises when we consider the actual process of interpretation. Schleiermacher developed this problem of the **hermeneutic circle** in three general directions. First, in relation to grammatical interpretation, Schleiermacher pointed out that even at the level of the sentence, that is, the linguistic expression of a complete thought, we cannot understand its general meaning without first understanding the meanings of its constituent words; conversely, however, we cannot understand the meanings of the words within a sentence without grasping the meaning of the entire sentence. This dilemma, of course, applies just as well to the relation between paragraphs and chapters, chapters and an entire book, and so forth. Second, in relation to psychological or technical interpretation, we cannot understand the thought or concept of an author without understanding the general biographical and historical context in which the thought or concept arose; however, we have no knowledge of what contextual factors are relevant without first encountering the thought or concept itself. We cannot, for example, understand what Descartes meant by "reason" without understanding the broader philosophical discussions of his day, but we cannot understand the nature of those discussions without understanding the role which Descartes' conception of "reason" played in them. Finally, and in the most general sense, all human understanding functions in the same manner as its paradigm, textual interpretation. Understanding is the dual and circular process of working through the always partial and limited experiences of a text, an artwork, another human being, or whatever, in order to grasp it as an organic whole, and of grasping the significance of the various partial experiences on the basis of an understanding of the whole of which they are parts.

Of course, while the hermeneutic circle clearly poses a logical conundrum at the level of theory, in practice it is not a vicious circle, since we do in fact gradually come to understand not only the meaning of texts as wholes but also how the whole text achieves its meaning in relation to its various parts. Similarly, while we learn a language by first learning specific words and phrases, at some point we become able to speak the whole language itself and recognize when particular instances of it do or do not obey its rules. For Schleiermacher as well as for later hermeneutic discourse, one of the most important conclusions that follows from this is that human understanding, by its very nature, involves a circular process that cannot be captured by the linear models of logical reasoning. This does not mean that it is without its own principles and methodological constraints but only that the understanding of human texts and the experience that they express cannot be adequately described or characterized by the logic appropriate to the natural world.

Wilhelm Dilthey: Hermeneutics as Methodology of the Human Sciences

Wilhelm Dilthey (1833–1911) is the most important figure after Schleiermacher in the nineteenth-century development of hermeneutics as a modern critical discourse. Like Schleiermacher, Dilthey shared the Romantic concern to respect the uniqueness and richness of individual experience and opposed any attempt to reduce it to either rationalist logical categories or empiricist sensory data. He called his general viewpoint a *Lebensphilosophie*—a philosophy of life. When used in this sense, the notion of life was not principally biological but indicated the total texture of meaningful human experience and its cultural expressions. Since no philosophical system could ever exhaust these, Dilthey also shared Schleiermacher's suspicion of any grand intellectual syntheses.

Dilthey conceived the task of *Lebensphilosophie* as a hermeneutic one, based on the general formula of **experience, expression,** and **understanding.** All human meaning arises from the lived experience of individuals already located and actively engaged in the relationships that make up the cultural and historical world. Within lived experience one encounters no pure facts but rather things and events that are already laden with meaning and values. The "objective" counterpart of lived experience is its expression in a rich diversity of cultural forms, including language, art works, practices, and institutions. Culture is thus the **objectification** of the meanings that make up lived experience. Understanding is the process by which we interpret these objectifications of lived experience in order to gain access to the lived experience that they express. This understanding of lived experience through the interpretation of its cultural expressions is the proper task of the human sciences, among which Dilthey counted philology, literary criticism, and history in addition to psychology, sociology, and anthropology. Hermeneutics thus becomes the linchpin joining the most basic processes of life and its meaningful expression in culture with the human sciences whose aim is to understand lived experience through cultural expressions. For Dilthey, hermeneutics is thus at once a basic and defining feature of human existence as well as the characteristic methodology of the human sciences. Hermeneutics as a methodology is but a more explicit and self-conscious articulation of what human beings constantly practice in lived experience.

The significance of Dilthey's ideas for the development of hermeneutic discourse was profound. First, as we have just seen, he believed that all forms of human activity and production were expressions of understanding. Understanding became not just one human faculty among others, as Schleiermacher tended to suggest, but comprised all human faculties and constituted our basic human condition. Reason, feeling, aesthetic appreciation, and so forth were all merely different manifestations or modalities of understanding. It followed from these assumptions that even Schleiermacher's general hermeneutics failed to describe the full extent of the hermeneutic project. If understanding included the whole range of expressions of distinctively human activity, or life, as Dilthey defined it, then hermeneutic issues were inseparable from the most fundamental philosophical considerations involving human existence. Dilthey's expansion of Schleiermacher's general hermeneutics thus became the foundation of the **philosophical hermeneutics** of the twentieth century. Further, this meant that hermeneutics could no longer be viewed as principally concerned with written texts. Rather, the object of hermeneutics was nothing less than the whole realm of human culture and its history. Thus, with Dilthey, the term *text* was first expanded to include any and all cultural products; from there, hermeneutics could be conceived of as a comprehensive critical discourse concerning culture. Finally, Dilthey's broad theory of human understanding as intrinsically hermeneutic allowed him to address methodological issues in the human sciences in a way that did not fall back into the more specialized interpretive approaches fashionable in the nineteenth cen-

tury, especially in legal theory and historiography. Rather, Dilthey sought to connect the human sciences directly to the most basic processes of human understanding—a linkage that until then had not been attempted.

Martin Heidegger:
Phenomenological Hermeneutics of Existence

Martin Heidegger (1889–1976) was by any account one of the seminal thinkers of
the twentieth century. The impact of his views extends well beyond the critical
discourse of hermeneutics, significantly influencing the critical theory of the
Frankfurt School and a good deal of poststructuralism as well. Still, it was within
the discourse of hermeneutics that Heidegger's ideas received their most explicit
development, just as his own thought was to a considerable extent a development
of the hermeneutic ideas of Dilthey. The major problem in assessing Heidegger's
influence on the critical discourses of the twentieth century lies in the fact that
Heidegger's basic concerns were overwhelmingly philosophical, to an extent not
encountered in most of the other figures we have thus far considered. This allowed his ideas to be appropriated in many different contexts, often with widely
varying practical results. Further, Heidegger's still hotly debated involvement with
the German national socialist movement in the early 1930s led some to deny influences on their own ideas that in fact ran deep. Still, some familiarity with Heidegger's views is important, especially in any attempt to understand the development of the critical discourse of hermeneutics in this century.

In his "phenomenological hermeneutic of existence," Heidegger developed three
themes of crucial significance for later hermeneutic theory. First, Heidegger
stressed that any hermeneutic enterprise, whether directed toward ascertaining the
meaning of our own existence or toward other ends, presupposes that we are already located and engaged in the world, as reflected in the term he coined for human existence, *Dasein* (roughly, "being there"): In a very literal sense, we can begin
any interpretive process only "from where we're at." In order even to formulate a
question of the meaning of something, we must have some **preunderstanding** of
what it is we are asking about as well as of what might count as an appropriate response to our question. Thus, any interpretive questioning will be guided both by
the understanding and concern out of which it arises and by the purposes we envi-
sion it accomplishing. It therefore makes no sense to seek some valid, impartial, or
objective interpretation, since no interpretation can have either a totally disinterested starting point nor aims completely removed from the purposes of the interpreter. Rather, every interpretation will reveal something both about what the interpreter already understands about her or his world and about the interests of the
interpreter in pursuing a given line of interpretation—that is, about the "from
which" and the "toward which" of the questions posed by the interpreter.

Of course, any interpretation involves (at least potentially) an **articulation** of
the meaning of what is being interpreted. Whether we are interpreting a poem or

reflecting on the meaning of our own existence, the "saying" of its meaning is a crucial element in the process. However, this "saying" typically refers to or focuses on the thing under discussion, leaving "unsaid" both its context of preunderstanding and its underlying interests. While "saying" reveals something about our understanding of the matter at hand, it equally conceals a good deal about our broader context and interests. Every interpretation therefore involves a complex interplay whereby the very process of framing, focusing on, and articulating a particular subject or text simultaneously also conceals and obscures something about it. This is not a matter of deliberate deception but part of the finite and located nature of human understanding. Thus, the task of hermeneutics is not merely one of "saying" what something means, but also of attending to what is "not said," to what the "saying" itself suppresses or obscures. This notion of understanding as simultaneously a revealing and a concealing, and of interpretation as a process whereby what is revealed is brought into connection with what is concealed, is the second major contribution of Heidegger to hermeneutics as a critical discourse.

Finally, Heidegger radicalized the conception of the consciousness of time as the foundation for all other engagements with meaning by showing how **temporality** forms the ultimate horizon of human existence. Heidegger employed the term *temporality* to call attention to his view that time was ultimately of the order of meanings, not that of things, and that it constituted the ultimate horizon for the meaning of lived experience and its understanding. Analogously, rather than speaking of past, present, and future as if they were somehow three different sets of events or entities to be distinguished by an appropriate dating process, Heidegger preferred to speak of **thrownness, circumspective concern,** and **projection.** In order to emphasize their relation to human existence, Heidegger calls these **temporal ek-stases,** ways in which the human being "stands out or away" from itself in its existence. By speaking of "thrownness" instead of "the past," he is calling attention to the manner in which we "always already" find ourselves cast into a world not entirely of our own making and nonetheless immediately relevant to us. The past, whether our own or of all history, is not experienced as some indifferent and dead body of facts or moments but as events that are meaningful to us in that they have been understood as forming part of the world into which we are "thrown," that is, part of the given historical conditions of our existence. Likewise, the present as experienced has little to do with the position of the hands on my watch. Rather, the lived and meaningful present has to do with those things, persons, and events that I care about in the world around me, things that I value, persons with whom I share relationships, causes to which I am committed. Heidegger called this perspective **circumspective concern.** Finally, the future is not experienced either as some empty and indeterminate void that lies ahead or as what must necessarily come to be because of some law of nature. Rather, in my projection of what I wish to do, the sort of person I want to become, or the kind of world I desire for my children, the future discloses itself to me as meaningful.

Heidegger dealt with the historical character of human existence in terms of his analysis of temporality. In describing *Dasein* in terms of temporal *ek-stases*, Heidegger meant that each represents a distinctive and irreducible dimension of any instance of understanding and thus of hermeneutics itself. While Heidegger agreed with Dilthey that any hermeneutic undertaking occurs within the necessarily finite and limited horizon of history, he preferred to use the term **historicity** to indicate that this includes not only the place of hermeneutic practice in relation to past events or discourses but also its present concerns and future commitments. It is this aspect of Heidegger's thought that most opens the prospect for hermeneutics as a genuinely critical discourse, since hereafter it becomes viewed as involving, not just an interest in texts of the past nor in the cultural world of the present, but an engaged appropriation of what is significant from the past, growing out of present concerns, in anticipation of a meaningful future.

In Heidegger's writings after *Being and Time*, which he regarded as the first part of a larger project (it was never completed), his thought underwent a dual shift in emphasis. First, he came to suspect that seeking the "access to Being" through an analysis of human being or Dasein might somehow skew the most important questions in a subjective direction, when his original intention had been nothing less than to discover and understand the meaning of "Being itself." Second, Heidegger came to focus more on language than on the temporality of human existence as the ultimate horizon for the understanding of Being. In a famous phrase, he claimed that "language is the house of Being." This suggested that rather than thinking of meaning as created out of the matrix of the temporal existence of Dasein, we should view it as something retrieved or appropriated from the historically developed resources of language. This, in turn, led Heidegger to begin questioning the very linguistic resources with which such fundamental questions can be raised within the European tradition—what he called the "destructive recovery of the history of metaphysics"—which provided the foundations for the later critical discourse of poststructuralism. However, well before this, Heidegger had begun pressing the implications of his philosophical hermeneutics for cultural critique in two directions.

Beginning with *Being and Time* and continuing into his later writings, the threat to meaningful human existence posed by **technology** became a central concern. Although Heidegger, like many of his contemporaries, was struck by the fact that the human race might be enslaved or even extinguished by its own technological creations, the real issue ran much deeper—it was, in the first instance, a hermeneutical problem. For Heidegger, the ever increasing domination of the modern world by technology should be regarded as a symptom of a deeper and widespread loss of a sense of the intimate connection between human being (*Dasein*) and Being itself (*Sein*), which *Being and Time* had been a first attempt to articulate. Although this process of alienation from the existential roots of our human being had already commenced with the Greek origins of European philosophy, it became dramatically intensified with the establishment of the modern sciences at the beginning of the modern era. The scientific attitude and its technological fruits increasingly interposed between human being and nature a world of artificial objects permitting an unprecedented degree of control over natural forces. The price to be paid, however, was a loss both of the fundamental meaning of human existence and of the resources of thought necessary to recover it. Modern thought itself, in thrall to the **calculative** discourse of the sciences, had itself become technological, reducing all truth to a function of statements and their logical connections rather than its more fundamental sense as a disclosure of Being within human being. Heidegger believed that the only path to recovering this sense and establishing a new relationship to our own technological productions was a sustained hermeneutic discourse aimed at disclosing the most fundamental ways in which understanding orients us with respect to the world and allows us to live meaningfully within it. Heidegger deliberately drew on the hermeneutic model of understanding as pointing the way to this new mode of thinking, which he sometimes called **meditative** as opposed to calculative. Such thinking opened the prospect of a critique of technology that would not merely serve to reinforce it, as had earlier attempts, but that would permit new relations to be established with technology.

A second dimension of hermeneutic-oriented critique in the later works of Heidegger involved an increasingly important role for art, and in particular, poetry. Many of Heidegger's most profound insights are expressed in his interpretive readings of poets such as Rilke, Hölderlin, and Trakl, whose use of language, in particular, Heidegger regarded as providing examples of discourse outside the pervasive influence of calculative attitudes. Heidegger's movement away from the more subjective stance of his earlier project toward the disclosure of Being in language was worked out, to a great extent, in the process of his poetic interpretation. His actual readings and his interpretive procedures have provided yet another important basis allowing later thinkers to link the philosophical concern with hermeneutics to a critique of technology, scientific modes of thought, and ultimately the entire historical tradition in which they rose to dominance.

Hans-Georg Gadamer: Philosophical Hermeneutics

Hans-Georg Gadamer (b. 1900) is the most influential of those who have developed the implications of Heidegger's thought for hermeneutic discourse. In fact, many who understandably find Heidegger's own texts impenetrable—especially those in fields such as literary criticism, history, and theology—have found in Gadamer an important avenue of access to contemporary hermeneutic discourse. Although Gadamer should not be read in every instance as a reliable guide to Heidegger (nor does he view himself as such, despite the fact that Heidegger was his teacher), it is clear that Heidegger's influence on Gadamer was profound. It is probably also true that Heidegger's ideas would not be nearly so widespread or so influential had it not been for Gadamer's writings, especially his *Truth and Method* (1960).

Anyone concerned with critical discourse who reads this work against the background of Heidegger's thought will be struck by an ambiguity in its critical stance. On the one hand, Gadamer's views are articulated in ways that are often more directly attentive and relevant to such other disciplines as aesthetics, historiography, literary criticism, and theology. On the other hand, and in seeming contradiction, Gadamer very explicitly wants to remove his philosophical hermeneutics from any concern with specific methods—indeed, he sees truth and method as antithetical—and from any direct implication for cultural critique or political practice. If Heidegger's position with respect to the sort of critique with which we have been concerned is difficult to determine, Gadamer's views, which sometimes seem to function at an even greater level of abstraction, are even more remote.

Still, Gadamer's philosophical hermeneutics takes up questions posed by the earlier hermeneutic tradition that Heidegger appears to have minimized or left behind. In the first place, Gadamer's discussion in *Truth and Method* continually returns to the question of **textuality**. While he certainly does not regard his views as limited exclusively to the interpretation of texts, the notion of the text does function in his thought in a much more explicit way than it does in Heidegger's, which remains focused on the question of Being. Whereas Heidegger could never be justly accused of textualizing the world, whatever else he may do, it is not clear that Gadamer could escape such a charge. Secondly, Gadamer's assessment of the Western intellectual tradition is much more positive than Heidegger's. Whereas one of Heidegger's recurrent themes was the covering over of the most basic questions of human existence within that tradition, requiring a sort of reflective break with or reversal of it, Gadamer tends to emphasize our inescapable and even productive continuity with our tradition. In a sense that runs contrary to Heidegger, Gadamer views himself as reaffirming, though with important qualifications, a version of the European humanist tradition. Finally, while Heidegger, especially in his later thought, tends to stress the necessity of a "passive listening" to Being as revealed in language, Gadamer does not want to lose sight of the active and productive nature of our appropriation of the past in the interpretation of historical texts.

Drawing on some of Heidegger's suggestions, Gadamer wishes to assert the irreducible unity of **hermeneutic experience** in the face of modern attempts to reduce the subject to the object or vice versa. If there is any general critical stance in evidence in *Truth and Method*, it is that neither the modern quest for objectivity, characteristic of the natural sciences born in the Enlightenment and other disciplines that emulate their methods, nor the subjectivity so emphasized by Romantic aesthetics and interpretation theory is an adequate basis for a genuinely philosophical hermeneutic viewpoint. Rather, the task of philosophical hermeneutics is to **dialectically** articulate the various concrete ways and dimensions in which subject and object are in continual interplay with one another. We should note immediately that when Gadamer uses the term *dialectical*, he does not intend it in the methodological sense of Marx's dialectical materialism but in an earlier sense that is more closely connected with the etymological cognate *dialogue,* a sort of open play of question and response.

Like Heidegger, Gadamer viewed understanding as more than just one among several human faculties or than a result to be reached through the application of a given method. He saw it as the universal and inescapable condition of human existence. As he put it, the hermeneutic problem is truly universal, since the interpretive activity of understanding is the condition for the emergence of any truth, prior to and independent of any subsequently adopted method. In his view, no method could ever guarantee truth. Rather, the disclosure of truth within the interpretive process of understanding is what first makes possible the choice, criterion, and warranty of any method. Philosophical hermeneutics therefore has no direct methodological consequences for the natural or human sciences, nor will it result in a general canon of hermeneutic principles equally applicable to any inquiry. Rather, it seeks to elucidate the conditions of understanding as engaged with truth prior to any question of method.

Gadamer employed the term **horizon** (derived from Husserl and Heidegger) to indicate those conditions within which human understanding exists and functions. In his analysis, **historicality** and **linguisticality** together constitute the ultimate horizon of all human understanding.

Drawing on Heidegger's analysis of temporality, Gadamer asserted that all interpretation occurs within a tradition, that it involves an attitude of **receptiveness** or **openness** to tradition, and that it moves toward the **disclosure** within understanding of what was initially concealed or hidden. In his discussion of tradition, Gadamer, like Heidegger, holds that all interpretation begins in preunderstanding, constituted by a set of received **prejudgments** or **prejudices**. He especially faults the skeptical turn of the Enlightenment, which we have already encountered in such thinkers as Bacon and Descartes, for discrediting the notions of prejudice and tradition, as if we could somehow establish a transhistorical standpoint free of them. In contrast to these thinkers, Gadamer viewed understanding as radically and inescapably historical and interpretation as a creative appropriation of the past, made possible only on the basis of the prejudgments inherited from the tradition in which we stand. This means that one cannot speak of a "right" or "correct" interpretation, since no two interpreters, or even a single interpreter at different times of her or his life, will confront a given text from within exactly the same horizon. As our historical horizons shift (as they continually do), so will our understanding of the meaning of a given text.

However, Gadamer insisted that this by no means implies a Romantic subjectivism, that any text means only what someone, at any given point in time, thinks that it does. Rather, any historical text (to use Gadamer's paradigm case) was produced by an author with her or his own historical horizon, which is necessarily reflected within the text itself. Understanding is thus the event whereby we bring the prejudgments of our own tradition to bear on the historical horizon of the text itself, through interpretation. Gadamer called this event of interpretive understanding a **"fusion of horizons"**: In any reading of a text, the text's historical horizon comes to fuse with our own in a unique creative act of appropriation, of making the text relevant to our own historical condition without thereby reducing it to our own subjective meaning-constructions. In this sense, Gadamer claimed, the hermeneutic experience always involves an application or engaged relating of the past to our present questions and concerns; for hermeneutics, there can be no artificial separation of theory and practice.

Gadamer thus rejected any tendency to equate the meaning of a text with either the subjective feelings of the interpreter (sometimes called the **affective fallacy**) or with the intentions of the author (sometimes called the **intentional fallacy**). In his words, "A placement between strangeness and familiarity exists between the historically intended, distanced objectivity of the heritage and our belongingness to a tradition. *In this 'between' is the true place of hermeneutics.*" To further specify this idea, Gadamer described interpretation as a dialogue between interpreter and text. On the basis of our own historical horizon and its prejudgments, we begin by "putting a question" to a text, bringing to a text what is initially understood and of concern to us. The text itself, however, is an answer, perhaps to a quite different question posed by the author. In an authentic hermeneutic experience, the text confronts our original question with one of its own, and a deepened understanding results from allowing the question posed by the text to guide our own subsequent responses and further questionings. In particular, we must come to understand not only the historical question to which the text was a response but the range of possible responses of which the text itself represents a specific instance. In interpretation, that is, we must attend not only to what the text says but also to what it leaves unsaid.

For example, we in the later twentieth century and in the wake of World War II come to Goethe's *Faust* with different questions than a mid–nineteenth-century German. However, in an authentic hermeneutic experience of the text, we will allow our own present questions, perhaps about how the German tradition could lead to the debacle of national socialism, to be directed by the broader questions posed in *Faust* about the nature of human striving, the infinitude of human aspirations in the face of finite human abilities, and so forth. In this dialogical play, the authentic hermeneutic experience should lead us both to reformulate our own initial questions and to see both the historical horizon of *Faust* and our own horizon in a new light. It is in such an event that the truth of our own and of the text's historical horizon as they relate to one another is disclosed. We might, for instance, come to see that *Faust* is not merely a document of German literary or political history but one way of responding to questions that we might well pose to ourselves about the nature of human accomplishment in a world infected with evil. Of course, this appropriation in turn will become part of our own **historically operative consciousness**, thus influencing the prejudgments and questions with which we approach other texts as our own historical horizons continue to change.

Gadamer's discussion of the historicality of understanding is intimately related to his notion of its linguisticality. If interpretation presupposes a fusion of horizons, this fusion is possible only because of the intrinsically linguistic nature of all understanding. Just as Heidegger claimed that "language is the house of Being," so Gadamer pointed out that it is only through language that a world opens up for us: To have a language is to have a world. The true significance of language for understanding is missed if it is regarded simply as a tool for communication or an arbitrarily constructed system of signs. Rather, like the air we breath, language for Gadamer is the medium in which we live and by which we are able to share a common world with others. We do not possess a language so much as we belong to it. But the same can be said of every producer of texts, however ancient or remote. It is only because both author and reader exist within a linguistic horizon that we are able to enter into the world of the author and relate it to our own. While every text is the realization of a particular possibility of its language and has its own subject matter, it is also the disclosure, at the same time, of the entire world constituted by its linguistic horizon. The dialogical event of interpretation must continually move from the question posed by a text toward the entire world that it discloses in the fusion of its linguistic horizon with our own.

Hermeneutics After Gadamer

While Schleiermacher's initial distinction between general and specialized hermeneutics underwent a number of important modifications in the development of this discourse, it suggested an underlying tension that has yet to be resolved. On the one hand, the discourse of hermeneutics has sought to explore, at a more fundamental and philosophical level than liberal humanism, the roots of human culture in the most fundamental linguistic processes of speaking, writing, reading, and interpreting, thus making hermeneutics especially fruitful in such disciplines as literary criticism. However, as a universal philosophical theory of understanding, the concrete implications of hermeneutics for cultural critique become difficult to assess. This is reinforced by the tendencies of some of its most important representatives to deny that the general or philosophical side of hermeneutic discourse has any relevance for questions of concrete methodology. At most, we can say that the critical import of philosophical hermeneutics lies in attempting to effect a change of attitude or consciousness with respect to the individual's relation to culture and history. In particular, it warns us against the modern tendency to accept the worldview of the natural sciences as adequate to the texture of lived human experience or to believe that the discovery of "truth" requires a prior determination of a "correct" method. On the other hand, in hermeneutics' concern with texts as the paradigmatic focal point of both the understanding's expression and interpretation, a much more concrete element enters. Unlike the universality of understanding, every text presents a unique cultural formation posing specific problems for interpretation, for which purpose a philosophical hermeneutics can be at best suggestive.

"Applied" Hermeneutics and Contemporary Social Science: Geertz's Approach to Anthropology

Anthropology (or, more properly, its subdivisions ethnology and ethnography) has long been the discipline most directly concerned with the study of culture. Consequently, it has been the social science most directly affected by the development of various discourses of cultural critique. The work of **Clifford Geertz** provides one of the clearest and most controversial examples of the influence of hermeneutics on the discipline of anthropology. In the writings of Geertz we can perceive the influences of the ideas of such figures as Dilthey, Gadamer, and especially Paul Ricoeur (whom Geertz frequently has cited).

In *The Interpretation of Cultures* (1973), Geertz maintains that the ethnographer, whatever else she or he may do in gathering and organizing data about a culture, will ultimately be engaged in a process of "thick description." Geertz asserts that culture consists of "webs of significance [the human being] has spun . . . and the analysis of it [is] therefore not an experimental science in search of law but an interpretive one in search of meaning." More specifically, cultural phenomena should be regarded as texts to be read rather than as objects to be observed. To the repugnance of many of his colleagues, Geertz goes so far as to claim that hermeneutic disciplines such as literary criticism are more germane to the methodology of anthropology than models drawn from the natural sciences. Like written texts, cultural phenomena have an irreducible linguistic dimension. This means that the ethnographer's search for cultural meaning can never stop at mere observation of action or analysis of cultural systems but also must take into account, as an essential element, what an action or institution means to the participants as they articulate it. In other terms, all human cultural activity exists within a linguistic horizon that is an essential and inseparable feature of the activity itself.

The necessity of **thick description**, in which the ethnographer is always involved, stems from the various dimensions of the linguisticality of all cultural phenomena. First, at the level of the participants' discourse, a given action can be described and thus interpreted by various participants in different ways. What one person may describe as a wink another may describe merely as a twitch of the eye and yet another as the placing of a curse. The point is that even at the level of the participants' own descriptions, there can be no single or unequivocal datum constituting the object of ethnography. Secondly, when dealing with a culture that employs a language with which the ethnographer is unfamiliar, she or he typically must make use of informants (persons who are native speakers of the language but who also speak the ethnographer's language). Their descriptions of actions and events in another language add another interpretive stratum to the texts that the ethnographer must interpret. Finally, the ethnographer must write his or her own account of these other descriptions in such a way as to communicate to yet other readers the "web of meanings" that make up a given culture. As Geertz succinctly summarizes his notion of thick description, "[W]hat we call our data are really our own constructions of other people's constructions of what they and their compatriots are up to."

From this follow several points already familiar from our survey of the hermeneutic tradition. Because Geertz views ethnography as an interpretive process, there can never be a final, correct description of a culture or its practices. The temporality of interpretation dictates that understanding will always remain incomplete and open-ended. However, this does not lead to subjectivism, because all cultural phenomena are, like texts, ultimately public, rule-governed, and in principle accessible. As Gadamer emphasized, the focus of interpretation is not so much on the private intentions of the author or actor or the affects of the reader as it is on the text's own significance, the questions it poses and the answers that it suggests. Geertz would generalize this to include all cultural phenomena. Finally, the aim of interpretive ethnography, like that of any hermeneutic experience, is engagement in a dialogue or conversation, whereby the interpreter's understanding is expanded and his or her own stance with regard to the text is altered. In Geertz's words, "The whole point . . . is, as I have said, to aid us in gaining access to the conceptual world in which our subjects live so that we can, in some extended sense of the term, converse with them."

Concluding Reflections

The status of hermeneutics as a critical discourse of culture has been from the outset and remains somewhat ambiguous. That it has profoundly influenced the way in which culture is approached and indeed the contemporary meaning of culture is beyond dispute. Its suggestions that cultural phenomena be understood as texts and that our understanding of them be guided by this metaphor have had a significant impact on almost all contemporary critical practices, however much they may differ in other respects. The real problem lies in determining the extent to which hermeneutics remains merely philosophical or descriptive, or in fact makes possible a genuinely critical standpoint on the basis of which prevailing practices and institutions can be challenged.

From the perspective of large-scale historical trends, hermeneutics might well be defended, though with important qualifications. In the first place, hermeneutic discourse was the first to challenge many prevailing ideas of the mainstream Enlightenment tradition. In particular, hermeneutic discourse, from its inception, has served as a warning against invoking a preconceived notion of rationality as a fundamental or defining feature of cultural existence. From the hermeneutic perspective, rationality is only one form, and a very limited one, in which human understanding can manifest itself. Secondly, hermeneutics has functioned as a continual critique of the tendency to idolize the methodologies of the natural sciences and has insisted that human phenomena be approached in a radically different manner. Thirdly, it provided the first example of a discourse with broadly interdisciplinary implications, a medium in which the increasing compartmentalization of the disciplines might be overcome. Finally, it has been a constant reminder that human knowledge and practice, as well as all critical discourses about them, are always historically located, beset by their own prejudices, and incapable of adopting a transcendent, ahistorical perspective.

However, from the point of view of other, later critical discourses that we will discuss in the next few chapters, hermeneutics, while critical of certain shortcomings of liberal humanism, has failed to extricate itself from others. In its most general form, the recurrent charge against hermeneutics has been that it remains trapped in subjectivism and idealism. By making meaning largely a function of the interpreter's understanding, it is reduced to invoking the authority of a subject, which ultimately implies relativism or nihilism. It has also been pointed out that the origins of hermeneutic discourse in biblical criticism led it to shroud all cultural texts in the sort of mystification characteristic of sacred texts themselves. Such criticisms are reinforced by the markedly idealistic treatments of history and language as mysterious superentities that somehow determine the contours of all human existence. On this basis, it could be argued that while hermeneutics shed some of the baggage of liberal humanism, such as the faith in scientific methodology and progress, it reinforced other aspects, such as an idealized notion of human freedom, a humanistic individualism, and the selective affirmation of tradition. To some, hermeneutic discourse thus appears not very different in its political implications from the later liberal humanism of Matthew Arnold, albeit articulated on a more elaborate philosophical foundation. Most contemporary critical discourse therefore has kept a wary distance from the hermeneutic tradition as a general approach to cultural critique.

However, at a more restricted level, where hermeneutic discourse has dealt explicitly with the reception of texts, the cultural processes involved in the transmission of texts, and the relation between textual understanding and methodology, important contributors to contemporary critical discourse from such areas as literary history and interpretation have drawn heavily on its insights, while rejecting its broader claims. Although hermeneutic discourse might have failed to establish its own critical stance, some have employed its insights as a basis on which a critical stance developed elsewhere can be grafted. We will see later how this occurred—for instance, in the work of some members of the Frankfurt School of critical theory. Thus, in reading works of contemporary cultural criticism, it is not unusual to find certain aspects of hermeneutic discourse being employed, even as the author maintains a decidedly critical stance toward hermeneutics as a general viewpoint.

Bibliographic Essay

There is a great deal of literature, both primary and secondary, on hermeneutics. The best general survey in English, as well as an accessible introduction to the thought of four of the major figures whom we have discussed, is *Hermeneutics: Interpretation Theory in Schleier-*

macher, Dilthey, Heidegger, and Gadamer, by Richard E. Palmer (Evanston, Ill.: Northwestern University Press, 1969). Although it does not approach hermeneutics from the point of view of cultural critical discourse, this book was nonetheless extremely helpful in preparing this chapter. While I generally avoid citing references to works in languages other than English, mention must be made of by far the most comprehensive and scholarly treatment of the early history of hermeneutics, the three volumes by Joachim Wach, collectively entitled *Das Verstehen: Grundzüge einer Geschichte der hermeneutischen Theorie im 19 Jahrhundert* (Tübingen: Mohr, 1926–1933). At least two anthologies of primary texts in the hermeneutic tradition are available: *The Hermeneutics Reader,* ed. Kurt Mueller-Vollmer (New York: Continuum, 1989), which contains an introduction offering a survey of hermeneutic thought much briefer than that of Palmer but still very helpful; and *The Hermeneutic Tradition: From Ast to Ricoeur,* eds. Gayle Ormiston and Alan Schrift (Albany, N.Y.: SUNY Press, 1990).

In the latter volume, the reader will find four essays, two each by Gadamer and Habermas, which not only serve as a good brief introduction to Gadamer's basic orientation but also present critical responses by Habermas, the most important contemporary representative of the Frankfurt School of critical theory. Within recent debates over the status of hermeneutics as a critical discourse, Paul Ricoeur has defended hermeneutics even as he surveyed its limitations, opening up new avenues for rapprochement between it and other critical discourses. The most succinct summary of Ricoeur's own hermeneutical views can be found in *Interpretation Theory: Discourse and the Surplus of Meaning* (Fort Worth: Texas Christian University Press, 1976). For his bridge-building efforts between hermeneutics and the social sciences, see the collection *Hermeneutics and the Human Sciences,* ed. John B. Thompson (Cambridge: Cambridge University Press, 1981), especially the very influential essay "The Model of the Text: Meaningful Action Considered as a Text." See the essay "Hermeneutics and the Critique of Ideology" in the same volume for Ricoeur's typically balanced response to the Gadamer-Habermas controversy mentioned above.

For a concrete example of an attempt to develop a distinctly critical stance from a hermeneutic position, see Charles H. Long, *Significations: Signs, Symbols, and Images in the Interpretation of Religion* (Philadelphia: Fortress, 1986). For the relevance of hermeneutic discourse to literary theory, see Joel Weinsheimer, *Philosophical Hermeneutics and Literary Theory* (New Haven: Yale University Press, 1991). *Reading Material Culture,* ed. Christopher Tilley (Oxford: Basil Blackwell, 1990) contains an essay by Eric Silverman entitled "Clifford Geertz: Towards a More 'Thick' Understanding," which presents Geertz's overall position together with a critique from the standpoint of poststructuralist ethnography.

For a scathing general critique of hermeneutics from a post-Arnoldian liberal humanist standpoint, see *Hermeneutics as Politics,* by Stanley Rosen (Oxford: Oxford University Press, 1987). Rosen paints hermeneutics in broad strokes, viewing it as symptomatic of the entire modernist project. His treatment is particularly interesting for its emphasis of the differences (where most critics have seen mainly similarities) between hermeneutics and later versions of liberal humanism.

3
The Materialist
Critique of Culture

In the early seventeenth century, the French philosopher and mathematician **René Descartes** (1596–1650) introduced into modern European intellectual discourse a doctrine known as **dualism**. According to this view, which Descartes intended to serve as the philosophical foundation for the newly emergent natural sciences, all things could be categorized in one of two classes: *res cogitans,* or things that think, and their ideas; and *res extensa,* or extended things, that is, objects that occupy space and hence are material. In other words, Descartes held that reality consists solely of minds and matter, and that everything real is either one or the other.

Descartes himself was a committed rationalist, so he naturally tended to place a decisive emphasis on the priority of minds and ideas over matter. He claimed that our first and most unshakable certainty was in our own existence, not as physical beings but as thinkers, as "subjects." On this basis he argued that mathematical ideas, in particular, were the privileged vehicles by which the scientific laws of material nature could be known. Descartes's emphasis on the mental was backed by his claim to have proven the existence of a deity (an immaterial, mental-like entity, of course), which "guaranteed" that so long as our thinking remains within the quantitative realm of mathematics, matter will, without fail, turn out to obey the mental laws of mathematics. Thus, *matter* for Descartes was the rather inert field over which thinking subjects, their mathematical ideas, and the power of an immaterial deity held sway. This philosophical view, which assigns a marked precedence to mind over matter, has come to be called **idealism** (not to be confused with the very different and more practical or ethical question as to whether someone is an idealist or a realist in their worldview).

Both the discourse of liberal humanism and that of hermeneutics can be regarded as idealist in that they take the subject, its ideas, and the cultural expressions of them as the starting point for any critique. During the Enlightenment, the way from idealist to materialist critical discourse was prepared intellectually by the writings of **Baruch Spinoza** (1632–1677) and practically by changes in how the sciences approached the explanation and control of nature. Spinoza, beginning with some of Descartes's methodological views, attempted to show, in effect, that any phenomenon could be explained equally well from the assumption of ideas or of matter as the basic reality. In his philosophy, the order of the mind and that of nature turned out to be strictly coordinate and complementary, and the preference of one over the other concerned only what one wished to accomplish by one's explanation. Further, as the seventeenth century turned into the eighteenth, and with the rise of Newtonian physics, the **empiricists** came to challenge the **rationalist** view of science as principally deductive and geometrical and increasingly to emphasize the notion that material nature had its own laws that the scientist "discovers" by observation and not by projecting onto nature mathematical ideas innate in the human mind.

Toward the end of the eighteenth century, a small but important group of critics had begun to turn the tables completely on the idealist implications of Cartesianism (as Descartes's general outlook had come to be known). Rejecting Cartesian dualism as logically incoherent and any exclusively idealist alternative as a mystification of more straightforward processes, these critics resolutely declared that genuinely scientific explanation required only the assumption of matter and its inalterable natural laws, which were discoverable through controlled observation and experiment. Further, in viewing the emergent science of economics as the only properly scientific approach to the study of human affairs, materialist critics of the later Enlightenment began laying the groundwork for what would become, in the work of Karl Marx and Friedrich Engels, a new materialist critical discourse.

In its fully developed form, materialist critical discourse differs dramatically from that of liberal humanism and of hermeneutics in several important respects. First, the primary emphasis of materialist critical discourse is on the notion of critique itself. While liberal humanism and hermeneutics could, with elaboration, become stances from which to launch a practical critique of specific cultural formations, most materialist views were oriented toward critique from the very beginning. In fact, determining the proper stance for cultural critique is almost always one of their overriding concerns. Put in other terms, for materialists, any view that is not self-consciously aware of its own critical position and import must be judged "abstract" and irrelevant to real human concerns. This especially applies to any view that begins from idealist assumptions, as do liberal humanism and hermeneutics.

Secondly, while most materialist views do not deny the existence and influence of ideas on human beings (any more than Descartes denied the existence or causal efficacy of matter), they tend to claim that mental phenomena and their cultural expressions are in some sense reflections of or responses to more fundamental, material forces. Materialist critics are rarely simplistic reductionists, but they do see a major function of critique as explaining how our ideas about the material world are themselves reflections of features of the material world. In the most basic sense, this problem of **ideology** is not an attempt to explain away mental and cultural phenomena but rather to show how ideas, philosophies, cultural formations, and general worldviews arise from material forces, mystify or conceal the nature of their origins, and then present themselves as putative realities that can appear to have a life of their own, independent of their material bases.

Thirdly, materialist discourse is rarely presented as external to or independent of the development of the human or social sciences. After all, the social sciences emerged as an attempt to apply the methods of the natural sciences to human phenomena, with a view toward understanding and controlling these phenomena in the same way as the natural sciences had done with regard to material nature. Materialist discourse saw in the social sciences, especially economics, the potential for cultural and historical transformation, but only if they were purged of their idealist elements and their tendencies to assume that human phenomena could be approached by straightforward adaptations of the basic methods of the natural sciences. Throughout its development, materialist critical discourse has maintained both a decidedly critical stance toward the scientistic methodological assumptions and potential for social manipulation of the mainstream social sciences, even while drawing from, interacting with, and often influencing them in various ways.

Fourthly, and more particularly, when a materialist perspective is brought to bear on human affairs, the emphasis does not fall primarily on the politics of civil society and the rights of the individual, or on the understanding of texts and their meanings, but on the material processes by which human beings collectively produce the means by which their basic needs are met, reproduce themselves as a species, and configure their social arrangements in such a way that through the exchange of their productions, their basic material existence can be secured and enhanced. This implies that in one sense or another, materialist discourse relates much more closely to economic concerns than to more abstractly political or literary paradigms. As we shall see, this does not mean that materialist discourse does not have very significant implications for political practice or literary interpretation, but only that material economic concerns take precedence and provide the major access to considering questions of political right or cultural meaning.

Finally, history, as it is characteristically viewed in materialist discourse, plays a much more prominent role in this critical discourse than in most others. Materialist discourse has tended to radicalize Vico's dictum that "what is true or knowable is what is created" into the sweeping claim that all of history is produced by human beings collectively securing the means of their own material survival. From this it follows not only that the underlying laws of history can be known because they arise from the process of human production itself, but also that historical formations can be changed by the same concerted human productive activity that brought them into existence in the first place. Of course, there has been considerable disagreement within materialist discourse about the degree to which historical knowledge or change is possible; but the assumption that history is neither inscrutable to human understanding nor absolutely resistant to practical human intervention seems operative in virtually all forms of modern materialist discourse.

Materialist Discourse Before Marx: The Struggle Against Philosophical Idealism

The Enlightenment has sometimes been called the Age of Ideas. The reason for this characterization probably lies in the fact that many of the Enlightenment's most prominent representatives, such as Voltaire, Diderot, and Condorcet, firmly believed that history was a process by which true ideas came gradually to replace false ones, and that these true ideas, especially those scientifically discovered and articulated, possessed an innate force sufficient to transform the social and cultural world. A common contemporary interpretation of the French Revolution held that it was born in the philosophical discussions that occupied the famous salons of the eighteenth century. Whatever its origins, anyone who observed the bloody course of the French Revolution, the rise of Napoleon Bonaparte as military dictator and later emperor, and the conservative reaction following his fall must have entertained profound doubts about the ability of ideas to direct history in the long run.

However, even before the French Revolution, a few advocates of the premier importance of the natural sciences and their methods had begun to doubt both the validity and the efficacy of extrascientific political or philosophical speculation. Such figures as **Julien Offroy de La Mettrie** (1709–1751) and the **Baron d'Holbach** (1723–1789) deliberately turned against the idealistic doctrines spawned in the wake of Descartes, which were designed to provide a metaphysical foundation for the natural sciences. Rejecting both the mainstream Enlightenment and the superstitions and prejudices born of organized religion, they likewise discounted the need for recourse to a creator-deity or an immortal soul, which many philosophers, who regarded themselves as **deists**, continued to affirm. For these materialists, human beings themselves were thoroughly material parts of the whole of material nature, the physical laws of which were all that was required for its explanation. For them, all of the rationalist and empiricist philosophical speculations of the Enlightenment were merely idealistic weeds that had grown up around the essentially "true" materialist trunk of the natural sciences, and their critical aim was to prune these obscuring outgrowths away. La Mettrie, in fact, had published a controversial work entitled *Man the Machine*, in which he suggested that from a rigorously materialist perspective, all human beings have an equal right to sensual gratification regardless of artificial social station, and that to continue to regard human beings from any other (idealist) perspective would merely serve to perpetuate the current injustices of the status quo.

During the same period, the development of economics also served to focus attention on the more materialistic processes underlying human society and culture. While the **Physiocrats** in France and political economists such as **Adam Smith** (1723–1790) in Great Britain could by no means themselves be regarded as materialists (as Marx would later be at great pains to demonstrate), they did begin exploring the social processes of the production and exchange of wealth and their relationship to labor, which would provide the basic scaffolding for the materialist critique of political economy. Just as the older materialists attempted to prune the idealist foliage from the trunk of materialist science, so Marx later attempted to do the same for the idealist mystifications inherent in the classical conception of economics.

Though materialist themes had begun to come to the forefront toward the end of the Enlightenment, their influence was largely checked in the years that followed the French Revolution by the development in Germany of a new and explicit form of idealism. Beginning with Kant, who yoked a global project of philosophical critique with a concerted defense of many of the idealistic themes of Enlightenment thought, **German idealism** succeeded in shaping these ideas into comprehensive and militantly antimaterialistic philosophical systems. The most fully developed and influential was that of **G.W.F. Hegel** (1770–1831). Hegel's self-described **absolute idealism** became the flashpoint for a new generation of materialist critics. This group, sometimes called the Young (or New) Hegelians, included **Ludwig Feuerbach** (1804–1872), the most important modern materialist prior to Marx and a crucial influence on the latter's thought.

However, before the critical project of Feuerbach (and subsequently Marx) can be presented, some acquaintance with the general contours of Hegel's absolute idealism is required. The reader should be aware that Hegel presented a very sophisticated and extremely complex philosophical viewpoint, of which what follows is merely a gloss of only those aspects most relevant to the development of materialist critical discourse. According to Hegel, all knowledge arises from experience, which is the process of comprehending the particular in the universal. Mere sensation yields no knowledge at all; rather, a given type of knowledge emerges only when the particulars of experience come to be characterized by a general concept. For instance, I can walk around a garden all day long, but I will know nothing about gardening until I am able to group the various individual plants that I perceive into general classes with common characteristics. But these general classes and common characteristics are concepts or ideas produced within the experience of the knowing **subject** as it relates its particular perceptions to universal concepts. In its most basic sense, Hegel's idealism thus consists in his claim that for the experiencing and knowing subject, reality is not individual, unique, and disjointed sensations but the universal concepts by which order and intelligibility are brought into the chaos of perception. In Hegel's famous phrase, "the real is the rational, and the rational is the real."

If experience is this process of comprehending what is more particular in terms of what is more general or universal, then experience must be progressive and cumulative, moving in the direction of ever higher conceptual generalities. Every conceptual level reached may be reconsidered from yet a more general or universal perspective, which latter will in turn determine its predecessor's level of conceptual reality. The subject itself, which is the productive source of these concepts, thus undergoes an expansion in each case, as it comes to comprehend increasingly more of reality through ever expanding concepts. Hegel calls the underlying structure of this process of the self-expansion of the subject in generating ever higher and more universal concepts **dialectic**. Most important for understanding this concept as Hegel (and later Marx and Engels) employed it is that all that we regard as making up reality—nature, culture, and even ourselves—is essentially a process of change and development, not a set of static structures. The term *dialectic* is employed to indicate the underlying logic of these developmental processes.

Probably the most controversial claim of Hegel's is that this dialectical development of the subject and its knowledge does not continue into an endless infinity. Rather, it will eventually reach a point of maximum expansion in a concept that will include all others and therefore all human experience itself. Religion has given us the first intimation of this in its concept of a supreme being that is the creator and sustainer of all that exists and is thus, at the same time, the absolutely first or primary being and the highest or most inclusive concept. Religion, however, presents this idea in the form of an image or representation. The task of idealist philosophy, then, is to articulate in logical and conceptual form the idea that is already present, although limited by its representational form, in religion. Thus, Hegel claimed that his philosophy of absolute idealism was nothing less than the explicit, rational articulation of the truth already implicit in religion: The "system of absolute knowledge" was the ultimate account of reality understood in the philosophical sense, that is, as conceptual and universal.

Although any modern subject is in principle capable of rising to this absolute standpoint, Hegel was at pains to show that all of history prepares the way and provides the "materials" that allow the subject to do so. History, for Hegel, is thus the broad, dialectical process of the gradual unfolding of absolute knowledge over time. By retraversing in its own experience the path that history has already traced, the modern subject becomes capable of actualizing in its own experience the standpoint of absolute knowledge at which history has already arrived. In a sense, then, the modern subject, thanks to history and dialectical philosophy, can occupy the place of the deity of religion and, from that point of view, see "the real as the rational and the rational as the real."

Hegel's argument had a deeply conservative thrust, since implicit in his absolute standpoint was the view that all historical conflicts and oppositions are ultimately resolved, that things have been and are exactly what they not only *should* be but as they *must* be. Whatever Hegel's own critical stance toward his contemporary world might have been, the radical Young Hegelians saw in his philosophical system a powerful and extended apologia for the status quo, an argument for a resigned acceptance of conditions that they regarded as intolerable. Further, based on their reading of Hegel's philosophy, they believed that the root of the problem could be traced back to Hegel's initial idealist assumptions, to which they opposed their own novel interpretation of materialism.

However, perhaps more than any other of the Young Hegelians (aside from Marx), Ludwig Feuerbach realized how formidable Hegel's philosophical system actually was, how thoroughly it had succeeded in assembling all the reactionary prejudices of the day and interjecting them into contemporary political and cultural attitudes and discourses. He thus appreciated the fact that no future critical discourse could avoid beginning with a critique of Hegel. Feuerbach found Hegel's greatest vulnerabilities to critique in three general areas: His dismissal of particular sensuous experience in favor of general concepts, his idea of religion as the penultimate form of truth, and his idealist account of the nature of human discourse.

In most popular accounts of Feuerbach, the almost humorous phrase "You are what you eat" is usually cited. Feuerbach himself might have meant this in a somewhat wry or ironic way, but it does convey an essential idea of modern materialist discourse. For Feuerbach, the first and always primary reality is what our senses give us—in particular, in those concrete, sensuous activities by which our biological life itself is maintained. Before we can think, worship a divinity, or construct a philosophical system, we must first eat, clothe ourselves, construct a place of shelter, and so forth. Whereas Hegel asserted that the realm of thought or the concept was the principal human reality, Feuerbach responded that prior to and presupposed by this realm is the more fundamental, material reality of maintaining our physical existence. In this sense, we must first "be what we eat" before we can "be what we think."

Religion, for Feuerbach, presented a paradigmatic case of Hegel's reversal of basic human priorities. Feuerbach was one of the first modern demystifiers of religious claims that demanded the subordination of secular to divine imperatives. Rather than offering us absolute knowledge in the representation of a supernatural realm on the basis of which all terrestrial travails and conflicts should be understood and evaluated, religion for Feuerbach was the product of human psychology in projecting an imaginary world unafflicted by the concrete difficulties and tensions of the actual world in which we daily live. It is our dissatisfaction with our present conditions that leads us to religious faith, not some higher form of knowledge or experience in which these conditions find their resolution. Of course, the same could be said of Hegel's own attempt to construct an absolute philosophical system: like religion, idealist philosophy was an attempt to reconcile, in the medium of thought, actual contradictions that continue to exist in the material world but are obscured by the idealist illusion of intellectual omnipotence. The real human problem is not to overcome contradictions in thought but to alter those concrete conditions that give rise to otherworldly impulses.

Finally, against Hegel's progressive dialectical method Feuerbach counterposed a critical procedure designed to undermine it at every point. This procedure, sometimes referred to as **transformational criticism**, deeply influenced the early thought of Marx. Hegel's idealism implied that the highest reality was equivalent to the most universal concept. Since, logically considered, the subject of a sentence should refer to what is most substantial or self-standing, while the predicate refers to one of its dependent attributes, Hegel often articulated his views in sentences that to most readers must seem quite unnatural. For instance, Hegel was led to assert such things as "The Absolute is the ground of the individual," or "The state is the truth of the citizen," or "Thought is the real element of sensation." In Feuerbach's transformational criticism, each of these sentences, and others like them that take the general to be more real or substantial than the particular, should be rewritten with the terms reversed. In privileging the general over the particular, Hegel intellectualized and thus mystified everything he touched, and his philosophy could be demystified only by a determined and thoroughgoing reversal of his terms. Thus, for Feuerbach, it is the individual who, in its thinking, gives rise to the concept of an absolute; the concept of the absolute is an arbitrary product of our own thought and imagination, not we of it. Or, as Feuerbach would claim, the state is nothing substantial in itself, but is merely an arbitrary way of referring to the manner in which individuals can act collectively; that is, the state is a historical accident of human will, not a substantial entity of which we are mere replaceable functionaries. This, of course, was by no means very sophisticated, but it inaugurated a process, later taken up by Marx, that allowed materialist discourse to critically engage its idealist opponents instead of merely dogmatically asserting its own counterassumptions, as had most previous advocates of materialism.

The Dialectical Materialism of Marx and Engels

Any discussion of Marxian critical discourse should probably begin with the eleventh and last of Marx's *Theses on Feuerbach* (1845): "The philosophers have only *interpreted* the world, in various ways; the point, however, is to *change* it." This may well be the only statement in the entire Marxian corpus that has received the unqualified assent of every participant in the critical discourse of materialism. The writings of Marx and Engels have been criticized, revised, supplemented, and contested so often and in such a wide variety of ways, even within the materialist tradition itself, that there sometimes seem to be as many Marxes as there are readers of him. However, this will come as no surprise to anyone who remembers two central features of modern materialist discourse: first, that it places a maximum premium on thoroughgoing critique, even within its own discourse, and second, that its emphasis on the historical character of knowledge implies that all theories and strategies must undergo constant revision in order to reflect changing historical circumstances. The writings of Marx and Engels no more present some settled and authoritative body of doctrine than did the works of Bacon or Schleiermacher for their discursive traditions. Certainly the ideas of Marx underwent considerable change and development throughout his own career. However, efforts, for example, to distinguish an early from a late or mature Marx may be of interest to historians or those seeking some doctrinal support for their own ideas, but it is of little consequence in trying to understand, in a broad sense, the role of Marx and Engels in the development of materialist critical discourse. Even less helpful would be a review of the many polemics directed against Marx's and Engels's thought on the basis of what can only be regarded as the distortions that it underwent in the hands of a Stalin or a Tito.

Here we will focus on some of the concepts, strategies, and issues that are crucial for understanding the subsequent development of Marx's version of materialist discourse. With the goal of providing a general overview of Marxian thought as it bears on the broader issue of cultural critique, I have organized the following discussion under the headings of some of these concepts and themes, arranged so as to suggest a broad framework in which their relations may be further explored, rather than in the actual chronological order of their development. In so doing, I have assumed that the thought of Marx and Engels has no less (but no more) unity than any of the other critical discourses thus far discussed.

Materialism Old and New: The Scientific Status of Critique

From the time of his earliest writings, Marx clearly recognized that any effective critique of existing society could align itself neither with the philosophical tradition running from Plato through Hegel nor with the operative assumptions of the modern natural sciences. He had learned from Feuerbach's critique of Hegel that philosophy in whatever form would ultimately wind up assuming, if not explicitly asserting, some form of idealism, the precedence of thought over material existence. On the other hand, the materialism implicit in the natural sciences and made explicit by earlier materialist thinkers represented no viable alternative. Nonetheless, both had something important to offer, even if it was presented in defective ways. Hegel was right, Marx thought, in affirming the priority of activity or process in his dialectical approach, but wrong in seeing this simply as a function of the development of ever more abstract ideas. Likewise, the earlier materialists were right to reject idealist mystification and attempt to bring thought "down to earth," but wrong in looking to the formal mathematical structures of the natural sciences as the true description of reality. Even for Feuerbach, who emphasized sensation over thought, the element of concrete human activity within the process of history was absent. Marx thus sought to develop a critical viewpoint that would join the dialectical or process-oriented approach of Hegel with the materialist insistence on the concrete material dimensions of human social existence. This critical viewpoint later came to be called **dialectical** (or **historical**) **materialism**.

Marx claimed that this new form of materialism was scientific in a way that the old form was not, however closely the latter might adhere to the assumptions and methodologies of the natural sciences. For while the old materialism might have been adequate as a theoretical basis for the study of natural, non-human phenomena (and there is evidence that Marx later came to doubt even this), it must ultimately be judged unscientific on its own criteria when applied to the dynamics of human social existence. The scientific method demanded that no essential or determining factor be arbitrarily disregarded or left out. In considering human historical and social phenomena, the effect of any given social practice or institution on the human actors involved in it is always an element of the highest importance, since it is from the situated human agent that such practices or institutions originate in the first place. To treat human activity, which is always affected by and in turn affects existing social formations, as if it were somehow indifferent to its own institutions and processes would therefore itself be unscientific. Yet, in Marx's view, this was exactly what the old materialism did in addressing phenomena of the human and cultural order. A genuinely scientific materialism would therefore have to attend carefully not only to the objective, material features or results of human social activity, but also to its subjective effects on the human beings involved in them.

Alienation

In his *Economic and Philosophic Manuscripts of 1844*, written at about the same time as the beginning of his collaboration with Friedrich Engels, Marx devoted a good deal of attention to analyzing the effects of the current economic system and its cultural expressions on its human participants. He declared the sum of these effects to be **alienation** or **estrangement** (the German term was *Entfremdung*). It is important to realize from the outset that unlike the term's later uses, *alienation* for Marx represented an objective feature of the impact of modern economic and social organization on its members. While alienation can and often does have subjective manifestations at the level of individual feeling and conscious awareness, for Marx it could never be reduced to these. Rather, it should be regarded as characterizing certain forms of objective relations between individuals and the contemporary socio-economic world that obtain whether or not a given individual happens to feel alienated.

At the root of this problem was the institution of **private property** and the associated notion of labor, so often defended by liberal humanists as well as classical economic theorists. Marx, radicalizing Feuerbach's demystification of Hegelian idealism, noted Hegel's description of the dialectical movement of thought as a "labor of the concept," but employing his own transformational criticism, Marx held that "real" labor concerns the material processes by which the means for physical existence are secured. In the afterword to the second German edition of *Das Kapital*, Marx made explicit his relation to Hegel in these famous (and often misquoted) words: "With him [the dialectic] is standing on its head. It must be turned right side up again, if you would discover the rational kernel within the mystical shell." The subject matter for Marx's attempt to right the dialectic already existed, albeit in its own mystified form, in the analysis of labor and property offered by classical economists such as Adam Smith and David Ricardo. However, in a manner similar to Hegel's, the classical economists had presented their economic theories as if they were universal natural laws, the effect of which was to vindicate the status quo as being what it *should* be because it was only what it *must* be. However, for Marx, what they had actually described, in an abstract and mystified form, were the principles of **capitalism**—a specific, historical, and thoroughly contingent form of economic organization. Marx's initial task was thus to reveal the dialectical interactions among economic agents and the capitalist economic system of which they were a part in a way that made clear their historical specificity and highlighted their real human effects, both of which classical theory mostly ignored.

In Marx's analysis, there are four principal aspects of alienation.

The first and most basic is what is sometimes called the **alienation of the thing.** One of the defining features of capitalism, as analyzed by the classical economists, was that while human labor was the principal source of economic value (the **labor theory of value**), the objects produced by human labor did not belong to the worker. Instead, the worker was paid a wage for the time she or he spent laboring, whereas the product was the **property** of the **capitalist** who paid the wage. Under such a system, the worker was alienated from the very things that she or he produced in the strict legal sense of being denied their possession. The effect was that workers found themselves in a world of objects of their own making that nonetheless did not belong to them and from which they were alienated not only legally but also psychologically. In *Das Kapital,* Marx would further develop this idea by analyzing what he called **the fetishism of commodities,** the fact that under capitalism, products of human labor take on an independent value of their own within a system of monetary exchange, producing an entire "world of economic value" apparently autonomous of its real bases in human labor and alien to them.

Second, a system based on **wage labor** (as opposed to independent producers who could dispose of their own products as they saw fit) implied that labor itself was a **commodity** that could be bought and sold on the market. That is, the worker's own **productive activity** became a commodity to which a price, a wage, was assigned. Marx called this **self-alienation** or **self-estrangement.** Anyone who has worked for an hourly wage at some repetitive and mechanical task will realize not only how one's own physical activity can come to appear alien but also how easily (for instance, if one daydreams too much on the job) she or he can be replaced by another person willing to do the same work.

From the alienation of the worker's own productive activity, a crucial reversal of natural human priorities occurs. For Marx, it is the nature of human beings to express themselves through their productive activities; in the natural order of things, we should live in order to express ourselves creatively. However, under capitalism, this natural order is reversed, and we engage in productive activities merely in order to sustain life; we labor in order to live. Marx referred to this as the **alienation from our species-being,** our estrangement from our distinctive features as human beings, productive creativity and self-expression. Marx regarded the worker's status under capitalism as that of an animal or worse.

Finally, these aspects of alienation, operating together, result in a generalized condition of alienation permeating all parts of capitalist society. Workers and owners find themselves alienated from one another in their opposed interests; owners are at odds with one another in economic competition; and workers themselves vie with one another in the labor market for available jobs. In every case, each person judges another based solely on their adversarial positions in the social context. Marx called this the **estrangement of human being from human being,** and in his description, the phenomenon resembles nothing so much as Hobbes's "war of all against all," inscribed in the very heart of the civil society that was supposed to have overcome it.

The Dynamics of Capitalism

From this beginning, the better part of Marx's career was spent attempting to uncover in detail the underlying dynamics of industrial capitalism, which produced
such humanly devastating effects. He spent most of the last twenty years of his life
on the project that was published in three large volumes (he also wrote part of a
fourth) under the title *Das Kapital*. Here we can only indicate some of Marx's basic and most influential ideas in overview.

According to Marx, one of the most decisive tendencies of modern economic
history was toward an increasing **division of labor**, with a single worker or group
of workers performing ever narrower and more specific functions. For example, a
medieval artisan might have acquired and processed the materials, made a pair of
shoes from beginning to end, and sold those that he and his family did not need at
a town market, while the worker under industrial capitalism (in a factory, for example) tended to perform a single repetitive function: tanning leather, cutting the
pieces, or perhaps sewing them together. Even more important than this segmentation of the production process, however, was the increasing division between
the functions of labor and ownership, to the point where one **class** of persons
were solely engaged in production for wages while the other, who owned the
means of production and the commodities produced, exchanged them for **profit**.
The former class Marx called the **proletariat**, the latter the **bourgeoisie**.

According to Marx, the profit that accrued to the bourgeoisie was the basic in-
centive to ownership; from their point of view, it was the reason why they owned
and invested in the means of production to begin with. However, Marx, who
strictly affirmed the labor theory of value already suggested by classical economists, held that the sole source of real economic value was the labor that had gone
into the production of a commodity; mere ownership or exchange of private
property produced no real value. The profit gained by the bourgeoisie in the sale
of a commodity produced by the proletariat was nothing other than the difference between the cost of producing the commodity and the total value that labor
had created in producing it. Put more simply, profit was the part of the labor-
value that had gone into a commodity but that was not returned to the worker in
the form of wages and hence was stolen from her or him. Roughly, then, profit
was, for the most part, the difference between the total value of a commodity
(what it was sold for on the market) and the wages paid to the worker for producing it. Marx referred to this difference as the **surplus value** of a commodity.

As classical economists had already asserted, the aim of the bourgeoisie was to
maximize profits and minimize losses. Two general types of adjustments were
thus possible. On the one hand, losses to the capitalist could be reduced by paying
the lowest wages possible. Marx found significant confirmation of this in the **Iron
Law of Wages** formulated by the classical economist David Ricardo, which held
that wages at any given point could rise only slightly above the minimum necessary to secure the basic necessities of the worker, thus enabling the worker to con-

tinue to labor and reproduce other workers. On the other side, profits could be maximized, for instance, by producing more commodities through increased division of labor and technological innovation in the means of production. This dual pressure of requiring more productivity for the same or lower total wages, necessitated by capitalist competition, led directly, according to Marx, to all the major abuses of nineteenth-century industrial capitalism: longer workdays, the exploitation of women and children (who could be paid less than men), dangerous working conditions, unemployment when market prices sank, and so forth.

Marx, however, saw these processes inherent in the nature of industrial capitalism as ultimately self-defeating. For what was gradually happening in the process of the specialization of labor was that the bourgeoisie was becoming increasingly irrelevant to the actual processes of production. While the means of production, as they became technologically more sophisticated, required a more specialized labor force, the bourgeoisie became ever more remote from the actual processes of production, often owning stock in distant companies about whose productive processes they knew nothing at all. Prone to boom-and-bust cycles in which overproduction, falling prices for surplus goods, and unemployment were followed by periods of economic recovery that ultimately would again lead to overproduction, industrial capitalism appeared intrinsically unstable to Marx. As the situation of workers became increasingly intolerable, Marx believed that they would ultimately come to recognize the contradiction between the facts that they alone were responsible for the operation of the economic system and that they benefited least from it.

Marx's revolutionary vision was that the workers would unite behind the recognition that they were a single class, the proletariat, and that this class was the true "engine of history." Taking possession of the highly developed means of production and unleashing its full potential (which had been restricted by the boom-and-bust cycles of capitalism), they would abolish the irrelevant bourgeoisie and its condition for existence, private property; would establish "a free association of producers under their [own] conscious and purposive control"; and would finally overcome the conditions that led to the alienation of human beings in modern society. For the first time, then, human beings, acting collectively, would become the conscious makers of history rather than its slaves.

Marx's Critique of Culture and Ideology

While the terms have not always been clearly distinguished, Marx's economic theory outlined above has sometimes been called **dialectical materialism** to contrast it with his related view of society, culture, and ideology, called **historical materialism**. Although the former has been challenged and rejected on many points, the latter has been most decisive for the materialist tradition of critical discourse.

As mentioned earlier, Marx, like Feuerbach, sought to explain the processes by which social and cultural expressions served to reinforce existing economic tensions by both reflecting and obscuring them. The most trenchant summary of this **ideo-**

logical effect can be found in *The German Ideology* (1845–1846, coauthored with Engels), and is worth quoting at length. With specific reference to Hegel, they write:

> No. 1. One must separate the ideas of those ruling for empirical reasons, under empirical conditions and as empirical individuals, from these actual rulers, and thus recognize the rule of ideas or illusions in history.
>
> No. 2. One must bring an order into this rule of ideas, prove a mystical connection among the successive ruling ideas, which is managed by understanding them as "acts of self-determination on the part of the concept." . . .
>
> No. 3. To remove the mystical appearance of this "self-determining concept" it is changed into a person—"a self-consciousness"—or, to appear thoroughly materialistic, into a series of persons, who represent the "concept" in history, into the "thinkers," the "philosophers," the ideologists, who again are understood as the manufacturers of history, as the "council of guardians," as the rulers. Thus the whole body of materialistic elements has been removed from history and now full rein can be given to the speculative steed.

Although Marx and Engels had in mind the absolute systems of the German philosophy of their time, the structure of this process can be applied to any ideology or its cultural expression. First, a cultural formation must be distinguished and lifted out of the material conditions and interests governing its production. To gain our assent, it must appear to be autonomous of the historical conditions of its production, as if its existence were entirely natural and its truth obvious. Second, it can achieve this only if it appears to take its place within its own idealized historical context. That is, it must relate to and cohere with other ideas or formations of its kind, forming a kind of surrogate world counterposed to the actual material world from which it derives but which it partly distorts and obscures. Finally, it must be repersonalized in the sense that it appears part of a world populated not by concrete human beings but by idealized cultural types or subjects that are in fact its own products.

Television advertisements offer a good example for such an analysis. Because we can recognize that they are produced out of specific economic motives—to make us buy a product—they have the intended effect only if their creators can skillfully conceal this fact and make the ads appear to present useful information or a natural experience with which we can associate. Every TV ad, of course, is part of a broader television culture, and most ads refer not to the economic realities from which they arise but to other elements of that constructed and imaginary culture—for example, to the "wonderful world of Disney," of fashion, or of popular entertainment. Finally, the "deal is closed" when viewers themselves adopt or unconsciously associate with the satisfied consumer or authority figure presented in the ad. As Marx and Engels suggested, we will have detached our viewing experience from the real bases of its production, entered the world referenced by the ad, and ultimately identified with the proper subject-place that it prepared for us.

The Conceptual Background of Historical Materialist Critique

Although an ideology that operates successfully can almost completely obscure the connection between its idealized world and the real world of concrete economic existence, the connection between the two nonetheless persists, and Marx believed that it could be given considerably more theoretical specificity.

Marx drew an important distinction between the **economic base** or **infrastructure** and the **superstructure** of a given society. Whereas infrastructure refers (roughly) to the economic means of production—the material processes by which commodities are produced and basic needs satisfied—superstructure concerns the entire variety of social and cultural institutions, practices, values, and ideologies to which a specific economic form of organization gives rise. This latter is roughly equivalent to what Marx called the **relations of production**. Engels summarized the connection between the two in the famous phrase, "Just as the hand plow produces the feudal system, so the steam engine produces capitalism." In other words, in order to understand the social practices, institutions, and culture of a given historical period, we must look to the organization of the underlying economic forces from which they spring.

However, despite later exaggerations of this thesis, neither Marx nor Engels believed that the relationship between the material, economic infrastructure and its social and cultural superstructure was one of pure determinism, that is, that the infrastructure could be regarded as the cause of the superstructure in any simple or direct sense. Rather, as we have already seen, various features of the superstructure, especially politics and its attendant ideologies, could function in complex ways to mask the underlying economic configuration, to forcefully protect it in times of instability, and to reinforce it through religious, legal, artistic, and philosophical justifications.

For Marx and Engels, then, materialist critique must always involve three elements operating together. First, it must elucidate the dynamics of the structure of economic production existing at any given time, never failing to include in this the effects of the economic structure on participants. Second, it must identify and demystify the principal ways in which the infrastructure is ideologically distorted by various social and cultural institutions and practices, not only laying bare their basis in material processes but showing how they serve at once to obscure and to reinforce the existing economic system. Finally, materialist critique must place this process of interaction between infrastructure and superstructure within the dialectical development of history itself, not only revealing that any existing configuration is itself contingent and hence alterable but indicating as well the direction in which the existing historical tensions and oppositions might be resolved.

The general view of culture associated with this conception of critique continues, despite controversies over details, to characterize materialist discourse. Within this discourse, culture will always be regarded as the general reflection in human social intercourse of a particular mode of economic production. However, culture's relation to its materialist basis remains problematic, since it obscures its basis at the same time that it serves to reinforce it. Because of this, culture appears in materialist criticism as a mystification that demands an uncompromising attitude of suspicion and demystification. Finally, every cultural configuration must be regarded as thoroughly historical. Rejecting all extrahistorical values invoked by liberal humanism and all privileged hermeneutic experience by which authentic meaning might be disclosed, materialist discourse insists that both cultural value and interpretation arise within a specific material-historical nexus and reflect the economic, class, and ideological interests of their advocates. It is on these points that any further consideration of culture must be based.

Lenin and Soviet Marxism

After Marx's death in 1883, Engels initiated the process by which his and Marx's critical discourse was gradually developed into a more rigid set of theoretical doctrines. Two directions in Engels's later thought particularly influenced the future development of Marxism as a political ideology. The first was Engels's increasing concern with articulating the operative principles of dialectical materialism as a universal method, of which the methods of the natural sciences would be merely local or restricted applications. In effect, he hardened the notion of the dialectic, which had been employed quite flexibly by Marx, into the oft-cited triadic schema of thesis-antithesis-synthesis, which he regarded as a universal law of nature. Secondly, impressed by Darwin's demonstration that nature itself had a history, nature and history in Engels's thought were fused in a single, deterministic process governed by "the laws of the materialist dialectic." An important result of this conception (which Marx himself almost certainly would have resisted) was to drastically reduce cultural phenomena to a mere reflection of economic contradictions in the human psyche and their subsequent collective expression in social intercourse. In the later Engels, the strong element of engaged cultural criticism in Marx was eliminated in favor of a deterministic "dialectical natural history" in which cultural phenomena played an ancillary role at best.

It was the Marxism developed by the later Engels that won the adherence of **Vladimir Ilyich Lenin** (1870–1924), the major figure of the Russian Revolution and the architect of Soviet communism. Lenin's concern with theory and critique was almost exclusively a product of his political activism, and by and large, remained subordinate to it. (The same can be said of **Mao Zedong** [1893–1976], who occupied a position in relation to the Chinese Revolution similar to that of Lenin in relation to the Russian; Mao regarded himself as a Marxist-Leninist.) From his student days, Lenin was convinced of the absolute necessity of revolution, and his philosophical and critical writings were composed almost solely in the service of this practical cause. Although Lenin's dedication to radical activism has often served as an example and inspiration for other materialist critics and his texts are occasionally cited as valid interpretations of Marx's views, his contributions to the development of materialist critical discourse were more strategic than substantive in nature. As materialist discourse continued to develop after Lenin, the strategic paths that the leader had charted for the Soviet state came to be regarded in a negative light, as an example to be avoided rather than embraced. Most materialist critics, like Georg Lukács, chose to return to Marx himself rather than accept the ideological orthodoxy that Stalin, Lenin's successor, conferred on Marxism-Leninism as the official doctrine of the authoritarian Soviet state.

Several of Lenin's strategic ideas have been singled out for particular critique and revision. Even as Lenin vigorously defended the general tenets of dialectical materialism, he rejected any implication (such as that perhaps present in the writings of the later Engels) that historical necessity somehow eliminated the need for deliberate human intervention. In particular, he did not believe that the proletariat left to its own devices would gradually become conscious of its historical role and spontaneously form a revolutionary force. Thus, he stressed that the real engine for historical change must be a highly organized, rigidly controlled, deliberately indoctrinated, and militant **party** that would educate and mobilize the proletariat for its historically appointed task. Even more specifically, he believed that the party required a dedicated and professional **revolutionary vanguard**, especially of socialist intellectuals, which would be responsible for articulating political doctrine and maintaining the consistency of that doctrine. In this view, which was put into practice after the Russian Revolution, the party, in the name of the proletariat, would constitute the **state apparatus,** which would oversee the transition from capitalism to communism. As we know, however, the gradual "withering away of the state" in favor of an organic association of free producers did not occur. Under Stalin, the Communist party continued to entrench itself and became what even many materialist critics outside the Soviet Union regarded as a de facto authoritarian dictatorship. Certainly by the 1930s, the Leninist-Stalinist ideology of the Soviet Union was widely regarded outside that country as a perversion of Marxian ideas, and many figures of the materialist critical tradition, while challenging capitalism on the one side, sought equally to distance themselves from Soviet ideology on the other.

Another of Lenin's characteristic ideas later provided Stalin and other Soviet leaders with a rationale for the authoritarian state's continued existence, which ran contrary to classical dialectical materialist theory. Lenin applied Marx's economic reflections on a global scale. He emphasized that the current world economic system had reached its final stage in **monopoly capitalism** and that its further expansion required that it move beyond national borders through economic and cultural **colonialism** and its attendant **imperialism**. Such forces would require active opposition and resistance on a global scale, especially in light of the fact that various nations were at **uneven levels of economic development**. Without active Soviet support, the socialist movements in the less developed countries would be eradicated by the colonialist onslaught and eventually the socialist experiment of the Soviet Union itself would be threatened with strangulation by the forces of monopoly capitalism. Under Stalinism, this view undergirded a virtual paranoia that was used to justify the continuation of the authoritarian state. One hardly need add that it was soon answered by a similar paranoia on the part of the capitalist nations, which set the stage for the cold war that so dominated recent history.

Marxist Revisionism and Humanism: The Search for a New Critical Stance

By the 1930s, the Marxist-Leninist version of dialectical materialism, which under Stalin had become entrenched as the official doctrine of Soviet communism, held little appeal for many materialist critics outside the Soviet Union. Two major areas of difficulty in previous Marxist thought, particularly its Leninist interpretation, were frequently cited.

The first was that earlier Marxist criticism (by its own theory) was itself a creature of nineteenth-century industrial capitalism and therefore was unable to deal successfully with the newly emerging social and economic trends of the twentieth century. The development of the mass media, with their potential for propagandistic manipulation; the rapid rise of fascist and national socialist movements; and the spread of new international capitalist formations all posed novel and serious challenges to earlier materialist criticism. The realization of these, along with an aversion to Stalinist authoritarianism, spawned a number of **revisionist** critical projects that sought to update, modify, or supplement the more traditional Marxist theory. This took a number of different directions. Among them were attempts to recover a more "authentic Marx" by returning to the Hegelian roots of his thought (Georg Lukács, Alexandre Kojève); efforts to recast Marxist criticism in light of the new developments in the mass media (Walter Benjamin); and a rethinking of the whole project of materialist criticism from a perspective more receptive than Marx's had been to Enlightenment notions such as democracy, political liberty, and rights (the Frankfurt School of critical theory). We will consider some of these developments in a later chapter.

The second objection often leveled against the more doctrinaire forms of Marxist critique was that Marx himself, having started with the alienating effects of modern society on the concretely existing individual, came to abandon (or at least to deemphasize) this essentially humanistic orientation in favor of a more systemic and determinist approach to critique. Convinced that Marx's general project of critique in the interest of human liberation from political and economic domination was sound but that its focus must remain on the free development of the concretely existing individual, a significant group of critics began articulating a viewpoint that is sometimes called **Marxist humanism**. Particularly influential in Eastern Europe (at that time under Soviet dominance) as well as in France, Marxist humanists elaborated the phenomenological, ethical, and aesthetic dimensions of Marx's economic and political theories that had been absent, in their estimation, from the mainstream of Marxist critical discourse. They sought to replace the earlier historical determinist tendencies of Marxism with a reaffirmation of the individual human responsibility actively to intervene in ending the alienation of modern human beings in exploitative social structures and to develop new political and cultural forms which would support the free expression and development of its participants in nonmanipulative environments.

Especially in France, Marxist humanism was a result of attempts to graft certain Marxist economic and political views onto a foundation provided by the development of Husserl's phenomenology, known as **existentialism**, the best-known proponent of which was **Jean-Paul Sartre** (1905–1980). Sartre's significance for materialist critical discourse has been mainly as an example or warning against attempts to ground materialist analysis on an essentially subjectivist and idealist theory of consciousness and freedom. Earlier in his career, Sartre had vehemently opposed dialectical materialism on the grounds that it treated human existence, the essence of which was the radical freedom of individual consciousness to determine its own meaning, as if it were a mere cipher or placeholder in history and society. After World War II, however, he seemed to modify his views, holding that material scarcity was the most deadly threat to the concrete realization of human freedom. He even went so far as to claim both that existentialism was the privileged vehicle by which Marxism could be recovered from its deterministic ossification and that, conversely, Marxism was "the ultimate philosophy of our age." Most readers of Sartre were quick to point out that the "subjectivism" and "radical freedom" on which existentialism was based were logically incompatible with materialist assumptions and that Sartre had ultimately failed to show how they might be squared with one another. Sartre's Marxist humanism was a blind alley for materialist critical discourse, but it undoubtedly played a historical role in warning later critical discourse away from seeking its grounds in any phenomenological notion of subjectivity or consciousness.

Antonio Gramsci:
Power, Hegemony, and the Engaged Critic

The writings of **Antonio Gramsci** (1891–1937), one of the founders of the Italian Communist party and later a prisoner of the Italian Fascists, provide a crucial link between the earlier materialist views of Marx and Engels, their development into an explicit revolutionary program by Lenin, and the discourse of contemporary cultural studies. Having influenced both Raymond Williams and Stuart Hall, two of the latter's prominent spokespersons, Gramsci continues to be cited with regularity in the literature of cultural studies. More than any other figure, Gramsci brought the distinctive problems posed by modern culture to the forefront of the agenda of materialist critical discourse.

Gramsci saw the historical events of his time, especially the rise of European fascism, as posing two major problems for Marxist-influenced materialist discourse. First, he was struck by the resilience of the modern state in commanding the allegiance of its populace in the face of severe economic dislocations and crises. What kept the people from revolting against the dominance of the privileged classes, when according to classical Marxist theory, all the necessary conditions for revolution were present? Second, as a committed communist, he could not help wondering why fascism had been able to defeat its communist resistance in many of the developed countries of Europe. What could be done in order to assure that this did not occur again?

Gramsci's attempt to answer the first question involved challenging what he regarded as the overly simplistic schema that traditional Marxism had employed in describing the relation between the economic base and the political and cultural superstructure. In particular, Gramsci doubted that their relationship was a "one-way street," with economy determining superstructure, and that the latter was a mere reflection of the former, as Marxism-Leninism asserted. Rather, he argued that the relationship between economy on the one hand and culture and politics on the other was that of **reciprocity**, involving mutual influence. Further, Gramsci held that at the interface of economics and culture stood the continually contested question of which groups would exercise **power** in a given society. Marxism had failed to confront this more complex question of power, which could be answered neither solely from the economic nor exclusively from the cultural sphere.

In analyzing the way in which power functioned in the modern state, Gramsci gradually developed elements of a new conceptual framework for materialist discourse. He first observed that power in modern societies was based on two distinguishable functions. On the one hand, the state could coerce its members through **direct domination**, the threat and actual use of physical force, to which it often had to resort especially in times of crisis. However, in a less overt but usually more effective manner, an entire ensemble of cultural formations, including education, the organization of family life, associations in the workplace, religion, and popular culture, worked together to infiltrate the daily private lives of individual members of civil society, producing a texture of beliefs and relationships that guaranteed the allegiance of the individual to the state. This Gramsci called **hegemony**, the cultural dominance of civil society over the individual even in the absence of the threat of overt force by the state. Employing a vivid military metaphor, Gramsci described hegemony in this way: "The superstructures of civil society are like the trench-systems of modern warfare. In war it would sometimes happen that a fierce artillery attack seemed to have destroyed the outer perimeter; and at the moment of their advance and attack the assailants would find themselves confronted by a line of defence which was still effective. The same thing happens in politics, during the great economic crises." Of course, this could also serve as a description of the problem faced by the European communist movements in the face of entrenched cultural attitudes that the fascists had proved more effective at exploiting.

Although hegemony, as Gramsci developed the concept, was still an element of the superstructure, it was nevertheless broader than the traditional Marxist concept of ideology in two respects. First, an ideology, while it has a tendency to obscure or conceal itself, can be articulated in fairly conscious terms, while hegemony so interpenetrates all dimensions of social and cultural practice that its operation is largely unconscious, definitive of what is at any given time taken to be natural, and consequently quite resistant to any intellectual critical analysis. Second, the operation of hegemony is such that it can even accommodate conflict between opposite ideological positions (such as the unending polemics between the Democratic and Republican parties in the United States), while preventing such conflict from greatly affecting the everyday lives of individuals.

However, according to Gramsci, the nature of modern society is such that hegemony can never be absolute. For one thing, various more traditional communities in modern states tend to compete with or disrupt the hegemonic culture. The Pennsylvania Amish, pockets of traditional culture in the American South, and immigrant groups that retain strong ethnic allegiances are examples. For another, new groups continually emerge whose interests are opposed to those of the hegemonic culture and **marginalized** by it. As a result, there will inevitably be **counterhegemonic** movements that will resist assimilation into the hegemonic culture, making culture a site of struggle among competing interests and their expressions. Anyone familiar with the current "culture wars" over curricular diversity at universities in the United States will understand the practical force of this phenomenon. In fact, it was Gramsci, more than any other thinker, who first asserted within the materialist tradition the idea that cultural criticism was an essential and indispensable element of any broader political or economic struggle and that materialist critique must pay special attention to the operation of hegemony at the level at which popular culture affects everyday life.

Despite its unconscious and ubiquitous character, hegemony does not come about simply as a result of impersonal historical forces. Rather, Gramsci held that both hegemonic and counterhegemonic movements involved not only sets of cultural practices and institutions but specific ways of feeling and thinking about them and seeing how they cohere or fail to cohere. Gramsci used the term *intellectual* in referring to those who performed the specific social function of formulating and institutionalizing frameworks in which the practices of everyday life could be understood and interpreted. Being an intellectual had little to do with native intelligence and was not an "essentialist" feature of any individual. Rather, in the case of "hegemonic intellectuals," it was a matter of functioning effectively in one of the social roles that supported the prevailing culture; in the case of "counterhegemonic intellectuals," it had to do with the leadership involved in articulating forms of resistance to hegemonic culture.

Gramsci described both hegemonic and counterhegemonic intellectuals within capitalist systems as necessarily **organic**, that is, concerned with making sense of the full range of cultural phenomena as they appear in everyday practices. The social function of the former is to maintain cultural hegemony by establishing both what is to count as socially valuable knowledge and to certify the self-guaranteeing methods by which it can be established. For Gramsci, earlier scholastic religious authorities and later academic philosophers and party ideologists preeminently served this function. Today, perhaps, the role is filled by journalists of the mass media, editors of scholarly journals, university department chairs, and members of professional societies. But Gramsci emphasized the particular need for counterhegemonic, organic intellectuals, who would avoid flights into theoretical abstraction and resist professional cooptation, remaining in continuous engagement with the struggle against hegemonic marginalization while articulating the need for new forms of knowledge and experience deemed irrational by hegemonic culture.

In line with this general theory of cultural hegemony, Gramsci was led to contest the monolithic notion of social classes presupposed by Marxism-Leninism. Since the notion of hegemony implied the possibility of a shifting set of strategic political allegiances among both dominant and marginalized cultural groups, he came to reject the need for cultivating a universal proletarian consciousness under strict party control. Instead, he favored a **pluralistic** development of more local interests that would recognize the hegemony of capitalist culture as their common opponent and thus would join together in a broadly socialist cause.

Louis Althusser: Structural Marxism

The work of **Louis Althusser** (1918–1990), a lifelong member of the French Communist party and a major figure in the discussions following the French student revolt of 1968, is quite different from that of Gramsci in critical orientation and approach, although it clearly shows the latter's influence. Throughout his career, Althusser functioned as an agent provocateur, contesting not only humanist variants of Marxism but challenging their emergent poststructuralist critics as well. While many of his views, especially those regarding the interpretation of Marx and the significance of Lenin for materialist critique, remain controversial even within the materialist tradition, several others, especially those presented in his essay "Ideology and Ideological State Apparatuses" (1969), have had considerable impact on contemporary critical discourse.

Althusser's general critical orientation, which changed somewhat over time, may be summarized under four general headings.

First, vehemently opposed to the "humanist" tendencies of such existentialists as Sartre and of others who preferred the early, Hegelian-influenced version of Marx, Althusser insisted that only the Marx of *Das Kapital* deserved serious attention. A self-professed **antihumanist**, Althusser argued that Marxism should be regarded exclusively as a scientific theory, based on Marx's "objective" critique of classical political economy; to link it to any general theory of consciousness or of an autonomous subject would spell its immediate fall into idealism and mystification. On this point, he cited Lenin as a reliable guide.

Second, instead of seeking an underpinning for Marxism in the "subjectivity" explored by phenomenology and existentialism, Althusser looked toward the

structuralism that had been developed by anthropologist Claude Lévi-Strauss and others in the 1950s. (The work of Lévi-Strauss will be discussed in a later chapter.) He was particularly impressed by the aspect of the structuralist approach that held that social and cultural phenomena should be regarded as consisting of "relatively autonomous" structures that determined what "places" individuals occupied, rather than as creative productions of freely acting individuals or "subjects." Simply put, in Althusser's view, subjects were produced by structures rather than producing them. Pushing this even further, Althusser insisted that even history, if regarded as a chronicle of the aggregate actions of autonomous subjects, must be called into question by a structuralist approach.

Third, employing this structuralist approach, Althusser questioned both the traditional Marxist view of capitalism and its analysis of this in the overly simplistic terms of base and superstructure. While Althusser generally endorsed Marx's analysis of capitalism in *Das Kapital,* he pointed out that in any given society, a number of different modes of production are always simultaneously operative— in other words, that there is no "pure" example of capitalist society discoverable *in concreto.* Further, while he affirmed that the economic base would be "ultimately determinant," it would not always be the dominant social structure. Rather, society must be viewed as a totality of "relatively independent" structures, any of which could at least in principle be dominant at a given time. For example, religion, at one time, might be the dominant social structure (as in the European Middle Ages), later superseded by the Enlightenment and the secular humanist system of education, all occurring "relatively independently" of the economic transition from feudalism to capitalism. In no case, however, could one establish any direct causal relation between an economic base (itself always diverse) and the dominance of a particular structural sector of society.

Finally, in order to explain the dynamics of such a complex set of systems operating as a totality, Althusser, expanding the traditional Marxist view, claimed that each structure involved its own characteristic **internal contradictions,** or tensions between opposed intrinsic forces. In addition, however, he referred to such contradictions as **overdetermined**, meaning that due to a given structure's external relation to other internally contradictory structures, its own internal contradictions always carried more significance (they were "supercharged," as it were), by virtue of their relations to other structures that were equally unstable internally. In such a system, what might seem a minor issue—for example, student demands for changes in the curriculum of public universities (as in France in 1968)— might become the focus of a much larger social upheaval due to its becoming symbolic or representative of (in other words, overdetermined by) other oppositions in other social spheres relatively remote from it. The thrust of this view was that unlike traditional Marxism, which emphasized almost exclusively the necessity of mobilizing the working class against the bourgeoisie, the potential for social disruption was distributed throughout the various systemic structures constituting modern societies and could break out at any number of points.

However, like Gramsci at an earlier period, Althusser also came to ask, after May 1968, what held the social system together and allowed it forcefully to re-assert itself in the face of widespread social and economic disruption. His most concise answer was contained in the 1969 essay, "Ideology and Ideological State Apparatuses," which has become something of a classic of modern materialist critical discourse.

He begins by making a distinction, closely paralleling one drawn by Gramsci, between a **repressive state apparatus** and an **ideological state apparatus** (often abbreviated respectively as RSA and ISA). The RSA includes the government, ad-ministration, police, courts, prisons, and so forth, and operates through the use or threat of violence. By contrast, ISAs function without the overt threat of violence, through specific institutions such as churches, the educational system, the family, the communications media, the arts, popular culture, and so forth. Also like Gramsci, Althusser emphasized that whereas the RSA functions in the public do-main, ISAs principally influence the private sphere, thus representing various ways in which the state intrudes on and maintains dominance over daily life.

How, then, do ISAs achieve their effects in promoting **ideologies**? Althusser wrote, "Ideology represents the imaginary relationship of individuals to their real conditions of existence." It is crucial to see that in this view, ideology always in-volves a simultaneous **allusion** or reference to real economic conditions together with an **illusion** or imaginary construction of them. Ideology is thus always a dis-tortion of conditions to which it is nonetheless related, and it can never be re-garded as wholly fictitious or false. Indeed, its allusion to the real world is what makes ideology so difficult to critique (much like stereotypes, which usually have some basis in fact however much they may distort it).

According to Althusser, ideology is always, in the first instance, a function of specific, observable institutions, not merely ideas lodged in the minds of individ-ual subjects. In promoting ideologies, the institutions that constitute ISAs act on concrete individuals, turning them into subjects. "Subjects" are thus created by in-stitutions through ideology, rather than ideology being the product of the thought or cognition of preexisting subjects. Althusser uses the term **interpella-tion** to indicate the manner in which ideology addresses concrete individuals and elicits appropriate responses, establishing them as its subjects (in the multiple senses of this loaded word).

For example, an individual's response to the question "Who are you," posed by a potential employer in a job interview as an invitation to articulate one's own self-conception, will inevitably reflect the prior operation of ideology: I am presently employed at the University, I have been married for three years, I have one child, I am an avid sailor, and so on. Not only the content of all these re-sponses, but the very fact that I take just these and not others to be obvious and relevant responses to the question, indeed even the fact that I realize that I am be-ing addressed by another under specific conditions, immediately reveals the prior workings of ideology in constituting me as a "subject." Notice as well that none of these answers to the question posed are, in the usual sense, "false." Rather, they represent elements in a broader system of signification that is presupposed by and appears to be entirely natural to both questioner and respondent, yet that as a whole structure, establishes an imaginary and distorted though shared relation to the real world of economic production and exchange.

It is because of this utter naturalness and obviousness of ideology, of our ordinary inability to conceive of things being any other way than the way they are (in other words, the way in which we imagine them, under the influence of ideology), that Althusser insists on a rigorously scientific basis for materialist critique. As he put it, "It is necessary to be outside ideology, i.e., in scientific knowledge, to be able to say: I am in ideology (a quite exceptional case) or (the general case): I was in ideology." Of course, the "scientific knowledge" to which Althusser was referring was none other than the scientific materialism of the mature Marx as interpreted by Althusser through the dual lenses of Leninism and structuralism.

Such claims as the ability of his structural Marxism to provide a relatively "ideology-free" standpoint for critique raise obvious problems. However, many of Althusser's ideas, especially his discussion of the relation between ideology and the subject, have been utilized in the critique of a wide diversity of social phenomena. They have been particularly prominent in contemporary discussions of such aspects of popular culture as fashion and commercial advertising, where everything depends on the successful interpellation of ideologically constituted consumer-subjects.

Contemporary Materialist Discourse

Althusser's obituary in the French leftist periodical *Le Monde* (31 October 1990) referred to him as "the last Marxist philosopher." This, of course, is false, if taken literally, and a premature historical judgment in any case. Nonetheless, it does point to some complex problems posed for any attempt to assess the current state of materialist discourse. In concluding this chapter, the soundest approach may be simply to indicate some of the basic issues and typical responses to them, since we are currently in the midst of a heated debate among numerous and widely diverse parties, the outcome of which cannot yet be predicted.

The most immediate issue to be confronted concerns the relationship between materialist critical discourse taken in a broad sense and its more specific Marxist inflection. As a general historical gloss, it is probably fair to say that since the late nineteenth century, Marxism has been by far the dominant form that materialist critical discourse has taken. From Engels through Althusser, almost every materialist critic in one way or another has been aligned with the Marxist tradition. To some degree, this has been as much a function of practical or historical necessity as of theoretical preference, since through a considerable period of recent history Marxism has been the only vital materialist option in the political arena. Even a figure such as Sartre, whose philosophical project was so drastically opposed to any theory of history that evoked shades of determinism, was led to acknowledge the Marxist version of materialism as the primary political force with which he had to reckon. However, we have seen that dialectical materialism is by no means the only form that materialist discourse can assume. So the question arises, To what degree is the fate of materialist critical discourse linked to that of its specifically Marxist inflection?

This has become especially problematic since the momentous events of 1989 and after: the collapse of the Soviet Union, the reemergence of a "free" eastern Europe, the unification of Germany, the (at least partial) opening of the People's Republic of China to trade and capitalist enterprise, and the significant decrease in the influence of leftist parties in most west European nations. If communism and its Marxist theoretical basis have been "defeated" and "discredited," as has been widely claimed in the mainstream media, what effect will this defeat have on materialist critical discourse, which was for so long aligned with them?

One possible response might be that Gramsci and Althusser already prepared the way beyond the historically discredited "vulgar Marxism-Leninism" that ultimately will permit a revitalized materialist discourse, disengaged from the Marxist tradition. In particular, one could use certain of the strategic devices that Gramsci and Althusser employed, such as the concepts of hegemony and ideology, without taking on their Marxist baggage as well. To a great extent, this seems to have been the approach adopted by a fair amount of work in contemporary cultural studies, following the paths charted by Raymond Williams and Stuart Hall, among others. While such critical projects have been in a broad sense materialist and counterhegemonic, they have stopped short of explicitly aligning themselves with traditional Marxist theory or communist political movements. To a certain degree, then, contemporary critical studies is a continuation of materialist discourse, although in a form different from traditional Marxism.

Deciding what attitude to adopt toward the Marxist tradition has been considerably complicated by the rise of poststructuralist modes of discourse in the period since World War II. We have already encountered Althusser's deliberate attempt to make use of structuralist methods of analysis and join them with Marxist-Leninist dialectical materialism, producing a structuralist-Marxist hybrid form of critique. Such a hybridization of Marxist discourse continued as it interacted with the poststructuralist critique of both structuralism and Marxism, which poststructuralists regarded as outdated, totalizing or global theories of a reality that is fragmentary and resistant to any form of universal analysis. In most cases where a confrontation of Marxism and poststructuralism has occurred, such as in the post-Marxist writings of Ernesto Laclau and Chantal Mouffe, Marxism has given way to new forms of radical pluralist and yet, in a broad sense, materialist discourse.

Still, a number of thinkers, such as Fredric Jameson and Terry Eagleton, have reaffirmed an explicitly Marxist stance in the face of poststructuralist critique, though with considerable revision and at times compromise with its opponents.

Jameson and Eagleton, both beginning from literary theory and criticism, have attempted to demonstrate the continuing fruitfulness of Marxist discourse for interpreting cultural texts as well as the succession of standpoints from which they have been interpreted. In particular, they have continued to argue for the necessity of exploring both cultural productions and their critical reception in relation to the social and economic processes that make up their historical context. Jameson, in fact, has gone so far as to argue that the rise of postmodernism can only be understood in conjunction with the development of international capitalism in the period following World War II and that only a broadly Marxist stance can elucidate the phenomenon of postmodernism.

Finally, since the nineteenth century there has been a continuing materialist strand of the mainstream (here, that is, non-Marxist) social sciences, which has insisted on explaining cultural phenomena with reference to the processes of material production and reproduction. Explicitly anti-Marxist, although just as emphatically materialist, the contemporary anthropologist Marvin Harris has argued the theoretical case for what he calls **cultural materialism**, offering impressive empirical evidence in its favor. In Harris's view, whereas Marxism is "burdened with nineteenth-century philosophical assumptions which reduce [its] plausibility and usefulness for twentieth-century anthropologists," such terms as infrastructure and superstructure, modes of production and relations of production can be formulated in such a way as to provide a framework for the scientifically rigorous empirical investigations of culture by the anthropologist.

Thus, even if at this point in time the Marxist version of materialist discourse is in retreat, materialist discourse itself seems still vital and open to considerable further development.

Bibliographic Essay

Although there is no anthology specifically devoted to the writings of the early materialists, many collections devoted to the Enlightenment include selections by them. (See the references in the Bibliographic Essay of Chapter 1.) All of Hegel's major works have been translated into English and there are a number of readily accessible anthologies of shorter selections, such as *Hegel: The Essential Writings*, ed. Frederick G. Weiss (New York: Harper Torchbooks, 1974). The reader might wish to start in that volume with the preface to Hegel's *Lectures on the Philosophy of History* and the final section, entitled "Absolute Spirit," of his *Encyclopaedia of the Philosophical Sciences*. For the critical response to Hegel prior to Marx (which includes selections by Feuerbach), see *The Young Hegelians: An Anthology*, ed. Lawrence Stepelevich (Cambridge: Cambridge University Press, 1983).

The works of Marx and Engels are also readily available in numerous formats. A convenient anthology of selections from the major writings is *The Marx-Engels Reader*, 2d ed., ed. Robert C. Tucker (New York: Norton, 1978). In this volume, particularly helpful for the beginner are the "Economic and Philosophic Manuscripts of 1844," "Theses on Feuerbach," "The German Ideology: Part I," the *Grundrisse* (selections), "Manifesto of the Communist Party," and Engels's later essay, "Socialism: Utopian and Scientific." An invaluable source for a broad range of materialist thought after Marx is *Marxism: Essential Writings,* ed. David McLellan (Oxford: Oxford University Press, 1988). This includes key selections by (among others) Lenin, Lukács, Gramsci, Stalin, and Mao. Some of the key texts for and against attempts to reconcile Marxism and existentialism are contained in *Existentialism Versus Marxism: Conflicting Views on Humanism,* ed. George Novack (New York: Dell, 1966). Several anthologies of the writings of Gramsci are available. Of special interest is *Antonio Gramsci: Selections from Cultural Writings,* ed. David Forgacs and Geoffrey Nowell-Smith (Cambridge, Mass.: Harvard University Press, 1985). The major ideas of Althusser can be found in *For Marx* (New York: Vintage, 1969) and *Lenin and Philosophy* (New York: Monthly Review Press, 1971). The latter work includes his crucial essay, "Ideology and Ideological State Apparatuses."

Important perspectives on the current state of materialist discourse can be found in various works by Fredric Jameson, especially "On Interpretation: Literature as a Socially Symbolic Act" in *The Political Unconscious* (Ithaca: Cornell University Press, 1981) and the first chapter of *Postmodernism, or The Cultural Logic of Late Capitalism* (Durham, N.C.: Duke University Press, 1991). Finally, *Cultural Materialism: The Struggle for a Science of Culture,* by Marvin Harris (New York: Vintage, 1980), is one of the major defenses of the materialist approach to culture outside the Marxist tradition.

As one might expect, there is a tremendous amount of secondary literature dealing with particular topics and specific figures. For brief sketches of some of the figures discussed in the present chapter, see *Social Theory: A Guide to Central Thinkers,* ed. Peter Beilharz (Sydney: Allen & Unwin, 1991). *A Survey of Marxism,* by A. James Gregor (New York: Random House, 1965) is helpful as a general and balanced introduction to intellectual influences on Marx and on his thought as well as on its further development by Engels and Lenin. Unfortunately, there is no general history of materialist, or even more specifically, Marxist, thought that can be recommended. I believe the present chapter to some degree fills that gap.

There are many texts in which a materialist approach is brought to bear on a specific cultural formation or historical phenomenon. To see Marxist theory in operation, the best place to start might be Marx's own *The Eighteenth Brumaire of Louis Bonaparte,* parts of which are included in *The Marx-Engels Reader.* Two more recent demonstrations of materialist critique are *Ways of Seeing,* by John Berger (London: BBC/Penguin, 1972), which focuses on the visual arts, and *Decoding Advertisements: Ideology and Meaning in Advertising,* by Judith Williamson (London: Marion Boyers, 1978), which includes vivid and contemporary illustrations of Althusser's notion of ideology, supplemented by other Marxist and poststructuralist insights. Finally, virtually any work by Raymond Williams will shed considerable light on the concrete practice of materialist critique. Williams's contribution is also discussed in more detail in Chapter 8 of this volume.

4

Psychoanalysis and
the Critique of Culture

At almost the same time that Karl Marx died in London, a young medical student was completing his internship in Vienna and making plans for an academic and research career in neurology. At the time, nothing could have been farther from his mind than the sort of large-scale political and cultural critique that had occupied Marx. Nevertheless, **Sigmund Freud** (1856–1939), although working in a direction almost totally opposite that of Marx, did ultimately found a new critical discourse that proved no less fertile or controversial than Marxism. For while Marx tended to view the psychology of the individual as primarily a product of social and historical contradictions, Freud gradually came to view history and culture as manifestations of powerful, mostly unconscious conflicts operating at the deepest levels of the human psyche.

Freud, from 1896 on, began referring to his project as **psychoanalysis**, deliberately contrasting it to the prevailing medical field of psychiatry. Originally, psychoanalysis was little more than certain new clinical techniques that Freud was developing to treat some forms of mental disturbance that were resistant to standard medical treatment. These techniques centered around the famous "talking cure" and featured its method of **free association**, in which patients were encouraged to say whatever occurred to them, regardless of how disconnected, insignificant, or absurd it might sound. In free association, the patients' dreams figured prominently and appeared to present special interpretive problems to the clinician. As Freud gradually fought his way toward understanding the significance of such phenomena and connecting them with the symptoms of his patients, general patterns began to emerge that suggested to him certain ideas regarding structures and operations of the psyche never before explored. Psychoanalysis was thus expanded to include not only certain clinical techniques but also their broader theoretical basis. As Freud elaborated this basis, he became increasingly convinced that psychoanalysis was not only a new method of studying human behavior, psychology, and its cultural expressions, but a body of knowledge about them sufficiently well grounded to establish a new discipline. In time, Freud even came to regard psychoanalysis as, in effect, a new philosophy or master science with far-ranging implications not only for unraveling the most vexing problems of individual existence but also for critically addressing some of those same large-scale social and cultural issues that had occupied Marx.

Particularly in the last sense, psychoanalysis came to constitute a distinctive discourse that developed in many, often opposed, directions and that influenced other discourses (in much the same way as did Marxism). Like Marx, Freud developed his views over a long period, often reinterpreting, revising, and sometimes even rejecting earlier stages of his thought. Nonetheless, as in the case of Marxism, Freud's version of psychoanalysis has a substantial core of basic terms and assumptions that no future discussion of culture could ignore. The first section of this chapter will be devoted to presenting these in overview. While Freudian psychoanalysis, from a rather early stage, spawned a wide range of competing views that borrowed the term from Freud (among many others, those of C. G. Jung, Alfred Adler, and Wilhelm Stekel), it is Freud's own distinctive views to which most subsequent critical discourse has continued to return. While these other variants of psychoanalysis have had their influence, one can discern a certain Freudian mainstream, on which we will concentrate here. Finally, while Freudian psychoanalysis has had no lack of critics both inside and outside its own discursive contours, recent feminist critiques of Freud have been especially important and will be discussed as indicating some of the most highly contested issues that psychoanalytic discourse must now confront. In later chapters, we will see that certain Freudian ideas have been appropriated, often in highly reworked forms, by other critical discourses, especially poststructuralism and the critical theory of the Frankfurt School; we also will explore these developments.

To begin with, however, it will be helpful to review several of the basic themes and issues that tend to recur in psychoanalytic discourse as well as in critical responses to it. What most distinguishes psychoanalysis from the liberal humanist and hermeneutic discourses (and in significant ways allies it with Marx's version of materialism) is the assumption that our natural confidence in the clarity, certainty, and truthfulness of consciousness must be regarded with thoroughgoing suspicion. Psychoanalysis makes the radical claims that we do not understand our real motivations and purposes, and furthermore, that we are in principle incapable of doing so by any traditional means, such as self-reflection or self-examination. From a psychoanalytic perspective, no deliberate philosophical attempt to respond to the Socratic charge to "know thyself" can ever hope to succeed, nor can any interpretive attempt to confer meaning on our own existence or any cultural text manage to do more than add another layer of obscurity to what is already opaque to us—without, that is, a detour through psychoanalysis. Thus, to borrow a term from the Marxist tradition, we as individuals continually and unavoidably exist in a condition of **false consciousness**.

However, psychoanalysis offers itself as a discourse through which such a condition of misrepresentation of self and others can be mitigated to some extent. Psychoanalysis does, in fact, involve a type of interpretation (a hermeneutic in a specific sense), but it is intimately connected with certain biological features of the human organism as well as with a larger theoretical framework dealing with the construction of the meanings that form the texture of conscious experience. For psycho-analysis, human meaning neither exists in itself (in classic texts, for example) nor in the mind of an author or reader; rather, it arises from fears and desires deeply rooted in the dynamic processes by which the human biological organism gradually develops a psychic organization and, at a quite late stage, a sense of self. Psychoanalysis thus locates itself at the dynamic interface between matter and mind, biology and psychology, desire and meaning. The combination of biology and psychology that is characteristic of Freudian psychoanalysis has led to some of the most heated debates surrounding the discourse. In particular, many have seen an essentialism and a biological determinism operative here, which, they argue, should be eliminated in favor of a more contingent and culture-relative construction of the self.

At a very early stage of his work, Freud came to believe that the key to understanding how unconscious desires produce conscious meanings must be sought in the arena of **human sexuality**, especially in the earliest stages of its development in the individual. In one of his accounts of the development of his ideas, Freud notes his surprise at the **resistance** of his patients to his suggestions that their symptoms might have a sexual origin. He soon came to encounter such resistance again and again on a much broader scale, as his psychoanalytic theories of sexuality were subjected to derision by the medical profession and the prevailing culture at large. Particularly his idea that newborn infants are already sexual beings and his broad conception of sexuality as including any form in which the organism experiences pleasure (or its absence) met heavy cultural resistance from late Victorian society. However, Freud had decided early on that the validity of his interpretations to a considerable extent could be gauged by the amount of resistance that they provoked, so he remained convinced of the importance of his discoveries in the domain of sexuality. Although Freud's views on sexuality have undergone far-ranging revision and critique over the years, by Freud himself as well as by others, they continue to serve as an important point of reference for much contemporary discussion of this topic.

While not originally a theory of culture, psychoanalysis, as Freud developed it, proved provocative and fruitful when expanded from the realm of individual psychic development to the sphere of interpersonal human relationships and their cultural expressions. Exploring the more collective forms of human experience, such as art, religion, and politics, Freud perceived trenchant examples of his theories "writ large." Just as he had previously employed his psychoanalytic techniques and their underlying theories to diagnose and ameliorate the symptoms of his patients, so he came to believe that whole societies and cultures might suffer from "collective neuroses" that psychoanalysis could be used to diagnose and perhaps to help remedy. Though Freud himself stopped short of postulating as did his student Jung the notion of a "collective unconscious," his often tentative suggestions about the connection between individual psychic organization and its social and cultural context established a critical agenda that remains in the forefront of much contemporary discussion.

Freud's First "Topography":
The Unconscious, Repression, and Interpretation

In attempting to explore the dynamics of the human psyche, Freud believed that he was moving through uncharted territory. The complexity of the "data" of his early clinical experience suggested that a general map of the terrain would be required by which he could orient himself, and so he developed various "topographies of the mind" that allowed him to assign different psychic phenomena to one or another of its "regions." Freud gradually adjusted his topographies as his explorations continued, but two major configurations may be described as dominant. In this section, we will discuss the earlier one, which in one form or another was operative in his thought until the early 1920s. Later, we will consider the second.

In an important sense, the beginning of Freudian psychoanalysis (he first used the term in a paper of 1896) can be dated to his introducing a distinction between **conscious** and **unconscious** psychic functions or processes, based on a fixed principle. While Freud was by no means the first to use the term *unconscious*, he was the first to identify it as the result of a dynamic process that he called **repression**. Whereas the conscious comprises any mental content of which we are immediately aware—images, ideas, perceptions, and so forth—the unconscious is comprised of psychic materials that have been repressed, that is, put out of the reach of conscious awareness. However, if we understand the conscious as comprising anything of which we are immediately aware at any given time, then a further distinction is required. Clearly, there is much in our minds that we can voluntarily access, as when we try to remember yesterday's meeting or the address of a friend; other things that we think of by association with present experiences; and much else that seems to just pop into our heads. Mental images and ideas of which we are not continuously conscious but of which we can voluntarily become aware Freud calls the **preconscious**. Thus, Freud's first topography involved an initial distinction between processes (and their results) of which we are aware at any given time—in other words, the conscious—and those that escape our awareness, or the unconscious. However, the unconscious in this broad sense includes both those processes of which we are not yet aware but about which we can become aware—in other words, the preconscious—and those that have been repressed and that we cannot voluntarily access, although they continue to affect our conscious thought processes—that is, the unconscious proper. (Henceforth, we will always use the term *unconscious* in this narrower or strict sense, as Freud himself almost always did.) So Freud's first topography involved distinctions among the **unconscious, preconscious, and conscious** (these are sometimes abbreviated as Ucs., Pcs., and Cs.), where the crucial process of **repression** sets the Ucs. off from the Pcs.-Cs. system by rendering the former's contents inaccessible to any voluntary attempt on the part of the latter system to become aware of them.

Freud elaborated on this idea with another distinction involving **primary processes** and **secondary processes**, both of which are connected with the notion of **repression**. Freud used the term **drive** (sometimes misleadingly translated as instinct) to refer to the psychic counterpart of an urge inherent in the human organism's biological make-up, that is, the form in which the biological necessities for our existence enters the mind. The most basic drives involve, for example, the desires for the intake of nourishment, the elimination of biological waste materials, and physical contact with another organism. Freud sometimes referred to such drives collectively as the **libido**. Prior to the separating out in the individual of the three regions, the human infant experiences either pleasure or displeasure associated with the satisfaction of these libidinal drives or with the lack thereof. In the case of lack of satisfaction, Freud held that the infant **hallucinates** or **fantasizes** satisfaction based on "memory traces" of past satisfaction, but that this continually ends in frustration and disillusionment, since the actual biological urge remains unsatisfied. The primary process is thus the drive toward immediate and complete satisfaction, which if left unfulfilled, ultimately results in increasing tension in the organism. This tension, Freud claimed, becomes the psychic region of the unconscious, which he further described as a "reservoir of psychic energy" seeking discharge, although almost always unsuccessfully.

The inevitable failure inherent in the primary processes to secure immediate and complete gratification leads to an adaptive development in the psychic structure of the organism. In order to assure eventual satisfaction, it is necessary that the drives involved in the primary processes be blocked, censored, or postponed—in short, repressed. Instead of fantasy or hallucination, which makes no distinction between internal and external sources of gratification, secondary processes emerge by means of which such a distinction is first established. The secondary processes link part of the amorphous or free-floating drives of the unconscious with particular mental representations and (eventually) words, which operate to repress most of the psychic energy of the unconscious while permitting partial satisfaction. This, according to Freud, is the original function of the preconscious. This linking of certain originally amorphous drives with particular mental representations Freud called **cathexis**, a sort of supercharging of images and words that remain available in the preconscious. These cathected images and words focus the unconscious drives enough so that they can be used to partially satisfy the conscious region of the psyche.

Two features of this topography are essential to bear in mind: First, the repressed drives by no means vanish from the psyche. Rather, they and the hallucinatory attempts to satisfy them remain active in the unconscious and continue to exert their subterranean influence on the preconscious-conscious system. Second, however, the development of the preconscious and its secondary processes forever seals off the drives involved with the primary processes from any direct or voluntary access on the part of consciousness. Just as in order to achieve partial satisfaction or to emerge at all in consciousness the psychic energy of the primary drives had to undergo repression and then be bound to images and words (cathexis) in the preconscious, so any access to them (such as there can be) on the part of consciousness can only be achieved by means of a detour through the preconscious. That is, there can be no direct access to the unconscious that does not go through the cathected images and words of the preconscious.

Nonetheless, it was one of Freud's early and cardinal discoveries that these unconscious drives can sufficiently disrupt the surface of consciousness to permit a sort of access to them. As early as 1899, Freud had come to believe that in phenomena that had previously been regarded as mere curiosities or anomalies, such as slips of the tongue (now called Freudian slips, or to use the more technical term, **parapraxes**), jokes, the language and behavior of neurotic and psychotic patients, and especially dreams, the unconscious had commandeered the images and language of the preconscious, allowing its drives a more direct release than the preconscious ordinarily permitted. In particular, in his landmark work of 1899, *The Interpretation of Dreams,* Freud attempted to demonstrate how a specialized hermeneutic could be developed that would give the analyst access to the dynamics of the unconscious unavailable to consciousness through any ordinary reflective processes.

Dreams and the "Dream-Work"

Freud's original topography suggested to him that the principles of operation of the primary or unconscious processes and the secondary or preconscious processes were fundamentally different. The preconscious made available to consciousness a stock of cathected words and images that formed the basis for all the logical principles governing ordinary experience and constantly employed by consciousness (for example, the relation of cause and effect, the distinction between internal and external, and the temporal sequence of before and after); the archaic fantasy realm of the unconscious seemed to obey no such laws. However, Freud's clinical practice convinced him that the unconscious had its own distinctive structure, however illogical it might appear by the standards of consciousness. It was through the interpretation of dreams that he first discerned this structure. The problem was thus to begin mapping how the principles of the unconscious could be translated into representations of which we could then become conscious.

Freud realized that neither the clinician nor the patient had any direct access to the unconscious. The clinician had only the report of the patient about the dream, which was hardly the full experience of the dream itself. Such a conscious account of a dream, the text provided by the patient to the analyst, Freud called the dream's **manifest content**, and this, together with what he knew about the history of the patient, was all he had to work with. Freud realized that this manifest content had already undergone a complex process of repression, filtering, and reconfiguration on the part of the preconscious before it reached the level where it could be consciously narrated. However, anyone who has tried to tell another about a dream will realize that one's narrative is always full of gaps, abrupt discontinuities, unrecognized faces and places, and illogical images and words.

Moving backward from the distorted narratives of dreams, Freud postulated on the basis of his topography that there must be a psychic mechanism whereby the primary fantasies of the fulfillment of unconscious drives were translated into the conscious text of the dream as reported. This he called the **dream-work.** Freud believed that the dream-work was closely analogous to the process by which the preconscious was originally formed and that it was able to function when the organization of the conscious part of the mind relaxed during sleep. In Freud's view, the unconscious attached its drives to certain images that functioned as objects of wish fulfillment, and these dream-thoughts constituted the original unconscious text of the dream, which he called its **latent content.** This text would then become subject to the operation of the dream-work, producing the manifest content of the dream as related to the analyst. The task of the analyst was thus to reconstruct the text of the unconscious, latent content of the dream on the basis of the manifest content.

In order to do this, however, the analyst would need to understand the principles by which the dream-work translated the latent content into the manifest content. As Freud's clinical experience with reports of dreams grew, he began identifying certain recurrent types of transformations that seemed to be involved in the dream-work. Among them, Freud prominently cited the processes of **condensation** and **displacement.** In condensation, a variety of unconscious wishes are combined by the dream-work (along with their "bound psychic energy") into a single image. These unfulfilled unconscious wishes thus would be amalgamated by the dream-work into a single, hypercathected or supercharged image, which would find its way into the text of the manifest content. A classic example is the famous Rosebud of *Citizen Kane,* the name of a sled into which were condensed the hero's early childhood experience, his relation to his mother, a sense of early innocence, an unresolved conflict with his father, and so forth. By contrast, displacement operates by presenting an image or detail in the manifest content as if it were insignificant, although in the latent content it was absolutely crucial. In other words, in displacement the dream-work has decathected a highly cathected unconscious thought so that it can enter into consciousness. In one of Freud's famous cases, an apparently incidental reference to the color red provided the clue by which he was able to interpret an entire dream, much else of which subsequently appeared of little relevance to its latent meaning.

Thus armed with a number of principles by which the dream-work operated, Freud believed he was able, through a special form of interpretation, to reconstruct the latent content of dreams, gradually explain them to his patients, and in some cases alleviate the symptoms that had brought the patients to him in the first place by helping them to understand the basis of their problems in unconscious conflicts. It was not long before Freud and many others recognized the power of such a hermeneutic for understanding other phenomena closely connected with the conscious manifestation of unconscious processes such as artistic creation, religious discourse, political ideology, and the whole range of cultural production. In a manner that paralleled Marx's reflections on how economic organization produced ideological superstructures and how the latter could be demystified by the cultural critic, Freud opened the way for interpreting the manifest productions of consciousness in terms of unconscious processes operating beyond the view of consciousness itself. Both men believed that what seemed most natural, obvious, and deliberate must be viewed with the deepest suspicion.

Beyond Interpretation:
Explaining Psychic Processes

Freud's work on the interpretation of dreams, important as it was, had raised as many new questions as it had answered old ones. Over the next two decades, Freud explored a wide range of psychic phenomena drawn not only from his clinical practice but also from the arts, anthropology, history, and popular culture. He always worked back and forth between empirical evidence and theoretical elaboration, continually adjusting and augmenting his theoretical framework to fit his ever expanding body of data. Eventually, in the 1920s, he superimposed another topography over the ones we have just discussed, but we must first understand some of the investigations that led him to do so. Three closely related themes are of particular importance in this respect, and each seemed to indicate to Freud a particular limitation of his original position.

Human Sexual Development

Almost immediately after his work on the interpretation of dreams, Freud began exploring more closely the connection between psychological processes and human sexuality. His previous clinical experience had alerted him to the fact that many of his patients' symptoms involved sexual disturbances, and his interpretations of dreams reinforced his convictions regarding the centrality of sexuality in understanding the dynamics of the psyche.

One of Freud's most controversial (and widely derided) hypotheses was that of **infantile sexuality**, that newborns were, almost from the moment of birth, already on the path of sexual development. This claim was possible because of the very broad way in which he defined sexuality, which he viewed as comprising anything by means of which the organism experienced pleasure. Although Freud never went so far as to claim that all psychic phenomena were exclusively sexual in origin (as has sometimes been asserted), there is no doubt that he sometimes flirted with such an idea.

Freud came to distinguish four stages of human sexual development. The earliest he called the **oral stage**, during which the mouth was the central focus of the derivation of pleasure. Freud noted that the tendency of infants to continue sucking even when the mother's breast or a bottle was not present suggested both the operation of fantasy at this stage and the fact that much more was involved than the mere taking of nourishment. Because the infant was completely dependent on its environment for suitable objects of satisfaction, it could only hallucinate the pleasure they provided at the inevitable times of their absence. At some later age, roughly at about a year and a half, the focus of pleasure changed to the infant's own waste products, the first objects that it could produce by its own devices; Freud called this the **anal stage**. Usually during about the second year of life, the pleasure derived from defecation and urination was brought under control in toilet training, which required a more specific adjustment on the part of the young child, for which fantasy was no longer adequate. The third stage, the **phallic**, was usually entered toward the end of the third year, when the child discovered that by manipulating its sexual organs, it could produce its own pleasurable sensations, beyond the mere fantasy of the first stage and the restrictions imposed on it during the second. Freud held that at this stage male and female sexual development began to diverge, in the first place because of differences in human physiology. We will consider this later in more detail in connection with the notorious Oedipal complex. These three phases taken together Freud called the **pregenital period**, which he believed occupied about the first five years of life. After the pregenital period, sexual development entered a period of latency, followed, with the onset of adolescence, by the **genital stage**, in which the desire for pleasure was directed toward intercourse with members of the opposite sex.

Several things should immediately be noted about Freud's theory of sexual development. First, while these stages are not clearly demarcated from one another in practice and may involve considerable overlap, they present human sexual development as involving several discrete tasks requiring quite different resolutions, especially in the area of constituting different relations between the organism's drives for pleasure and their various objects. Second, for Freud, the heuristic value of such a theory of sexual development lay in his view that interference with or disturbance of "normal" sexual development at any given stage would produce characteristic psychological disturbances, deviance, or particular character traits that would surface at a much later period of life. For example, a person whose toilet training was overly severe or traumatic might later experience exaggerated feelings of guilt, a compulsive desire for extreme order or cleanliness, or even sexual impotence. Finally, Freud tended to present his theory of sexual development as a normative or natural progression against which other "deviations" could be gauged. In focusing his account on male heterosexuality as the normal outcome of human sexual development, Freud virtually guaranteed that female sexuality and homoeroticism would be regarded as marginal or deviant. This aspect of Freud's theory remains one of the most disputed.

Narcissism

Implicit in Freud's theory of sexual development was his conception of **narcissism**, which figured ever more prominently in his theoretical formulations. Freud theorized that in the pregenital period the infant's own body provided the object of pleasurable experience, although that pleasure came in three different forms. As the focus of pleasure moved from the mouth to the anus and its products and then to the sexual organs, an increasing localization of erotic zones of the infant's own body occurs, while remaining in the confines of the organism itself. While other, external objects, such as the mother's breast, can be cathected, or charged with significance as potentially satisfying the organism's libidinal drives, they always immediately refer back to the pleasurable excitation of the infant's own body. As Freud sometimes formulated the idea, such objects remained under the dominion of the **pleasure principle**, appearing to the infant as extensions of its own body and its capacities for pleasure. This self-contained or monadic condition of the infant was transformed only when the object of satisfaction was perceived as lying outside the body of the organism, when the original self-love (or ego-love) of the organism was shifted to an object-love, a love of something perceived as external. Only in the process of overcoming this **primary narcissism** did the notions both of a discrete self and a reality or world outside it become possible. In this way, the original pleasure principle governing the self-contained organism was checked and limited by the **reality principle**, giving rise to a whole set of further adjustments, the result of which was the formation of a self and its distinctive character. It should, of course, be noted that this is intimately connected with the passage from the phallic stage, which is pregenital and hence narcissistic, through latency, to the genital stage, which presupposes the overcoming of primary narcissism in directing its libidinal drives toward an object independent of itself.

The Oedipal Complex

Very early in his investigations, Freud had identified the set of relationships involved in the phallic phase as decisive for the later psychic development of the human organism. He believed that the triangle of mother-father-child posed a unique set of problems to the developing child, the resolution of which would influence, in the most profound ways, all later psychic development. More than any other single point in psychic evolution, the manner in which this resolution was accomplished would determine not only the sexual identity of the individual but also the basic structure and content of its ideals, values, socialization, and manner of locating itself in relation to the world beyond. Freud was repeatedly drawn back to considering this stage of development throughout his career, and his views on it changed considerably over time. Here we can only indicate his thought in a broad and schematic way.

Freud referred to the principal set of problems posed to the organism at the phallic stage by the term **Oedipal complex**, invoking the famous figure from Greek mythology and tragedy who killed his father and became incestuously involved with his mother, though at the time unwittingly. Put very roughly at first, we can say that the Oedipal complex confronts the child with the problem of the perceived loss of its (until that time) principal object of satisfaction, the mother, under the threat posed by the figure of the father. This problem, of course, is not yet amenable to conscious or deliberate response on the part of the child, since such devices are not yet at its disposal; so the form taken by its resolution must be understood as resulting in an entire restructuring of the child's psychic apparatus, which the child will carry into the subsequent, genital phase, and thereafter, throughout its life.

To explain how this complicated series of psychic adjustments occurs, it will first be necessary to introduce several technical terms that Freud employed in his writings on this topic: **ambivalence**, **identification**, and **introjection**. Freud sometimes vacillated on whether these three could be clearly differentiated, having observed early on that most psychic drives appeared to have a double inflection, to involve a sort of "love-hate" relationship. On the one hand, we are erotically drawn to objects that provide satisfaction for drives, and we seek to become one with them—for example, by consuming or possessing them. On the other, because of the reality principle, this sought-after unity can only be partial or sporadic, giving rise to frustration and ultimately aggressive impulses directed toward the very objects of desire. (As we will later see, this led Freud to postulate a theory of two opposed instincts, libido and aggression, which are intermingled in almost all of our experiences with the objects of our drives.) Freud called this experience of erotic attachment to an object, coupled with aggression occasioned by its absence, **ambivalence**, and held that it characterized virtually all "object-relationships." However, in the world of early childhood, where inner and outer, psyche and reality, self and world had not yet become clearly differentiated, it was possible for the child to view an object of its drives as included in its own psychic life. That is, a child, in the process of **identification**, could effect a unity with its desired object by regarding the object as a part or an extension of itself. The object would thus come, as it were, to constitute a part of the organism's own psychic makeup, independent of the object's real status. Finally, although this identification could be only fantasized and partial, certain features associated with these highly cathected objects—for example, their attitudes, values, prohibitions, and so forth—could be internalized as permanent and enduring parts of the child's psychic apparatus, forming a significant part of the self-identity and character of the emerging individual. Freud referred to this process by which a major part of the self was constituted as **introjection**.

One further point: When Freud wrote of the mother or father, he was referring to a role rather than a particular person. These words did not necessarily indicate the biological parents, and indeed, in some cases they were used in referring to more than one person playing the same role.

The developmental crisis involved in the Oedipal complex can now be more clearly specified—although, according to Freud's account, the path taken toward its resolution by males and females diverges quite dramatically. To begin with, both male and female children who reach this stage will have experienced ambivalence with regard to their first object of gratification, the mother's body, since although it remains desired, it is present only intermittently, occasioning aggressive responses such as biting, fits of rejection, or temper tantrums. These ambivalent feelings will already be present in the fantasized identification with the desired object and thus active in the child's own attitudes toward itself. Thus, even prior to the entry on the scene of a competitor for the mother's affection, the psychic life of the organism is already highly volatile. (Freud later found the bipolarity or ambivalence implicit in sadomasochistic phenomena instructive in this regard.) However, once the child has entered the phallic stage of development, with the possibilities for self-gratification which it opens, this implicit ambivalence soon becomes aggravated dramatically. For the ability for self-gratification won by the identification with the mother-figure, thus establishing the child as both giver and receiver of pleasure, is soon threatened.

The entry on the scene of the father (or father-figure) has several extremely important consequences for the developing child, which will also prove decisive for Freud's later cultural critique. First, it signals the end of primary narcissism, eventually terminating all infantile fantasies centered exclusively on its own body as source of pleasure. In other words, it is the point where the pleasure principle most decisively gives way to what will later appear as the reality principle. Second, it destabilizes the processes of identification with the mother, since the father now enters the scene as a perceived competitor for the actual mother's affections, establishing the mother as a cathected object in her own right. Third, it represents the initial point at which the child begins to be socialized, when it comes to realize that an intersubjective world exists beyond the processes of its identification with the mother. Fourth, this initial step toward socialization is attended by extreme anxiety, which will persist throughout the life of the individual. The further psychic adjustments of the child in the face of this anxiety will then increasingly begin to assume the form of an introjecting of values and attitudes derived from this father-figure as a subsequent form of identification. Finally, the entry of the father simultaneously occasions the beginnings of sexual differentiation between male and female out of the previously androgynous state of primary narcissism, giving rise to different paths of development for male and female children. Nothing in Freud's psychoanalytic theory is as decisive for his view of culture and its critique as this binding together of the end of primary narcissism, the beginning of socialization and the reign of the reality principle, the internalization of basic values and attitudes, sexual differentiation, and the anxiety accompanying all of this, brought to a focus in the Oedipal complex. When Freud later entertained the idea that the price to be paid for civilization was an all-pervasive anxiety, guilt, and neurosis, he sought the origins of these feelings at this stage in the child's psychic development.

So far we have provided a general description of the effects of the Oedipal complex and its resolution, which in one form or another have remained key to Freudian critical discourse. However, many theorists have parted ways with Freud over the specifics of his analysis of this crisis and its resolution, particularly as concerns sexual differentiation; it is this highly contested area that we must now consider.

The onset of the Oedipal complex as depicted by Freud attends the entry of the child into a phallic stage of psychic development, where the primary center of pleasure has become localized in the penis (for the male) or the clitoris (for the female). (Note that Freud regarded the female clitoris as the anatomical counterpart of the male penis, though in a stunted or underdeveloped form.) Once such localization has occurred, the principal threat presented by the father will be initially translated by the child solely in phallic terms, that is, it will be represented in the child's psyche as the threat of **castration**, which Freud understands as the loss of the penis. Initially, this threat of castration posed by the father will, for both male and female children, set up a dual set of ambivalences directed toward the mother and father. The implicit ambivalence in the identification with the mother will be aggravated by the prospect of a loss of the child's initial love-object to a competitor. The mother as the primary object of identification and source of gratification thus will begin to appear a potential coconspirator with the father to deny such gratification. Likewise, the father will appear both a potential threat to identification with the mother and an object of identification in his own right, thus allowing the child to effect a vicarious possession and union with the mother. At this point, that is, both male and female children will experience the wholly ambivalent feelings of jealousy of and desire for identification with both parents.

However, this dual set of ambivalences experienced by both the male and female child become unbalanced and asymmetrical with the recognition of the biological differences between them. For the male child's part, somehow realizing that the mother and female child lack that organ that is shared by him with the father (exactly how this comes about Freud is never entirely clear), his own subsequent development will revolve around three factors. First, the male child will experience fully the threat of castration with its attendant anxiety, which cannot be an issue for the female child. Second, he will come to identify more strongly with the father as occupying a structurally analogous role in relation to the mother as erotic object. Third, he will experience a murderous sense of competition with the father for the affections of the mother, which he is nonetheless entirely ill-equipped to win. In compensation, he will come to introject into his own psyche both the father's values as well as his prohibitions backed by the threat of castration. The former will appear to make him a more worthy competitor, the latter to insure his survival as potential rival. It is with the introjection of the father-figure, in the form of both basic traits and prohibitions (which Freud will later discuss under the heading of the formation of the superego) that the male child ultimately resolves the Oedipal crisis and is able to continue in his psychic development, ultimately coming to occupy the position of the father himself at the genital stage, which accompanies the onset of adolescence.

For the female child, the situation is quite different. Rather than fear of castration, so important to the male child, the female comes to realize (again Freud is not clear how) that she lacks a penis and experiences feelings of envy, inferiority, and anger at her mother for permitting her to be born without a penis. Her initial response, as Freud has it, is to focus her desire on the father, wishing to substitute for the mother as his sexual partner. Since this will prove unsuccessful, she normally will repress her desires for the father and return to an uneasy identification with the mother, while continuing to compete for the father's attentions. In so doing, she will normally introject some of the mother's own values and attitudes, while at the same time, in a state of great ambivalence, she internalizes some of the same prohibitions derived from the father as does the male child, though in her case not backed by the threat of castration. The female child's resolution of the Oedipal crisis is thus achieved when she has repressed her desires for the father, introjected certain traits of the mother together with paternal prohibitions, and is thus equipped, at the onset of adolescence, to assume the role of the mother in the genital phase.

Later, we will consider some of the more important critical responses to this view. For the moment, it is most important to realize how crucial the Oedipal complex is in Freud's overall view, since it represents the watershed between infantile narcissism under the rule of the pleasure principle and social integration under the reign of the reality principle. For Freud, the Oedipal complex is a genuine and universal rite of passage, and for that reason, its importance cannot be overestimated.

Freud's Later "Topography": The Development of the Ego

In the previous section, we summarized the more important issues that Freud explored after the *Interpretation of Dreams*. As we suggested at the beginning, these investigations led Freud to realize some of the crucial limitations of his original topography of unconscious-preconscious-conscious. This topography highlighted the role of repression in the formation of the Ucs. and its division from the Pcs.-Cs. system and provided Freud with a schema for understanding certain distortions that emerged in the conscious realm as a result of the pressures of repressed material in the unconscious. However, Freud's later studies convinced him that this schema was inadequate as a comprehensive view of the human psyche into which his new results could be integrated. Three major limitations of the first topography should be mentioned. First, it tended to homogenize the phenomena of repression and the unconscious into a more or less unified set of operations and their products. In particular, Freud came to doubt whether a view that placed so much responsibility on the preconscious as the principal agency of repression was adequate to the available evidence. He became convinced that in order to account for such diverse phenomena as dreams, anxiety, guilt, and sexual

Figure 4.1   Freud's Diagram of Id-Ego-Superego

dysfunction, factors in addition to the operation of the preconscious must be considered. In fact, he conjectured that every "psychic region" might have its own characteristic forms of repression, functioning as **defense mechanisms** by which the organism protected itself against threats of dissolution. Second, his original topography was, to a large degree, a static schema. As Freud became increasingly interested in questions of psychic development, he found that his original map helped him little in describing how the various aspects of the psyche developed in relation to one another. Finally, as the conflicts between the pleasure principle and the reality principle and between the drives emerging from the biological constitution of the organism and the more external pressures exerted by other persons and society loomed ever more important in his thought, Freud found it necessary to revise his original schema, which had been geared markedly toward the former types of psychological processes and their manifestations in individual patients. In other words, Freud needed a new topography that would allow him to explain the emergence and dynamics of a distinct ego or self, rather than one that merely mapped the psychic processes of an already constituted individual like those he encountered in his clinical practice.

The best way to introduce Freud's new topography (or what is sometimes called his structural model) is to consider Freud's own diagram, first presented in his *New Introductory Lectures* of 1933 (although he was employing its terms at least a decade earlier; see Figure 4.1).

Freud's new topography is clearly superimposed over the original topography of conscious (to which he now affixes "Pcpt."—that is, perception, or the immediate sensory awareness of the external world), preconscious, and unconscious.

Indeed, its typography indicates that now the focus will be on the system **id-ego-superego**, which does not directly correspond with the system unconscious-preconscious-conscious, although it has important relationships with it.

The Id

Id, the usual translation of Freud's German term *das Es* (literally, "the it"), indicates the part of the psychic apparatus that is most primitive or elemental. Existing prior to the emergence of a distinct self, or *I*, the id is closely related to the biological constitution of the organism and its natural drives, hence the open part of the diagram at the bottom. While the id is in part made up of repressed materials, it also includes biological drives (sometimes called instincts) that derive from the organism independently of repression. In this sense, the earlier unconscious, which Freud tended to regard as exclusively the product of repression, can be seen as a part of the id.

The id and its drives constitute a realm lacking any sense of time or logic as well as any ability to signify through language or other signs, and wholly governed by the pleasure principle—that is, always seeking the drives' own immediate and entire satisfaction regardless of the consequences. The id, then, is more remote from any conscious or preconscious processes than was the unconscious in the earlier topography, more dependent than it on the biological constitution of the organism, and thus even less accessible to any hermeneutic deciphering.

Viewed from a developmental perspective, the id can be roughly equated with the pre-Oedipal, narcissistic state of the infant, although the id's demands do not cease with the infant's further development.

The Ego

Ego, the common English translation of Freud's *das Ich* (literally, "the I"), emerges as the drives of the id come to be controlled or harnessed under the sway of the reality principle. That is, as we have already seen, the inevitable frustration and defeat of the id's drives toward immediate and complete gratification in the face of the limitations posed by the external world gives rise to a set of adaptive mechanisms that mediate between the id's incessant demands and their potential for only partial accommodation in reality. Note that the ego is a system that develops out of the id but also that it is never completely separated from it; rather, the two tend to merge and coexist in a state of uneasy tension. From the diagram, we can see that the ego includes both the earlier preconscious and conscious systems, though its roots go deeper into the id and the unconscious than the earlier topography suggested. The ego is clearly divided from the id only in the area of specifically repressed content but elsewhere remains continuous with it.

Freud did intend that the ego be understood as what we more ordinarily regard as the self, but his suggestion was that the self be equated neither with immediate consciousness nor with its preconscious memory traces but conceived as including a good deal more as well. For Freud, to speak of a self is to make reference not only to whom we might consciously claim to be and what memories we might be able to access, but also to certain dispositions, character traits, and even unconscious desires, which make us who we are even without our own conscious awareness of them. It also should be noted that the ego itself plays a significant role in the repression of certain drives as it adapts itself under the influence of the reality principle.

The ego develops in asserting partial control over the id through the acquisition of language, the development of a sense of time and of cause and effect, and the learning of the logic by which reality can be manipulated in the interests of the ultimate though always only partial gratification of the id's drives. While the ego, due to its partial merging with the id, will never be totally rational, rationality will nonetheless be one of the instruments at its disposal for adjusting the irrational drives of the id to the demands of the reality principle.

Viewed developmentally, the ego begins its emergence at the point where primary narcissism begins to fade and the child discovers the rupture between its fantasized omnipotence and a world that frustrates its own efforts at self-gratification. The structures that make up the ego begin to form through a series of object-identifications in which objects, values, and traits become "introjected" into the psychic apparatus of the developing organism, prior to but overlapping with the Oedipal crisis.

The Superego

Superego, the usual English translation of Freud's term *das Oberich* (or *the super I),* consists of two closely related subsystems: the **ego-ideal** and **conscience**. Whereas the ego-ideal is the internalization or introjection of various objects or traits learned from the parents as commendable or praiseworthy, conscience consists of a set of prohibitions associated with punishment and particularly connected with the Oedipal threat posed by the father. Indeed, it is in the attempt to resolve the Oedipal conflict with the father that the individual first comes to identify with and internalize the father's prohibitions as a way of defending itself from the perceived threat posed by the father. Further, the ego, through introjection, constructs an ideal that if fulfilled would induce the father's affection. Roughly speaking, then, the superego is the internalization of various norms and prohibitions, especially those of the father, which having been at first externally imposed, come to govern the thought and behavior of the individual even in the absence of threat by an authority figure. It is the locus of what is sometimes referred to as the *moral sense,* but can include much else as well.

According to Freud, the relation of the superego to the id and ego is complex and often ambiguous. Referring to the diagram, we can see that on the one hand, the superego is in some ways even more in touch with the id than is the ego itself, since unconscious drives provide much of the energy for the superego's operation. It is possible for the superego to conspire with the id against the ego, producing powerful feelings of inferiority and guilt in the ego and ultimately resulting in various neurotic disturbances. On the other hand, the superego and ego can enjoy a certain degree of interchange that is denied the ego in its relation to the repressed part of the id. In more concrete terms, enough of the superego approaches the Pcs.-Cs. system to allow the ego to become aware of certain (though never all) of its ideals and values and to alter them or direct them into productive channels.

Freud summarized the results of this new topography in the following way: "We are warned by a proverb against serving two masters at the same time. The poor ego has things even worse: it serves three severe masters and does what it can to bring their claims and demands into harmony with one another. These claims are always divergent and often seem incompatible. No wonder that the ego so often fails in its task."

Who are these "three masters"? The first is the id, constantly demanding complete and immediate satisfaction of its drives under the influence of the pleasure principle. The second is the external world, which, as the reality principle, directly opposes exactly what the id demands. The third, of course, is the superego, yet another set of ideals and prohibitions that the ego, in its development, has in effect imposed on itself but that often appears as an autonomous force foreign to the ego. For Freud, this embattled and anxiety-riddled ego or self, attempting to accommodate and to compromise the demands of the external world, its own internal drives, and its moral ideals and prohibitions, is both the creator and the ultimate victim of cultural forms.

The Theory of the Instincts: Eros and Thanatos

As if this stark account of the task facing the individual were not enough, Freud, in the last phase of his career, came to reconsider the nature of the basic instinctual forces driving this entire psychic apparatus. The notion of a dual system of instincts had occurred to him much earlier. Initially, he tended to distinguish between those drives bound up with sexual pleasure (libido proper) and those directed toward self-preservation (about which he otherwise said relatively little). However, as was the case with many European intellectuals, the terrible events of World War I and its aftermath intensified Freud's interest in exploring what psychoanalysis might have to offer for understanding the dynamics of a contemporary society that, contrary to all rational judgment, seemed intent on self-destruction, even at the very height of its civilized development.

In his essay of 1920 titled "Beyond the Pleasure Principle," Freud began postulating two basic but opposed instincts that seemed to underlie all other psychic processes and to act as engines driving them on, separately as well as in various combined forms. It should be noted that this remained a postulate in Freud's mind—that is, something philosophical or speculative, which he relegated to the area of what he called **metapsychology**. Nonetheless, he came to believe that it contained considerable explanatory power, and in particular, provided a requisite link between his ego psychology and his broader social theory.

The first of these basic instincts he called **Eros**, which he associated with all tendencies on the part of the organism to form unities with other objects in the surrounding world. The realm of Eros ran from such elementary processes as the consumption of food to identification first with the mother and later with other persons as love-objects, to the formation of social communities. Eros thus represented an instinctual centrifugal tendency on the part of the organism, driving it to unify itself, to extend its life-oriented processes into ever larger communities, and to maintain its existence. Opposed to this was the **death instinct**, sometimes called *Thanatos* (the opposite of the Greek term *Eros),* which was a principle of dissolution, of the violation or breaking up of unities, and ultimately of the cessation of the organism's life processes. Given his broad notion of sexuality, it was natural for Freud to associate Eros with what he had earlier called libido, and Eros maintained this intimate connection with sexuality and its development. However, Freud's idea of sexual development was also closely connected with repression, which intensified the drive on the part of the archaic unconscious to return to an earlier state before repression, which at its antipode would be a purely inorganic condition—the death of the organism.

Three important features of this dual theory of instincts must be noted. First, while Freud regarded these instincts as deeply rooted in the id and hence in the biological constitution of the organism, they tended to pervade all psychic processes, which Freud's later topography envisioned as overlapping at many points with one another. While the id remained the primary locus of the death-instinct, it nonetheless communicated its negative energy in various forms into other, more conscious psychic processes as well. Correspondingly, although Freud regarded the ego as the primary mechanism by which Eros was sustained and enhanced and Thanatos repressed and held in check, he believed that under certain circumstances the death-instinct could manifest itself in the processes of the ego as well. The deliberateness with which the European nations had focused their aggressive tendencies in mobilizing for war provided Freud with ample grounds for this belief.

Because they operated through "object-cathexes," as we have already discussed, Eros and Thanatos can rarely be observed in a pure or pristine form. Rather, they manifest themselves in various combinations in almost any psychic phenomenon. The consumption of food, for example, involves not only the maintenance of the life of an organism, hence its erotic component, but at the same time entails the reduction of the object consumed to the inorganic state characteristic of the death-instinct. On a broader scale, while a nation's engagement in war for its self-preservation or aggrandizement involves a strong communal bonding, war itself also involves a willingness to die for the cause of the nation.

Finally, it should not be thought that Freud regarded the death-instinct as something unqualifiedly evil or something to be eradicated in all cases. In the overall economy of the psyche, the death-instinct, when properly counterbalanced by Eros, limits the absorption of the individual into its various objects or higher cultural unities; and the **aggression** associated with the death-instinct, under the right circumstances, can even serve to secure the very conditions for the further expression of Eros. However, this issue of a balance between the two intimately connected instincts will always remain problematic, since the death-instinct taps into biological forces even more primitive and archaic than those accessed by Eros and thus tends to overpower it in many situations, as happened during World War I.

Psychoanalysis as Theory and Critique of Culture

Unlike Marx's version of materialism, Freudian psychoanalysis was not explicitly designed as a vehicle for cultural critique. In fact, Freud himself admitted that he was by temperament rather apolitical, and he remained somewhat tentative and uneasy when attempting to extend his scientific work into what he regarded as more speculative areas. As a result, the position of psychoanalysis in the broader history of critical discourses has remained (appropriately enough) ambivalent, even as it has deeply influenced many other discourses.

Freud's Applications of Psychoanalysis to the Critique of Culture

One of Freud's most direct applications of psychoanalysis to cultural production was formulated relatively early in his career in his essay of 1907 entitled "Creative Writers and Daydreaming." Drawing on his earlier work on the interpretation of dreams, he suggested in this essay that imaginative works of literature (and by extension other examples of artistic creativity) might be productively viewed as an extension of the play of fantasy involved in childhood narcissism under the sway of the pleasure principle. The artist, he writes, "creates a world of phantasy which he takes very seriously—that is, which he invests with large amounts of emotion—while separating it sharply from reality." The creative process is based on what Freud calls **daydreaming**, thereby suggesting that artistic productions might, with certain qualifications, be interpreted according to the same principles that he had explored in *The Interpretation of Dreams*. Like the manifest content of the dream, the artistic work does not present the artist's narcissistic dream-thoughts in their raw form, which would be unpleasurable for creator and audience alike. Rather, the artist reworks them into a surrogate, aesthetic form, from which both the creator and the audience derive pleasure precisely because this form places them squarely in the realm of the imaginative play of fantasy. Culture, in this early view of Freud's, thus appears as a vehicle whereby the repressed content of the unconscious can find expression in **sublimated** forms that can be experienced as pleasurable. The production and consumption of cultural products thus take place in strict accordance with the drive of the unconscious, under the pleasure principle, to oppose itself to the reality principle and recover something of the narcissistic gratification sought in the common infantile human condition. Culture therefore becomes the "return of the repressed" in sublimated forms, and like dreams, provides yet another set of possibilities for entry into the dynamics of the unconscious.

When Freud turned from the cultural phenomenon of artistic creation to that of religion, things became considerably more complicated. Unlike art, which even in depicting the most violent or offensive material can nonetheless produce a pleasurable cathexis due to its distance from reality, religion clearly brings into play its own set of repressive and pain-inducing taboos, prohibitions, and anxieties, since it does not present itself wholly (or in some cases even in part) under the guise of fantasy. This suggested to Freud that where the origin of artistic creation lay in early narcissism, that of religion must be principally sought in the Oedipal challenge to narcissism. In his most important writings on religion, especially *Totem and Taboo* (1913), *The Future of an Illusion* (1927), and *Moses and Monotheism* (1939), Freud interpreted religions as various collective symbolic representations of the Oedipal crisis and its resolution.

Based on his study of contemporary anthropological literature, Freud theorized that the most primitive religions were founded on the **incest taboo**, a prohibition against sexual relations with certain persons in a given circle of kinship, which could ultimately be traced to the Oedipal fear of castration by the father attendant on the child's desire for the mother. Further, the identification of the tribe with a totem animal, including both its veneration and its ritual sacrifice and consumption, were based on transference of the ambivalence toward the father-figure to a mystical being, which was both idealized in its attributes of power and debased in its slaughter and consumption. Such attributes, according to Freud, continued into monotheistic religions, where, as in Christianity, the divinity has both an omnipotent, patriarchal aspect (God the Father) and a human, suffering element (God the Son), in whose demise and incorporation by consumption the believer participates in the ritual of communion. While Freud regarded religion in one sense as an important mechanism for the maintenance of psychic integrity, he also believed that it nonetheless represented a continuation of infantile and prerational patterns of experience and thought that should ultimately be replaced by the clear-sighted "truth" provided by modern science and its worldview. With a guardedly critical attitude, Freud could write, "Men cannot remain children forever; they must in the end go out into 'hostile life.' We may call this 'education to reality.'"

In his essay most explicitly devoted to the foundations of communal and political life, *Group Psychology and the Analysis of the Ego* (1921), Freud continued to extrapolate the structures of individual psychic development to the social and cultural spheres. Directly comparing the behavior of crowds or masses with that of children, Freud suggested that both were narcissistic, motivated by the desire for immediate gratification, and that neither was interested in "truth" but operated under the sway of fantasy, tending to fixate on specific, highly cathected symbols, words, or slogans that resisted any rational analysis or critique. (Here, of course, are the rudiments of Freud's version of the origin of ideologies.) Groups are formed from the infantile state of crowds or masses when the libidinous energy of individuals comes to be directed toward a leader as the collective ego-ideal of the group, performing the same function as the father-figure at the level of the individual. In internalizing the same ego-ideal, the members of the group also come to affirm their solidarity with one another to the exclusion of all nonmembers, whose ego-ideal differs from their own. In an almost Hobbesian fashion, Freud asserts that the idea of the political equality of individuals is predicated on their equal inequality when compared to the leader or father-figure that embodies the shared ego-ideal. Characteristically, Freud's view of the origins of groups and more complex political associations in the patriarchal nexus of the Oedipal conflict places severe restraints on any competing theory that would seek a rational or political solution to human conflict.

Freud radicalized this line of reflection in what is probably his most famous work on cultural theory, *Civilization and Its Discontents* (1930). Delving beneath even the Oedipal origins of religion and politics, he mobilizes his theory of the instincts to offer what appears the most critical and pessimistic account of culture and civilization since Rousseau's *First Discourse*. Why, Freud asks, given the abundant fruits of modern progress and civilization, do so many people still feel disaffected, alienated, and even aggressive toward themselves and the world around them? The answer he proposes turns on his assumption of the conflictual coexistence of the sexual and death instincts (Eros and Thanatos). Precivilized human beings, dependent on the vicissitudes of nature though with minimal social constraints, under most circumstances could gratify both their sexual and aggressive drives rather directly and immediately, thus experiencing a correspondingly low degree of repression. However, the price paid for this was an extremely insecure existence, and at best, short-term satisfaction. Like the individual, collective humankind gradually relinquished part of the realm of the pleasure principle to the dictates of the reality principle in order to make more secure the now-delimited region of the pleasure principle. For the sexual drive (Eros), this meant that some of its libidinal energy had to be rechanneled into social and cultural production in order to secure the conditions for longer-range gratification. That is, a certain part of the sexual drive had to undergo repression and sublimation in less immediately gratifying activities. Labor, a sublimated form of erotic activity, thus served as an outlet for some libidinal energy while dictating that a good deal more immediate sexual gratification be deferred. This was attended, as is all loss or deferral of gratification, by a rise in the level of aggressive impulses, directed in the primary instance toward other persons as now unavailable love-objects. However, since the work of cultural production required social cooperation, the aggressive or death instincts became redirected toward the ego through the agency of the superego. This resulted in pervasive feelings of guilt, arising from fantasies of aggression toward others but turned inward on the self by the agency of the superego.

According to Freud, then, the growth of civilization extracted a high price from the individual: repressed sexual drives that could rarely if ever find complete outlet in productive activity, and heightened aggression that, turned inward, produced neurotic feelings of guilt and attendant symptoms. It followed that the more developed the level of civilization of a particular culture, the more likely its constituent members were to experience psychic disturbances, including anxiety, anger, and sporadic outbreaks of unrest and violence. As Freud wrote, "If the development of civilization has such a far-reaching similarity to the development of the individual and if it employs the same methods, may we not be justified in reaching the diagnosis that, under the influence of cultural urges, some civilizations, or some epochs of civilization—possibly the whole of mankind—have become 'neurotic'?"

In this work, Freud offered no panaceas. Perhaps, he suggested, psychoanalysis might help us to ameliorate the symptoms of those most afflicted by the "curses of civilization," and to a limited degree, to enhance our understanding of the causes of those symptoms, thus counseling tolerance. However, he discounted any such solution as Marxian socialism, since, in his analysis, the basic problems did not arise from any specific economic configuration but from civilization itself, with or without private property. Indeed, Freud believed that the acquisition of private property itself offered an important outlet for libidinal energy in modern societies and that socialist societies were capable of being just as repressive of the instincts as were capitalist ones, if not more so.

When we realize that Freud was writing in the wake of World War I and as a contemporary observer of the rise of Stalinism and of European fascist regimes, we can perhaps sympathize with the pathos of his conclusion to this famous work: "And now it is to be expected that the other of the two 'Heavenly Powers,' eternal Eros, will make an effort to assert himself in the struggle with his equally immortal adversary. But who can foresee with what success and with what result?"

Radical Developments of the Psychoanalytic Theory of Culture

On the face of it, classical psychoanalysis seems a rather incongenial bedfellow for radical social movements. To many radical critics, the individualism, determinism, essentialism, and pessimism inherent in the Freudian theories of character and culture could lead only to a defeatist attitude with respect to the possibilities for significant social change. Taking psychoanalysis at its literal word on such issues, most communist, socialist, and even progressive parties viewed it as a new, insidious version of bourgeois ideology. Still, there have been several significant attempts to muster psychoanalytic theory into the service of social critique and transformation on the part of those willing to give up the prevailing orthodoxies of the existing psychoanalytic and radical movements. Generally speaking, for those who have attempted a rapprochement between Marxism and psychoanalysis, certain aspects of each have had to be significantly altered or jettisoned. In the next chapter, we will consider the work of Herbert Marcuse of the Frankfurt School, who began with a critical social theory and attempted to support it with certain insights derived from psychoanalysis. Later on, we will see how Jacques Lacan's poststructuralist reading of Freud provided the basis for such new forms of social critique as that of Louis Althusser.

Appropriations of Psychoanalytic Discourse

To complete our survey of the critical discourse of psychoanalysis, brief note must be taken of its widespread appropriation by other creative and critical practices. Like all of the critical discourses that we are considering, psychoanalysis offered a new theoretical framework and vocabulary in which to pose novel questions and explore a range of alternative responses to them. Even in Freud's own lifetime, some of the basic ideas and themes of psychoanalysis came to influence not only other critical discourses concerned with culture (such as Marxism and the Frankfurt School of critical theory) but also many figures directly involved in cultural production. Among the latter can be counted such authors as Thomas Mann, D. H. Lawrence, and James Joyce; visual artists involved in the Dadaist and Surrealist movements, including Max Ernst and Salvador Dali; and composers such as Arnold Schoenberg, Alban Berg, and Richard Strauss, whose operas explicitly drew on key Freudian notions.

Literary criticism (and its cousin, media criticism) has employed psychoanalytic insights in particularly productive ways. While few literary or media critics would consider their approach exclusively psychoanalytic, many have drawn on various psychoanalytic ideas in their attempts to interpret the multiple dimensions of cultural texts. In his book *Literary Theory: An Introduction* (1983), Terry Eagleton provides a helpful classification of approaches to literary works that have employed psychoanalytic insights. There he distinguishes among psychoanalytic interpretations that focus on a work's **author**, its **contents**, its **formal construction**, and its **reader**.

As we have seen, Freud himself first pointed the way toward reading cultural texts as manifestations of the unconscious psychic conflicts of the author, suggesting that they be approached by analogy to the manifest content of dreams, that is, as products of the author's daydreams and fantasies. By a more or less straightforward appropriation of Freud, cultural texts can provide ready examples for exploring the psychodynamics of the individual outside the rarefied context of clinical psychoanalysis. From a more critical perspective, such analyses remind us that cultural products are never completely under the control of even the most deliberate author but reveal a complex interplay between unconscious desire and conscious representation that constantly overruns the author's intentions. For some critics, psychoanalytic approaches to cultural products indeed help us understand their authors better than those individuals understood themselves. The critical writings of Ernest Jones and Harold Bloom provide some of the best known examples of this approach. Perhaps even more interesting from a critical perspective are attempts to psychoanalyze the collective author of commercial productions such as television series, advertisements, film genres, or political campaigns, where collective patterns of repression and neurosis often manifest themselves.

Similar points can be made with respect to the contents of various cultural productions. From a psychoanalytic perspective, the selection and presentation of a particular subject matter for cultural products is governed by the highly charged object-cathexes first established in the unconscious. The use of phallic and uterine symbols in artistic and commercial productions are the most obvious examples of this unconscious overdetermination of content. Even entire cultural genres such as the Western, the thriller, and the soap opera have been shown to revolve around primal Oedipal conflicts and resolutions, which reveals much about the psychological tensions present in authors and audience alike. For example, a virtual cottage industry has developed in cinematic theory centered around the psychological analysis of films by Alfred Hitchcock, which are purported to unveil important insights about contemporary neurotic obsessions and psychopathology.

The psychoanalytic approach to the form of cultural productions is somewhat more complex. As Freud points out in *The Interpretation of Dreams,* the manifest content of a dream is the result of the structural transformation of the unconscious thoughts by the dream-work into a form amenable to conscious narration. Operative in this process are various defense mechanisms, such as condensation and displacement, which permit pain-inducing or aggressive impulses to achieve nonthreatening forms at the level of conscious experience. Focusing on the surface-level narrative structure of a cultural production in conjunction with the psychoanalytic account of the emergence of the ego and superego from the id, such an approach may reveal something of the distorted and repressive character of widely circulating and influential cultural narratives. To take a simple case, the tendency of many novels and films to begin with a crisis and conclude with a happy ending may be read as a direct narrative reversal of the disruption of primary narcissism by the Oedipal crisis, which itself permits no final resolution. Narrative structure might thus be one of the mechanisms by which pre-Oedipal wishes are fulfilled in fantasy. On a more restricted scale, many literary critics following the lead of Kenneth Burke have productively utilized parallels such as those between Freud's notions of condensation and displacement and the literary devices of metaphor (a single word carrying multiple significations) and metonymy (a particular aspect of something signifying the whole). A number of theories about literary form have emerged in an attempt to map the whole range of literary devices or tropes onto the various defense mechanisms explored by Freud.

Finally, various ideas borrowed from psychoanalysis have been used to elucidate the psychic processes and effects involved in reading cultural texts. Literary critics such as Simon Lesser and Norman Holland, for example, have proposed that works of literature evoke unconscious fantasies that provide pleasure to the reader even as they provoke various defense mechanisms or resistances that counter this effect, in a process of dynamic interchange. A story, novel, or film, for instance, may allow us to identify, though at an unconscious level, with a character's sexual ambivalence or antiauthoritarian aggression, even as our conscious processes erect various defense mechanisms or prohibitions against doing so. This dynamic can have especially interesting implications when applied to commercial productions, which may be viewed as attempting simultaneously to elicit a strong sense of unconscious identification with a particular product or personality and to break down conscious resistance to such identifications.

As things stand at present, few if any cultural critics would subscribe to the classical Freudian theory of culture. Likewise, large-scale attempts to wed psychoanalytic theory to radical social critique seem passé in light of prevailing poststructuralist suspicions regarding any variety of overarching or totalizing theory. Though the constructive influence of psychoanalytic discourse has by no means ceased, it continues for the most part either in the sort of partial and fragmentary forms that we have just discussed, or thanks to Lacan's radical reformulations, as an important dimension of poststructuralist discourse. Paradoxically, however, perhaps the most significant influence of psychoanalysis in recent times stems from its serving as a highly contested area for various types of feminist criticism; this has led to a renewed interest in its earliest origins and its classical Freudian formulations.

Feminist Critique of Psychoanalysis

From its outset, psychoanalysis was inextricably entwined with issues involving the psychology of women. Much of Freud's own early and most important clinical experience involved work with female patients. Women also figured prominently in the earliest circles of clinical analysts, which included such pivotal theorist-practitioners as Helene Deutsch, Karen Horney, and Anna Freud, Sigmund's youngest child. In addition, Freud frequently returned to the explicit consideration of female sexuality throughout much of his career. Historically, the discourse of psychoanalysis was and has remained more open to contributions by women than have the natural sciences, other clinical professions, or even other critical discourses. Indeed, psychoanalysis was the first critical discourse in which issues surrounding sexual differentiation were explicitly raised and thus it could not fail to attract the attention of thinkers with feminist concerns. However, Freud's own writings on female sexuality (not to mention those of many of his followers) have often and understandably provoked a wide range of critical responses. Whether the discourse of psychoanalysis has anything constructive to offer feminist cultural criticism remains even today a highly contested issue.

How one decides this question depends a great deal on how one interprets the nature and significance of psychoanalysis, and to a considerable extent, how one reads Freud himself. Despite the serious feminist objections raised against psychoanalysis in general and Freud's version of it in particular, both continue to find defenders among the ranks of feminists; the status of psychoanalysis in relation to feminist critique is by no means clear-cut. Here we will consider some of the most important types of objections that have been raised, noting that in each case, well-considered responses also have been offered, often in the form of dramatically different readings of the primary Freudian texts. It also should be noted that objections to Freudian psychoanalysis have been raised from critical positions other than feminist ones.

It will be convenient to group the critical responses to psychoanalysis under three headings. The first concerns problems of **methodology** and basic philosophical assumptions made by Freud, especially those of **determinism** and **essentialism**, which tended to pass into the subsequent discourse of psychoanalysis. This type of criticism is by no means exclusively feminist. The second type turns on certain cultural assumptions that involve the notion of patriarchy. The third type of criticism focuses more particularly on some of the specifics of Freud's account of female sexuality in relation to the Oedipal complex.

The Scientific Status of Psychoanalysis and Its Underlying Assumptions

In the concluding essay of *New Introductory Lectures on Psychoanalysis* (1933), entitled "The Question of a *Weltanschauung* (Worldview)," Freud stated without qualification that psychoanalysis "is a part of science and can adhere to the scientific *Weltanschauung.*" Although Freud's emphasis in this essay was on the difference between a religious and a scientific orientation toward the world—that is, on the contrast between the "illusions" of religion and the "truths" of science—he suppressed one crucial feature of the scientific worldview: its implicit determinism. Elsewhere, however, Freud had made no secret of his view that "anatomy (or biology) is destiny," nor of his closely related conviction that the later psychological lives of individuals are determined by their early sexual development. Because Freud was convinced that "the intellect and the mind are objects for scientific research in exactly the same way as nonhuman things" and that consequently psychoanalysis was a bona fide "special science," he quite consistently embraced biological and psychological determinism.

Whatever may be the truth of Freud's strong claims about the status of psychoanalysis as a science and the metaphysical baggage this notion carries, they have found few supporters even among those who otherwise adhered to Freud's ideas. Some of the earliest psychoanalytic theorists, such as Alfred Adler, Karen Horney, and Clara Thompson, moved quite early to reject Freud's biological determinism, arguing in one form or another that sexuality and its various forms of expression were at least as much a matter of social and cultural construction as of biological necessity. Generally, they also held that human psychological development could not be adequately conceived of as simply the playing out of a scenario written in the first years of life.

Such critical advocates of psychoanalysis were later seconded by many of the founders of contemporary feminist critique, although the latter also went on to express suspicions that psychoanalysis was so tainted that it might have to be excluded as an approach for feminist criticism. Such figures as **Betty Friedan, Shulamith Firestone**, and **Kate Millett** emphasized that the real issue that critical discourse must confront was neither biology nor sexuality (as Freud had thought) but **power**, which although it was not entirely disconnected from biology, played itself out in the sphere of politics and culture. Raising suspicions about Freud's clinical practices in relation to his female patients and his tendency to accept prevailing Victorian notions of male and female sexuality in the context of the nuclear family as normative, they tended to view psychoanalysis as yet another intellectual ruse cloaked in the mantle of science, by which prevailing power relations were maintained and promoted. Like all brands of determinism, Freud's thus appeared to underwrite the status quo by elevating what is cultural, historical, and hence changeable to the status of a universal and inalterable scientific law. As a result of the work of these and other Anglo-American feminists (with the notable exception of Nancy Chodorow), psychoanalysis has come to be regarded in Anglophone countries as something of a pariah, a situation quite different from feminist thought on the continent, where the dramatic revision of psychoanalysis by Jacques Lacan has been most influential.

Closely related to the notion of determinism is that of **essentialism**. To say that anatomy is destiny is to claim that biological differences constitute organisms having essentially different natures and that these natures are fixed in ways that no subsequent development can alter. Counter to this tendency, **Simone de Beauvoir**, in *The Second Sex* (1952), forcefully drew a distinction that has been widely employed in much subsequent feminist thought. There she suggested that classical psychoanalysis failed to recognize the crucial distinction between **gender** and **sex**. While *sex* is properly descriptive of biological features and processes, *gender* refers to the various social and cultural roles and formations constructed on the basis of biological differences. To speak, for example, of distinctively male and female traits is already to have passed from the sphere of biology to that of the always contingent and variable cultural construction of meaning. In collapsing these two very different discursive spheres into the term *sexuality*, classical psychoanalysis was led to an essentialist view of sexual identity that denied the fact that "one is not born, but rather becomes, a woman." For de Beauvoir, psychoanalytic essentialism was ineffective in addressing the process of gender-identity development in the nexus of prevailing cultural constructions.

Cultural Assumptions and the Problem of Patriarchy

In addition to the more general problems of determinism and essentialism attendant on Freud's definition of psychoanalysis as a natural or biological science, many feminist critics have noted other substantive cultural biases enmeshed in the psychoanalytic discourse. In feminist thought, **patriarchy**, the rule of the father, has come to signify the entire complex of psychological, social, and cultural formations that establish and promote the historical dominance of men over women. Psychoanalysis has often been criticized for resting on patriarchal assumptions and reinforcing prevalent patriarchal attitudes and institutions.

While the term *patriarchy* had been used earlier by anthropologists and social theorists (including Marx), the significance it has achieved in recent feminist thought can be traced to Kate Millett's *Sexual Politics* (1970). Millett regarded patriarchy as a type of ideology and argued that it was the paradigmatic example of all cases of differentials in social and political power. In her view, unless the underlying patriarchal ideology of contemporary society, which guaranteed the subordination of women to men, was transformed, no other genuinely significant or constructive social change could occur.

Millett cited what she called neo-Freudianism as promoting this patriarchal ideology. While Millett credited Freud with opening up the area of human sexuality to critical discourse, she condemned many of his followers as tending "to rationalize the invidious relationship between the sexes, to ratify traditional roles, and to validate temperamental differences." From her perspective, while Freud launched a discourse with distinctly constructive possibilities for social and cultural change, its institutionalization coopted it into the support of the very patriarchal ideology that it should have challenged. Millett was especially critical of neo-Freudian clinical practice, which views the role of therapy as helping women become better adjusted to prevailing social conditions while failing to see that the patriarchal bases of modern society are ultimately the source of many of the difficulties experienced by women in the first place.

Perhaps the most evenhanded account of the patriarchal assumptions and biases of psychoanalysis can be found in *The Reproduction of Mothering: Psychoanalysis and the Sociology of Gender* (1978) by **Nancy Chodorow**, who explicitly attempted to preserve the constructive insights provided by psychoanalysis while rejecting its more dubious patriarchal elements. Chodorow was forthright in citing some of Freud's most notoriously patriarchal and sexist statements, especially those in his essays on the psychic consequences of the anatomical distinction between the sexes (1925), female sexuality (1931), and femininity (1933). She traced such attitudes to two basic assumptions made by Freud about sex and gender: "First, Freud defines gender and sexual differentiation as presence or absence of masculinity and the male genital rather than as two different presences; second, Freud maintains a functional/teleological view of the 'destiny' reserved for anatomical differences between the sexes. Patriarchal assumptions about passivity and activity, and the necessity for men to aggress sexually, are cloaked in the idiom of 'nature.'"

Freud's assumptions, questionable on the grounds both of clinical evidence and of other aspects of basic psychoanalytic theory, led him to reiterate a whole litany of patriarchal prejudices, including the normative character of male heterosexual development, the natural passivity of women, the difference between the moral outlook of abstractly just males and maternal, caring females, and the equation of civilization with the historical passage from matriarchal to patriarchal cultural formations. Admitting that Freud was very much a product of his own patriarchal cultural milieu, Chodorow concluded that such assumptions, while neither empirically nor theoretically warranted, were likewise not required by a suitably developed psychoanalytic viewpoint. Thus, for Chodorow, while classical psychoanalysis was historically intertwined with patriarchal ideology, there was no reason why contemporary psychoanalysis should remain so. However, it should be added that many other feminist thinkers have not been so sanguine about the prospects for extricating psychoanalysis from its patriarchal heritage.

More Specific Targets of Feminist Critique

While such authors as Chodorow and **Juliet Mitchell** (*Psychoanalysis and Feminism*, 1974) have defended revised versions of psychoanalytic theory as an indispensable element of feminist critique, others have argued that the most basic concepts of psychoanalysis are so misogynistic that any adequate revision would no longer be recognizable as psychoanalytic discourse. At the center of this controversy is the classical Freudian account of female sexuality in the nexus of the Oedipal complex.

According to the classical account, the condition of infantile sexuality prior to the onset of the Oedipal conflict is undifferentiated, or as Freud sometimes suggested, bisexual. Involved in the commencement of the Oedipal complex is the recognition by the male child that he possesses a penis, which the female child lacks (or possesses in the "stunted form" of the clitoris). This recognition, in turn, determines that the relations to the parents of the male child will be different from those of the female. While the male child will come to identify with the powerful figure of the similarly endowed father, even as the father is simultaneously seen as a competitor for the affections of the mother, the female child will experience what Freud called "penis envy," seeing herself and her mother as lacking, inferior, and inadequate.

For Freud, this penis envy on the part of the female child had portentous consequences for female psychological development. On the one hand, the female child would experience feelings of anger at her mother for allowing her to be born incomplete or deformed like the mother herself. On the other hand, she would desire the father's penis as the fulfillment of her own deficiency. In normal psychological development, the female child would resolve this Oedipal conflict by substituting the desire for a male child for her original desire for the father's penis. If this desire for motherhood did not occur, Freud believed that the female child would either become inhibited and neurotic or would assume "masculine traits," which Freud regarded as abnormal. Under the assumption of biological determinism, women were destined to regard themselves as inferior to men, to aspire to motherhood and all its associated traits as part of "normal" development, to experience feelings of competition with and aversion to their mothers and other females, and to be less "civilized," "rational," and "moral" than males, due to their having identified less completely with the father during the formation of their superegos.

Some feminist critics called this complex of Freud's ideas **phallocentrism**, because it underwrote male authority on the basis of the female's "lack" of a penis. Viewing phallocentrism as the psychological basis for patriarchal attitudes and institutions in the cultural sphere, some feminist thinkers have argued, in effect, that if patriarchy does not represent the natural or necessary condition of human society, then any theory that logically implies it must be wrong as well. Many thus have rejected psychoanalytic discourse as incurably phallocentric and hence unsuitable as a basis for feminist critique. Others, following Juliet Mitchell, have come to regard the classical psychoanalytic account as a more or less accurate depiction of the construction of gender in a patriarchal society, without presupposing that there are no alternatives to such a social formation.

The Current Status of
the Discourse of Psychoanalysis

Psychoanalysis has been the subject of continual controversy from the very outset. It is therefore difficult to draw any firm conclusions about the role of psychoanalytic discourse in the context of contemporary cultural critique. A few tentative observations must suffice. First, it is probably fair to say that even among clinicians, psychoanalysis has failed to achieve the status of a science in the sense asserted by Freud, although this may have as much to do with changing conceptions of science as it does with the limitations of psychoanalysis. Second, various, often dramatic revisions of classical psychoanalytic discourse, such as that of Jacques Lacan, have continued to renew and refocus interest in its potential for cultural criticism. While few critics today would subscribe to the classical view, many current approaches to cultural formations draw on revised forms of the classical theory, often in conjunction with other critical discourses, such as semiotics. Finally, thanks to such novel readings of Freud as that by Paul Ricoeur, psychoanalytic discourse, if no longer viewed as a science, continues as an important dimension of contemporary debates concerning interpretation. Authors such as Jane Gallop and Naomi Schor, for example, have recently argued for a new rapprochement between psychoanalytic and feminist literary criticism. Though often under heavy revision and in various hybrid forms, the discourse of psychoanalysis remains a conspicuous landmark on the current critical landscape.

Bibliographic Essay

The complete works of Freud have been critically edited and translated into English (usually quite reliably) in *The Standard Edition of the Complete Psychological Works of Sigmund*

Freud, trans. and ed. James Strachey (New York: W. W. Norton, 1966). In addition, most of the major works have been issued by Norton individually and are readily available. There are many general as well as more topical anthologies of Freud's works. Probably the best general selection, topically organized but representative of the development of Freud's thought in each area, is *The Freud Reader,* ed. Peter Gay (New York: W. W. Norton, 1989). A representative selection of writings by some of Freud's earlier followers, though with a decidedly clinical focus, can be found in *An Outline of Psychoanalysis,* rev. ed., ed. Clara Thompson (New York: Random House, 1955).

   The secondary literature on Freud and psychoanalysis is massive. A basic, brief, and standard introduction to classical psychoanalysis, though heavily biased toward Freud's later thought, is *A Primer of Freudian Psychology* by Calvin S. Hall (New York: Mentor, 1954). More difficult but also more detailed is *An Elementary Textbook of Psychoanalysis,* rev. ed., by Charles Brenner (New York: Doubleday, 1973). *Freud and the Post-Freudians,* by J.A.C. Brown (Baltimore: Penguin, 1961), provides a very accessible account of the history of the psychoanalytic movement after Freud. Also very accessible is *The Freudian Left: Wilhelm Reich, Geza Roheim, Herbert Marcuse* (New York: Harper & Row, 1969), which explores some of the better known attempts to wed psychoanalysis to Marxist social critique. The most comprehensive historical account of the entire psychoanalytic movement is *A History of Psychoanalysis,* by Reuben Fine (New York: Columbia University Press, 1979).

   The three most often cited works exploring the cultural implications of psychoanalysis are *Freud: The Mind of the Moralist* (New York: Doubleday, 1961) and *The Triumph of the Therapeutic* (New York: Harper & Row, 1966), both by Philip Rieff; and *Man, Morals, and Society,* by J. C. Flugel (New York: International Universities Press, 1970). More recently, cultural historian Peter Gay has written several works dealing with Freud and psychoanalysis in the context of modern intellectual history. His *Freud: A Life for Our Time* (London: Dent, 1988) is the most recent biography of Freud, supplementing the massive *Sigmund Freud: Life and Work,* 3 vols., by Ernest Jones (London: Hogarth, 1953–1957). Gay's *Freud for Historians* (Oxford: Oxford University Press, 1985) is especially interesting as an exploration of the significance of psychoanalysis for research in history. *Sigmund Freud,* by Robert Bocock (Chichester, England: Ellis Horwood, 1983), offers an assessment of the significance of Freud's work for the discipline of sociology.

   One of the most thoughtful assessments of the philosophical implications of Freud's work from the perspective of a major figure in the phenomenological-hermeneutic tradition is *Freud and Philosophy: An Essay on Interpretation,* by Paul Ricoeur (New Haven: Yale University Press, 1970). Richard Wollheim's anthology of essays exploring various philosophical dimensions of psychoanalysis, including problems surrounding its status as a science, appears under the title *Freud: A Collection of Critical Essays* (New York: Anchor Doubleday, 1994).

   An excellent sourcebook for the entire range of feminist thought regarding various psychoanalytic concepts is *Feminism and Psychoanalysis: A Critical Dictionary,* ed. Elizabeth Wright (Oxford: Basil Blackwell, 1992). This work includes extensive bibliographies of feminist writings on most of the major figures and ideas of the psychoanalytic movement. For readers unfamiliar with its range and contours, *Feminist Thought: A Comprehensive Introduction,* by Rosemarie Tong (Boulder: Westview, 1989), is highly recommended and might well be read as a counterpoint to the present text. See especially the chapter titled "Psychoanalytic Feminism." The most prominent defenses of psychoanalysis by authors with feminist concerns are *Psychoanalysis and Feminism: Freud, Reich, Laing, and Women,* by Juliet Mitchell (New York: Random House, 1974), and *The Reproduction of Mothering: Psychoanalysis and the Sociology of Gender,* by Nancy Chodorow (Berkeley: University of California Press, 1978). For classic attacks on psychoanalysis, consult Betty Friedan, *The Feminine Mystique* (New York: Dell, 1974); Kate Millett, *Sexual Politics* (Garden City, N.Y.: Doubleday, 1970); Shulamith Firestone, *The Dialectic of Sex* (New York: Bantam Books, 1970); and of course, the indispensable *The Second Sex,* by Simone de Beauvoir, trans. and ed. H. M. Parshley (New York: Vintage, 1974).

For the impact of psychoanalysis on cultural production, especially literature, the section on this topic in Terry Eagleton's *Literary Theory: An Introduction* (Minneapolis: University of Minnesota Press, 1983) is the best concise account. For a broader ranging discussion, see *Freudianism and the Literary Mind,* by Frederick J. Hoffman (Baton Rouge: Louisiana State University Press, 1967). Probably the best known practicing Freudian literary critic is Harold Bloom, whose *The Breaking of the Vessels* (Chicago: University of Chicago Press, 1982) provides a convenient outline of his critical stance. While most current uses of psychoanalysis in film theory and criticism are of a decidedly Lacanian bent, *The Imaginary Signifier: Psychoanalysis and the Cinema,* by Christian Metz (Bloomington: Indiana University Press, 1977), presents the basic contours of the psychoanalytic approach as a prelude to his own more semiotic orientation. *Channels of Discourse,* ed. Robert C. Allen (Chapel Hill: University of North Carolina Press, 1987) contains a chapter on psychoanalytic approaches to television, including some specific applications.

5

The Critical Theory
of the Frankfurt School

Like the old adage about the Holy Roman Empire, the Frankfurt School of critical theory was not continuously located in Frankfurt, nor could it without considerable qualification be regarded as a school in either the institutional or intellectual sense of the term. While it did constitute one of the most influential critical discourses of the twentieth century, certain of its characteristics markedly distinguish it from the discourses that we have thus far considered.

In the first place, the Frankfurt School rejected from the very beginning any attempt to formulate or adopt a standard or doctrinaire position. Although most participants in this movement regarded themselves as aligned in some general way with the earlier, Marxist tradition of materialist social analysis, a wide range of views was not only tolerated but encouraged. What the movement's participants shared was a conviction that historical developments, especially after World War I, demanded a thorough reconsideration, revision, and in some cases rejection of some of the most entrenched assumptions of the materialist critical tradition.

At the most fundamental level, the critical theory developed by the Frankfurt School came to focus, in a deliberately self-reflexive manner, on the meaning, methods, and inherent limitations of the very notion of critique in the context of contemporary society. Unlike the other critical discourses that we have considered, both the significance and possibility of cultural critique always remained an open question, though one of paramount importance. Rejecting any notion of some firm foundation—empirical, moral, methodological, or otherwise—on which cultural critique might proceed, the thinkers of the Frankfurt School returned again and again to the question of how any genuinely oppositional critique might be conducted in the all-assimilating context of contemporary society and culture, especially in light of the explosion of the mass media early in the twentieth century.

Their rejection of ultimate doctrinal or methodological foundations for critique allowed these thinkers much leeway to draw on other existing critical traditions as they attempted to construct their own dynamic notion of critical practice. Thus, over the course of its development, various thinkers of the Frankfurt School assimilated into their critical views a good deal of the idealist tradition of

Kant and Hegel, which the materialist critique had rejected; attempted to establish a place in their views for the results of the empirical social sciences; sought a rapprochement between materialist social theory and psychoanalysis; and engaged in lively interchanges with contemporary representatives of both the liberal humanist and hermeneutic traditions.

As a result, there can be no straightforward presentation of some core set of essential views or doctrines of the Frankfurt School. Indeed, it would be difficult to decide whether certain thinkers, such as Walter Benjamin or Erich Fromm, should be counted as bona fide members of the Frankfurt School at all, even though they were clearly related to this movement in important ways. For this reason, it is perhaps best to define critical theory as an attempt to formulate a new set of questions and an agenda for critical discourse in the novel historical conditions presented by the twentieth century. One must acknowledge that, in the course of this formulation, a wide range of opinions persisted as to what form the answers might take. Since many more individuals were involved with the Frankfurt School at one time or another than can be discussed here, we will focus on some of the most influential aspects of the works of **Max Horkheimer** (1895–1971), **Theodor Adorno** (1903–1969), **Herbert Marcuse** (1898–1979), and **Jürgen Habermas** (b. 1929), who are generally recognized among its most important representatives.

However, since the critical theory of the Frankfurt School originated in a very specific set of historical circumstances and subsequently developed in response to their dramatic transformations over a turbulent half-century, it will be helpful to begin with a brief overview of the Frankfurt School's historical development.

A Brief History of the Frankfurt School

In the first years of the 1920s, Felix Weil, the wealthy son of a commodities merchant, began organizing and financially underwriting a series of forums and research projects involving intellectuals and scholars with broadly Marxist views. At that time, such independent Marxist thinkers as Georg Lukács, Karel Korsch, and Friedrich Pollock were facing a serious historical and personal dilemma. On the one hand, in the wake of the Bolshevik Revolution in Russia and the failure of parallel revolutions in central Europe and especially Germany, Lenin had come to assert the leadership of his own brand of Marxism in the international struggle against capitalism. However, many European Marxists had grown increasingly suspicious of the authoritarian course that the revolution in Russia was taking under Lenin and had come to reject the Russian model and its Marxist-Leninist ideology as both historically inapplicable and politically intolerable for Western, industrialized societies. On the other hand, some former Marxists had thrown in their lot with the liberal and socialist parties participating in the newly formed Weimar Republic in Germany, a move that most of Weil's early circle regarded as merely postponing rather than solving the problems with which they had long been concerned. As a result, independent Marxists welcomed a forum in which they could develop their own unaligned views. What all shared, and what would become a continuing theme of the Frankfurt School, was a strong sense that the Marxist tradition of materialist discourse required a thorough reconsideration and revision in light of changed circumstances.

Out of these early, unofficial activities, the **Institute for Social Research** was organized in 1923 under the auspices of the German Ministry of Education in loose affiliation with the University of Frankfurt. Carl Grünberg, an economic and social historian, was named its first director, and in line with his own interests, he saw the primary aim of the institute as sponsoring empirical research on concrete social issues from a generally materialist orientation, with a minimum of theoretical discussion or speculation. For Grünberg, who regarded Marxism as a social science rather than a philosophy, the principal questions to be addressed were purely empirical—namely, how it happened that communism had triumphed in Russia, while contrary to Marx's own predictions, the movement had apparently collapsed in the far more industrialized countries of the West, and what social and political implications these findings might have on the future of Europe.

Following Grünberg's retirement due to a stroke in 1929, the directorship of the institute passed to Max Horkheimer in 1930. In his inaugural statement of 1931, "The Present Situation of Social Philosophy and the Tasks of an Institute of Social Research," Horkheimer made it clear that the entire direction of the institute would henceforth change dramatically. Harking back to the birth of modern social theory with the great idealists, Kant and Hegel, Horkheimer asserted that the institute's "ultimate aim is the philosophical interpretation of the vicissitudes of human fate—the fate of humans not as mere individuals, however, but as members of a community." While empirical research would remain part of the program of the Institute, it would henceforth be pursued strictly in the service of the more comprehensive development of a new critical philosophical program. This change was underscored by the addition in 1932 of the neo-Hegelian Marxist social theorist Herbert Marcuse to membership in the institute.

With the National Socialist consolidation of power in 1933, the institute was banned in Germany and most of its members eventually followed Horkheimer into exile in the United States, there to continue their work in loose affiliation with Columbia University. During this period, the institute under Horkheimer's leadership added new associates, most notably Theodor Adorno; began exploring the most important and characteristic themes associated with its critical theory; and sponsored a good deal of empirical research, especially that involving psychoanalytic-influenced analyses of the relation between the individual and contemporary society and studies of Nazism and anti-Semitism (for example, *The Authoritarian Personality*).

After the war, in 1950, the institute returned to Frankfurt, although several of its key members, especially Herbert Marcuse, remained in the United States. During the postwar period, the Frankfurt School came to be a major intellectual influence not only on European philosophy and social science, especially in Germany, but later, primarily through the works of Marcuse, on the rise of the New Left in the United States during the 1960s.

With the deaths of Adorno in 1969 and Horkheimer in 1973 and the dissipation of the student movements in Europe and the United States, the influence of the original institute began to decline, although many of its characteristic concepts, themes, and ways of posing questions had found their way into the work of the generation of philosophers and social scientists who began to take their academic posts in the postwar period. In particular, Jürgen Habermas, a student of Adorno, and his own students in turn, have continued to pursue and develop many of the themes and ideas of the original institute, carrying forward and expanding their predecessors' critique in new directions.

What Is Critical Theory?

Horkheimer's programmatic essay of 1937, "Traditional and Critical Theory," is a classic general statement of the theoretical stance of the Frankfurt School. As its title suggests, this essay develops the notion of a "critical" theory in opposition to what Horkheimer refers to as "traditional" theory. In this essay, Horkheimer characterizes traditional theory very broadly as any view that makes three basic assumptions. First, it assumes that the world is an ensemble of objective and observable facts that the knower passively registers. Second, it presupposes that knowledge consists of propositions that are formulated so as to correspond to these facts and that hence can be regarded as true. Finally, traditional theory aims at logically joining these propositions in such a way that their systematic interrelations with one another are clearly revealed as standing in seamless logical or mathematical relations of necessity with one another. In the course of the development of critical theory, these assumptions also came to be viewed as constituting what the Frankfurt School variously called **scientism** or **positivism**.

Horkheimer's critique of traditional theory and presentation of his own critical alternative proceeds on two levels. At the level of these basic assumptions, he maintains, against the first, that what any science takes to be its relevant facts is already the result of a complicated process of the prior experiential interaction of the knower with her or his world, a practical reciprocity in which operative values are ever present. Indeed, that something qualifies as a fact implies a value judgment, conferring on the alleged fact a certain significance or relevance for the knower's own project. Against the second assumption of traditional theory, he responds that propositions are not merely value-neutral expressions of fact but are implicated in a whole pretheoretical texture of essentially social discourse and are in themselves meaningless if regarded as independent of this discursive nexus. Finally, he counters that the organization of true propositions into a systematic totality not only obscures actual tensions and controversies inherent in the growth of knowledge but produces the illusory impression that what has been totalized is unassailable by further criticism and inalterable by practical human activity. Horkheimer emphasizes that all of this is especially problematic when the question is one of human society, culture, and history.

However, the most serious problems with traditional theory, according to Horkheimer, are much broader. Traditional theory, for all its concern with facts and objectivity, has failed to reflect on its own status in the context of contemporary society and history, always proceeding on the assumption that the scientist or researcher is somehow autonomous or removed from the social and historical nexus in which she or he functions. What traditional theory has failed to grasp is that its assumptions and worldview, which arose roughly with the beginning of the Enlightenment in the seventeenth century, are themselves historical phenomena rooted in the economic and social changes that European society has been undergoing. Expanding on ideas familiar from Marx, Horkheimer points out that, contrary to its self-representation as neutral and objective, traditional theory has always been directly and inextricably implicated in the social and economic processes directed toward the control of nature through the increasing rationalization of production and of the social relations necessary to reach this end. The modern scientific enterprise, far from merely producing objective knowledge, has its own hidden internal teleology: to make possible the technological control of nature and society by those who command its resources by virtue of their economic, social, and political ascendancy. In terms reminiscent of Rousseau's earlier invective, Horkheimer claims that scientism, however beneficial its results in certain senses, ultimately effaces human spontaneity and autonomy in the interests of a functional system that is taken to be fully self-justifying and hence rational.

What is needed to counter this pervasive scientistic or positivistic orientation of modern society, according to Horkheimer, is a new critical theory. He wrote:

> We must go on now to add that there is a human activity which has society itself for its object. The aim of this activity is not simply to eliminate one or another abuse, for it regards such abuses as necessarily connected with the way in which the social structure is organized. Although it itself emerges from the social structure, its purpose is not, either in its conscious intention or in its objective significance, the better functioning of any element in the structure. . . . But the critical attitude of which we are speaking is wholly distrustful of the rules of conduct with which society as presently constituted provides each of its members. . . . The separation between individual and society in virtue of which the individual accepts as natural the limits prescribed for his activity is relativized in critical theory.

In line with this programmatic statement, Horkheimer suggests several conditions that critical theory must fulfill. First, it must position itself as a continual and vigilant critic of the dominant scientism of modern society. In particular, while Horkheimer does not reject wholesale the methods or results of the existing empirical social sciences, he believes that critical theory must function as a continual **oppositional discourse** against the uncritical acceptance and use of the results of empirical science. It falls to critical theory to propose broader frameworks in which scientific activities can be accorded their proper and limited places. Second, critical theory must be explicitly and deliberately engaged in both theoretical and practical activities the goal of which is the **emancipation** of human beings from conditions that threaten or deny their fundamental autonomy and freedom. Third, critical theory must rigorously maintain an openness to its own **self-critique**—that is, it must view itself as concretely situated in given social and historical circumstances and renounce any claim to producing an alternative totalizing system of its own. Finally, it must continually strive to overcome the opposition between the private individual and the public social context that is inherent in the scientism of modern society. In particular, it must reject any social theory based on the radical separation of individual and community, especially one that places the social theorist in some objective or privileged position to describe or prescribe norms for society as a whole. Since modern society is permeated by **contradictions**, especially that between the progressive rationalization of society and the autonomy of the individual, critical theory must acknowledge these contradictions and project the conditions for their elimination from out of the concrete historical circumstances in which they exist at any given time.

While the objections of critical theory to traditional theory (especially as represented by the empirical social sciences) are clear, it may be helpful to consider briefly how critical theory also differs from more traditional Marxist theory, to which it is in many respects more closely aligned. To begin with, critical theory, while self-admittedly standing in a dialectical relationship with its own historical milieu, rejects the deterministic notion of history characteristic of dialectical materialism. At the core of critical theory is the more Kantian and idealist conviction of human autonomy, which any overarching theory of historical development must ultimately deny. Second, critical theory, despite its critical stance with regard to the empirical social sciences, views them not as elements of an ideological superstructure to be rejected out of hand but rather as limited projects that might at least in part find their place in a broader self-critical theoretical framework. Third, critical theorists reject the key Marxist notion of class struggle between the proletariat and the bourgeoisie as an adequate characterization of the changed face of capitalism in the twentieth century. In particular, against such otherwise neo-Hegelian thinkers as Georg Lukács, they maintained that changes in modern society and economics since the time of Marx had in part fragmented and in part eliminated the proletariat as a possible source of social change. Because they believed most European workers had been largely coopted, the Frankfurt School tended to seek possible instruments of social change elsewhere than in the more traditional workers' movements. Finally, the critical theorists concluded that Marx did not and could not have anticipated the scale and depth to which the most distinctive feature of twentieth-century society, the growth of mass culture propagated principally through the media, had come to influence psychological propensities and cultural attitudes. They thus came to regard the old Marxist distinction between economic infrastructure and ideological superstructure as too crude to assist in the analysis of phenomena that clearly cut across such a distinction.

The Dialectic of Enlightenment: The Historical Stance of Critical Theory

The Frankfurt School's exile in the United States during the rise of European fascism and World War II was a period of painful crisis, both institutionally and personally, for the critical theorists—all the more so since many of them were Jewish. Not only were their hopes of a Marxist victory dashed, but fascist totalitarianism had triumphed in Europe and promptly set about violently extending itself over the face of the globe. These events called into question the earlier Marxist leanings of the critical theorists, seemingly demanding a reconsideration of the entire progressive Enlightenment tradition to which Marxian socialism had regarded itself as heir. The crucial question now was not only why Marxist movements had failed in the most advanced countries in Europe but also why the liberal humanist tradition, embodied in the democratic experiments following World War I, had itself so rapidly succumbed to totalitarian mass movements such as fascism and national socialism.

The attempt to grapple with this difficult question can be found in the collection of essays by Horkheimer and Adorno composed between 1942 and 1944 and published in 1947 under the title *Dialectic of Enlightenment*—a work that remains the classic statement of the views of the Frankfurt School in exile. Assembling virtually all of the most characteristic and eclectic themes associated with this group, this work presented, first and foremost, a new theory of history that squarely opposed both the ideology of progress of the Enlightenment and the optimistic Marxian view of historical materialism, which recent events had so decisively discredited.

The key point of the view of history presented here is that history must be understood as an ongoing, open-ended dialectic between **mythology** and **enlightenment**. Returning to the ancient Greek classic the *Odyssey,* Horkheimer and Adorno argue a two-sided dialectical thesis. On the one hand, they claim that mythology is an attempt to impose order and secure human control over the irrational fate dictated by external nature and the irrational impulses and instincts of internal or human nature. On the other hand, they assert that the enlightened critique and rejection of mythology, especially in the modern age, has its own internal countertendency to construct a new mythology. Just as mythology is already a step firmly on the way to enlightenment, so enlightenment ultimately culminates in new mythological stances and attitudes. As the authors themselves put it, "Mythology itself set off the unending process of enlightenment in which ever and again, with the inevitability of necessity, every specific theoretic view succumbs to the destructive criticism that it is only a belief—until even the very notions of spirit, of truth and, indeed, enlightenment itself, have become animistic magic."

A concrete, contemporary reference for this dramatic claim can be found in the role that the Nazi movement accorded to ancient Teutonic myths, which led to their "scientific" doctrines of racial superiority, all under the aegis of further modernizing the most economically progressive country in Europe at that time.

At the heart of critical theory stands the philosophically problematic notion of reason. Borrowing heavily from the work of the sociologist **Max Weber** (1864–1920), the members of the Frankfurt School maintained that with the beginning of the modern world in the Reformation and the Enlightenment, the basic conception of reason dramatically changed. Whereas the ancient Greeks and medieval Christians had regarded reason as essentially teleological, that is, as specifying in itself certain natural ends or values to be realized in human life and society, the modern world had severed the connection between means and ends implicit in the earlier concept of reason. Henceforth, reason came to be viewed as a purely formal, objective, and value-neutral mechanism for directing human action toward ends that arose elsewhere and were therefore essentially irrational, or outside the proper sphere of rational discourse. The latter was now concerned merely with the most efficient means for securing these ends. Such a view of reason, which they called **instrumental**, thus drove a wedge between facts and values, science and ethics, technology and the human consequences of its applications. Most of all, however, it made any attempt such as that of the Frankfurt School to question the rationality of contemporary society appear irrational, ruled out of court by the prevalent notion of reason as purely instrumental and value neutral.

This modern notion of instrumental reason ensured that the very notion of enlightenment would be transformed into a new mythology. True, the liberal humanism of the Enlightenment had emphasized the liberty and rights of the individual against the domination of religious dogma and aristocratic excess, but a high price had been paid for this. In place of the former structure of domination emerged an even more insidious complex of structures: the alienation of human beings from nature, which now appeared merely as a field for technological manipulation and control; the blind mechanism of the capitalist market, which while potentially satisfying individual human desires, resulted in the division of society into competing and mutually hostile classes based on human exploitation; and the bureaucratic administration of the social system, replacing any sense of human community or solidarity with its own impersonal and purely formal procedures. Even philosophy itself, once a vehicle for genuine critical thinking, had succumbed to the temptations of instrumental reason, having come to view itself either like the positivists, as concerned with the value-free logic of the sciences, or like Hegel and his heirs, with the construction of overarching metaphysical systems that aimed at the seamless explanation of all events at the expense of human freedom and spontaneity.

Two key terms, which although they were not coined by the critical theorists, were continually employed by them in analyzing such phenomena, deserve special note. The first is **reification**. Drawing on Marx's well-known analysis of the "fetishism of commodities" in the economic sphere, critical theorists developed his line of thought further, asserting that the entirety of modern culture evidenced a distinctive and pervasive tendency to convert everything—including values, ideas, works of art, and even human beings—into objects of scientific analysis, economic consumption, and bureaucratic manipulation. Closely connected with this concept was the idea of **totalization**. In line with the basic assumptions of traditional theory, *totalization* designated the tendency of modern enlightenment to extend its knowledge and domination over the entire range of reified human experience and social existence. That is, the real counterpart of its seamless epistemological web of necessarily related true propositions was a seamless totality of rationally controlled and administered social relations and processes that excluded as irrational any possibility of theoretical critique or practical opposition. Later, the result of this process of totalization would be referred to simply as "the system."

The result was that enlightenment itself (and the historical period bearing the same name), once institutionalized in modern society, had become a new mythology the aim of which was to reify, totalize, and rationalize all dimensions of human experience, a mythology whose articles of faith were now in turn accepted as unquestionable and self-justifying. On these grounds, Horkheimer and Adorno thus drew the extremely unpopular and controversial conclusion that the rise of modern totalitarianism was neither some unfortunate and unprecedented disturbance of the naturally progressive development of modern society nor the result of some moral indiscretion or lack of vigilance on the part of certain contemporary societies. Rather, it was the natural culmination of a one-sidedness that was implicit in the modern historical Enlightenment project from its beginning and that presented a continuing danger to any philosophy or society that subscribed to the basic tenets of the Enlightenment. Expressed in its boldest form, the thesis of the Frankfurt School was that totalitarianism was nothing other than an extension of the basic aims of the Enlightenment as it established itself as its own mythology. Even more, it suggested the pessimistic conclusion that the defeat of totalitarian regimes by "enlightened" powers would not end the "dialectic of Enlightenment" but would give rise to ever more subtle reifying and totalizing forms of domination so long as the underlying assumptions of the Enlightenment remained beyond the reach of genuinely critical thought.

The Cultural Theory of the Frankfurt School

Another way of highlighting what has already been said regarding the Frankfurt School's relation to earlier liberal humanist and materialist views is to say that its critical theory came to focus preeminently on contemporary culture as opposed to liberal politics or Marxian economics. Characteristically, however, the Frankfurt School's view of culture unfolded as a continuing dialogue that proposed new questions and issues rather than arriving at any stable doctrine or accepted set of answers.

Walter Benjamin's Materialist Theory of Culture

Walter Benjamin (1892–1940), an avowed though by no means orthodox Marxist materialist with wide-ranging interests in history, literature, and the arts, was a key provocateur for the Frankfurt School's cultural theory. Benjamin's continuing commitment to revolutionary workers' movements on the basis of an admittedly idiosyncratic version of their Marxist theoretical underpinnings ensured that he would find no comfortable niche in the Frankfurt School. However, his works on modern history and contemporary culture constituted an important backdrop and often a stimulating foil for many of the critical theorists, especially Theodor Adorno, with whom he was most closely associated.

Benjamin's most important work on contemporary culture appeared in the Frankfurt School's periodical, *Zeitschrift für Sozialforschung*, in 1936 under the title, "The Work of Art in the Age of Mechanical Reproduction." This was a time, it will be remembered, when critical theory was just taking shape and well before the Frankfurt School had begun devoting sustained attention to concrete questions of contemporary culture. As such, it can be regarded as an important starting point for the cultural theory of the Frankfurt School.

Benjamin, whose materialist assumptions and approach were more pronounced than those of the major figures of the Frankfurt School, closely followed this tradition, asking how recent changes in the material basis of the production of cultural products altered the nature of those products and the social relations bound up with them. His principal thesis can be explained in this way: Just as the invention of printing in the fifteenth century had begun the process of revolutionizing the sphere of culture by promoting the widespread dissemination of knowledge and ideas beyond a cultural elite to an ever growing literate public, so the modern development of new mechanical reproductive media, beginning in the graphic arts and photography, signaled another, potentially even more revolutionary phase in the cultural sphere. In Benjamin's essentially Marxist view of history, the trajectory of these developments was always in the direction of the enhancement of the consciousness, and hence empowerment, of the masses and the corresponding weakening of the grip on culture traditionally exercised by a privileged elite. The development of such media as photography, sound recording, and film signaled, for Benjamin, the dawn of a new epoch in the democratization of culture and hence in the revolutionary potential of the proletarian class.

This was especially true in the area of the fine arts, or what had previously been viewed as high culture. According to Benjamin, for example, a painting by a master, under conditions of cultural production prior to the advent of mechanical reproduction, possessed a certain **aura**. This aura had several components that dictated the work's cultural and economic value and hence its inaccessibility to the masses. Most important, a traditional work of art such as a painting was unique, existing as a single instance at a particular place and time. Its uniqueness meant that as a commodity, its supply was a negative limit case (since it was one of a kind), thus ensuring that its monetary value on the art market remained high. Closely related to this is the question of the work's authenticity. To ensure uniqueness, paintings must be certified by experts as the genuine work of an established master, thus reinforcing the cult of genius surrounding those artists accepted as authoritative for a tradition. Finally, this leads to the notion that the traditional work of art is autonomous, standing as a self-sufficient value detached from the socio-historical circumstances of its production and consumption and hence, as "art for art's sake," inaccessible to the normal processes of social interpretation and critique.

According to Benjamin, such media of mechanical reproduction as photography, sound recording, and film had begun the process of removing this aura from the traditional work of art. With the advent of mechanical reproduction techniques, the masses were able to gain access to images, music, theatrical performances, and literature, which were formerly reserved for the privileged classes. However, the most profound effect of this new technology was the change it introduced into the notion of cultural interpretation. The aura of traditional works of art was maintained by and in turn reinforced specific historical traditions, or what would later be called canons, which specified which works were worthy of experience and study and which were not. Since these traditions of great works had the circular character of self-justification—the canon of great works itself provided the criteria for judging all other works—all criticism of them must be purely aesthetic, never economic or political. With the loss of their aura through mechanical reproduction, however, these works' quantitative availability to the masses issued in a qualitative change in how they were received and interpreted. Standards of aesthetic taste, dictated by a tradition based on a canon of great works, gave way to new and diverse standards that called the tradition itself into question on economic and political grounds; that is, aesthetic criticism gave way to political critique. No longer the privileged possession of the elite, traditional works of art could now be interpreted according to the emancipatory interests of the masses, and at least in certain cases (the paintings of Van Gogh of peasant life offer good examples), appropriated as their own.

Beyond this, however, Benjamin suggested that alterations in the means of cultural production also opened opportunities for the creation of entirely new artworks through the devices of new media such as photography and film. These new artworks could serve as vehicles for the new expression of populist, democratic, and emancipatory ideas in forms widely available to the masses whom such ideas served. In Benjamin's rather optimistic view, art for the masses could now, for the first time, be made in which the masses' own aspirations and critical stances were expressed, in turn further enhancing their own critical consciousness. For Benjamin, like his sometime collaborator Berthold Brecht, the new art could thus provide the engine for historical transformation. In contrast to the contemporaneous fascist tendency to absorb politics into art by making politics itself an "aesthetic event," as in the elaborate staging of the 1936 Olympics or the

Nuremberg rallies, Benjamin concluded his essay with the claim that "Communism responds by politicizing art."

The Frankfurt School's Distinction
Between Mass Culture and Affirmative Culture

The conclusions of Benjamin's optimistic theory of culture, based on a broadly Marxist theory of history, clearly ran counter to the fundamental conviction of the critical theorists that traditional Marxism, as an integral part of what they came to call the dialectic of enlightenment, could not, without extensive revision, continue to serve as a basis for cultural critique. Nonetheless, Benjamin had announced some of the most important themes that would become integral parts of the cultural theory of the Frankfurt School, even if the latter drew radically opposed conclusions from them. To mention the most important of these themes, Benjamin had placed squarely on the agenda the assessment of the influence of new forms of cultural production on contemporary culture and society, thus ensuring that an analysis of the mass media would occupy a central place in the cultural discourse of the Frankfurt School. He also had at least implicitly introduced a new form of the crucial distinction between high culture and mass culture into the discussion of the critical theorists. In particular, he had indicated the lines along which both sides of this distinction must be reinterpreted in light of the advent of mechanical reproduction and the mass media, in effect destabilizing the more rigid and "undialectical" distinction that one finds, for example, in Matthew Arnold and his liberal humanist followers. Finally, Benjamin's own concrete analyses, which highlighted the social production and **reception** of cultural artifacts rather than their formal and aesthetic properties, established a precedent that would be followed closely in the cultural analyses undertaken by critical theorists.

The principal point of contention between the cultural theory of Benjamin and that of the Frankfurt School was in their assessment of the social and political consequences of the advent of the mass media. By 1947, Adorno and Horkheimer had coined the term **culture industry** to refer to the processes of production of a mass culture based principally on the new resources of the mass media. Indeed, the title of one of the essays in *Dialectic of Enlightenment* made their attitude abundantly clear: "The Culture Industry: Enlightenment as Mass Deception." In their view, rather than seeing in the production of mass culture the anarchy of Arnold or the potential emancipation of the masses of Benjamin, Horkheimer and Adorno claimed that the culture industry was an integral, characteristic, and even essential element promoting the processes of domination involved in the reification and totalization of "enlightenment become mythology." True to their overall view, they saw in modern journalism, film, and (presciently) in television not a potential counterforce to fascist propaganda but a massive and insidious expansion of the very devices that fascism had so skillfully employed. According to Horkheimer and Adorno, the culture industry was no neutral medium that could be appropriated for some externally chosen ends, but by its very nature, promoted two crucial tendencies inherent in the modern project of enlightenment. The first was the production of **cultural homogeneity**, that is, the blurring of cultural and class distinctions and the eradication of genuine individual spontaneity through the leveling of taste to an innocuous least common denominator. As they put it: "Film, radio and magazines make up a system which is uniform as a whole and in every part. . . . All mass culture is identical." Second, they noted that in line with the tendency of modern enlightenment processes to ensure complete social control, the culture industry reproduced in its products and their consumption the sort of **predictability** aimed at by enlightened social administration at large. Rather than challenge the viewer's beliefs or stimulate the viewer to autonomous critical thought, the products of the culture industry were designed to conform to the viewers' uncritical expectations, to require a minimal amount of thought or response on the part of consumers, and to promote social norms that ultimately, though beneath the level of consumers' conscious awareness, served the interests of the industry and its cultural nexus. They did not hesitate to note, of course, that these goals were entirely consistent with those of totalitarian propaganda, even when the mass media were employed in the service of liberal ideologies.

Critical theorists contrasted what they called **affirmative culture** (a term first introduced by Marcuse) to the homogenous and predictable mass culture produced by the culture industry. This was neither an attempt to revert back to the high culture defended by Arnold nor to invent new forms of mass culture championed by Benjamin. Rather, Adorno, who with Marcuse especially elaborated this notion, attempted to delineate a sphere of authentic art that transcended and hence escaped both the elitist canon of Arnold and the mass culture optimistically invoked by Benjamin. Since art had assumed much of the former role of religion in representing an ideal world of human fulfillment and emancipation in contrast to the sordid realities and alienation of the real world, it had established for itself a potentially critical standpoint from which to challenge existing beliefs, judge current practices, and imagine more humane futures. Of course, not everything we call art actually fulfills these aims, but the Frankfurt School was convinced that considerable hope lay in certain types of art that possessed such potential.

Affirmative culture, therefore, must be sought in works of art possessing certain specific characteristics. First, although it might qualify as part of "high culture" by virtue of prevailing social structures, the significance of authentic art would not be defined or exhausted simply by its conformity to some traditional canonical standards. Rather, an essential element (which the tradition would tend to overlook or deemphasize) would be its very function of calling the relevant tradition itself into question. Second, it would be a type of art that did not aim to demonstrate technical skill for its own sake or to invoke some experience of "beauty" on the part of its audience but that confronted its audience with the limitations and potential for domination inherent in contemporary experience and culture and stimulated its members to imagine new, more humane conditions. Finally, rather than fulfill the expectations of the viewer or come with some obvious and prepackaged message or interpretation, it should serve to mobilize the critical resources of the audience, creating a space where the individual is thrown back on her or his own resources to construct a meaning or interpretation that will shed new light on personal existence as well as that of society. On the basis of these ideas, Adorno and others championed the aesthetic experiments of abstract painting and twelve-tone music.

For the thinkers of the Frankfurt School, one could not expect such affirmative culture to completely coincide with traditional high culture (though there was room for some overlap), but neither could it be expected to emerge from the processes of the culture industry. They regarded the realm of art as one still capable of harboring affirmative tendencies but held out the proviso that any art product, however affirmative, runs the continuing risk of being commodified and reinterpreted as a possession of the elite or as yet another vehicle of mass culture.

Psychoanalysis and Critical Theory: How Adorno Watched Television

The original members of the Frankfurt School were primarily sociologists working within a revisionist Marxist framework. While they were certainly aware of the development of psychoanalysis by Freud and his followers, deep theoretical conflicts between psychoanalysis and Marxism stood in the way of any immediate embrace of Freudian discourse on the part of the Frankfurt theorists. I mentioned above Freud's own rejection of Marxist social theory as a "regressive collectivist fantasy." The denunciation of psychoanalysis by Marxists as a new form of "bourgeois subjectivist ideology" was no less vehement; in fact, it was so strong that psychoanalysis was totally banned in the Soviet Union from an early date. However, given the research program and theoretical concerns of the Frankfurt School, which were aimed at exploring the dynamic influences of contemporary social structures and individual psychology on one another, it was not surprising that the discourse of psychoanalysis gradually was integrated into their own critical project. As early as the 1930s, psychoanalyst Erich Fromm was playing a central role in research series such as Studies in Authority and the Family. The psychoanalytic current grew even stronger in the 1940s in such enterprises as Studies in Prejudice, a series of publications in which the psychosocial roots of anti-Semitism were explored; of these works, *The Authoritarian Personality* is the best known. By the end of the war and the return of the institute to Europe, many of the basic ideas of psychoanalysis had become integral parts of the still evolving discourse of the Frankfurt School, albeit in suitably "revised" forms. In 1955, Herbert Marcuse in *Eros and Civilization*, which we will consider later, attempted a full theoretical fusion of revised Marxian and Freudian ideas.

A year before, in 1954, Theodor Adorno had published a groundbreaking essay entitled "How to Look at Television," in which psychoanalysis figured as a cornerstone of the analysis. In this pioneering statement, Adorno sketched a program of investigation into the then novel medium of television that drew on earlier studies of cultural media such as popular music but employed distinctively psychoanalytic concepts. Adorno focused primarily on the relation between the psychodynamics of the consumption of the new medium and its contemporary social context. This essay is one of the best examples of the concrete application of the discourse of critical theory, after it had fully assimilated psychoanalysis, to the realm of popular culture.

Adorno proposed as his basic methodological assumption an interpretive framework drawn from Freud's *Interpretation of Dreams*. Drawing on a familiar Freudian schema, he suggested that television programs, like dreams, must be approached as **multilayered structures**. Every program conveys a **surface** or **overt message** as well as a series of **depth** or **hidden messages**, all superimposed over one another. Although television programming, like other common mass productions of the culture industry, appears straightforward and transparent—mere entertainment—this is an illusion that masks its deeper psychological effects and arrests our critical capacity to see them in relation to existing social configurations. The illusion is strongly reinforced by the pleasure of viewing, which works hand in hand with our psychological tendency to regress from painful confrontation with the reality principle back to the infantile state of the pleasure principle. To critically interpret television programming, it is therefore necessary, as in dream analysis, to interpret each level of this multilayered structure as it dynamically interacts with the other levels.

The production of television programming, Adorno suggested, borrowing a phrase from his Frankfurt School colleague Leo Lowenthal, is "psychoanalysis in reverse." That is, the cultural industry might be regarded as employing multilayered meaning not, as in psychoanalysis, to liberate the individual from her or his obsessions or neuroses, but "to ensnare the consumer as completely as possible and . . . engage him psychodynamically in the service of premeditated effects." Here we see the usual hostility of the Frankfurt School to the potential of mass culture for social domination, but now placed squarely on a psychoanalytic foundation. Adorno added that the question was not so much one of the deliberate projection of the producers' desires on the consumers as it was of the general function of a medium that was commercial, collective, and fully integrated into the prevailing social system. From the perspective of production, the nature of the medium dictated that there was little hope for positive change.

Adorno focused attention on the multilayered effects of programming on consumers in the hope of making them more self-consciously aware of what was involved in the viewing process. Using many concrete examples from early television, Adorno indicated a number of specific ways in which television programming reinforces social domination by influencing the unconscious processes and attitudes of the viewer under the illusion of the medium's straightforward, overt content.

The first is a general effect that he called **pseudorealism**. Pseudorealism has two aspects: On the one hand, because most programming presents itself as an image of the real world or a slice of life (soap operas especially come to mind here), the consumer is led to accept what is essentially a particular version of reality as reality itself. The consumer in turn projects this pseudoreality offered by television back on the world of her or his own experience, interpreting the latter in terms of the hidden plots, forbidden liaisons, and covert criminal activities that are the stuff of much programming. Put in psychoanalytic terms, this was clearly a kind of regression in fantasy back to the Oedipal threat. On the other hand, television programming, especially in its comic genres, such as the still popular sitcoms, tends to reconcile us to our existing circumstances through the sublimating effects of laughter. By introducing a comic dimension into otherwise painful social issues such as unemployment, racial prejudice, sexism, or exploitation in the workplace, television sublimates any potentially liberational thought or action in which we might otherwise engage through the defense mechanism of laughter.

Second, Adorno asserted that as in the case of popular music, television programming was **standardized**, functioning within a narrow range of set formulas that utilized interchangeable elements. Employing such familiar genres as light comedy, westerns, cops-and-criminals, and mysteries, television programming drew on and reinforced the established expectations of its audience. The viewer often knows from the very first seconds or minutes of a program who the major characters are and what the outcome is likely to be. When such expectations are satisfied, which they generally are, the viewer is unconsciously led to accept the state of affairs portrayed by the program as entirely natural and necessary. ("There's a lot of crime out there, but the police will ultimately deal with it.") Of course, like many dreams, television's catering to viewer expectations is nothing other than a sort of wish fulfillment, appealing to our psychological tendencies to project on the world our own attitudes, beliefs, and fantasies.

Finally, Adorno pointed to **stereotyping** as a particularly complex and pervasive effect of television programming on its consumers. Corresponding to his previous notion of pseudoreality is that of **pseudopersonalization**. By this Adorno meant the tendency to accept characters presented in television programming not only as actual personalities but as representative human types. When such unconscious associations are made, not only does the viewer tend to approach other real persons in terms of the qualities and categories of media characters, but she or he comes to believe that real social problems, which are matters of much broader historical structures, are merely functions of individual personalities. Again, in psychoanalytic theory, these tendencies are deeply rooted in our early processes of identification with and aggression toward mother and father figures who variously serve, in an alternating and complex process, as givers of pleasure and enforcers of repression. While such processes provide the bases on which television programming can be so engaging and influential, they also induce a regressed state on the part of the viewer that remains powerfully resistant to rational critique.

Critical Theory, Psychoanalysis, and the New Left: Marcuse

While most members of the Frankfurt School returned to Germany after the war, Herbert Marcuse (1898–1979) remained in the United States, teaching at Brandeis University and the University of California. Unlike most other members of the institute, which he joined in 1932, Marcuse's background was specifically in philosophy and included previous study with both Husserl and Heidegger. However, although Marcuse was probably the most theoretically inclined of the group, his work during the war for the U.S. State Department in the Eastern European section and his postwar concerns with continuing patterns of domination in the postwar United States lent his work a somewhat more engaged tone and radical edge than that of his colleagues. However, while some aspects of Marcuse's thought pointed in directions different from those of his Frankfurt School colleagues, the theoretical underpinnings of his views were largely consistent with the concepts that we have already considered. In fact, it was to a great extent through Marcuse's writings that the work of the Frankfurt School achieved its widest hearing and most concrete practical influence, especially on the American New Left.

Marcuse's major contributions to the critical theory of the Frankfurt School can be grouped under three headings: his attempt to fully integrate psychoanalysis into radical social theory; his theory of the one-dimensional character of contemporary culture and society; and his concept of cultural opposition and liberation, which especially influenced the American New Left and counterculture of the 1960s.

A New Rapprochement Between Freud and Marx

In 1955, Marcuse published *Eros and Civilization: A Philosophical Inquiry into Freud,* a work in which he attempted to provide theoretical foundations for the mixture of materialist and Freudian discourses that had already come to characterize the work of the Frankfurt School. Whereas the Marxist tradition had always emphasized the historical and economic nature of social contradictions and their possible resolution and tended to exclude the individual's role, the psychoanalytic tradition had attempted to locate social contradictions in the biological and psychological features of the individual, at the expense of historical and economic factors. Put more simply, the basic issue dividing the two discourses concerned whether human social and cultural formations were purely a product of human history and could be altered by purely historical means, or whether they were rooted in certain natural or given features of the individual human organism and must therefore be accepted as ultimately inalterable. In responding to this apparent dilemma, Marcuse pursued a dual strategy. On the one hand, he argued that while psychoanalysis was correct in pointing to the biological and psychological bases for human social formations, it failed to see that that these natural forces also harbored a powerful dynamic for radical social change. On the other hand, while Marx was right in emphasizing the essentially historical nature of any given social configuration, he was wrong in his optimistic assessment that the expansion of technology under capitalism would necessarily be accompanied by growing self-consciousness and ensuing political action on the part of a proletarian class. Ultimately, then, Marcuse's view was that while social domination and oppression were historical facts, liberation would arise not from a class war but out of the basic biological instincts of oppressed human beings. It was principally to this revision of Freud that *Eros and Civilization* was devoted. Marcuse saved his critique of traditional Marxist theory in light of contemporary historical developments for a later work, *One-Dimensional Man* (1964).

Eros and Civilization starts out with a discussion of psychoanalytic theory as presented in Freud's *Civilization and Its Discontents*. There Freud had offered the gloomy thesis that the advance of civilization went hand in hand with increased psychological repression—especially that of the sexual instinct—which was necessitated by more specialized labor, more rigid codes of social conduct, and increasing bureaucratic administration. The results were pervasive aggression, alienation, and neurosis in the most highly civilized societies. This view was reinforced by Freud's theory of the instincts, whereby the instinct toward ever greater assimilation and identification with the external world and other persons, or Eros, was continually opposed by the instinct to regress to a more primitive state and ultimately to inorganic matter (Thanatos, or the death instinct). In response, Marcuse argued that the tendency to turn our instincts in destructive directions is by no means a biological given as Freud had argued, but a function of particular historical configurations of society. That is, Freud had posited the existence of a destructive instinct manifested in civilization generally, when he should have seen that certain forms of society provoked the transformation of an originally productive and creative force into a destructive one.

More specifically, Marcuse pointed to the fact that the degree of repression demanded by any society was directly related to the level of scarcity in that society. Scarcity was defined as a function of the structure of individual needs involved at a given historical point in the development of a society. Whereas the satisfaction of basic needs as well as "higher" cultural needs (for example, recreation, artistic expression, and the like) do require a certain degree of **necessary repression**, a feature of modern society is the generation of **surplus repression**. In place of the reality principle, to which individuals living in any historical period must adjust through repression, modern society has substituted a **performance principle**. That is, modern economic development has made competition, excess production, and massive consumption needs pursued for their own sake, independently of the basic needs of the individual. Even more extreme repression is required in order to satisfy these additional needs dictated by the performance principle (as witnessed by the workaholic and the shopaholic, for example), and Marcuse called this phenomenon "surplus repression." In his view, the aggression, anomie, and neurosis that Freud saw in civilization in general were actually a function of the surplus repression demanded by advanced, expansionist economies and enforced by their ever more extreme structures of social domination.

Where, then, should we look for prospects of eliminating surplus repression? According to Marcuse, human biological instincts themselves contain the seeds of liberation. Discarding Freud's pessimistic conclusion that in modern society the death instinct appears to be vanquishing eros, Marcuse claimed, or at least hoped, that the increasing irrationality of modern society in its demands for surplus repression will lead to a revolt of the instincts against its system of domination—something that Marcuse later referred to as **The Great Refusal**. The surplus repression of the biologically creative instincts by advanced industrial society will increasingly appear unnatural, a case of historically alterable human culture violating our natural capacities for creative expression and self-determination.

Marcuse's revisionist reading of Freud established a radically new agenda for critical social theory: Such transformative theory must abandon its role of merely describing and explaining existing society or designing new but unrealizable utopias. Instead, linking up with other affirmative aspects of art and culture, it must attempt *to imagine new, emancipated forms of society based on the possibilities latent in existing society.* Marcuse's thought seems to have followed two directions that often competed with one another in his writings. On the one hand, Marcuse at certain points appeared to suggest, along more traditional Marxian lines, that an intensive development of a humanized technology will eliminate the need for surplus repression under prevailing conditions of continuing scarcity. On the other, he sometimes wrote as if the elimination of surplus repression could be accomplished by a reduction in technological growth and the adoption of simpler, perhaps more communal lifestyles. In either case, Marcuse seems to have believed, like some of Freud's more radical followers, that two hallmarks of any more liberated society would be diminishing levels of specifically sexual repression (and a corresponding reerotization of other dimensions of our existence with the energy thereby freed) and enhanced, genuinely democratic social determination through the dismantling of current structures of repressive domination.

"One-Dimensional Man"

Having established the emancipatory potential inherent in human biological instincts and thus having answered Freud's pessimistic assessment of the price paid for civilization, Marcuse turned his attention to an analysis of the contemporary historical situation, which he termed **advanced industrial society**. Like most other members of the Frankfurt School, Marcuse was convinced that the defeat of fascist regimes during World War II by no means signaled an end to the totalitarian tendencies of contemporary society. Rather, a renewed critique was necessary in the postwar era in order to expose the structures of domination operative in

the "softer" but in many ways more effective forms of totalitarianism that characterized both the "liberal democratic" and the "bureaucratic socialist" societies.

Marcuse's departure from traditional Marxist critique is most apparent in his
claim that ideology in advanced industrial societies is no longer a relatively autonomous element of the superstructure but has been absorbed into the production process. That is, ideology and the technological means of production can no
longer be meaningfully distinguished from one another, rendering impossible a
critique of one by reference to the other, as more traditional materialist forms of
critique attempted. Marcuse offered a long list of factors pointing to this novel
feature of advanced industrial society:

> Concentration of the national economy on the needs of the big corporations, with
> the government as a stimulating, supporting, and sometimes even controlling force;
> hitching of this economy to a worldwide system of military alliances, monetary
> arrangements, technical assistance and development schemes; gradual assimilation of
> blue-collar and white-collar population, of leadership types in business and labor, of
> leisure activities and aspirations in different social classes; fostering of a preestab-
> lished harmony between scholarship and national purpose; invasion of the private
> household by the togetherness of public opinion; opening of the bedroom to the me-
> dia of mass communication.

As a result of all this, the traditional Marxist proletariat, which was supposed to
have been the historical engine of radical social change, had itself become totally
absorbed or coopted into the system of production and reproduction. Rather
than maintaining an alienated critical standpoint from which to oppose the dominant ideology, the former proletariat had itself become a major factor in promoting the underlying ideology of advanced industrial capitalism.

To explain how this had happened, Marcuse invented a term that drew on a key
psychoanalytic notion. While psychoanalysis regarded sublimation as an important defense mechanism in the rechanneling of repressed sexual energy into productive and pleasurable paths, a basic feature of advanced industrial society was
the reverse process, what Marcuse called **repressive desublimation**. By this he
meant that in advanced industrial society, all phases of production and consumption—work, leisure, advertising, commodities, and so forth—are sexualized, producing a highly pleasurable effect at the same time as they promote the domination of the individual by the system. Through the immediate gratification
produced by repressive desublimation, advanced industrial societies, in Rousseau's
famous words, "hang garlands of flowers on the iron chains that bind us."

Ideology, now woven into the entire material and psychological fabric of contemporary society rather than functioning as a part of the superstructure, plays a
key role in this process. Marcuse especially noted that the meaning of freedom, the
central notion of liberal humanist critical discourse, has changed from qualitative
human autonomy and self-determination to a quantitative range of choices among
many different commodities. In advanced industrial society, we exercise our free-

dom not through direct political action or meaningful discourse but by choosing among a wide variety of consumer products—failing to realize that behind their dazzling packaging they are all essentially the same. This is true whether we are selecting breakfast food, automobiles, or candidates for public office.

In such a situation, human beings become increasingly unable to distinguish between their true and false needs and interests. Inherent in the functioning of advanced industrial society is the systematic creation of false needs, especially through the media and its pervasive advertising and through the fostering of economic expansion and consumption for their own sake. This results in the surplus repression analyzed in detail in *Eros and Civilization.*

Perhaps the greatest human catastrophe of advanced industrial society, however, is its *tendency to debase and neutralize language,* the very medium in which any critical thought or discussion might otherwise occur. Due to the pervasive effects of the mass media, language has been reduced to buzzwords, formulas, slogans, and jingles that we repeat continually to ourselves and others, with no critical regard for their truth or falsity: America is the greatest country on earth; men are from Mars, women are from Venus; if you try hard enough, you will succeed. However, not just the mass media but philosophers and scientists themselves have succumbed to this tendency, the former in holding that the uses of ordinary language are the ultimate criteria of linguistic meaning, the latter in demanding that every term be definable by the operations used to verify the statements in which it occurs. In all cases, the traditional tension between the real and the ideal, between what is and what ought to be, is lost. To lose this tension is to eliminate the very opening in which critical reflection and discourse might occur.

All of these tendencies converge in a condition that Marcuse called **one-dimensionality**. Society becomes a monolith without oppositional elements, human beings become uncritical ciphers in the pleasurable processes of production and consumption, and language becomes assimilated to the most ordinary and clichéd slogans circulating through the system. The result is a "soft" form of totalitarianism that has no external boundary and that is increasingly able to absorb all attempts at internal critique.

Prospects for Liberation: Marcuse and the New Left

Marcuse's *One-Dimensional Man* appeared in 1964, not long after the "Port Huron Statement," the founding document of the U.S. student movement called the New Left, and about the same time as the appearance of the counterculture of the 1960s and the first wave of civil rights legislation. How much Marcuse borrowed from these movements and how much they took from him would be difficult to determine with any precision. What is clear is that these three movements were concrete historical manifestations of the three areas from which Marcuse believed any prospect for liberation from the one-dimensionality of advanced industrial society must emerge. Marcuse suggested in *One-Dimensional Man* that although advanced industrial society for the most part raises the general standard of living, it also produces an ever greater disparity in the distribution of wealth, as wealth continues to accumulate at the top of the social pyramid. As a result, it tends to marginalize large segments of the population, disenfranchising them from social decisionmaking and stunting their capacities for self-expression. Under such conditions, the surplus repression demanded by advanced industrial society will appear especially irrational to these groups, and acting on what Marcuse regarded as a biological imperative, they will revolt. Marcuse thus concluded that students, by virtue of their dependent status and repression by an increasingly technocratic educational system, and racial minorities and other marginalized groups, by virtue of their own long-standing economic and cultural oppression, would be among the first to react to the inherent irrationality of the system. Further, drawing on the long-standing conviction of the Frankfurt School that the potential for genuine critique was still alive in the aesthetic imagination, Marcuse argued that the revolt against the system would initially be a cultural revolution.

Marcuse's reputation as an important critical thinker waned as movements spawned in the 1960s dissipated; but he was one of the first observers of the American scene to explore the emancipatory potential of popular culture. While other critical theorists continued to maintain an unremittingly hostile attitude toward mass culture, Marcuse, who had earlier ascribed to such a view, gradually began to see, especially in light of the rise of the counterculture in the 1960s, a potential for liberation operating in the dynamics of mass culture. In particular, Marcuse noted how the counterculture had reappropriated certain aspects of mass culture (rock music, dress, posters and films) for its own ends, thereby turning mass culture against itself in an overtly critical manner. While Marcuse did not go as far in exploring the dynamics of this process as did later critics, he clearly anticipated, at least in a general way, many of their basic themes and approaches. However, sounding a less optimistic note, Marcuse also warned of the resilient capacities of contemporary society to neutralize and absorb such challenges back into itself through what he called **repressive tolerance**. That is, any attempt to turn mass culture against itself, as occurred in the 1960s, was always subject to recommodification, to becoming yet more grist for the mill of the culture industry. Although the original Woodstock was a true populist countercultural phenomenon, Woodstock II was a purely commercial media event, fully integrated into the "system" and lacking all critical content.

Habermas and the Present State of Critical Theory

As an identifiable discourse explicitly concerned with the critique of contemporary culture, critical theory has been said to have run its course with Marcuse. Why it allegedly ceased to be a viable critical discourse has been variously explained by transformations in contemporary society that invalidated some of its

basic operative assumptions, its identification with the limited agendas of a specific group of thinkers, the taking over of many of its major themes by discourses
better equipped to deal with them, and its own internal contradictions and ambiguities. Among the latter, its inability to account for how its theories might find
practical application, its increasingly unscientific and speculative character in
light of other developments in the social sciences, its continually ambivalent attitude toward technology, and its increasingly strong streak of historical pessimism
have all been cited as contributing to its demise. However, despite critical theory's
reported decline, the many radically new questions formulated by the Frankfurt
School established the most fundamental themes and underlying assumptions of
most other critical discourses now current. Critical theory's eclecticism, particularly in combining psychoanalysis and progressive social theory; its problematiz-
ing of mass and popular culture; its insistence that both liberal democracies and
socialist bureaucracies utilize essentially totalitarian means of social control; and
its continuing conviction that the realization of human autonomy requires an extension of democratic participation together with a humanizing of technology
are a permanent legacy. Such views, hard won by the Frankfurt School, were by no
means operative assumptions of the liberal humanist and materialist discourses
that dominated the era of its inception.

   Whatever one's attitude toward the institutional existence of the Frankfurt
School, the work of **Jürgen Habermas** (b. 1929), a student of Adorno, is still often
cited alongside that of such figures as Albrecht Wellmer, Alfred Schmidt, and
Claus Offe, as constituting a second generation of social theory, or a neocritical
school, descended from the original Frankfurt School. The work of the prolific
Habermas, the best known representative of this group, illustrates the similarities
and differences between contemporary **neocritical theory** and the critical theory
of the Frankfurt School. Below I have summarized the most conspicuous.

   1. While the Frankfurt School from its beginning was highly critical of existing
empirical social sciences of the day as inherently "positivistic," to the point of
largely abandoning them for theoretical reflection, Habermas has always attempted to build bridges between the empirical social sciences and theoretical reflection. He constantly utilizes current empirical research in ways that earlier critical theorists generally did not.

   2. While earlier critical theorists were highly critical of the idea of enlightenment as involving a progressively totalitarian cycle of domination, Habermas
tends to see the basic ideals of the Enlightenment's liberal humanism as an unfinished project rather than an intellectual snare. That is, while the historical unfolding of modernity might have experienced certain disruptions and aberrations, the
basic ideals of individual freedom, democratic participation, and controlled scientific and technological progress remain as desirable human aims.

   3. While the thinkers of the original Frankfurt School tended to focus on cultural and aesthetic issues both as important ways of accessing social contradictions and as potential arenas for exercising the critical imagination, Habermas is

much more concerned with explicitly studying existing social configurations. Like the older, Marxist materialist critics, he tends to see cultural phenomena as explicable on the basis of a broader theory of society rather than as an inextricable element of it.

4. Although his predecessors often pointed in the direction of the idealist tradition of Kant and Hegel and borrowed from it when appropriate, they rarely saw their own theoretical project as directly continuous with idealism. Habermas, by contrast, often formulates his views in terms directly borrowed from the idealist tradition, believing that traditional philosophical enterprises such as ethics, political philosophy, and philosophical anthropology are still viable though as yet incomplete projects.

5. In line with this, Habermas is principally concerned with the constructive project, along broadly Kantian lines, of formulating the foundations and operative principles of a "discourse-based" social ethic that could be defended as normative for the sphere of public discourse, an enterprise almost entirely neglected by the earlier critical theorists.

6. In most ways, Habermas is even farther removed from the Marxist tradition than were the earlier critical theorists. Not only does he jettison the notion of a historically efficacious proletariat class, but he rejects as well any sort of labor- or production-based analysis in favor of one that focuses on human communication as the fundamental form of social interaction.

Habermas's own most influential theoretical contribution to critical discourse is probably his analysis of the complex ways in which **communicative action** functions at the heart of human social existence, an idea that draws heavily on the American pragmatists, especially George Herbert Mead. Looking first at contemporary society, Habermas holds that our emancipatory interest is principally engaged by the fact that much contemporary social interaction is based on **systematically distorted communication**. In a way reminiscent of Adorno, Habermas claims that much of the discourse involved in the media and popular culture as well as in contemporary political affairs has the structure of a "manifest level" that presents in a systematically distorted way a deeper, "latent" level of repressed desire and motivation.

Because of this, Habermas recommends the critical discourse of psychoanalysis as a methodological model for critical reflection, suggesting that like the psychoanalyst, the emancipation-minded social critic must learn to translate the "surface level" of cultural and political discourse back into the "deep structures" of desire, repression, and the will to power, which give rise to it. In the process, the would-be social analyst should also gain self-reflexive knowledge of her or his own propensities for being trapped in such distorted discourse, hence initiating the process of her or his own emancipation from them.

Further, Habermas goes on to argue that the notion of systematically distorted communication presupposes a more positive model of what undistorted communication would be. In his most extensive work, *The Theory of Communicative Ac-*

tion (2 vols., 1984), he attempted to demonstrate that the very structure of human communication itself presupposes certain "transcendental-pragmatic" principles, principles that must be presupposed if any successful communication is to occur at all and that form the basis for a "social ethic of communication." Bringing to mind Kant's application of the categorical imperative to social communicative interaction, Habermas claims that undistorted communication presupposes an initial condition in which all persons potentially affected by the topic under discussion are allowed to participate, that each has equal access to express her or his own views of the matter, and that each accepts certain minimal rules for rational argumentation that will, in the optimal case, lead to consensus, and in other cases, will permit all participants to agree that they are rationally justified in accepting the results of the process because it has accommodated their own interests.

In his broader social theory, Habermas differentiates "the system," which comprises external nature as well as economic and technological forms of social administration, from the "life-world," which indicates the potentially free sphere of human social communicative interaction. When formulated in this way, the key question occurring at the interface of the system's own imperatives and the life-world of communicative interaction is one of **legitimation**. In order to legitimate and gain acceptance for its own actions and policies, especially under conditions of modern capitalism, where the requirements of the system will constantly be at odds with the desires and norms operative in the life-world, the system resorts to systematically distorted forms of communication (the most extreme case of which would be overt political propaganda). Critical reflection must unmask the systematically distorted character of legitimations offered by the system, opposing them with its own normative and essentially democratic model of undistorted communication. The result should be a constant and progressive subjection of distorted communication to the imperatives of a free and democratic public discourse based on an ethic of communicative action.

In conclusion, it must be said that the rather complicated, abstract, and in some ways idealistic theories of Habermas and other neocritics have not yet had as great an influence on contemporary critical discourse about culture as has the older Frankfurt School. While certain aspects of neocritical theory are occasionally used as theoretical platforms from which to challenge the poststructuralist and postmodernist discourses that have been ascendant during the last two decades or so, they have yet to produce any substantial body of the sort of concrete cultural criticism at which such Frankfurt School thinkers as Horkheimer and Adorno excelled. Whether the sphere of culture can or will be suggestively addressed in the neocritical framework remains to be seen.

Bibliographic Essay

Most of the writings of the figures discussed in this chapter are readily available in English. As yet untranslated and sometimes more difficult to obtain are works by some of the lesser known members of the institute and parts of some of the large-scale research projects that the institute sponsored.

Max Horkheimer followed up his *Dialectic of Enlightenment* (New York: Continuum, 1990), coauthored with Adorno, with a solo attempt to develop its ideas further, *The Eclipse of Reason* (New York: Oxford University Press, 1947; reprint ed., New York: Seabury, 1974). Since it was originally composed as a series of public lectures, it is notable for its clear and concise manner of presentation and is highly recommended as an introduction to the thinking of the Frankfurt School in exile. Many of Horkheimer's most important essays and addresses have been collected and translated in *Between Philosophy and Social Science: Selected Early Writings*, tr. G. Hunter, M. Kramer, and J. Torpey (Cambridge, Mass.: MIT Press, 1993).

The best introduction to the work of Walter Benjamin is the anthology *Illuminations*, ed. Hannah Arendt (New York: Schocken, 1968). See especially the last two essays in this volume, "The Work of Art in the Age of Mechanical Reproduction" and "Theses on the Philosophy of History."

Theodor Adorno's major works available in English (besides, of course, *Dialectic of Enlightenment)* include *Negative Dialectics* (New York: Seabury, 1973); *Minima Moralia* (London: New Left Books, 1974); *Prisms* (London: Spearman, 1967); *Philosophy of Modern Music* (London: Sheed & Ward, 1973); and *Aesthetic Theory* (London: Routledge & Kegan Paul, 1984). A number of examples of his concrete cultural criticism are available in English translation in various journals devoted to the topics under discussion.

Herbert Marcuse's major works in English include *Reason and Revolution: Hegel and the Rise of Social Theory* (New York: Oxford University Press, 1941); *Eros and Civilization: A Philosophical Inquiry into Freud* (Boston: Beacon, 1955); *Soviet Marxism: A Critical Analysis* (New York: Columbia University Press, 1958); *One-Dimensional Man: Studies in the Ideology of Advanced Industrial Capitalism* (Boston: Beacon, 1964); and *An Essay on Liberation* (Boston: Beacon, 1969). The last, growing out of his experience in the 1960s, is probably the best general introduction to his most influential views. *Negations: Essays in Critical Theory* (Boston: Beacon, 1968) brings together a number of his shorter works; especially important for cultural critique is the essay "The Affirmative Character of Culture."

Among the many works of Jürgen Habermas available in English, the most important are *Knowledge and Human Interests* (New York: Beacon, 1972); *The Structural Transformation of the Public Sphere* (Cambridge, Mass.: MIT Press, 1989); *Communication and the Evolution of Society* (New York: Beacon, 1979); *Legitimation Crisis* (New York: Beacon, 1976); *The Theory of Communicative Action*, 2 vols. (Cambridge, Mass.: MIT Press, 1984–1989); and *Moral Consciousness and Communicative Action* (Cambridge, Mass.: MIT Press, 1990). In addition to constructively developing his own views, Habermas has engaged in critical (and often polemical) discussions with representatives of many of the other contemporary discourses. *The Philosophical Discourse of Modernity* (Cambridge, Mass.: MIT Press, 1988) is an especially interesting and lively survey and critique of current cultural theory from Habermas's own neocritical perspective.

Several anthologies containing selections from the works of the Frankfurt School are available. For broadly representative collections, see D. Ingram and J. Simon-Ingram, eds., *Critical Theory: The Essential Readings* (New York: Paragon, 1992) and A. Arato and E. Gebhardt, eds., *The Essential Frankfurt School Reader* (New York: Urizen Books, 1978). Another particularly helpful collection, oriented more toward the significance of critical theory for the social sciences and including some essays important for the historical background of the movement as well, is P. Connerton, ed., *Critical Sociology* (New York: Penguin, 1976).

There are several histories of the Frankfurt School. The pioneering history of the beginnings up to the return to Germany is Martin Jay, *The Dialectical Imagination: A History of the Frankfurt School and the Institute of Social Research, 1923–1950* (Boston: Little, Brown, 1973). A more recent work, by Rolf Wiggershaus, *The Frankfurt School: Its History, Theories, and Political Significance* (Cambridge, Mass.: MIT Press, 1994; orig. ed. 1986 [in German]), draws on a good deal of new material that has become available since the appearance of Jay's book, including the work of Habermas and other neocritics and covering developments through the mid-1980s. For a discussion of the more specifically cultural theory of the Frankfurt School, including the intellectual ferment out of which the institute was born, see Susan Buck-Morss, *The Origin of Negative Dialectics: Theodor W. Adorno, Walter Benjamin and the Frankfurt Institute* (Hassocks, England: Harvester, 1977).

The secondary literature on critical theory continues to grow. Among the works that a beginning student of this school might find helpful are Tom Bottomore, *The Frankfurt School* (Chichester, England: Ellis Horwood, 1984); David Ingram, *Critical Theory and Philosophy* (New York: Paragon House, 1990); Douglas Kellner, *Critical Theory, Marxism and Modernity* (Baltimore: Johns Hopkins Press, 1989); David Held, *Introduction to Critical Theory: Horkheimer to Habermas* (Cambridge, Mass.: MIT Press, 1980); and of particular interest with regard to the cultural theory of the Frankfurt School, Ronald Roblin, ed., *The Aesthetics of the Critical Theorists: Studies on Benjamin, Adorno, Marcuse, and Habermas* (Lewiston, N.Y.: Edwin Mellen, 1990).

6
Formalist, Structuralist, and Semiotic Analyses of Culture

The critique of cultural productions and institutions based on an analysis of their underlying forms or structures is not a uniquely modern idea: It can be traced all the way back to Plato. However, Plato viewed forms or structures as independent of the cultural phenomena that they were employed to analyze, as preexisting any concrete exemplar, and as unchanging or invariant over any process of historical change. After the intrinsically historical nature of cultural discourse and critique came to be accepted during the nineteenth century, however, the operative notion of form or structure was transformed as well. No longer viewed as autonomous metaphysical entities occupying a separate realm (the Platonic world of forms or ideas), the basic structures underlying culture and its expressions came to be seen as firmly rooted in history yet sufficiently detachable from their concrete instances to permit powerful new forms of explanation, interpretation, comparison, and critique to be developed through their systematic analysis.

This transformation of the notion of form or structure resulted in a new, distinctly modern type of critical discourse that took as its basic question not *what* meaning a cultural institution or product might have (as did the hermeneutic tradition), but *how* any cultural phenomenon produces the meanings attributed to it. Clearly, the question of meaning stands at the heart of any formal or structural approach, bringing it closer in its basic aims and orientation to the earlier hermeneutic and psychoanalytic approaches and distancing it somewhat from those of the materialists and the Frankfurt School. However, in its own basic assumptions and methods, structural analysis represents a novel point of departure for critical discourse and constitutes a distinctive and continuous strand of cultural critique during the twentieth century.

Before we explore these basic assumptions further, a brief comment about the variety of methodological approaches discussed in this chapter may be helpful. For purposes of the present discussion, we will distinguish between the formalist, structuralist (in the more specific sense specified below), and semiotic strands of a broader discourse that we will refer to as Structuralism. (In this chapter, I have capitalized this term and its cognates when the generic and inclusive sense is intended. Elsewhere in this book, *structuralism* should be understood in the broader sense unless otherwise noted.) The **formalist** approach is most closely associated with the type of literary and cultural analyses pursued in Russia in the first half of the twentieth century, of which **Vladimir Propp** is today probably the best known representative. **Structuralism** (in the specific sense) is most closely identified with the work of anthropologist **Claude Lévi-Strauss**, beginning in the 1930s, and is still a vital approach in certain areas of the social sciences and humanities. **Semiotics** (or **semiology**, the root of which is derived from the Greek word for sign) is generally held to have commenced with the works of philosopher **Charles S. Peirce** and of linguists **Ferdinand de Saussure** and **Roman Jakobson** in the early twentieth century (a bit earlier, in the case of Peirce) and continues in the approaches of critics such as **Roland Barthes, Umberto Eco,** and **Julia Kristeva.** One should not, however, think that these various strands of Structuralism are entirely autonomous of one another, since a good deal of cross-fertilization has occurred among them, even at relatively early dates. Viewed broadly, all three strands share a number of common assumptions.

1. The question of a proper methodology for cultural analysis and critique stands at the forefront of Structuralist concerns. Like several of the discourses that have already been discussed, early Structuralism also involved the conviction that the methodology of the natural sciences was inapplicable to the human creation of meaning, or in other words, to cultural production. However, unlike most of these other discourses, Structuralism assumed that specific alternative methodologies could be developed independently of the natural sciences and that these would lead to equally precise and fruitful explanatory and interpretive results.

2. Because of this, many Structuralists tended to regard their enterprise as, in its own distinctive way, scientific. Saussure especially regarded himself as founding a new science of semiology that would discover and explore laws governing "the life of signs within society." The aspiration toward scientific rigor and precision in methods and results tends to distinguish this approach from most of its modern competitors.

3. Virtually all Structuralists, in one way or another, take human language as the basic paradigm for the development of their discourse. Almost all have regarded the development of the science of linguistics, beginning in the nineteenth century, as the crucial turning point in the study of culture and often have conceived of their own broader enterprises as extensions of it. Indeed, much Structuralist discourse of the twentieth century takes as its explicit starting point the linguistic views of Saussure and Jakobson.

4. While Structuralists generally operate with a very broad notion of meaning, viewing all human activity as essentially meaningful and hence amenable to Structuralist methods, they also agree that meaning is never rooted in external nature or timeless ideas of the human mind and hence fixed once and for all. Rather, they believe that *meanings are (relatively) arbitrary constructions* based on their place in a

broader context of other meanings. Most Structuralist views are therefore decidedly **antiessentialist** in holding that meaning is a purely cultural construction.

5. Structuralists further maintain that the **systems** in which meanings function are themselves cultural and historical constructions. Because they operate according to their own laws (*sui generis*), they can never be adequately described or explained according the usual principles of the empirical social sciences. Although the Structuralist can study and describe the metamorphoses of these systems over time, even in connection with other more empirical disciplines such as history, sociology, and economics, the emphasis of Structuralist analysis must remain on the meaning-creating systems themselves, which no amount of purely empirical observation or description alone can supply or exhaust.

6. An important result of the foregoing is that Structuralist approaches tend to *deemphasize the role of the individual subject* in the essentially social processes of the production and interpretation of meaning. Rather than looking toward the production and reproduction of meaning (as did the materialists and the critical theorists of the Frankfurt School) or to the existential engagement of the individual with a work or tradition (as does hermeneutics), Structuralism focuses on the ways in which the meaning of a text or product is constituted in relation to its own constituent parts and to the range of possible meanings inherent in the system in which it functions. Any individual or subjective variants in the interpretation of a text are thus viewed as derivative from the objective structures and processes operative in the system under consideration, not as essential constituents of the meaning itself.

The Linguistic Foundations of Structuralism: Saussure and Jakobson

Both **Ferdinand de Saussure** (1857–1913) and **Roman Jakobson** (1896–1982) were principally concerned with linguistics, not cultural critique. However, both realized that their linguistic ideas, first presented in the opening decades of the twentieth century, contained the seeds of a much broader theory of culture and method of critique that others would develop as a distinctly Structuralist discourse. One could not claim that their ideas were entirely unprecedented, since systematic reflection about language regarded as a sign-system can be found as early as Aristotle, the first in a long line that included Raymond Lull, G. W. Leibniz, J. H. Lambert, and Charles Peirce, a contemporary of Saussure. However, it was on the basis of the works of Saussure and Jakobson that this approach became established as a dominant critical discourse of the twentieth century.

Saussure's major contribution took the form of three series of lectures at the University of Geneva during the years 1906–1911. The contents of those lectures are available only in the form of a reconstruction of Saussure's notes under the title *Course in General Linguistics,* which first appeared in 1915. Jakobson became familiar with the work of Saussure at an early date and openly acknowledged the importance of the work of Saussure for Russian formalism and its development, in which he himself played a key role. Jakobson began from certain key concepts and distinctions developed by Saussure, refining and extending them during his long and productive career, to the point where they could be directly applied in a new form of cultural critique.

Saussure's Linguistics and the Project of a General Science of Semiology

The principal agenda of Saussure's lectures was the reform of linguistics as it had been pursued up to his time through establishing it on a new foundation. Saussure believed that nineteenth-century linguistics, by focusing its attention on a broad and motley set of empirical phenomena such as phonology (a study of the various ways in which the human voice produces meaningful sounds), linguistic change over time, the comparison of diverse grammars, and the geographical distribution of languages and dialects, had failed to establish the firm foundations necessary in order to win the discipline the status of a science. According to Saussure, lying at the root of this was the fact that earlier linguists had entirely missed the most characteristic feature of language, namely its wholistic or systematic aspect.

In order to make this point, Saussure introduced one of his most important distinctions: that between *parole* (or speech) and *langue* (or language). *Parole* concerns the psychophysiological process of a speaker producing sounds that are understood as meaningful by a listener, whereas *langue* indicates the entire set of formal structures and rules that must be shared by speaker and listener in order for communication to occur at all. In other words, *speaking presupposes a structurally determinate language in which to speak*. While earlier linguists had much to say about speech, they had almost entirely overlooked the most essential features of its indispensable presupposition, language as a determinate system of signification.

In his lectures, Saussure summarized the key differences between parole and langue as follows. These contrasts are particularly important because they form the conceptual basis for most subsequent Structuralist discourse.

1. While speech is subject to a virtually unlimited set of physiological, psychological, and contextual variations, a language is a well-defined and stable object. In particular, language is not dependent on the particular capacities of any individual subject, but is, as Saussure says, "the social side of speech, outside the individual, who can never create or modify it by himself."

2. Language, unlike speech, can be studied independently of all the other extraneous factors that enter into actual instances of speech, such as the virtually unlimited variations observable in pronunciations and dialects as well as in contextual background. Indeed, scientific linguistics depends on language being separable from these factors.

3. Along the same lines, while speech constitutes a heterogeneous field involving physiology, phonology, psychology, history, and so forth, language is homoge-

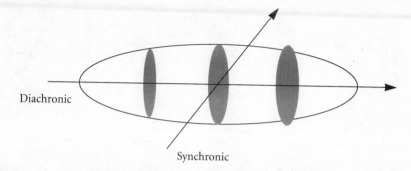

Diachronic

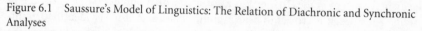

Synchronic

Figure 6.1   Saussure's Model of Linguistics: The Relation of Diachronic and Synchronic Analyses

neous in the sense that it involves only signs and their systematic interconnections, based solely on the immediate psychological association of a sound-image with its meaning.

4. Language is as concrete as speech, although in a different sense. The concreteness of language, and hence its suitability for scientific study, consists in the fact that linguistic signs can be translated directly and completely into fixed visual images such as graphic symbols, hieroglyphs, or writing, whereas empirical instances of speaking can be described only partially and always inadequately.

Another way in which Saussure called attention to these points was by making a distinction between **synchronic** and **diachronic** types of linguistic analysis (see Figure 6.1). Whereas a diachronic analysis studies the changes of parts of language over time, a synchronic analysis concentrates on the structural characteristics of an entire language-system at a particular point or cross-section of time. Ideally, of course, a fully developed science of linguistics would undertake both; but according to Saussure, any diachronic analysis presupposes the existence of a synchronic characterization (that is, a total picture) of the language in question. Saussure's polemic against prior linguists is that in being preoccupied with parole rather than langue, they naturally pursued inherently incomplete diachronic projects, while failing to provide the synchronic analyses of langue on which any valid diachronic study would have to be based. While Saussure was speaking only of linguistics, the terms he used would be applied later in other fields as well, such as anthropology and sociology.

On what, then, should the linguist focus in her or his synchronic study of language, if not on speaking? According to Saussure, language consists of signs and their interrelations. For Saussure, a **sign** must always be understood (in a way rather different from our ordinary notion of this) as a relation between a **signifier** and a **signified**. A signifier, in Saussure's definition, is any sensory image that is immediately connected with (or gives rise to) a specific mental concept or idea; a signified is

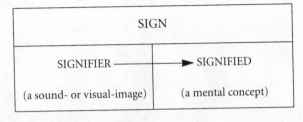

Figure 6.2   The Relation Between Signifier and Signified

the mental concept or idea that is thus associated with a signifier (see Figure 6.2). In reading Saussure, it is crucial to bear in mind that a sign is never identified exclusively with either the signifier or the signified; rather, it is the *relation* between the two. For instance, although most would tend to identify a stop sign with the red octagonal object on a street corner, this is actually only a potential signifier that will not function as a sign unless the concept of bringing our car to a halt is immediately associated with a visual image of it. A child or someone from another culture can certainly see the object, but they will not understand it as a sign until they have learned to associate its image with the idea of stopping an automobile.

A crucial point follows from Saussure's definition of a sign as a relation between a signifier and a signified. According to Saussure, there are few if any natural connections between signifiers and their signified concepts. There is no good reason, for example, to stop at red lights and go at green, other than socially established conventions; any other pair of recognizably different colors would have served just as well. Likewise, there is no natural connection between the spoken or written word *book* and my concept of a book. Indeed, the word for book in other languages can be entirely different, such as *livre* in French or *biblios* in Greek. For this reason, Saussure claims, the relation between any signifier and its signified (thus any sign) is arbitrary, in the sense that this connection is based solely on cultural rules or conventions and not on any natural resemblance between the two.

If this is so, how does any meaningful correlation between signifiers and signifieds arise at all? In response to this, Saussure invites us to think of the set of signifiers of a given language and the set of concepts that are signified as two distinct but correlated realms or spheres. Every sign in a language can thus be defined as a point where a particular linguistic signifier is immediately correlated with its specific conceptual signified. Given this, we can read in either direction, that is, from linguistic signifier to mental concept or from mental concept to linguistic signifier. For the purposes of linguistics, however, our principal concern is with the first, since mental concepts are unavailable to direct observation; that is, the concern of the linguist is to study the structure of linguistic signifiers as a means of access to the structure of mental concepts. Extending this idea, Saussure suggested that we understand the differences between languages (and the conceptual structures with which they are correlated) as involving different sets of correlation be-

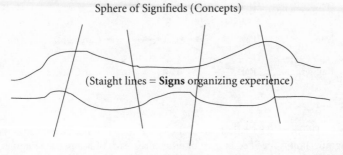

Figure 6.3   Signs as the Correlation Between the Two Separate Spheres of Signifier and Signified. [Note that there is no natural fit or correlation between the sphere of signifiers and that of signifieds, as indicated by the two wavy lines.]

tween signifiers and signifieds, that is, as different ways in which the continuum of possible sound-images is specifically correlated with the continuum of possible mental concepts, thus determining the different ways in which human experience is segmented (see Figure 6.3).

Having offered this model of the relation between signifier and signified, Saussure proposed that systems of linguistic signifiers be approached in the following manner. First, he suggested that we begin by determining the basic units of meaning in the system of signifiers. These are called **morphemes** (Saussure actually used another term here, but this terminology was later recognized as an improvement). It must be immediately added, against the most obvious view, that these will not necessarily be identical with the individual words of a language. Since there is no natural connection between signifiers and signifieds, one cannot appeal directly to concepts to determine the meanings of morphemes. Rather, Saussure held that different morphemes can be distinguished from one another only by the ways in which each differs from the others, that is, through their own **system of differences**. For example, let's assume that *cat, bat, bag,* and *car* are all morphemes, that is, units of meaning irreducible to any simpler elements. Since none of them have any natural connection to their respective concepts, the differences in their meaning can only arise from the system of differences in their spellings or pronunciations, that is, from the differences in their sound-images or visual images. Thus, changing the *c* in *cat* to a *b* alters the meaning of the word from a feline to a flying rodent, just as a subsequent change of the *t* in *bat* to a *g* alters its meaning to a container for groceries. The point is that the meanings of these linguistic signs are strictly dependent on the system of differences constitutive of the English language, not on anything intrinsic to the individual signs themselves or their correlated concepts (see Figure 6.4).

However, not only words can be morphemes; most prefixes and suffixes also qualify. Following Saussure's suggestions, there is always a **differential test** for

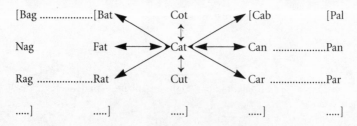

Figure 6.4   Differential Specifications of the Word *Cat*. [This diagram illustrates how the word (signifier) *cat* is specified by a set of differences, each of its opposed signifiers being in turn defined by its own system of differences. Obviously, the diagram could be extended in all directions.]

this—if the addition of another element alters the meaning attributed to the original, then what is added will also be a morpheme. For example, let's assume that *joy* is a morpheme. Then we add the suffix *-ful* and ask whether the meaning or concept of the original word has been altered. In this case, we have changed the meaning from a certain positive emotion to an adjective describing something else, perhaps a movement of a symphony. Thus we must conclude that *-ful* is also a morpheme. We can reapply this test for the addition of the suffixes *-ly* and *-ness* as well as the prefix *un-*. In each of these cases, the addition alters the meaning; so all qualify as morphemes.

When Saussure claimed that the signs constituting language were arbitrary, he meant that there was no natural or predetermined meaning for any given unit of language. However, he did not mean that once a linguistic system was in operation one could, as Humpty Dumpty claimed, make anything mean whatever one wanted it to. Rather, he regarded language as a fully interlocked and determined system of differences that could be understood also as a set of rules specifying, for any speaker of the language, the sorts of signs, together with their combinations and transformations, that can count as meaningful in that language.

Expanding a bit on Saussure at this point (and following Roland Barthes's suggestions), we can say that there are three basic sorts of rules involved in any linguistic (or, more broadly, semiotic) system. To understand them, an analogy with the game of chess may be helpful. The first type of rule is determined simply by the list of elementary units or morphemes that make up the language. In speaking a language (at least if we want to be understood), we can only make use of the available units of meaning that count as constituent elements of that language. By analogy, in chess each player receives, at the beginning of a game, a fixed set of pieces—no more, no less, and no different than what the rules of the game allow. Second, there is a limited number of other words that may meaningfully be substituted for any given morpheme or word. For example, in the sentence *The cat is on the stove*, a range a words can be substituted for most of the words in the sentence, for example, *dog* or *hamster* for *cat*, *range* or *table* for *stove*, even *was* or *will*

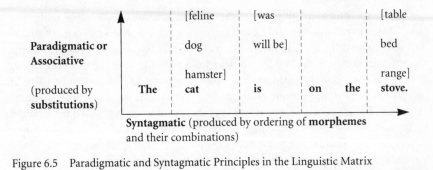

	[feline	[was			[table
Paradigmatic or	dog	will be]			bed
Associative					
	hamster]				range]
(produced by	**The** **cat**	**is**	**on**	**the**	**stove.**
substitutions)					

Syntagmatic (produced by ordering of **morphemes**
and their combinations)

Figure 6.5   Paradigmatic and Syntagmatic Principles in the Linguistic Matrix

---

be for *is*. Likewise, in chess, most pieces allow a given, though always restricted, range of different moves at any point in the game. The knight, for example, can move either two spaces forward and one over, or one space forward and two over. Of course, the outcome of the game, like the meaning of a sentence, will be determined by which choices are made. Types of rules that involve a set of permissible substitutions for given units Saussure called **associative,** based on his hypothesis that the mind tends to associate a given word with other words that can be substituted for it in the same linguistic place in a phrase or sentence. Later, such rules generally became referred to as **paradigmatic,** a term presumably less loaded with questionable psychological implications. Finally, in any given language, there are also rules that govern the sequential order in which various morphemes or larger units can occur. To refer back to our former example, while the sentence *The cat is on the stove* is meaningful in English, a sentence such as *Stove the cat on the is* is not. Rules governing the order of the elements rather than their allowable substitutions are called **syntagmatic,** a word derived from the grammatical term syntax. Again, in chess, there are certain restrictions on the order of play. For example, each player can move once and only once a turn; the pawns blocking the king, queen, bishops, and rooks must be moved before those other pieces can be moved; and so forth (see Figure 6.5).

The outcome of the interrelated workings of these three sorts of rules can be envisioned as follows. If we allow that there are a finite number of morphemes that constitute the basic elements of any sign system (as Saussure seemed to believe), it immediately follows that an even more restricted subset of these will be available at any given point for paradigmatic substitution. Likewise, the syntagmatic rules governing correctly formed sentences will significantly restrict the number of compounds that can be produced from the basic elements and their substitution-instances. What emerges is a view of any linguistic or significational system imagined as a sort of matrix. Theoretically, the matrix should be able to present all possible syntagmatic structures (represented, for example, by the horizontal axis) together with all possible paradigmatic substitution instances allowable in the various places constituting the syntax (represented by the vertical axis). In principle, then, all possible meaningful statements allowable under the rules of the given system could be exhaustively specified without reference to any concrete instance of speaking. The matrix would therefore structurally represent the entire field of possibilities for meaningful expression, and the meaning of any concrete instance of expression would be exhaustively determined by its place in the system, that is, the unique possibility that it realizes from all those theoretically available (somewhat like buying one square on a betting board determined by the last two numbers of the final score of a football game). Just as supercomputers are approaching the point of being able to determine ahead of time all the virtually uncountable (though nonetheless finite) possible games of chess, so the range of meanings that can be expressed in any sign system should be, in principle, determinable, so long as Saussure's basic assumptions are met.

In fact, Saussure himself never attempted so exhaustive an analysis, since he realized many of the theoretical and most of the practical problems such a project would involve. Rather than pursuing a hopelessly complex undertaking, Saussure was primarily concerned with establishing a new way of thinking first about linguistic and then about more broadly cultural phenomena. Saussure taught that in understanding any particular cultural product, the most important questions to ask are, What other possibilities were available from among which this specific one was chosen? and What rules seem to govern the manner in which its elements are ordered?

In his lectures, Saussure referred to semiology as "a science that studies the life of signs in society" and went on to claim that "linguistics is only a part of the general science of semiology," and that "[b]y studying rites, customs, etc. as signs, I believe that we shall throw new light on the facts and point up the need for including them in a science of semiology and explaining them by its laws." Thus, the real thrust of Saussure's thought was in the direction of extending the basic principles of the structural analysis of signifying systems to cultural phenomena in general, rather than some increasingly exhaustive attempt to render a completely determinant characterization of particular systems. It is in this spirit that the critical discourse of Structuralism has generally followed.

Extending the Structuralist Framework: Roman Jakobson

Roman Jakobson (1896–1982), a prolific scholar of exceptionally broad interests including philology, linguistics, literary theory, and aesthetics, probably did more than any other individual in helping to bridge the gap between Saussure's linguistic theories and their application to the wider field of cultural analysis and critique. Not only did he help found both the Moscow Linguistic Circle (1915) and the Prague Linguistic Circle (1926), but through his teaching and research activities in the United States beginning in 1941, he introduced Structuralist methods to yet another new audience, thus establishing Structuralism as a genuinely international critical discourse. Jakobson's contributions are too numerous to survey in any brief discussion, but three of his developments of Saussure's linguistic framework became fundamental to all subsequent Structuralist thought: his concepts of **binarism**, of the important distinction between **metaphor** and **metonymy**, and of the basic constituents of any act of communication.

As we have already seen, Saussure had emphasized the differential nature of language viewed as a system of signs. Whether one considers the sphere of linguistic signifiers or that of mental concepts or signifieds, Saussure held that the meaning or value of any term or concept was completely a function of the system of differences in which it operated, never some essential or intrinsic quality of the constituents of the signs themselves. Jakobson, seeking to identify the most basic structural feature underlying Saussure's notion of the differential nature of signification, observed that every differential system, however complex, can ultimately be analyzed into a set of binary oppositions, that is, oppositions involving only two elements. To return to our previous example, the location in the English linguistic system of the signifier *cat* can be (partially) determined by specifying a list of binary oppositions with other signifiers lying close to it: [*cat*, not *bat*], [*cat*, not *car*], [*cat*, not *rat*], [*cat*, not *cot*], and so on (where *not* simply indicates the binary opposition between the two signifiers listed in each case).

While this observation at first glance might not appear especially profound, it had several consequences that have been highly influential in the development of Structuralist discourse and its methods. First, Jakobson hypothesized on the basis of this linguistic observation that the human mind might operate according to essentially binary principles, that is, that thinking is, at its basis, a complex set of oppositional or binary operations. (At the time, he could not have known the importance that this view of human thought would have for later questions involving the alleged artificial intelligence of computers, which always operate in a binary fashion.) Second, it implied that the meaning of any sign can only be understood in terms of a set of other signs that might have been chosen instead but were not. For example, when a portrait painter includes a small dog at the subject's feet (a device popular during the seventeenth century), we might ask how the meaning conveyed would have been altered had the artist instead included a cat, a peacock, or a sleeping lion. That is, binarism would invite us to consider the artist's portrayal of a small dog as involving a set of binary choices between the animal actually chosen and others that could have been chosen but were rejected. In themselves, dogs may or may not be, say, gentle and faithful, but given the system of differences operative in European culture (at least at certain historical moments), they have come to be associated with such qualities in contrast to other animals with their own distinctive associations.

Most important for cultural critique, however, is that the underlying binary character of the human mind and its significations, when joined with the idea of associative or paradigmatic substitution developed by Saussure, suggested that we tend to order our thought in terms of parallel but opposed chains of terms. In such a schema, each term will be associated with the others in its own chain (and,

TABLE 6.1 Differential Signification: Generic Jeans vs. Designer Jeans

generic jeans	designer jeans
classless	upscale
country	city
communal	socially distinctive
unisex	feminine (or more rarely, masculine)
work	leisure
traditional	contemporary
unchanging	transient
THE WEST	THE EAST
NATURE	CULTURE

in a sense, substitutable for them) as well as contrasted with another term in the opposing chain. In his book *Understanding Popular Culture,* John Fiske presents the table above in order to characterize the differential signification between generic jeans and designer jeans (see Table 6.1).

The point, of course, is that neither generic nor designer jeans necessarily have any of these associations: Outside this system of differential oppositions, they are simply articles of clothing worn below the waist. However, when placed in the broader semiotic system of contemporary fashion and analyzed as elements of opposed significational chains of associated concepts, a definite binary pattern in our manner of viewing the world emerges. Similar analyses have been performed that are very suggestive for contemporary cultural critique, beginning with such common binary oppositions as male/female, Occident/Orient, straight/gay, white/black, rich/poor, sane/insane, and the like.

The second major contribution of Jakobson to the extension of Saussure's structuralist views significantly promoted their adoption in the field of literary analysis and criticism (and later in related fields). Since the Greco-Roman period of classical rhetoric, the study of **tropes,** or figures of speech, has been an important area of literary study. In particular, much effort has been devoted to the identification and classification of a bewildering array of many different types of recognized tropes. Drawing on Saussure's distinction between the fundamental linguistic operations of associative substitution and syntagmatic ordering, Jakobson proposed that two of the recognized tropes, metaphor and metonymy, must be regarded as preeminent among them. According to Jakobson, metaphor was the rhetorical or literary counterpart of the operation of associative substitution, involving a conceptual shift or substitution of meaning operating along the paradigmatic axis of language. For example, in the sentence *He was to us a fixed star,* the metaphorical signifier *fixed star* invites us to substitute in its place some further concept or signified such as *reliable guide* or *dependable leader,* thus serving to link together another realm of signifieds different from that suggested by the literal "astronomical signified" indicated by the metaphorical signifier. By contrast, Jakobson related

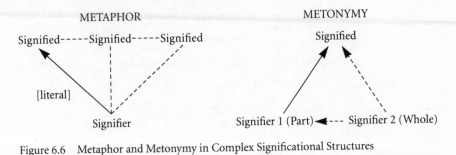

Figure 6.6   Metaphor and Metonymy in Complex Significational Structures

metonymy to the syntagmatic axis of Saussure's linguistic framework, maintaining that both of these concepts functioned through a principle of proximate or contiguous ordering. Thus, in the sentence *Her heart was not in her work today,* the metonym *heart,* a condensation or abbreviation for her entire psychological state of being attentive or concerned, depends for its meaning on the fact that *heart* is directly associated with certain mental attitudes or conditions. Metonyms are substitutions at the level of signifiers rather than that of signifieds: Because it is a part of our overall mental attitude, *heart* can replace a much more complicated phrase in order to convey the same signified (see Figure 6.6).

Having made this distinction, Jakobson suggested that metaphor and metonymy might be thought of as constituting two poles of a continuum along which various genres of literature, or even specific works, might be located: At one extreme would fall those, like lyric poetry, that depend heavily on metaphorical substitutions at the level of the signified; at the other, those, like the narrative novel, that are based on a sequential order of constituent signifiers (that is, a plot). In contemporary cultural critique, this notion has continued to prove fruitful in the analysis of complex significational structures, such as film, where sequential narrative elements are interwoven with individual shots suggesting metaphorical connections.

The third and probably most influential development of Saussure's linguistic views introduced by Jakobson was his structural analysis of the various constituents of any act of human communication. While Saussure had by no means neglected to treat the broader question of human communication, which provided the overall context for his more limited synchronic analyses, his remarks on this topic in the *Course* fell short of the scientific rigor that was his goal. Jakobson, then, proceeded to supply a structural analysis of the broader system presupposed by any linguistic or semiological research (see Figure 6.7).

The functions of **addresser** and **addressee** are, of course, obvious: Any act of communication presupposes both a speaker (or writer) and a hearer (or reader). The other functions, which concern the message sent from speaker to hearer, represent a novel and very important set of distinctions. The **context** concerns the dimension of communication wherein the ability to refer to things or ideas in a

CONTEXT

MESSAGE

ADDRESSER   ....   ADDRESSEE

CONTACT

CODE

Figure 6.7   The Structure of Communication

---

shared world is presupposed. Using a television commercial as an example, the context would involve such facts as that most members of the audience possess automobiles and that they understand that these must be periodically fueled. The **message** involves the content, or the what, that is being communicated. For example, the message of a commercial for petroleum products might be something like "Texaco makes the best fuel; buy our product." The **contact** has to do with the means, or medium, by which the addresser is connected with the addressee, which in the present example is television. Finally, the **code** concerns those features of signification that Saussure attempted to analyze according to morphemic, associative, and syntagmatic principles of signification. In the case of the television advertisement, several different codes are typically employed at once: the English language, the system of petroleum company logos, the story line of the commercial, and so forth.

Russian Formalism:
Propp's Analysis of the Russian Folktale

Having introduced some of the fundamental concepts of structural analysis developed on the basis of the study of linguistics in the early twentieth century, we will now turn to some of their more significant extensions beyond this field. We will begin with an early attempt by **Vladimir Propp**, a member of Jakobson's Moscow Linguistic Circle, to apply a syntagmatic analysis to the plot-structure of the Russian folktale. The type of analysis undertaken by Propp and the Moscow group is often referred to as **Russian formalism**.

As a movement, Russian formalism originated in the second decade of the twentieth century as a reaction against the prevalent modes of criticism, which it regarded as too subjectivist, either in overemphasizing the biographical details of the author's life (**biographism**) or how readers interpret a text (**psychologism**). Convinced that the study of literary texts should be objective, that is, that it should focus on the formal features of the construction of the text itself, the formalists proceeded to develop various methods for analyzing texts by isolating and describing the various **mechanisms** (a term often employed very literally) by which texts are organized and produce their characteristic effects. Such dimensions of literature as genre, images, metrics, and plot were carefully studied, utilizing both the linguistic theories of Saussure and Jakobson (the latter was an early member of this movement) as well as comparative methods based on quantitative statistics. It should be mentioned that these objective methods allowed the formalists to carve out a niche for literary scholarship in the repressive context of the young Soviet Union, establishing a tradition that persists in most countries of the former Soviet bloc today.

Vladimir Propp was primarily interested in the study of Russian folklore. His *Morphology of the Folktale* (1928, trans. 1958) contains an early statement of some of the most important methodological principles of Structuralist analysis as well as one of the most influential examples of the formalist analysis of plot, a type of structural analysis that would later be called **narratology**, that is, the study of narrative structures. It is especially noteworthy for demonstrating how formalist analyses can be combined with statistical comparison to yield a general characterization of a particular literary genre, in this case the Russian folktale. However, since Propp intended that his method have general application to any set of texts involving plot or syntagmatic elements analogous to it, it can serve as a representative example for this variety of Structuralist cultural analysis.

Propp described his project in this way: "We are undertaking a comparison of the themes of these tales. For the sake of comparison we shall separate the component parts of fairy tales by special methods; and then, we shall make a comparison of the tales according to their components. The result will be a morphology (i.e., a description of the tale according to its component parts and the relationship of these components to each other and to the whole)."

The basic procedure that Propp employed can be described as follows. It should be noted, however, that this procedure could be applied to many other sets of narrative texts, such as detergent commercials, Disney cartoons, television sitcoms, detective stories, horror films, and Italian operas.

1. Define and delimit the set of texts that one wishes to analyze. In Propp's case, this was a collection of more than three hundred traditional Russian folktales (with variants) that should hypothetically constitute a particular genre or type of literature.

2. Determine the basic units of analysis to be employed. (These might be referred to as the morphemes of the particular genre.) With respect to plot, Propp suggested that these would be various functions involved in the narrative; these might or might not always be identified with specific characters each of whom could perform a number of functions in the plot. Such functions might include leaving home, posing a task, struggle with an opponent, receipt of a magic agent (or helpful information), and so on. Obviously, every genre will have its own characteristic set of such functions.

3. Assume that the number of such functions is limited, even though they can be performed by various characters and the manner of their fulfillment might admit some variety in details. (Such possible substitutions in various functions are

analogous to Saussure's paradigmatic rules.) The main point is that there should
be as complete an enumeration of functions as possible, so that even if a particular text does not contain all of them, any text can be described by a certain sub-
group of the list of functions.

4. Diagram each text (ideally, using symbols for each function) so that the syntagmatic structure of every text will be clear in terms of the list of functions.

5. Compare the sequential order of whatever functions occur in a given text
with that of other texts. (This order of functions corresponds to Saussure's syntagmatic rules. Note that this is by far the most important dimension of such an
analysis.) Again, it is not necessary that all functions occur in every text. With regard to the Russian folktale, Propp believed he could demonstrate that there was a
basic and invariant sequential or syntagmatic order of functions that defined the
genre of the Russian folktale, even if not all of these functions occurred in any
given text. In other words, one could formulate general laws governing the sequence of a finite number of functions, thereby defining the genre. In cases where
this order was violated or where an unlisted function appeared, one could then
hypothesize that the deviant example might have come from another (for example, French or German) tradition of folktales or that it represented an introduction of modern literary elements into the folk tradition.

The Extension of Structural Analysis:
Lévi-Strauss

Claude Lévi-Strauss (b. 1908), one of the most important and controversial anthropologists of the twentieth century, claimed that the three most significant influences on his work were geology, Freud, and Marx, though one might well add
to this list the structural linguistics pioneered by Saussure and Jakobson. What all
shared in common, and what he found decisive in them, was the conviction that
in order to understand and explain any of the phenomena with which they dealt,
it was necessary to look beyond the level of observed **surface structures** to the
deep structures underlying them. Whether one considers surface rock formations, reports of dreams, political ideologies, or ordinary linguistic usage, any scientifically acceptable explanation must primarily look not to their history, which
will yield only further collections of surface data, but to their underlying deep
structures and laws, of which the observed surface structures represent only so
many variations. Lévi-Strauss's pivotal role in the development of structuralist
discourse was to develop generalized methods of structural analysis that could be
applied to large-scale cultural formations such as kinship, food production and
consumption, ritual, and especially myth. In approaching cultural phenomena
through such methods, he believed that structuralist research would ultimately
converge on certain basic and irreducible structural patterns governing both human thought and its manifold cultural expressions. In particular, we would come
to see that modern scientific thought was in no way qualitatively different from

primitive thought and that contemporary Western culture was simply another variant of universal deep structures underlying all cultures. Whether his predictions have proven true remains a matter of heated controversy.

To understand the distinctiveness of Lévi-Strauss's contribution to Structuralist discourse, one should begin with what he accepts from structural linguistics and what revisions to it he regards as necessary in order to render it useful for a broader analysis of culture. Lévi-Strauss, in his important essay "Structural Analysis in Linguistics and in Anthropology" (1945), affirms four basic principles established by the field of linguistics.

1. "Structural linguistics shifts from the study of *conscious* linguistic phenomena to study of their *unconscious* infrastructure." Likewise, in the broader field of culture Lévi-Strauss maintains that since the members of a culture are no more aware of the underlying structures governing their actions and institutions than is an individual of the rules of grammar when speaking a language, the focus of cultural analysis should be shifted accordingly.

2. "It (that is, structural linguistics) does not treat *terms* as independent entities, taking instead as its basis of analysis the *relations* between terms." In the realm of culture as well, Lévi-Strauss maintains that the basic structures with which he is concerned are, like Saussure's signs and Jakobson's binaries, relations between terms rather than fixed categories viewed as somehow meaningful in themselves.

3. "It introduces the concept of *system.*" In cultural analysis as in linguistics, the various parts or aspects of culture that we might identify receive their function and significance only through their place in the structure of an entire system. Conversely, such systems can never be viewed merely as sums or concatenations of their respective parts but possess their own irreducible features.

4. "Structural linguistics aims at discovering *general laws.*" Lévi-Strauss believed that just as linguistics had been able to determine certain basic laws of linguistic systems, so anthropology should, with suitable methodological adjustments, be able to formulate general laws governing cultural systems.

Lévi-Strauss's most explicit discussion of the modifications to structural linguistics required in order to make it suitable for cultural analysis appeared in an article entitled "The Structural Study of Myth" (1955) together with concrete examples of the application of his structuralist method. (The reader should be aware, however, that Lévi-Strauss never held that there was some single or fixed method that could be mechanically applied to any given cultural formation; rather, like the handyman, or *bricoleur,* the anthropologist or cultural critic must continually adapt the tools at her or his disposal to the task at hand, with the proviso that only certain structuralist tools are appropriate for the analysis of cultural phenomena.) The modifications of the principles of structural linguistics required for the analysis of culture, or in this particular case myth, include the following:

1. Whereas structuralist linguistics had commenced with Saussure's distinction between *parole* (speech as diachronic event) and *langue* (language as synchronic structure) in order to exclude the former as the proper object of linguistic study, myth clearly involves both dimensions. Myth is at once temporal and universal. It is temporal in the dual sense that it exists in the form of **sequential narratives**—stories that must be told—and that it refers to events long past, which are recounted in the present. However, it is also universal or timeless in that it employs atemporal structural features that allow it to function as an enduring and powerful explanation of the past, present, and future. Thus, while, as Lévi-Strauss says, "myth is language," it is language of a higher order in which the narrative's syntagmatic and diachronic dimension is inextricably bound to the paradigmatic and synchronic dimension. As a result, the goal of any structural analysis of myth should not be to separate its temporal and atemporal aspects (as occurs in structural linguistics) but to describe and elucidate their distinctive modes of interaction. In other words, myths, like orchestral scores, require a **dual reading**: on the one hand, an attention to the temporal sequence or linear flow of its narration or performance; on the other, an awareness of the recurrent themes and variations that lend it its characteristic structural unity.

2. According to structural linguistics, language is made up of basic units, variously called phonemes or morphemes. Myths, too, consist of basic elements, but they will again be of a higher order than their linguistic counterparts. Lévi-Strauss calls these elements "gross constituent units" or **mythemes**, and suggests that they be sought at the linguistic level of sentences. As a methodological rule of thumb, he suggests that the story of every myth be broken down into a set of simple sentences that can be compared, contrasted, and ordered with respect to one another.

3. Mythemes, in a manner analogous to Propp's functions, will constitute a set of sentences each of which expresses a specific relation. These relations can include actions of a subject on an object (or vice versa), kinship relations between the figures in the myth, and even the meanings of proper names introduced in the course of the narrative (a significantly broader range of materials than those included in Propp's formalist syntagmatic analysis).

4. When approached in this way, the real units of myth will turn out to be not merely the single relations expressed by its sentences but **bundles of relations** or classes of mythemes—that is, distinct groups of structurally similar relations that, although they may involve different personae and may occur at widely dispersed points in the narrative, constitute the deep structure on which a reading of the significance of the myth can be based.

To illustrate this analytic method, Lévi-Strauss offered the following chart (see Figure 6.8).

The sentences that Lévi-Strauss presents constitute the mythemes of the Oedipus myth. Reading from left to right and continuing down the page as usual, the reader can follow the basic narrative sequence of the Oedipus myth. However, if we consider the mythemes gathered under each column, we will immediately see that each column presents a bundle of parallel or analogous relations that are presented

Cadmos
seeks his sister
Europa, ravished
by Zeus

　　　　　　　　　　　Cadmos kills
　　　　　　　　　　　the dragon

　　　　　　The Spartoi
　　　　　　kill one another

　　　　　　　　　　　　　　　　　Labdacos (Laios'
　　　　　　　　　　　　　　　　　father) = *lame* (?)

　　　　　　Oedipus kills　　　　　Laios (Oedipus'
　　　　　　his father,　　　　　　father) = *left-sided*
　　　　　　Laios　　　　　　　　　(?)

　　　　　　　　　　　Oedipus kills
　　　　　　　　　　　the Sphinx

　　　　　　　　　　　　　　　　　Oedipus = *swollen
　　　　　　　　　　　　　　　　　foot* (?)

Oedipus
marries his
mother, Jocasta

　　　　　　Eteocles kills
　　　　　　his brother,
　　　　　　Polynices

Antigone buries
her brother,
Polynices, despite
prohibition

Figure 6.8　　The Structure of the Oedipus Myth

at widely dispersed points in the narrative sequence. Lévi-Strauss believed this other dimension in the relationship of mythemes was just as important as the first.

In the case of the Oedipus myth, the first vertical bundle concerns blood relationships which are overemphasized, or more highly stressed than appropriate. The second, in direct contrast, concerns opposite cases where blood relationships are undervalued, or not given their due weight. The third column concerns the slaying of monsters, while the fourth involves the common feature of names that refer to difficulties in walking straight and standing upright. Lévi-Strauss suggested a connection between the latter two: Monsters represent natural forces associated with the earth, which must be vanquished in order that human beings may flourish, implying that human existence on the earth is somehow unnatural. On the other hand, one associates difficulties in walking or standing with natural disabilities, underlining the fact that human beings are very much under the sway of natural forces and are hence "of the earth."

In interpreting the overall myth, Lévi-Strauss sees the set of contrasts involved in the first two columns—the problem of over- versus undervaluation of blood relationships—as analogous and closely related to the second two—the problem of deciding whether human beings are natural creatures born of the earth or whether they represent a violation of the natural order. The point is not, of course, that the myth resolves these deep-seated dilemmas in the human psyche, but that it functions through its underlying structure as a means of expressing universal and timeless conflicts in our relationships to nature and to other human beings. Ultimately, it signifies that as long as we remain undecided about whether we are natural beings or usurpers, we will also remain in conflict regarding the duties and prohibitions that ought to govern our relations with other human beings, especially those most closely related to us.

Semiotics and the Critique of Ideology: Barthes

Roland Barthes (1915–1980) is an enigmatic and Protean figure in the history of Structuralist discourse. Over the course of his career, he articulated the most extreme and rigorous version of semiotics that had yet appeared and then seemed to reject it entirely; he attempted to demonstrate how specific texts could be exhaustively reduced to their constituent codes and then came to emphasize the reader-oriented pleasure of the text; and while he often appeared to be speaking from a broadly Marxist stance, he also insisted on maintaining a pronounced critical distance, declining any overt or unambiguous political pronouncement. For such reasons, any straightforward association of his work with a specific discipline or even discourse would be misleading. However, several of his ideas were of crucial importance specifically to the development of Structuralist discourse and we will therefore consider them here.

As a general characterization of Barthes's contributions in this area, one could say that whereas Lévi-Strauss had demonstrated how Structuralist methods drawn from linguistics could be used to analyze cultural formations, Barthes showed how such analyses could in turn be employed in the service of cultural critique. With Barthes, that is, Structuralism moved from the realm of scientific description and analysis to that of genuinely critical and practical discourse. However, Barthes's importance is not limited to his having made this shift at the level of theory. More forcefully than any of his predecessors, Barthes demonstrated through his many Structural analyses of productions of both high and popular culture exactly how such a critical discourse should proceed. Because of this, his work has come to constitute the basis for a large segment of contemporary cultural critique, which would be virtually unthinkable without it.

By way of introducing the aspects of Barthes's work most relevant to Structuralist cultural critique, it will be helpful first to note how Barthes challenged some of the inherent limitations of the Structuralist thought preceding him. For Barthes, Structuralism was unduly restrictive in two opposed directions. On the one hand, while Structuralist methods may have sufficed for understanding the relatively simple plot-structures of Russian folktales or for organizing highly condensed versions of well-known myths, their adequacy for analyzing the far more complex structures of literary texts or contemporary cultural institutions remained unproven. In this respect, Barthes significantly extended the range of application of explicitly Structuralist methods. On the other hand, other Structuralists such as Propp and Jakobson had deliberately excluded from their analyses any reference to the social, historical, or political context, which they viewed as lying outside the particular significational system under consideration. By contrast, it was precisely the linkage between signifying systems and their broader ideological settings that Barthes sought to establish.

More specifically, the earlier Structuralists had insisted that the meaning or value of any morpheme in a system was rigorously determined by its place in the system of differences. Barthes, without abandoning this basic methodological principle in relation to a single or isolated system, nonetheless insisted that signs must be regarded as **polysemic**, that is, as capable of taking on various values or meanings depending on the various systems in which they almost always simultaneously functioned. To make this point, he introduced two terms that dramatically expanded the framework of earlier Structuralism—**denotation** and **connotation**—which he viewed as irreducible features of any system of signs. Further, taking up Lévi-Strauss's own central concern, Barthes reformulated and expanded the concept of mythology in a way that identified it with the very means by which cultural ideologies are established and maintained instead of with some atemporal structure or essential feature of the human psyche.

The idea underlying Barthes's distinctive analysis of mythology is that any sign, in addition to establishing a relation between a signifier and a signified, can also be employed as a signifier of other signifieds of a higher order that are also signs. This higher order of signification in which a sign signifies other signs Barthes called the level of **connotations**. At this level, a significational system encounters an extrasystemic dimension—namely, some prevailing set of historical and cultural meanings or codes. As an example, a photograph of a bald eagle is, at its most basic level, a signifier for a signified, which is simply the actual bald eagle photographed (or its mental image). Thus, the photograph itself is a sign that denotes a bald eagle. However, in addition to the first-order object, most of us would think almost immediately of other, related signs, such as the American flag, patriotism, or perhaps endangered species, all of which constitute part of the eagle's connotation for most contemporary Americans. Following Barthes, we can offer the following general diagram of the relation between the levels of denotation and connotation (see Figure 6.9).

Mapping our example above onto this schema would yield the following set of equivalences:

PRIMARY SIGNIFICATION	1. SIGNIFIER	2. SIGNIFIED
Denotation [Secondary signification]	3. SIGN (= a. Signifier)	(Another Sign) (= b. Signified)
Connotation	c. Sign	

Figure 6.9   The Relation Between Denotation and Connotation

1. Signifier = physical photograph;
2. Signified = the bald eagle as photographed, or a mental image of it;
3. Sign (a. Signifier) = photograph of a bald eagle, recognized as such (which is the level of **denotation**); (b. Signified) = patriotism, the American flag, or an endangered species (or whatever else might be associated with it in a given cultural code), which produces the level of **connotation.**

The question arises, What are we to call the "c.sign"? This brings us immediately to Barthes's discussion of **mythology**, which can be found in the concluding section of his book *Mythologies* (1957). According to Barthes, a mythology is "a second-order semiological system," based on a "first-order" system of denotation but operating at the level of connotation. In his use of the term, a mythology can be any higher-order cultural code that takes our primary significational systems (which can involve words, images, sounds, clothing, food, and so forth) and, by virtue of the various connotations immediately linked with them by a given society or culture, produces a system of higher-order significations, or mythologies, which taken together form the **ideological system** of that society or culture. To see this, we can refer back to our diagram, noting that it could in principle be progressively extended, with the sign becoming the signifier for yet other connoted signifieds. If we were to analyze many mythologies (as Barthes himself does in the first part of the book), we would see them converging on a basic set of higher-order signs that taken together would be nothing other than the prevalent ideology of our society, which many have called late, or postindustrial, capitalism. Barthes's schema for understanding mythologies was designed to show what the operative ideas and values of a given culture are and how they are produced and maintained, as well as to suggest ways in which they might be unmasked, criticized, and perhaps transformed.

More Recent Developments
in Structuralist Discourse

There is no question that Structuralist discourse remains a major component of contemporary cultural critique, although it would be difficult to catalog the many forms in which it has been developed and applied. It also continues to play a significant role as the starting point for much poststructuralist and postmodernist thought, although the attitude toward it there is generally highly critical. These critical responses to Structuralism will be discussed in the next chapter. To conclude the present section, we will briefly consider two developments illustrative of directions in which Structuralist thought has been extended since the writings of Barthes. Umberto Eco, an influential advocate of a highly elaborated semiotic approach, has attempted to temper Structuralism's seeming rigidity and probe its inherent limitations with a number of considerations drawn from hermeneutic discourse. In a quite different direction, Julia Kristeva, drawing on the work of Jacques Lacan (see the next chapter), has attempted to bring a semiotic stance into direct proximity with the psychoanalysis of desire.

Eco: The Role of the Reader and the Limits of Semiotics

Umberto Eco (b. 1932), best known to popular audiences for his two novels *The Name of the Rose* (1980) and *Foucault's Pendulum* (1988), continues to be an intriguing and provocative figure in the development of critical discourse. This is due in part to the fact that as an Italian, his intellectual background was neither the French structuralism of Saussure and Lévi-Strauss nor the Russian formalism of Propp and Jakobson. Rather, it was the far more traditional study of the sign-saturated aesthetics of medieval thinkers such as Thomas Aquinas.

The general focus of Eco's theoretical work can best be characterized as a detailed exploration of the interface between the processes of reading and interpreting texts and the semiotic systems or codes that constitute them. A chronology of his published works evidences a sort of dialectical tension between these concerns. His reflections in the early 1960s, especially *The Open Work* (1962), written before his "discovery" of semiotic methods of analysis, centered around the consequences of different types of texts for the kind of engagement with them required of the reader. During this period, these reflections were expanded to include texts generated by mass and popular culture. In the mid-1960s, Eco became acquainted with the analytical methods of structuralism and semiotics, and influenced equally by French structuralism and the American tradition of semiotics represented by Charles S. Peirce and Charles Morris, he ultimately produced his own elaborately developed approach in *A Theory of Semiotics* (1976). This work, a decided affirmation of the importance and usefulness of semiotic analysis, also included some crucial reflections on the limits of this type of approach, leading Eco to return once again to questions of reading and interpretation in *The Role of the Reader* (1979). Eco's intellectual odyssey has resulted in a suggestive hybrid of semiotic and reader-response forms of critique, which he has applied to a wide spectrum of cultural productions including literature, film, travel, politics, and history.

A continuous thread running through Eco's thought is a distinction between **open** and **closed texts**. He characterizes an open text or work as one that "tends to encourage 'acts of conscious freedom' on the part of the performer (and, we should add, interpreter) and place him at the focal point of a network of limitless interrelations, among which he chooses to set up his own form without being influenced by an external *necessity* which definitively prescribes the organization of the work in hand." By contrast, a closed work is one constructed in such a way as to minimize the range of interpretive choices, and hence the engagement of the performer or reader, by predetermining as many essential elements as possible. Eco sees openness as particularly characteristic of certain kinds of modern texts (especially of the avant-garde type) and cites as examples musical compositions by composers such as Stockhausen and Berio, in which the performer is required to choose the order of the notes or sections to be played; literary works such as Joyce's *Ulysses* and *Finnegan's Wake* and Mallarmé's *Livre*; and the mobiles of Calder. In contrast to these, most works of traditional art are more or less closed. Of course, in a somewhat different sense of these terms, all artistic works are open in that the reader is free to supply his or her own interpretation, and closed in that they constitute "unique organic wholes." What the modern open text (in the more specific sense with which Eco is concerned) explicitly highlights are the dramatic differences between the twentieth century worldview and those of preceding ages—that is, the modern tendency to see the world as a set of dynamic signs requiring completion through the virtually limitless processes of interpretation rather than as an already predetermined image or analogue of a static reality. In this new worldview, all texts, even the most traditional, come to be viewed as open, as parts of (as Eco might later say) a semiotic field demanding the active engagement of the reader.

In his *Theory of Semiotics* (1976) Eco appears to move in the opposite direction, offering a very complex and sophisticated framework for the analysis of sign-systems and their interrelations. It is important to note, however, that he regards semiotics as an enterprise with very definite limits, however fruitful it might be while operating inside them. In the short final chapter to this work, entitled "The Subject of Semiotics," Eco points out very explicitly that "semiotics cannot define these subjects [i.e., the actual persons involved in the process of communication] except in its own theoretical framework. . . . Either they can be defined in terms of semiotic structures or—from this point of view—they do not exist at all." This is not to deny that subjects are of the highest importance to the enterprise of cultural analysis and critique; but in order to deal with the "subject of semiotics" it is necessary to go "beyond the semiotic threshold"—toward, in Eco's case, a more hermeneutic or reader-centered inquiry.

Kristeva: Language and Desire

Julia Kristeva (b. 1941), a student of Roland Barthes and Lucien Goldmann as well as a practicing psychoanalyst, has explored yet another direction leading beyond the limits of Structuralist analysis. Dissatisfied with what she described as the "necrophiliac" tendencies of contemporary reflection on language, which has rendered it no more than an inert laboratory specimen awaiting dissection, Kris-teva outlined a new discipline that she called **semanalysis**. She characterized this discipline as a combination of semiology deriving from Saussure and of psycho-analysis as reinterpreted by Lacan (see next chapter). Semanalysis functions at the elusive and problematic point where the repressed desires of the Freudian uncon-scious find their way into expression in the significational structures of language, the point where the desiring organism of the human body develops into a dis-crete, self-conscious ego. It is this critical point that escaped both earlier semiol-ogy, focusing as it did on socially constructed and already objectively functioning codes, and psychoanalysis, directed primarily toward the prelinguistic dynamics of the unconscious. In Kristeva's words, semanalysis "conceives of meaning not as a sign-system but as a **signifying process**."

Kristeva used two other terms in *Revolution in Poetic Language* (1974) in a new way that is central to her enterprise. Giving each a dramatically different sense than they ordinarily possess, she distinguished between two heterogeneous ele-ments in signification: the **semiotic** and the **symbolic**. In her transformation of these terms, the *semiotic* is not to be confused with the discourse or methods of the same name, but instead indicates the basic drives recognized by psychoanaly-sis as they discharge themselves into language prior to any actual linguistic signifi-cation. Kristeva based her appropriation of this term on its Greek etymology, which includes the notions of "distinctive mark, trace, index, precursory sign," and so forth. By contrast, she employs the term *symbolic* to indicate the aspect of signification bound up with already established and functioning codes and rules of linguistic usage. Though she does not say this, one might suggest that her choice of this term also has an etymological basis: It indicates choosing or judging two or more things together, the basic process of forming a linguistic statement or proposition. At the level of language, the semiotic is particularly associated with the rhythm and tone of any act of signification, the symbolic with syntax, gram-mar, and the ability to form sentences communicating information to a receiver. Some languages, Kristeva suggests, can be purely semiotic, as is the case with mu-sic. Others can be characterized by various mixtures of the semiotic and symbolic aspects, like poetry, for example. Most important in this distinction, however, is Kristeva's constant insistence that language must always be approached as, in its first instance, the act of an **embodied subject**, not some formal system of codes, and that any use of language, even written communication removed from its au-thor, will still bear traces of its semiotic dimension.

Three particular features of the relation between the semiotic and symbolic di-mensions of signification are especially important to Kristeva's project. First, all instances of linguistic activity will be the products of interactions and adjust-ments between the unconscious desires of the subject and the formal structures constituting the various codes that it employs. Second, if we view the psychology of the subject developmentally, we can identify a **thetic** phase, which represents the point at which the semiotic impulses already at work in the body of the organism erupt into the symbolic order and break with the self-contained character of narcissistic desire. In other words, the thetic phase is the point at which the organism enters into the network of social linguistic codes, assumes a position there, and thus becomes a discrete individual. (In Freudian terminology, this would be the point at which the Ego begins to separate from the Id.) Not only would this be impossible without the prior functioning of the semiotic drives, but there would be no symbolic realm had the semiotic drives of the embodied organism not prepared its way. Third, once the "thetic rupture" has occurred, the possibility is opened for the semantic aspect to operate on the symbolic. This can be seen clearly in the manner in which poetry as well as the other arts employ various devices, such as metaphor, that tend to alter, disrupt, and even violate the codes operative in the symbolic dimension of language. Kristeva thus describes the relation between the semiotic and the symbolic as an "oscillation" in which the natural drives of the subject and the artificial codes of language mutually interact with one another in productive ways. She especially emphasizes the fact that the semiotic rupturing and subverting of the structures of the symbolic, as they occur in wordplay, poetry, and many other spheres of signification, are a primary source of pleasure, which leads back to the embodied, signifying subject, Kristeva's principal concern. On the basis of these ideas, Kristeva has played a very influential role in the development of French feminism, especially in her development of a new approach to ethics.

A consideration of recent contributors to Structuralist discourse such as Eco and Kristeva makes clear that while this tradition remains significant and vital to contemporary cultural critique, its inherent limitations also have been well recognized. As a result, Structuralist methods continue to play an important role in contemporary cultural critique, though generally embedded in some broader framework.

Bibliographic Essay

The Structuralist tradition has generated a daunting body of both theoretical and applied texts, ranging from treatments of significational systems in impenetrable formal languages to fanciful and entertaining arabesques on the most unlikely curiosities of popular culture. Fortunately, the foundational texts of Structuralism are relatively modest in number and for the most part quite readable. A good start would be *Semiotics: An Introductory Anthology,* ed. Robert E. Innis (Bloomington: Indiana University Press, 1985). This volume contains several essays and selections from longer works presenting many of the ideas discussed in this chapter. Of particular importance are the selections by Saussure, Lévi-Strauss, Jakobson, Barthes, and Eco. Additional basic reading should include Ferdinand de Saussure, *Course in General Linguistics* (New York: McGraw-Hill, 1966); Vladimir Propp, *Morphology of the Folktale* (Austin: University of Texas Press, 1968); Claude Lévi-Strauss, *Structural Anthropology* (Garden City, N.Y.: Anchor Books, 1967) and *The Savage Mind* (Chicago: University of Chicago Press, 1966); and Roland Barthes, *Mythologies* (New York: Hill and Wang, 1972) and *Elements of Semiology* (New York: Hill and Wang, 1967).

The last work, while difficult, is the most concise theoretical statement of the principal form in which Structuralist analysis has entered contemporary critical discourse; a careful study of it will repay the reader's effort. Its basic concepts are especially important as background for understanding poststructuralist critique.

The standard history of Russian formalism is Victor Erlich, *Russian Formalism: History-Doctrine* (The Hague: Mouton, 1955). The most representative collection of formalist works available in English is L. Matejka and K. Pomorska, eds., *Readings in Russian Poetics* (Cambridge, Mass.: MIT Press, 1971). Although there is no equivalent work on the history of French structuralism, Jonathan Culler's *Structuralist Poetics: Structuralism, Linguistics, and the Study of Literature* (Ithaca, N.Y.: Cornell University Press, 1975) could serve as a lucid and helpful start on such a project. Jacques Ehrmann, ed., *Structuralism* (New York: Anchor Books, 1970) is a useful anthology, charting the influence of Structuralist methods on a variety of diverse fields. For a survey of the range of application of semiotics as well as for a distinctive version of this approach, one can consult Umberto Eco, *A Theory of Semiotics* (Bloomington: Indiana University Press, 1979).

Among the many works written to introduce readers to this field, three are especially recommended: Terence Hawkes, *Structuralism and Semiotics* (Berkeley: University of California Press, 1977), Robert Scholes, *Structuralism in Literature: An Introduction* (New Haven: Yale University Press, 1974), and by the same author, *Semiotics and Interpretation* (New Haven: Yale University Press, 1982). While Scholes is mainly concerned with the area of literary studies, the latter work offers lucid examples that point toward greater generalization.

Since critically responding to Structuralism is a major preoccupation of poststructuralist discourse, we will indicate the relevant texts in the next chapter. However, an especially insightful and trenchant critique of Structuralism from a neo-Marxist standpoint can be found in Fredric Jameson, *The Prison-House of Language* (Princeton, N.J.: Princeton University Press, 1972). Jameson, it should be noted, is a major figure in the contemporary discussion of postmodernism, and this work forms the background for his later views on this topic. We have already discussed works by Eco and Kristeva, who, beginning from Structuralist standpoints, developed critical though sympathetic views of Structuralism. Eco's most fully developed work in this respect is *The Role of the Reader: Explorations in the Semiotics of Texts* (Bloomington: Indiana University Press, 1979). Kristeva's *Revolution in Poetic Language* (New York: Columbia University Press, 1984) is the first and most comprehensive statement of her views. For a sense of the breadth and influence of her later thought, the reader should also consult Toril Moi, ed., *The Kristeva Reader* (New York: Columbia University Press, 1986).

For readers interested in later Structuralist developments of a general theory of culture, Yuri Lotman's *Universe of the Mind: A Semiotic Theory of Culture* (Bloomington: Indiana University Press, 1990) might be consulted. In a quite different vein, Robert Hodge and Gunther Kress, *Social Semiotics* (Ithaca, N.Y.: Cornell University Press, 1988) represents an attempt to formulate a general Structuralist theory as a critique of ideology. This work is replete with concrete applications as well.

There are countless examples illustrating the application of Structuralist methods to specific cultural phenomena. The short essays written for the popular press and collected in the first part of Barthes's *Mythologies* are good starting points, though their informality and basis in French popular culture of the 1950s sometimes make it difficult to see clearly why he proceeds as he does. At the other extreme, Christian Metz has formulated a framework of staggering complexity with which to analyze film and has demonstrated its application in great detail in his *Film Language: A Semiotics of the Cinema* (New York: Oxford University Press, 1974). Two examples of works falling somewhere in between these extremes are Judith Williamson, *Decoding Advertisements: Ideology and Meaning in Advertising* (London: Marion Boyars, 1978) and Arthur Asa Berger, *Popular Culture Genres* (Newbury Park, Calif.: Sage, 1992). While neither is a pure example of the application of Structuralist methodology, both draw heavily on it and introduce its basic concepts with copious examples drawn from popular culture. Other individual essays employing Structuralist methods to analyze specific topics can be found in numerous journals and periodicals, including *Diacritics, Semiotica, Communications, Journal of Popular Culture,* and *Cultural Studies.* Beyond these, new titles continue to appear regularly.

7

Poststructuralist and Postmodernist Discourses

The critical discourses that we have considered so far typically present theoretical or methodological alternatives to other available discourses. With few exceptions, the practice of cultural critique has been founded on a constellation of assumptions, operative terms, and methodologies constituting an identifiable critical platform or stance that is arguably more adequate for cultural analysis and critique than other alternatives. In principle, at least, the more recent critical discourses of poststructuralism and postmodernism are aimed at something quite different. Their proponents wish decisively and finally to reject all recourse to some privileged and ultimately ahistorical theoretical or methodological stance in favor of a historically embedded and constantly open process of radical critique. This critical practice does take up other theoretical options, but only in order to reveal their internal instabilities and to challenge their implicit claims to historical privilege. Asserting that cultural productions, practices, and institutions are inseparable from basic assumptions and theories about them, these modes of critique are designed to show how any attempt to theorize culture objectively is already informed by its own cultural prejudices and becomes destabilized and self-undermining in the very process by which it attempts to conduct its critique.

More specifically, poststructuralist and postmodernist discourses maintain that cultural practices and theories about them both have a common root in manifold, complex, and ever shifting configurations of power. It is not the task of radical critique to propose yet another theoretical discourse but rather to force the specific configurations of power underlying any and all existing cultural discourses to show themselves. Because of this, it is difficult and even misleading to attempt to describe some characteristic theoretical or methodological position of these discourses. Rather, we should speak more of a set of shared attitudes and recurrent themes, and especially of critical strategies. Although the discourses included under these terms are sometimes in critical conflict with one another, they do share an archive of key texts, a range of stylistic similarities, and a set of common thematic emphases sufficient to allow them to be considered together.

No generally accepted account of the meaning of and relations among structuralism, modernism, poststructuralism, and postmodernism has yet emerged, despite the appearance of an extensive body of literature devoted to each. For present purposes, the following characterization is proposed, with the proviso that it represents one among a number of competing accounts, some of which will be considered later in this chapter. To begin with, it seems fair to say that **modernism** and **postmodernism** are terms that usually refer to large-scale historical and cultural trends, including various theoretical or philosophical views as well as developments in the visual arts, architecture, literature, politics, the media, technology, and so forth. More specifically, *modernism* has often been employed both in a historical sense, to indicate the period commencing with the Enlightenment in the seventeenth century and continuing into our own time, and in an aesthetic sense, to refer to a particular movement in the arts beginning in the late nineteenth or early twentieth century and continuing at least through World War II. Correspondingly, *postmodernism* has been used to signify both an alleged set of large-scale historical and cultural transformations thought to characterize the period beginning sometime after World War II as well as a more specific aesthetic reaction, especially in the visual arts, architecture, and literature, against the modernist aesthetic, which dominated much cultural production of the first half of the twentieth century.

By contrast, the terms **structuralism** and **poststructuralism** usually have a much more restricted signification. In Chapter 6, *structuralism* was defined as a methodology based on developments in linguistics in the early twentieth century and elaborated by such figures as Claude Lévi-Strauss and Roland Barthes into a distinctive type of approach in the social sciences and in cultural analysis. *Poststructuralism*, then, often indicates a set of specific critical responses to the theoretical assumptions and practical applications of structuralist methodology.

If this is a fair assessment, then we can regard structuralism as one among several movements or elements (probably the most recent) in the broader project of modernism (taken in either its historical or its aesthetic sense), and poststructuralism as one among several developments (probably the earliest) in the broader context of postmodernism. We might add that more specific textual strategies, such as Derrida's deconstruction and Foucault's genealogy, will appear in this framework as elements of the poststructuralist movement. In the present discussion, then, we will be employing these terms according to the schema shown in Figure 7.1.

It has frequently been observed that the structuralist/poststructuralist controversy was a defining feature especially of the French intellectual scene of the postwar era until 1968. The broader discussion of postmodernism, then, while arguably already underway in the arts, commenced in earnest in France and abroad only after the political agitation of the 1960s. While it would be misleading to assert some clear or definitive demarcation between poststructuralist and postmodernist discourses, there are enough differences in emphasis and outlook to warrant our presenting them somewhat independently.

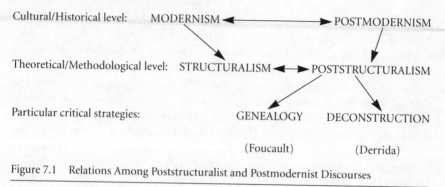

Figure 7.1   Relations Among Poststructuralist and Postmodernist Discourses

Poststructural Discourses: Decentering the Metaphysical Tradition

Historical Sources: Nietzsche and Heidegger

The most important historical forerunners of poststructuralist discourses were the German philologist and cultural critic **Friedrich Nietzsche** (1844–1900) and the philosopher **Martin Heidegger**, who had been deeply influenced by the thought of Nietzsche. (In the case of Heidegger, it should be noted that his earlier existential hermeneutic project was not as decisive for poststructuralists as was his global cultural critique that emerged in the early 1930s.) In fact, poststructuralism has often been characterized by various authors as either French Nietzscheanism or French Heideggerianism. The ideas and attitudes of these men that most influenced poststructuralist discourses are outlined below.

The Global Critique of Western Civilization.   Nietzsche was the first modern thinker to undertake a radical, comprehensive, and sustained critique of what has come to be called the Western tradition. According to Nietzsche, Plato's well-known distinction between an unchanging intellectual world of ideas and a mutable, perceptible world of change or flux established the fundamental opposition that would dominate the course of European thought and history. In Nietzsche's reading of Plato, this distinction was the first by which the real world, the world from which our biological life arises and in which we function as earthly beings, was devalued in contrast to a better or more perfect other world. Christianity, which Nietzsche once referred to as "Platonism for the masses," built on this essentially Platonic opposition in its doctrines of the fallenness of the temporal world and the need to deny and mortify the physical body in this life in order to gain a heavenly reward in the next. For Nietzsche, although the skeptical attacks of modernity on religion managed to undermine belief in the other world, they did not succeed in restoring to this world the meaning or value that Platonism and Christianity had so long denied it. The result was **nihilism**, a sense of meaninglessness and valuelessness that pervaded the whole of Western civilization, which Nietzsche aptly expressed in his notorious phrase "God is dead."

The turning point in Heidegger's thought from an essentially phenomenological to a globally critical project occurred, at least in part, as a result of his exhaustive study of Nietzsche. Nietzsche's indictment of Western culture generally took the form of a critique of morality and its religious and political foundations, but Heidegger saw the ethical nihilism of European culture as a symptom of something deeper. According to Heidegger, classical Greek philosophy and especially Plato had effected a decisive and historically portentous transformation in the meanings of *being* and *truth*. Heidegger maintained that prior to the foundation of Western metaphysics as the dominant philosophical discipline in Plato and Aristotle, thinking was a process by which the "meaning of Being" was uncovered and disclosed in the "openness" of its truth, as expressed in the earlier Greek poets, tragedians, and pre-Socratic philosophers. With Plato and Aristotle, however, the meaning of Being gradually became identified with various kinds of particular beings, including a "highest being," or god; and truth became not an open process of the disclosure of meaning but a logical function of individual propositions referring to the various kinds of beings making up the world. In Heidegger's analysis, the inception of Western philosophy, or metaphysics, which he took to be the ultimately defining feature of the Western tradition, represented the opening of an **ontological difference** between Being and beings, where beings became the sole focus of philosophical concern and Being as their ground became covered over and ultimately inaccessible to philosophy. From this fateful gesture flowed both the Christian identification of ultimate Being with God as the "highest being" and modern science as the rigorously methodological project of classifying and explaining all types of beings. The final stage appeared with the technological application of the sciences to the control of nature, and soon after, of human affairs.

In Heidegger's account, nihilism was inscribed in the origins of Western culture at the point where thought was barred from raising the most important question of all, that of the meaning of Being. The final result was the nihilism of the contemporary world, where science and technology, acting as virtually autonomous forces, had finally achieved dominance over all human affairs, while human beings themselves had lost any sense of meaning or value in their increasingly administrated and regimented lives. For Heidegger, the path beyond nihilism lay in the direction of a global critique of Western civilization, aimed at dismantling its deepest and most fundamental assumptions in order to clear the way for a new relation between Being and human being to emerge. What was required was not another philosophy or ideology, but new and more authentic ways of experiencing, speaking, and thinking than those dictated by logic, science, and the modern technological attitude.

As Heidegger developed this line of reflection, his writings became increasingly poetic and even mystical. Although the poststructuralists generally declined to follow Heidegger in this respect and in many ways remained closer to Nietzsche's critical stance, they adopted his general conviction that Western culture was ultimately defined by the discipline of philosophy, that European philosophy was essentially metaphysical, and that any critical project must be concerned, first and foremost, with destabilizing and dismantling the ensemble of assumptions and attitudes that were associated with Western metaphysics.

The Will to Truth and the Will to Power.　In his own search for the underlying mechanism driving the nihilistic trajectory of Western civilization, Nietzsche had asserted that although Western philosophy and its offshoots were characterized by a **will to truth**, this was but a historical variant of a more fundamental and universal principle, the **will to power.** In Nietzsche's analysis, the will to power was not merely a function of the desires of individual human beings but was itself a metaphysical principle defining all of nature, society, and even being, inasmuch as every being must be viewed as ultimately striving to maintain its existence by carving out its own metaphysical sphere of influence. Heidegger, for his part, tended to see Nietzsche's notion of the will to power as the culmination of Western metaphysics, the last great metaphysical idea expressing the ultimate meaning of the Western tradition, thus preparing the way for the dawning of new relations between Being and human being beyond the dictates of power.

For the poststructuralists, Nietzsche's will to power, as interpreted by Heidegger, suggested that the ultimate aim of global critique was to reveal how all cultural discourses, institutions, and practices, however innocent they might appear on the surface, were based on particular configurations of power and served to support and promote those configurations. While the Marxist tradition, with which most poststructuralists were at least somewhat sympathetic, shared something of this attitude in its theory of ideology, most poststructuralists tended to view the Marxist analysis of power in terms of economics, politics, and class structure as too restrictive to allow access to the most basic cultural levels in which power relations were insinuated and sustained. For them, questions of power were not merely features or side effects of a particular historical form of economic organization but were fundamental to any and all forms of social organization and discourse in ways that continually outstrip and defy any strictly political critique.

The Centrality of Language.　As in so much else, Nietzsche had prefigured the poststructuralist critical project in his famous assertion, in a fragment of 1873, that truth is

> a mobile army of metaphors, metonyms, and anthropomorphisms—in short, a sum of human relations, which have been enhanced, transposed, and embellished poetically and rhetorically, and which after long use seem firm, canonical, and obligatory to a people: truths are illusions about which one has forgotten that this is what they are; metaphors which are worn out and without sensuous power; coins which have lost their pictures and now matter only as metal, no longer as coins.

In a later reflection, Heidegger claimed that "language is the house of Being," insisting that the primary basis for the hold that Western metaphysics exercised over human experience and thought must be sought in its insinuation into our modes of discourse, and that the means of recovering the question of the meaning of Being must be established first and foremost in a new view of and relation to language.

In placing discourse and its concrete functioning in various texts at the center of their critical project, the poststructuralists drew on both Nietzsche's and Heidegger's insights. They viewed the connection between discourses and human relations as so intimate that the critique of the mechanisms operative in texts was tantamount to a critique of culture itself. Indeed, for the poststructuralists, *culture was the complex interplay of its discourses.* To critique culture was to reveal the manner in which the various devices employed in and across its texts manifested specific configurations of power, privileging certain terms, metaphors, and rhetorical figures while suppressing others equally essential to the meaning of the texts. Radical critique thus was aimed at revealing the "illusion of truth" created by cultural texts, laying bare the processes of privileging and marginalizing out of which they are constructed, and showing that the dominant terms and metaphors would lack all significance without those very determinations that they attempt to conceal and suppress. In other words, if language is a set of metaphors that become fixed as objective terms or true concepts when their metaphorical origins are forgotten, then the task of radical critique is to demystify their pretensions of stating the objective truth, by revealing their historical, contingent, and arbitrary genealogies.

We should note that the often seemingly impenetrable and idiosyncratic style of much poststructuralist critique is directly related to this view of language. Since the poststructuralists believed that language is essentially a complex and dynamic interplay of linguistic and rhetorical figures rather than something analyzable as a set of truth-bearing propositions, and since they wished to avoid at all costs the construction of yet another "true" or "conceptual" discourse, which would lead them into the very trap that they sought to critique, then their own style of presentation became an overriding and decisive issue. For the poststructuralists, the style of their critical discourses was rarely an arbitrary or capricious choice but rather was a vehicle for instantiating, mirroring, inverting, or playing with the terms of the cultural discourse being critiqued. An old joke asks, What do you get when you cross a poststructuralist with a mafioso? Answer: An offer you can't understand. While many on first reading might see some truth in this, the more serious point is that given the poststructuralist project of open-ended, radical critique, we could expect nothing else. Rather than attempting to state some true theses about a text under consideration, the basic poststructuralist strategy employed stylistic devices, deflections, and deviations in order (ideally) to teach the reader how to read and critique the text for her or himself, not to convince the reader of some true or objective textual interpretation. Whether such a strategy always, often, or even sometimes succeeds remains open to question.

Strategies of Decentering. As the modernist poet W. B. Yeats wrote around the turn of this century, "Things fall apart, the centre cannot hold; mere anarchy is loosed upon the world." Taken in a certain sense, this could well serve as the motto for the dominant critical strategies of the poststructuralists. Perhaps the best starting point for understanding the strategies of "decentering" employed by the poststructuralists is a brief glance at the philosophical system of G.W.F. Hegel, which is often regarded as the final and culminating synthesis of the Western metaphysical tradition. Hegel's grand philosophical synthesis was based on three inextricably interrelated claims.

First, referring to the development of modern philosophy beginning with Descartes's notion of the thinking self and its subsequent development by the German idealists Kant, Fichte, and Schelling, Hegel saw the crowning moment of the Western tradition as the final achievement of self-consciousness, that is, of human consciousness or subjectivity becoming aware of itself as the source of all reality, truth, and being. In his view, whereas Socrates had established the fundamental agenda of Western philosophy in the dictum "Know thyself," it was only in the post-Christian, modern world that this exhortation was finally fulfilled. Hegel thus established, in its most extreme form, the idea that consciousness or subjectivity, which in modernity had become fully self-transparent and lucid to itself, was the center of all truth and being, the ultimate, firm, and irrefutable court that must adjudicate all claims of truth, meaning, and human value. Nothing existed for him that could defy or resist absorption into the absolute and closed circle that self-consciousness represented: The self-conscious subject had no "outside" and no "other" and hence signified the true incarnation of the divine on earth, which Christianity had already anticipated, although in merely figurative or symbolic terms.

Closely related to these ideas was Hegel's view of culture and especially of philosophy as culture's highest manifestation. According to Hegel, the true and enduring monuments of Western civilization were the ideas and systems of Hegel's canon of great philosophers, each of which gave expression to his own age in the ultimate form of pure conceptual thought. That is, each embodied the highest self-consciousness or subjectivity of which his epoch was capable. Fundamental to his interpretation of culture and history was the conviction that all cultural texts were, in the final analysis, essentially philosophical and hence rational, since they all manifested to a greater or lesser degree the "truth" expressed most clearly by the philosophy of the age. For Hegel, however, to view a text as rational implied that it was an internally coherent, organic unity, articulating a single dominant idea or thought that informed and animated all of its parts. In other words, texts, interpreted according to the paradigm of Hegelian philosophy, should be approached as totally transparent media communicating directly and without distortion the rational, unitary thought of the author to the reader. For a philosophically self-conscious interpreter capable of grasping the essence or unitary concept animating a text, the particular textual details of content or style were irrelevant to its philosophical meaning and significance, which could only be coherent, unitary, and rational. Thus, Hegel's view of texts as rational, unitary, and centered was an exact counterpart of his notion of the self-conscious subject as the ultimate source of all texts.

Finally, this implied that history could never be adequately viewed as merely contingent sequences of empirical events or even as a complex texture of various traditions. Rather, history for Hegel was nothing less that the unitary, necessary, and rational unfolding in time of the development of the self-conscious subject of modern philosophy. The history of philosophy constituted the true essence and paradigm of history itself, and genuine history could only be conceptual and rational. At times, in fact, Hegel went so far as to describe history as the coming to self-consciousness of a universal, transpersonal "world spirit," constituting a single, unified, and undeviating narrative of preordained progress, which constantly overcomes all contingency and opposition by absorbing them into itself. To view history in this way was, in Hegel's famous phrase, to see that "the real is the rational and the rational is the real," and to interpret historical texts was merely to determine the particular role that they played in this overarching teleological process of the development of self-conscious subjectivity.

Although the comprehensive philosophy that Hegel articulated was abandoned by the generations of thinkers succeeding him, the basic convictions on which it was based continued to exercise their influence. Even otherwise anti-Hegelian movements as Marxism, phenomenology, and existentialism continued to rely on notions of a historically conscious subject, texts expressing unitary and coherent intentions of an author, and history as involving some overarching meaning or significance. In the broadest sense, the poststructuralists sought to lay these remnants of Western metaphysics to rest once and for all by pursuing critical strategies specifically designed to decenter these central metaphysical notions.

While the three major poststructuralists whom we will discuss have all, at one point or another, critically addressed each of these central ideas, their discourses have tended to focus on one in particular, and this aspect will be emphasized in what follows. It should also be noted that there has been a good deal of cross-fertilization between their critical discourses, so that any attempt clearly to demarcate their views from one another might be misleading. In what follows, then, we will consider the ideas of the revisionist Freudian psychoanalyst **Jacques Lacan** (1901–1981) as paradigmatic of a strategy aimed at decentering the notion of the **subject**; the work of **Jacques Derrida** (b. 1930) as it addresses the deconstruction of **texts**; and the archaeological and genealogical strategies of **Michel Foucault** (1926–1984), directed at destabilizing metaphysical assumptions about **history**. Before considering these critics individually, however, it will be helpful to review how structuralism provided the proximate background for the emergence of poststructuralist discourses.

From Structuralism to Poststructuralism

Structuralism originated in the linguistic writings of theorists such as Saussure and Jakobson and was developed by Lévi-Strauss as a methodology for cultural analysis in anthropology. By the 1950s, particularly in France, its influence had spread not only to other disciplines in the social sciences but via further narratological and semiotic elaborations by figures such as Barthes to fields such as literary criticism, historiography, and even philosophy. In France it was the dominant critical discourse of that decade, displacing the phenomenological and existential approaches of the 1940s. While some practitioners of structuralist discourse such as Barthes had already began to push beyond its inherent limitations by the mid-1950s, a new generation of critics, fortified by readings of Nietzsche, Heidegger, and a more literary tradition including **Maurice Blanchot** (b. 1907) and **Georges Bataille** (1897–1962), began to emerge in the late 1950s and early 1960s. These poststructuralist critics had much larger goals than merely the dismantling of structuralism, but since this was the dominant discourse of the day, it was a natural target for their critical strategies at this early stage. In general, the poststructuralists tended to regard structuralism as the latest form that all the metaphysical assumptions undergirding the Western tradition had assumed, so the dismantling of structuralist attitudes served as their initial access to the broader critique of Western metaphysics, which was their overarching concern.

The principal objection of the poststructuralists to structuralism was the latter's assumption that a clear line of demarcation could be drawn between the **surface structure** of a text or phenomenon and its underlying **deep structure**. To the poststructuralists, such a distinction merely reaffirmed the traditional metaphysical differentiations between becoming and being, opinion and truth, appearance and reality, phenomenon and noumenon, and so forth, with the latter term always being privileged. Instead, the poststructuralists wished to emphasize that like all of these others, each term is completely dependent on the other, so that the assumed difference between surface structure and deep structure is itself a product of the play of signification, not some real or ultimate difference. Not only must the structuralists' deep structures intrude on and reveal themselves at the surface level, but the surface level tends to defy, break apart, and cancel out the alleged logic of the deep structures. More concretely, for the poststructuralists, the meaning of any text is not to be sought in some dimension of depth behind or beneath the text itself, but in the constantly shifting play of signification of the text's own elements.

Among the more specific structuralist doctrines clustered around this assumed difference that the poststructuralists wished to challenge, the following deserve special mention.

The Relation Between Signifier and Signified.   One of the basic tenets of structuralism stemming from Saussure was the definition of a sign as the relation between a signifier and a signified, where the latter is regarded as a mental concept. Saussure maintained that this relation was arbitrary in the sense that there was no natural connection lying at its basis; however, once the association between signifier and signified had been established, the resulting sign tended to be viewed in the structuralist perspective as a relatively stable unit in the linguistic system.

Against this, the poststructuralists proposed a notion sometimes called the **sliding signified** (or its counterpart, the **sliding signifier**). Their idea was that in the actual use of language, the relations between signifiers and signifieds were constantly in flux, shifting and sliding so that various occurrences of the same signifier in different contexts or in different historical periods could expand, contract, or even dramatically alter in relation to the signifieds associated with it. Characteristically, the poststructuralists pointed to literary uses of language, especially poetic and rhetorical figures, to emphasize the essentially creative and indeterminate nature of signification in contrast to its structuralist ossification. Above all, they pointed to such devices as metaphor and metonymy as more characteristic of the actual nature of language than the literalism that often characterized the structuralist outlook. From the poststructuralist point of view, the sort of linguistic structures that the structuralists were describing were, as Nietzsche claimed, the residues of metaphors and other figurative uses of language that through constant repetition and circulation had lost their poetic patina. Genuine signification, they wished to assert, was Protean and ever changing, a quality that could not be captured by exclusive attention to stable linguistic structures.

The Langue/Parole Distinction and the Problem of Closure.   Along the same trajectory, the poststructuralists rejected the rigidity of the structuralist distinction between language as a system and speech. The poststructuralist view of the sliding relation between signifier and signified implied that the meaning-possibilities of a linguistic system could not be isolated from the actual uses of language in which this shifting occurred. Rather, the system itself was constantly being destabilized by new and innovative connections forged between signifiers and signifieds in the actual occurrences of linguistic acts. A language, therefore, was never a fixed, given, and closed matrix of possibilities for signification from which actual acts of speaking must select, but at best, a historical archive of linguistic innovations from which some possibilities were constantly being dropped as others were added.

The poststructuralists singled out for special criticism the structuralist assumption of the **closure** *(clôture)* of linguistic systems or texts generated from them, viewing this as a remnant of a paradigmatically metaphysical way of thinking. To this, they opposed a view of language and texts as radically open and **polysemic**, that is, conveying multiple meanings and susceptible to manifold interpretations. Language and texts were open spaces for the play of signification, not classical monuments demanding reverent contemplation.

Synchrony and Diachrony.   The structuralist outlook clearly privileged analyses focusing on the synchronic (cotemporal) dimension of languages, texts, or cultures over those attending to their historical, diachronic development. The poststructuralists had no desire to reinstate chronological historical narrative, but they were concerned with pointing out the artificiality and inadequacy of the distinction between synchrony and diachrony. Clearly, a "slice of time" is an abstraction from a more dynamic process, just as any dynamic process can be frozen at any given point to yield a temporal cross-section for structural analysis. The two are always, as it were, the recto and verso of the same phenomenon. More to the point for the poststructuralists, however, just as the systematic configurations sought by the structuralists' preferred synchronic analyses were actually an illusion produced by suppressing the play of signification, so the apparent continuity over time produced by diachronic analyses based on the structuralist model was an equally artificial effect of its operative assumptions. Not only were language and its texts open and polysemic when considered in themselves, but the history of their production, reception, and mutual influence could not be charted along some continuous or seamless arc. Rather, the poststructuralists wished to maintain that various linguistic productions and texts mutually influence one another over time in quite arbitrary and unpredictable ways, borrowing from one another, commenting on one another, and often undermining one another's apparent meaning. The poststructuralists sometimes used the term **intertextuality** to call attention to the interplay of texts over time, rejecting any notion of some overarching historical process of development while allowing the possibility of various localized islands of mutual influence and opposition.

Writing as Paradigmatic for Language. Saussure, like most of the tradition preceding him, viewed writing merely as a "sign of a sign," a sort of second-order or supplemental device for encoding spoken language with no genuine linguistic significance of its own. As a result, writing never appeared as an important theme in the structuralist program. The poststructuralists were quick to note that the suppression of writing was a typical feature of the Western metaphysical tradition that had been carried over into structuralism. While we will consider this in more detail in discussing the deconstructive strategies of Jacques Derrida, we should note here two important results of the poststructuralist reversal of the relative importance accorded by the structuralists to spoken and written language. First, the privileging of spoken over written language, of a living voice over a silent inscription, naturally induced the structuralists to speculate on some ultimate location or source of the structures in question in either the human mind or its conceptual (and hence metaphysical) thought processes. Lévi-Strauss himself occasionally entertained the notion that the structures he studied might be fixed and invariant features of human psychology or culture, thus implying the sort of essentialist view that the poststructuralists (and others) wished decisively to reject. Second, the assumption that speaking rather than writing was the paradigmatic occurrence of language tended to reinforce the theoretical blindness of the structuralists to the play and polysemy of signification by encouraging the idea that the meaning of any statement could, in principle, be clarified and fixed by further interrogation of the speaker. Although this is not possible in the case of most written texts, the idea of the presence of the meaning-authenticating speaker naturally carried over into the idea of writing. The result was that structuralists tended to understand texts as they did the language system itself, as closed and unitary totalities with a definite meaning corresponding to the intentional choices of an author in constructing the text.

For the poststructuralists, writing provided a much more adequate paradigm for understanding the actual functioning of language. In the most basic sense, writing presents itself as an array of physical marks on a surface separated by various spaces and other purely visual punctuation devices, usually in contexts where their producer is absent and unavailable for clarification. The very materiality of writing manifests its artificially constructed nature and its inevitable play between the "presence" of its signs and the "absence" of its spacings, that is, by the fact that it is a not a closed totality but a polysemic construction with many "open" points of interpretive entry and exit. Further, the absence of the author as an "authority" over her or his own inscriptions places the central emphasis on the activity of the reader in attempting to decipher, recode, and play with the written text in her or his own interpretive context, not merely to reproduce some intended meaning of the author, fixed by her or his choice of the structural possibilities available in a language.

Decentering the Subject: Jacques Lacan's Readings of Freud

Jacques Lacan (1901–1981), by training and lifelong vocation a practicing psychoanalyst as well as a theorist, was the first to employ many of the critical strategies that came to be associated with poststructuralism. This he did in the context of his central concern: the recovery of Freud's fundamental insights through a sustained and meticulous reading of his texts. Lacan began to emerge as an important if controversial figure in the psychoanalytic movement in the 1930s, well before the appearance of any distinctly poststructuralist discourses. At an early stage he came to view structuralist linguistics as the key to unlocking Freud's own most profound insights regarding the dynamics of the human psyche, claiming that Freud himself had often arrived at essentially structuralist views even though he could not yet have had access to their full development. However, as Lacan's structuralist reading of Freud progressed, it became clear to him both that Freud's own stated views tended to significantly qualify and limit structuralist methods as they were originally developed and that such a reading demanded certain revisions in at least the letter if not the spirit of Freud's texts. Thus, Lacan's reading of Freudian psychoanalytic texts from the standpoint of structuralist linguistics tended to destabilize both, anticipating as it did many of the attitudes, styles, and strategies that would later come to characterize poststructuralism.

The proximate motivation for Lacan's attempt to recover Freud was his conviction that the institutionalized psychoanalytic orthodoxy that had developed by the 1930s, as it was most conspicuously represented by the International Psychoanalytical Association, had transformed Freud's essentially open, rich, and multidimensional insights, concepts, and terms into rigid and petrified doctrines.

When applied in clinical practice, Lacan began to see its human results as a mere reprogramming of automatons to be reinserted back into the same contexts that to a great degree had created their symptoms to begin with. For Lacan, the crux of the issue was the tendency of "ego psychologists" to assume, wrongly citing Freud in their support, a model of the human subject or self as potentially unified, rational, and in control of the "dark forces" represented by the unconscious—in other words, as a version of the subject already delineated in the metaphysical tradition. The heart of Lacan's critical project was to recover in Freud's writings a notion of the "subject of psychoanalysis" as irreducibly multivalent, dynamic, open, and decentered. As it turned out, Lacan's antimetaphysical view of the self would become the starting point for most later poststructuralist stances, just as his readings of Freud in critical juxtaposition with structuralist linguistics would provide models for later poststructuralist textual strategies.

While Lacan's thought, like Freud's, ranged over many topics and many disciplines both theoretical and applied, we will concentrate here on the aspects that are most relevant to his decentering of the coherent, unified self.

The Linguistic Unconscious. In one of his most famous statements, Lacan asserted that "the unconscious is structured like a language." Citing Freud's earlier works, such as *The Interpretation of Dreams,* Lacan wished to challenge any notion (which could admittedly sometimes be found in Freud, especially in the later writings) that the unconscious was merely an inchoate and irrational reservoir of repressed energy or an inarticulate seat of purely biological instincts or drives. In such a model, which was characteristic of Freudian orthodoxy, the unconscious was conceived of as the antithesis of the preconscious-conscious system, which was the seat of linguistic expression, articulation, and ultimately rationality. Lacan was convinced that if this were really the case—if the unconscious could never reveal itself in manifest linguistic processes—then it must remain unknown and inaccessible both to the client and to the psychoanalyst. Lacan thought that Freud had attempted to make this point but had lacked the sort of linguistic theory that would allow him to demonstrate it decisively. However, drawing on the notion of the sliding signified of structuralist linguistics, Lacan attempted to analyze how language itself involved the constant configuring and reconfiguring of signifiers in relation to their signifieds, such that unconscious desires and motivations were constantly being revealed in the very texture of conscious discourse.

One particularly important result of Lacan's notion of the linguistic unconscious was his challenge to orthodox clinical practice based on its interpretation of Freud's famous dictum, "Where Id was, there Ego shall be." This dictum suggested to orthodox clinicians that the principal task of the analyst was to assist the client's ego in making conscious to itself what had been repressed into the unconscious, that is, in reclaiming on behalf of the conscious ego territory that had been taken over by repressed and unconscious drives and instincts, producing neurotic or psychotic symptoms. Lacan disputed this way of understanding Freud, arguing instead that in the process of psychoanalysis, it was not merely the conscious ego that the analyst must address but a complex symbolic construction, or subject, which even in Freud's mind was decentered and could never be identified solely with the ego, which was merely one element of a broader schema.

Ego, Subject, and the Other: Lacan's L-Schema.   Two of Lacan's most important insights, based on his refusal to identify the subject with the ego, were that both ego and subject are formed from the very beginning, not by biological drives originating in the human organism, but by encounters with something radically "other" than themselves, and that the subject, instead of the creator of language, is more fundamentally its creature. To see the force of this, consider what we mean when we use the personal pronoun *I* to refer to ourselves. The first thing to notice is that this signifier can indicate a number of different things, depending on the context in which it is used. It is, in other words, a paradigm of a sliding signifier. Sometimes this word serves to indicate the ensemble of my desires, fears, aspirations, and so forth, as when I say, "I am afraid of the dark" or "I don't like noisy people." At the other extreme, it can serve to indicate who I am in a social context, as in "I am a graduate of Yale University" or "I am a Republican." In the former case, the *I* speaks as the ego, giving expression to a desire that might be part of a much larger and in some sense mainly unconscious ensemble of motives, emotions, preferences, and the like. In the latter, the subject is taking a place already prepared for it in a larger linguistic and culturally determined set of signifiers. Clearly, the discourses of the desiring ego and the socialized subject intersect and influence one another at many points, but the main idea here is that it makes no sense to ask which *I* is more real or actual: In some sense, I am simultaneously both and neither, or I am the dynamic and continual interplay between both of these and their various intersections. And, in either case, my being an *I* presupposes that I have already entered the domain of language where the signifier *I* receives its meaning in the chain of other signifiers.

Lacan offered a diagram that he called the **L-schema** as his "map" of the set of relations that constitute the decentered self (see Figure 7.2).

To explain the axis o'-o, which Lacan called the **imaginary relation**, he invoked one of his own early contributions to psychoanalysis, the **mirror stage**. Sometime between the ages of 6 and 18 months, the human infant, which until then is, psychologically speaking, an undifferentiated totality with no sense of separation between its body and the external world, encounters its own image in a mirror (or some other device, such as the mother's gaze), by which a sense of its body as objectified and external is reflected back to it. When this occurs, the infant perceives its counterpart as simultaneously separate from and yet the same as itself. While it experiences a sense of jubilation in seeing itself as unified, to a degree that its own level of motor coordination does not yet actually allow it, it also feels a sense of envy and rivalry with its image. The ego is thus formed in the ambivalent process by which the infant both identifies with its image and experiences a sense of

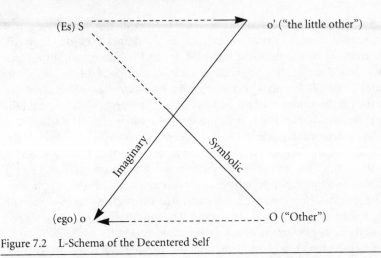

Figure 7.2   L-Schema of the Decentered Self

threat from it. The primary ambivalence and fragility of the ego established at the mirror stage will henceforth carry over into all identifications with other persons or objects ("the little others"), which will henceforth be experienced as *lacks* or *absences* that nonetheless, through identification, define the ego. In this sense, the ego is not something substantial in itself but is rather the lack or absence of the objects of its identifications: The ego is, literally, what it is not. Lacan called this axis or plane the imaginary relation, not because it has to do with the imagination as usually understood but because it functions in the realm of images that are idealized as objects with which the ego identifies.

Contrasted to but intersecting the imaginary axis is the **symbolic plane**, represented by the line S-O in the L-schema. In acquiring the ability to speak, the infant becomes inserted into a preexisting linguistic and cultural system and all that this implies, which Lacan called "the Other" (with a capital O). Again, just as the "little other" served to determine the ego through its absence, so the "big Other" presents a context in which the already determined position of subject must be assumed. Lacan labeled this symbolic plane "unconscious," consistent with his conviction that the unconscious is "structured like a language." In the act of speaking, of mobilizing one signifier after another, the subject is constantly being constrained and determined by the Other, the ensemble of linguistic and cultural codes that provides it a place, without being aware at any given moment of the operation of these laws in so situating it. It is as if the Other repeatedly recedes or hides itself in its totality as the subject proceeds from one signifier to the next. This hidden but constantly operative symbolic system of the Other constitutes the Lacanian unconscious.

Two important results that follow from this are indicated by the broken horizontal lines at the top and bottom of the L-schema. First, because the imaginary plane intersects with the symbolic, the linguistic discourse of the subject is constantly being deflected by the identifications of the ego with the "little others" that are the objects of its ambivalence, as indicated by the dotted lines in the top half of the diagram. These are the same interruptions and deviations within the discourse of a clinical subject that Freud observed in jokes, slips of the tongue, poetic figures, and above all, dreams—phenomena that he believed gave him privileged access to the psychodynamics of his patients. Second, Lacan held that beyond the primary identifications of the infant, the symbolic order (in other words, the Other) plays a determining role in the subsequent formation of the subject's desires (roughly, the top horizontal line) as well as in the further identifications of the ego (the bottom horizontal line). Not only is the subject determined by the place it comes to occupy in the symbolic order through signification, but the symbolic order in turn determines the subsequent structure of the desires of the self, providing it with its objects (the "little others") and underwriting its urgency and force through further determinations of the ego's identifications.

According to Lacan's L-schema, then, what the metaphysical tradition regarded as a unified self becomes multiply displaced and decentered. Not only is the psyche split between subject and ego—that is, a socialized self and a seat of identification and desire—but each is in turn spread out in the direction of the lacking other of desire and the continually escaping Other, which is the unconscious basis for language itself. In this fourfold field, there is no fixed point that could finally be identified with a unitary metaphysical self; rather, there are only the constant shifts, substitutions, and play among signifiers in which the four poles of the psyche reveal themselves in constantly varying combinations. We should especially note that for Lacan, there is no biological or psychological essence of the self that grounds this process, only the intersection of desire and culture mediated by the ongoing process of signification.

Beyond Biology: Lacan's Theory of Human Sexuality.   Lacan's account of sexuality has provided the primary channel through which his broader theory of the decentered self has been used in concrete critical analyses. It has been extremely controversial, both because its own complexity and Lacan's manner of presenting it have spawned much disagreement as to what he actually intended, and because many readers, especially some feminists, have found in it much that seems objectionable. Perhaps the best way to understand Lacan's theory of sexuality is to view it as an attempt to develop the linguistic and symbolic dimensions implicit (so Lacan thinks) in the Freudian account of sexuality. Whereas Freud tended to couch his discussions of sexuality in terms of the influence of biological factors on the development of sexual identity and differentiation, Lacan viewed this process as occurring primarily in the symbolic field of signification. While biological factors are never completely absent from Lacan's account, cultural determinations loom much larger in his view than they did in that of Freud.

Lacan agreed with Freud in locating the critical moment of sexual identification and differentiation at the stage of the Oedipal complex. To present his view of this

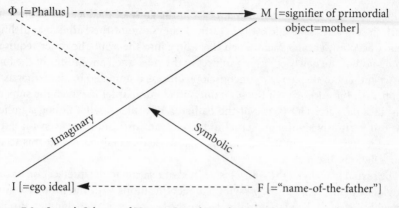

Figure 7.3   Lacan's Schema of Human Sexual Development

moment, Lacan offered a somewhat more complicated fourfold diagram overlaid on his L-schema; but for our present purposes, his major points can be made by employing the structure with which we are already familiar (see Figure 7.3).

Beginning with the imaginary plane (here, I-M), which is presymbolic and pre-social, the path leading to human sexual development, like the original formation of the ego, begins in the mirror stage. As mentioned earlier, Lacan understood the mirror not as necessarily a physical object but as anything that reflects an image of the infant back to it, setting in motion the process of identification, experience of lack, and ambivalent response that we have already described. In most cases, the gaze of the mother on the infant plays a central role in the earliest stages of the formation of the ego. As Freud had noted, the original identification of the infant with the mother (here, as always, understood as a signifying place or a function, not necessarily the biological parent) is highly problematic, given the infant's experience of the alternating presence and absence of its primary object of identification. Lacan viewed the ego ideal formed in this process at the prelinguistic and presocial level as structured by the other encountered as object of identification and at the same time as lack or absence. In his terms, M[=Mother] must be understood not as some particular individual or any associated biological functions but as a sliding signifier that assumes different values or meanings in a broader system of signification.

Intersecting this imaginary plane of primary identification with the Mother-signifier is the symbolic plane, which commences its operation with the infant's entry into the linguistic and cultural sphere. Lacan understood this critical point, where presymbolic identifications give way to identifications mediated by linguistic signification, as the onset of the Oedipal complex. In his discussion of the origin of sexual identity, Lacan maintained that the Other, that is, the preexisting linguistic and cultural systems in which the speaking subject must take its place, also determines the symbolic processes by which the subject acquires its sexual identity. Lacan called the Other, which appears in the guise of the locus or context in which the subject's sexual identity is formed, the **Name-of-the-Father**. Paralleling Freud's account, Lacan's maintained that entry into the symbolic order requires submission of the newly emerging subject to the rules and conventions of the linguistic and cultural sphere, an unconscious process dominated by the father as a signifier for the authority of the symbolic and cultural order in which the subject must take its place. This Name-of-the-Father is, of course, itself a sliding signifier that can variously signify an actual individual, an institution, or even (at later stages) a divine and omnipotent being (Lacan deliberately borrowed this term from religious discourse).

The sexual identity of the subject is defined in relation to the intersection of the imaginary plane, defined by presymbolic identifications with the Mother-signifier, with the symbolic plane, dominated by the law of the Father-signifier. Probably the most difficult and controversial of Lacan's ideas is his characterization of the sexualized subject in terms of the **Phallus**. Whereas Freud saw the crucial moment of the formation of sexual identity as the infant's realization that it either possessed or lacked a penis, thus leading to separate courses of sexual identification for males and females with the father or mother, Lacan insisted that the Phallus not be identified simply with a biological organ: Like other Lacanian terms, *Phallus* is a sliding signifier. Lacan's association of the socialized subject with the signifier *Phallus* indicates that the Oedipus complex hinges less on a purely biological fact than on a series of problematic and ambivalent identifications with the Name-of-the-Father. The *Phallus*, as Lacan employed this term, signifies the process by which the socialized subject "inserts" itself into the symbolic and cultural sphere as an already sexualized (or perhaps better described as "gendered") speaker and signifier. While the Freudian focus on the biological fact of the possession or lack of a penis is not irrelevant to this process, sexual identity has far more to do with the manner in which the gendered subject is determined by and relates, on the imaginary plane, to objects of desire, and connects on the symbolic plane with the linguistic and cultural codes that create the preassigned places (sexual roles, one might say) that can be occupied.

With regard to the differences between male and female sexual identities, we must begin with the realization that according to Lacan's schema, the position of both male and female subjects is defined by the Phallus-signifier. That is, as signifying or speaking subjects, males and females are equally "subject to" the Name-of-the-Father in inserting themselves into linguistic and cultural signifying systems as well as equally implicated in a context of social relations where the male form of sexual identity is privileged. In this sense, both male and female sexual identities are phallic. Likewise, both sexual identities are defined by lack in relation both to their objects of identification (the little others) and to the Other in the guise of the Name-of-the-Father. The difference lies in the nature of this lack, which defines desire. The major locus of the male lack occurs in the suppression of the identifications of the imaginary plane in favor of the authority that males enjoy in the symbolic order. The price for the male's ability to assume the Name-of-the-Father in the symbolic sphere is the exacerbation of the tensions and ambivalences already present in the identifications with the Mother-signifier in the imaginary plane. By contrast, the ability of the female to identify less ambiguously with the Mother-signifier reduces the importance for her of phallic participation in the symbolic order. While female sexuality is suppressed and devalued in the dominant patriarchal symbolic order, it is, in the imaginary plane, potentially more whole and intact and more subversive of the cultural order than male sexuality—a discovery of Lacan's that was soon exploited by a number of French feminist theorists.

Among the results of Lacan's theory of sexuality that have played a significant role in later employments of his theory by poststructuralist critical discourse, the following deserve special mention:

1. In comparison with Freud's, Lacan's theory of sexuality is decidedly antiessentialist. Based on structuralist models of signification rather than on biology, it reinforces the distinction, already familiar in feminist discourse, between sex and gender. While sex finds its place in the register of biological discourse, gender is a cultural construct that need not completely correspond with the male/female binary of biological classification. The proponents of the critical discourses of feminism and of gay studies have drawn on Lacan's views in their attempts to challenge culturally received attitudes about human sexuality and identity.

2. Even more than Freud, Lacan has emphasized the need to understand human sexuality as a complex phenomenon that involves ambivalent identifications at every point. In Lacan's decentered view of sexual identity, the Oedipal complex can never be completely resolved in favor of one identification over another, nor is there some normal manner in which this might be accomplished. Rather, like the decentered subject, our sexual identities remain throughout our lives spread out over the field defined by the fourfold determinations of our ego ideal, our situated role as speaking and desiring subjects, the particular objects of our desires, and the cultural system of codes that defines and structures sexual discourse and signification.

3. Particularly important in this ongoing process is the manner in which the symbolic order, the Other in the guise of the Name-of-the-Father, determines both the objects of our desires and our extrasymbolic identifications with them. Particularly in the area of the criticism of the media, Lacan's analysis of sexuality in terms of signification has provided a useful framework for understanding the dynamics of how sexuality is related to the production and reconfiguration of desire in film, television, and advertising and how these in turn affect our sexual identities.

4. By bringing sexuality out of the Freudian unconscious and into the nexus of cultural signifying processes, Lacan opened the door for critiques of existing power relations in society based on views of sexual identity underwritten by biological models. While Lacan has often been criticized by some feminists as contin-

uing to privilege male over female sexuality, particularly in his view of the central significance of the Phallus, his overall decentering of existing notions of sexual identity has provided a general framework that, with certain revisions, can serve as the basis for a critique of patriarchal systems and their underlying power disparities.

Decentering the Text: Jacques Derrida's Deconstructive Strategies

Jacques Derrida (b. 1930) did for the traditional notion of the text what Lacan did for the metaphysical self or subject: He showed why it can never be adequately regarded as some single, unitary, and internally coherent structure conveying to the reader a stable and determinate meaning. Despite the large body of Derrida's writings dealing with authors who are usually classified as literary, it should be remembered that Derrida was trained as a philosopher and that the careful reading of what are usually regarded as philosophical texts constitutes the backbone of his production. It is fair to say that Derrida's reflections commenced with his bringing phenomenology (as practiced by Husserl and amplified by Heidegger) into a critical juxtaposition with structuralism (especially as represented by Saussure and Lévi-Strauss) and that his subsequent work, while greatly expanding this project, has nonetheless remained informed by insights originally developed in these discussions. It should also be noted that more than any other poststructuralist, Derrida explicitly and continuously addressed the issues originally raised by Nietzsche and Heidegger regarding the foundations and limits of the Western metaphysical tradition. In pursuing the project of deconstructing this tradition, he has simultaneously provided a general diagnosis of its perennial but always suppressed presuppositions, traced their covert operations in a multitude of representative texts, and developed a number of critical strategies for reading texts, aimed at identifying and destabilizing these assumptions. At the heart of Derrida's thought lies the conviction that any tradition exists in the form of its texts; that every text is a nonunitary, unstable, and ultimately self-undermining construction; and that the only possible critique of any tradition lies in demonstrating the necessarily decentered nature of its texts in contrast to the manner in which they traditionally present themselves and are usually read.

Phenomenology, Structuralism, and the Decentered Text. Derrida's first writings appeared in the early 1960s, when structuralism and phenomenology (the latter, in its Sartrean, existentialist inflection) were two major axes of the French intellectual scene. Although their earliest founding documents were produced at roughly the same time, the discourses of phenomenology and structuralism pointed in drastically different directions. Phenomenology, as inaugurated by Edmund Husserl, sought to open up the sphere of human meaning underlying the objectivities of the natural sciences (and their everyday counterparts) by tracing all meanings, whether presented in language, the sciences, works of art, or other cultural productions, back to their origins in the activities of a "transcendental ego," the most fundamental stratum of the self. By contrast, structuralism from its very inception tended to move in exactly the opposite direction, focusing on meaning as a function of the operation of symbolic or linguistic systems and codes whose structures were indifferent to and determining for any self that might operate inside them.

Much of Derrida's early work involved a bidirectional critical strategy, a version of what he would later call a **double reading**, whereby each reading would serve as the starting point for a critique of the other. With regard to Husserl's phenomenological analyses, Derrida argued in works such as *Speech and Phenomena* (1967), from something of a structuralist perspective and in a manner reminiscent of Lacan's reading of Freud, that language and its differential structures permeate the entire enterprise of phenomenology to the deepest stratum of the transcendental ego itself. This implied, of course, that there was no founding center of meaning at any stratum of the self that could escape the play of differences constituting language. On the other hand, adopting a more or less phenomenological attitude, Derrida claimed in several essays in *Writing and Difference* (1967) that structuralism had obscured and suppressed a crucial feature of signification—its character as located, temporalized, and concrete events—in favor of the logic of closed systems. That is, any occurrence of signification or language involves, as a necessary component, a concrete and unique act or event that must escape and overflow the formal and generalized codes invoked in structuralist analysis.

Nevertheless, Derrida's double reading never aimed at any synthesis between phenomenology and structuralism but at a critique of both. In Derrida's view, we can no longer invoke the self in the form of an active, transcendental ego as the underlying basis of meaning, nor can we seek meaning exclusively in the operations of a formal, closed system. Rather, our only access to the questions that preoccupied the phenomenologists and the structuralists is through careful attention to concrete instances of signification—texts—from a stance that refuses to consider them either as transparent expressions of some subject or author or as mere instances of a unified and overarching system.

Beyond Phenomenology and Structuralism: The Critique of the Metaphysics of Presence.   In addition to his critical meditations on phenomenology and structuralism, Derrida produced a number of thoughtful readings of the later works of Heidegger. Following Heidegger, Derrida saw a common assumption underlying both the phenomenological and structuralist projects, one that placed them squarely in the broader tradition of Western metaphysics. This was the tradition's tendency to understand all of its major signifiers—*being, truth, meaning,* and so forth—in terms of some enduring and stable presence. Heidegger himself had already shown, with regard to the ontological difference between *Being* and *beings,* that the tradition beginning with Plato had covered over a more primordial notion of Being and truth found in the pre-Socratic philosophers, namely, that any revealing of

Being in the form of particular beings was, at the very same moment, a concealing of Being itself. In the register of linguistic signification, this meant that every saying or affirmation was at the same time a concealing or suppression of what was not said. Ultimately, the tradition of Western metaphysics had privileged presence over its necessary and inescapable counterpart, even though presence was unthinkable without its suppressed other. This characteristic privileging of presence over its suppressed counterpart continued to manifest itself in phenomenology's quest for the founding presence of the subject to itself, the transcendental ego, as well as in structuralism's assumption of a meaning-founding system of signification that was somehow present in and controlling for any concrete act of signification. Both moved completely in the ambit of a "metaphysics of presence."

Like Heidegger, Derrida believed that the ultimate task of critique was to begin dismantling, or in his own words, **deconstructing** the entire ensemble of assumptions and terms on which the metaphysical tradition was based. However, both emphasized that such a critique could never be accomplished by attempting to establish a place outside of that tradition, since such a move would only reestablish a new sort of presence, thus replicating the defining feature of the tradition itself. The only option was to reveal, in the texts and primary signifiers of the tradition, how the privileging of presence in them was threatened by the irruption of its suppressed counterparts and how it ultimately depended on them. In particular, at the level of the text this meant showing, by detailed and patient reading, how the manifest or overt meaning of the text was continually undermined by the very linguistic devices that it employed in the process of constructing that meaning. As Derrida always insists, the reader does not deconstruct a text in an external act of violence; rather, texts deconstruct themselves because their very linguistic medium constantly overflows and defies any attempt, however skillful, to muster its resources into the service of a unitary and stable meaning. For Derrida, the reader, in a sense, merely bears witness to this process through careful attention to the signifying devices operating in the text and to the ways in which they privilege certain meanings while suppressing others that nonetheless continually threaten to undermine them. The text itself, in this view, is intrinsically unstable, polysemic, and decentered.

Logocentrism, Phonocentrism, and the Impossible Science of Grammatology. Heidegger's groundbreaking attack on Western metaphysics focused on the ontological difference, that is, on the difference between Being and beings. For the most part, Derrida tended to regard even Heidegger's project as still ensnared in the trap of Western metaphysics, since *Being* remained, in his reading of Heidegger, a primary signifier. Derrida sought to radicalize the Heideggerian project by tracing the metaphysical privileging of presence back to the tradition's most basic assumptions regarding language, signification, and textuality.

In direct response to Heidegger's notion of the ontological difference, Derrida, in a difficult essay entitled "La Différance" (published in the collection *Margins of*

Philosophy, 1972), sought to disperse the "difference" that Heidegger emphasized between Being and beings throughout the entire breadth of signification. Heidegger's "difference," as Derrida viewed it, was but one instance, albeit an important one, of the interplay between presence and absence characterizing all signification. Invoking the structuralist notion of the differential nature of the sign—that the meaning of any sign is entirely dependent on the ensemble of its differences with other signs—Derrida introduced the signifier *différance*. Identical in sound with the French word *différence,* of which it at first appears a misspelling, it indicates the underlying process of opening or spacing that makes any concrete system of differences possible. Neither active nor passive, substantial nor insubstantial, determinate nor indeterminate, *différance* is presented by Derrida as a sort of intersection of temporality becoming spatialized. It underlies, intertwines, and penetrates all acts of signification, making possible the actual differences between signs that establish their meanings. *Différance* is neither signs nor the differences between them but a sort of open field of play out of which both arise. It is covered over or suppressed by every concrete act of signification, but it is also their ultimate source and precondition, a spacing (as Derrida has described it) but not a space, a temporalizing but not any particular temporal event, a continually receding or deferred trace of past and future significations in the present.

Différance, a signifier that Derrida himself invented, can only be expressed in writing, not speaking (since it is pronounced the same in French as *différence*)—a fact that points the way toward Derrida's distinctive critique of the metaphysical tradition, which is stated most forcefully in *Of Grammatology* (1967). According to Derrida, the metaphysical tradition can be characterized, from its origins in Plato and Aristotle, as a **logocentrism**, that is, as centered around and grounded on the Greek polysemic signifier *logos,* which includes among its many signifieds language, logic, science, and reason. In other words, the Western metaphysical tradition has taken as its principal task the formulation of "true statements," where "true" is understood as a function of language, governed by the formal laws of logic, in making present to the soul or mind that to which the statement refers.

Further, the underlying logocentrism of the metaphysical tradition is closely connected with another of its characteristic features, which likewise can be traced throughout its history from as early as Plato's criticism of written as opposed to spoken expression in the *Phaedrus*—a tendency Derrida calls **phonocentrism.** Phonocentrism for Derrida is the marked tendency of the tradition to privilege the spoken over the written occurrence of language as the form most adequate for making the "truth" present to the mind or consciousness. For the tradition, the paradigmatic case of language is that in which, on the one hand, the "truth" is present to the speaker in the form of his or her own internal monologue, and on the other, is communicated to another through the voice of the speaker, which as it is internalized by the hearer allows the "truth" to be present to the hearer as well. Under the regime of Western metaphysics, written language has always been devalued and repressed as nothing more than a "representation of a representation," a "(written) sign of a (spoken) sign," an inessential and deficient supplement to the fullness of vocal speech. In *Of Grammatology* and several essays, especially those appearing in *Margins of Philosophy,* Derrida traces this suppression of writing in favor of speaking from Plato, through such moderns as Condillac and Rousseau, up to Husserl, Saussure, and Lévi-Strauss.

In place of the still logocentric and phonocentric alternatives of phenomenology and structuralism, Derrida suggests a new project called **grammatology.** In what is perhaps his most important deconstructive critique, Derrida attempted to show (1) how the tradition has continually privileged speech over writing; (2) that the marginalized supplement, writing, properly understood, is the suppressed foundation for speaking, and thus the relationship between the two is the exact inverse of the presupposed hierarchy of speech/writing; and (3) what would be involved in a new type of inquiry, grammatology, which would take writing rather than speech as the paradigm of language. Clearly at the heart of this project was the written text. Detached from the presence that dominates spoken occurrences of language, written texts are autonomous of their absent authors, who can no longer exercise authority over their texts. Further, written texts are, in the most basic sense, an array of physical figures, inscribed signs, which stand out against their background only by virtue of the equally important spaces between them. Written texts, that is, physically exemplify the interplay of signs and their differences, of constructions and spacings, of presences and absences, in ways that the fullness of the voice in spoken language tends to obscure or obliterate.

Derrida does not dispute the claim that speaking has in fact preceded writing in some temporal or historical sense. Rather, he means to indicate that "mundane writing," that is, ordinary alphabetic writing, bears traces of a more fundamental **archi-writing** or **proto-writing,** which is the condition for any occurrence of language whatsoever—traces that the phonocentrism of tradition has suppressed. This archi-writing can be viewed as the primordial operation of *différance,* of the interplay between presence and absence or temporalizing and spatializing, from which something like a language, whether spoken or written, could first emerge as a determinate system of differences.

Grammatology, the science of writing, would thus be the inquiry into the ultimate conditions for language itself and their persistence, as suppressed traces, in actual written texts. Of course, Derrida adds that grammatology is an "impossible science," because its object, the operation of *différance,* can never be made present without reducing it to yet another metaphysical term. Thus, grammatology, while specifying a problem and suggesting a set of strategies for approaching it, must itself remain forever different from other sciences, and deferred in terms of producing the sort of results that we ordinarily expect from them.

Deconstructive Textual Strategies: Underlying Assumptions.   True to Derrida's "impossible program," most of his writings since the early 1970s have consisted of close readings of written texts drawn from a wide variety of genres, which trace in detail the concealed and subtle effects of the metaphysical tradition while serving as illustrations of various strategies by which these metaphysical assumptions can be brought to light, reversed, neutralized, and rewritten. Following are certain key assumptions, which have proven most important for contemporary cultural critique, about the nature of texts that are operative in Derrida's deconstructive readings.

1. By its very nature, no text can possess an entirely unitary and unambiguous meaning. This is not so much because, as hermeneutic discourse emphasized, the historical context and reception of texts alter (though these undoubtedly play a role), but because writing itself involves the continual interplay between "presence" and "absence," that is, what is said and what is not said or is suppressed.

2. As the etymology of the word suggests, a *text* is a weaving together of various, often conflicting or counteracting discourses or "strands" that originate in earlier texts and lead in the direction of other, new or different texts. Using a very revealing metaphor, Derrida sometimes describes texts as "tapestries" with discernible "figures" woven in their centers, though with "frayed edges" consisting of strands coming from elsewhere and leading in diverse directions. The task of deconstruction can thus be viewed as a process of unraveling the various strands of the tapestry, tracing them back to other tapestries in which they are already interwoven and following them where they might lead beyond the texts at hand. This, of course, is another image for what has been called the *intertextuality* of texts.

3. As the structuralists emphasized, language can never be completely under the control of an author. Writing involves the use of preexisting words, figures, and discourses whose meaning continually overruns any intention that may be attributed to its author. A text, to use yet another metaphor, is more like a material production employing preexisting materials, each possessing its own characteristic physical qualities, which can be bent or forced to serve the producer's purposes but which are never purely indifferent and malleable media of expression. As a result, such materials will often grind against one another, counteract each other's force, go their own ways, and sometimes defeat all efforts of the producer to control them.

4. From a broader critical perspective, the inherent privileging of certain terms or figures in a text and the suppression or marginalization of others is both a manifestation of and a means of propagating existing power-differentials in the text's cultural contexts. The deconstruction of texts has a necessarily critical, ethical, and political dimension, in that the identification, reconfiguration, and reversal of significational hierarchies operating in texts is, at the same time, a critique of the cultural systems which underwrite them. Whereas the conception of a text as possessing a unitary and more or less obvious meaning has the effect of making this meaning appear to be natural and unassailable, the destabilization of this notion opens the dual possibility of revealing the arbitrary and ideological bases of textual constructions and of initiating an internal critique based on their own self-undermining operations.

Decentering History: Michel Foucault's Archaeology and Genealogy

The writings of **Michel Foucault** (1926–1984) accentuate three dimensions that are often muted in Lacan and Derrida: first, an attentiveness to various ways in which texts interact with one another in broader historical contexts; second, a concern for extratextual practices, codes, and institutions that govern the production and circulation of texts; and third, a sharp focus on the specific ways in which power relations govern the structures operative in and among texts, as well as the conditions of their construction. Of course, one should not expect some overarching theory of history into which Lacan's decentered subject and Derrida's decentered text can simply be inserted, since Foucault was as resolute about decentering the metaphysical notion of history as were Lacan and Derrida with respect to their own primary areas of emphasis. Nonetheless, Foucault's project, when compared to those of Lacan and Derrida, unfolded at a more general level than that of the self or the individual text.

Foucault's basic units of analysis are discourses, or more precisely, **discursive formations**. Foucault introduced this idea in *The Archaeology of Knowledge* (1969) in the following manner: "Whenever one can describe, between a number of statements, such a system of dispersion, whenever, between objects, types of statement, concepts, or thematic choices, one can define a regularity (an order, correlations, positions and functionings, transformations), we will say, for the sake of convenience, that we are dealing with a *discursive formation*."

He then continued, in the same passage, to introduce another, closely related notion, that of **rules of formation**: "The conditions to which the elements of this division (objects, mode of statement, concepts, thematic choices) are subjected we shall call the *rules of formation*. The rules of formation are conditions of existence (but also of coexistence, maintenance, modification, and disappearance) in a given discursive division."

Notice that Foucault's "discursive formations" are located beyond the level of individual statements or any traditional grouping of them—a particular text, the oeuvre of a particular author, the writings of a specific historical period, or a traditionally recognized discipline—and indeed can intersect and play across all of these. Among the discursive formations that Foucault studied and analyzed were the discourses of madness, medicine, crime, sexuality, and "man" as the object of the social sciences. Note also that the "rules of formation" governing such discourses cannot be identified with (even if they are closely related to) structural codes governing the signifiers of any given text or set of texts. Rather, they also include considerations involving who may speak, on what subjects, in what contexts, with what authority, and so forth. They point, that is, beyond the internal workings of texts toward the practical and institutional conditions under which texts are produced. While Foucault continued to rework these early ideas as his thought unfolded, his focus on discourses and the institutional and practical conditions for their existence and transmutations remained a constant in his thought.

Foucault and Structuralism. Although there are discernible connections between Foucault's thought and structuralism, he is even farther removed from it than either Lacan or Derrida. In the clearest possible terms, he claimed: "My aim is not to transfer to the field of history, and more particularly to the history of knowledge *(connaissances)*, a structuralist method that has proved valuable in other fields of analysis. My aim is to uncover the principles and consequences of an autochthonous transformation that is taking place in the field of historical knowledge."

Like Derrida, Foucault firmly rejected the structuralist assumption of closed texts governed by an overarching system of differences. In the field of history, the discourses with which he was concerned were events rather than formal structures, and were characterized by **chance**, **discontinuity**, and **materiality**. That is, to the structuralist text or mythological system as an access to historical phenomena Foucault opposed a view in which discursive formations unpredictably irrupt in the interstices of other discourses, develop and operate according to their own rules of formation, relatively autonomously of other competing discourses, and exist on a plane thoroughly intertwined with material practices, institutions, and configurations of power. In Foucault, every structural approach must assume the very systematic determinism, continuity, and ideality that he decisively rejects.

Still, there are at least three important points at which his project and that of structuralism intersected. First, Foucault shared with structuralism the tendency to remove the subject as the locus or guarantor of meaning. Just as structuralism saw meaning as a function of systems of difference, so Foucault saw history as a function of discourses and their processes of displacement. Second, Foucault positively embraced the accusation of antihumanism often aimed at structuralism, declaring at many points that *man*, a mere signifier and a historical invention of the Enlightenment period, must die so that a new (poststructuralist) age could be born. Finally, while Foucault rejected as artificial and untenable the structuralist distinction between synchronic and diachronic analyses, one finds a counterpart to these in his notions of archaeology and genealogy.

Foucault's Decentering of History: An Overview. Before turning to the more specific forms that historical investigation took in Foucault's thought, it will be helpful to gain an overview (so far as is possible) of his decentered conception of history. To begin with, Foucault rejected all of the more traditional views of history based on a single organizing principle or overarching narrative structure. Christianity's doctrine of history as a divine plan of salvation, the Enlightenment's view of history as a continuous progression toward the vanquishing of superstition by scientific reason, Hegel's idealist view of history as the narrative of the "Spirit's becoming self-conscious," and Marx's economic history of the continuous development of the class struggle, as well as any view of history as a set of explicable connections between causes and effects—all impose on history a single, totalizing principle of organization, obscuring its essentially chance, discontinuous, and nonlinear character. While the historian can chart, in given discursive formations, certain commonalities, regularities, and systems of difference, there is no single, overarching narrative into which they can be inserted and given a rational order or significance. Rather, invoking Nietzsche's view that truth is perspectival and that the number of possible perspectives on any object or event is limitless, Foucault insisted that every discursive formation is a set of perspectives from which any other can be viewed. No one perspective, however, whether present or past, scientific or primitive, philosophically grounded or maintained by sheer prejudice or habit, can claim ultimate precedence over any other.

Foucaultian history, then, can never assume the form of a linear narrative about individuals, events, ideas, institutions, or underlying processes. Rather, Foucault distinguished between a **universal (or total) history** constructed on the basis of such continuous and centered narratives and a **general history** the task of which is to chart the "series, divisions, limits, differences of level, shifts, chronological specificities, particular forms of rehandling, [and] possible types of relation" that occur in and between various discursive formations. As he put it, "A total description draws all phenomena around a single center—a principle, a meaning, a spirit, a worldview, an overall shape; a general history, on the contrary, would deploy the space of a dispersion." In other words, a general history would not impose a unitary explanation or center on a chronological sequence of widely dispersed events and discourses, but employing a model more spatial than temporal, would seek to describe the various discourses and rules of formation in a field of differences and incommensurabilities.

A corollary concern is the appropriate focus for a general history. Foucault sometimes used the terms **macrohistory** and **microhistory** to contrast total and general history. Whereas macrohistory tends to focus on large-scale trends and continuities operating over a broad range of events and lengthy historical periods, microhistory focuses on small-scale and even unique events or junctures where differences, specificities, and discontinuities occur. For example, in contrast to the expansive and ponderous macrohistories of the development of the French legal system as it relates to the issue of criminal insanity, Foucault, in *I, Pierre Rivière* (1973), offered a single case of a multiple murder that occurred in nineteenth-century France at a time when the discourses of law, criminology, and psychiatry were just beginning to intersect over the proper understanding of insanity. Foucault refused to construct any general theory or overall narrative into which this case could be inserted, contenting himself with simply offering the reader a dossier on this case, accompanied by a few brief comments by way of clarification.

Archaeology: Foucaultian Synchronics. Foucault used the term **archaeology** to characterize his first three major historical studies: of the discourse of madness and its silencing *(Madness and Civilization,* 1961), of illness and its medical treatment *(The Birth of the Clinic,* 1963, rev. ed. 1972), and of the human sciences and their new conception of "man" *(The Order of Things,* 1966). In each case, Foucault was guided by the question, Given that our present field of knowledge and discourse is structured in certain definite ways, what specific historical transformations first made the discursive formations which today seem "natural" to us possible? For example, what transformations in discourse made it possible for us to speak of madness as mental abnormality or illness and to justify the incarceration and (later) medical treatment and social administration of the "insane"? How did the field of medicine acquire its authority over virtually all matters connected with the body and come to exercise the degree of social control that it now does? And how did the human sciences invent the idea of "man" as both subject and object of a "scientific investigation" into virtually all dimensions of human experience and activity, so that these sciences now function as major vehicles for the formation of social policy? Like the archaeologist who excavates, under an existing structure, the various levels or strata on which it has been constructed and the structural shifts from one to the other that have produced what is visible today, Foucault sought in the realm of discursive formations the historical conditions and transformations that first made them possible. And just as the archaeologist has only the evidence of physical materials, artifacts, and their placements with respect to one another with which to work, so Foucaultian archaeology deals almost exclusively with the texts produced in various discursive formations, charting their layerings, series, differences, and transformations with respect to one another.

In his archaeological investigations, Foucault made several noteworthy assumptions relevant to cultural critique.

1. All of our prevalent discursive formations are based on "the fundamental codes of a culture," which predetermine, for a given discursive field, how we perceive, what can be known, how it can be known, and therefore what counts as "truth." Foucault referred to such a fundamental code, which constitutes what he sometimes called the "historical a priori" of a given discourse, an **episteme** (from the Greek word for knowledge). True to his Nietzschean heritage, he regarded all such epistemes as completely historical and thus as subject to further transformations, but never (despite how obvious or natural they might seem to us) as privileged repositories of some "truth" beyond the limits of the codes themselves.

2. While Foucault rejected the historical periodization usually employed by other historians (based, for example, on important political events, great ideas, or cultural styles), his archaeological investigations parallel one another in pointing to several locatable historical breaks or discontinuities. Since Foucault was primarily interested in an archaeology of modernity, he often distinguished between epistemes characteristic of the Renaissance, the "Classical period" (the seventeenth and eighteenth centuries), and the nineteenth century, viewing the present as still emergent from the latter. While the Renaissance episteme was based on an elaborate symbolic system of resemblances in which things are explained by their likenesses to other things, the "Classical" episteme broke with the Renaissance and turned on contiguities and tables of classification, an essentially spatial and time-

less notion. The nineteenth century represented yet another break, focusing as it did on historical analogies and temporal succession, while our present period was heralded by a new episteme based on the decenterings and differences implicit in structural linguistics and psychoanalysis. The crucial point in each case is that in the transition from one historical episteme to another, "things are no longer perceived, described, expressed, characterized, classified, and known in the same way."

3. Underlying each of these historical ruptures or discontinuities are transformations in the rules of formation for each respective discursive formation. Not only what can be spoken about and how it can be validly formulated but also who is entitled to speak, under what circumstances, and with what authority changes from period to period. In *Madness and Civilization,* for example, Foucault charted the manner in which the "madman," whose voice was regarded during the Renaissance as possessing its own special inspiration and wisdom, was first silenced through incarceration in the seventeenth century, then socialized during the humanistic, reeducational experiments of the eighteenth and nineteenth centuries, and finally made the object of the scientific discourse of abnormal psychology in the later nineteenth and early twentieth centuries.

4. Foucault regarded the general historical trajectory operating through these various discursive transformations as the tendency of reason, first established in its modern form during the "Classical period," to extend its domination over any and every other discourse that might assert itself as an alternative. While modern reason originally emerged in opposition to the discourse of madness, which was necessary for its self-definition, it gradually came to incorporate this other discourse into its own by submitting it to scientific forms of explanation, analysis, and treatment. In particular, the other of the discourse of reason gradually came to be viewed as a merely defective version of itself under the sway of the powerful binary signifiers of normal/abnormal. Similar processes occurred in the areas of medicine (healthy/unhealthy), penology (law-abiding/criminal), and sexuality (normal/perverse). Foucault was thus concerned to establish the archaeology and trace the social consequences of the hierarchized binaries that one encounters in Derrida. For this reason, one might view Foucault's archaeology as a historical counterpart to Derrida's most important deconstructive textual strategy.

Genealogy: Foucaultian Diachronics.   In his inaugural address of 1970 (sometimes called "The Discourse on Language") to the Collège de France on being awarded the chair in the history of systems of thought, Foucault outlined a new departure for his future research. Invoking a term first used by Nietzsche, he called his new approach **genealogy** to distinguish it from his earlier archaeological research. Foucault did not intend this to signal a break in his thought but rather a widening of the field of analysis. Specifically, following Nietzsche's lead in his *Genealogy of Morals,* Foucault sought to relate the structural transformations of discursive formations to their basis in and effects on the material conditions of discourse, including "institutions, political events, economic practices and processes." In a similarly Nietzschean vein, he asserted that his research on discursive formations should now be conducted "in relation to the will to knowledge," which he regarded, as had Nietzsche, as the modern form of the will to power. Thus, in genealogy the emphasis falls not on discourses themselves, as in archaeology, but on the manner in which discourses become vehicles for the establishment and maintenance of power, both in their own spheres and in non- and extradiscursive areas of culture as well. Genealogy, then, operates at the interface of discourses and other cultural practices and institutions, seeking to describe how modern concentrations and dispersements of power have come to assume the forms that they now have. It should be noted that this shift of approach signaled the onset of a more practical and interventionist attitude on Foucault's part and was accompanied by his own increasing involvement in concrete political causes.

Foucault's two major projects employing this genealogical approach were *Discipline and Punish* (1975) and the multivolume (and unfinished) series *The History of Sexuality* (first volume, 1976). In both of these works, Foucault is concerned with tracing how the "speaking subject" of discourse is likewise "subjected" to discourses, material techniques for control, and institutions that serve to define it and assign it its "proper place" in broader power configurations. These studies may be regarded as historical specifications of the mechanisms of the symbolic plane earlier introduced by Lacan.

In these genealogical investigations, Foucault introduced an idea that proved decisive for the next generation of poststructural thought: the notion of the **body** as the ultimate material locus on which modern power is brought to bear and through whose structuring and control it most decisively functions. In *Discipline and Punish,* Foucault charts the transition from the classical "body/soul unity" as symbolic referent of a "juridico-political" form of power existing external to and dominating it, to the "embodied subject" of more recent times, in which power has been internalized and inscribed in its own discourses and bodily functions. To highlight this rupture between the classical and more modern view, Foucault contrasts the formalized and ritual-like public executions still practiced late into the eighteenth century with the nineteenth century's growing tendency to incarcerate criminals under conditions of enforced physical discipline. Symbolic of this historical fissure is Scottish social philosopher Jeremy Bentham's ideal plan of a prison, called the **panopticon**. In this arrangement (still typical of many modern prisons and other such institutions), prisoners are placed in cells arranged in a circle around a central observation tower so that each prisoner is constantly visible from the central point. For Foucault, the essential point is that in such an arrangement, the prisoners cannot tell whether they are actually being observed or not at any given time, so that they gradually come to internalize and obey the disciplinary rules of the institution even when no one is actually in the observation tower. The actual power represented by the guard in the tower does not require continual and explicit exercise due to the prisoners' own complicity in this process of discipline. For Foucault, this panopticon assigns to every embodied subject its proper spatial location, induces its own compliance with the discipline of the institution even in the absence of overt surveillance or force, and physically inscribes its structures into the bodily activities and processes of its subjects. As such, it serves as a metaphor for a wide variety of modern institutions, including hospitals, schools, and the workplace. In such contexts, power no longer appears as something purely negative and external but is dispersed throughout the entire physical arrangement and discipline of the subjects, who become complicit participants in its maintenance and reproduction.

In *The History of Sexuality,* Foucault challenged the prevalent **repressive hypothesis** underlying much modern discourse concerning sexuality. Rather than viewing modernity as involving an ever increasing repression of sexuality (as the Freudian and Marxist traditions tended to do), Foucault maintained that in modernity, sexuality had increasingly become the subject of various discourses that served on the one hand to deploy it in the interests of existing power configurations, and on the other, to "normalize" it by introducing purely historical discriminations between normal and abnormal sexual behaviors and orientations. In particular, rather than being repressed outright, sexuality had become the subject of a discourse that he called **scientia sexualis**, "sexual science," which had assigned sexuality and the sexualized subject a place in modern knowledge and controlled the potentially disruptive effects of sexuality through various "technical disciplines" aimed at the body and its activities. In Foucault's analysis, the recent proliferation of sex therapies, birth-control clinics, sex education, and even media talk shows devoted to such topics should not be seen as attempts to liberate us from an older, repressive regime but as elements of a newly emergent set of techniques for policing and deploying sexuality in the interests of modern power configurations. According to Foucault, **bio-power** now represents a major form, inscribed at the level of the body and its most intimate processes, in which social and political control and production are exercised and expanded.

Power/Knowledge and Strategies of Critique and Resistance.   Probably the most influential idea for cultural critique stemming from Foucault's poststructuralist decentering of history is that of **power/knowledge.** By the frequent use of this apparent binary, Foucault wished to emphasize several related points.

1. Although knowledge discourses (for example, the various recognized disciplines) might represent themselves as objective searches for or statements of truth, their genealogies indicate, without exception, that they ultimately function to produce, maintain, and reproduce power configurations. In this sense, power is the suppressed and concealed other of the modern disciplines concerned with knowledge, and Foucault's strategy is to reveal this suppressed hierarchy, reverse its terms, and reinscribe them in a new account of both power and knowledge.

2. The characteristic forms of power exercised in modernity do not take the form of brute physical force (as in premodernity) but are wrapped in the mantle of scientific knowledge. They establish the norms for rational discourse, systemat-

ically excluding any other discourses on the grounds that they are irrational, perverse, or insane. Foucault opposes to these normalized discourses his own genealogies and others like them, calling them "counterdiscourses" or "antisciences," not because they take issue with logical or scientific methods themselves but because they contest "the effects of the centralizing powers which are linked to the institution and functioning of an organized scientific discourse." In this sense, the practice of genealogy is an important critical strategy for contesting dominant and (implicitly) coercive forms of knowledge.

3. The manner in which power/knowledge operates in modernity can most clearly be seen in the institutions associated with the various scientific discourses. According to Foucault, each such discourse has institutional counterparts that involve the observation, manipulation, and control of the body. Under the idealistic rubric of "the best interest" of the individual or society, asylums, prisons, hospitals, schools, and workplaces are all institutional extensions of "scientific discourses" (psychopathology, penology, medicine, educational theory, and economics) where the power implicit in disciplinary knowledge is physically brought to bear on the living bodies of human beings. Foucault's own political activism was directed, to a great extent, toward challenging, at the level of such concrete institutions, the exercise of power through the scientific knowledge on which such arrangements are based.

4. Foucault's signal contribution to poststructuralist critical discourse was to show that we tend to think of power according to models that are more characteristic of premodern societies, overlooking the subtle and complex ways in which, in modernity, it has dispersed and insinuated itself into our most common and accepted institutions, practices, and even ways of speaking. Because of this, Foucault rejects any attempt to ally contemporary critical practice with large-scale political movements, preferring instead to challenge specific practices and institutions at the local or micro level, the level at which power actually exercises its effects. For Foucault, political ideologies are at best irrelevant and at worst complicitous in a context where real power is "a multiple and mobile field of force relations where far-reaching, but never completely stable effects of domination are produced."

5. To return to the themes with which we began this section, Foucault's view of power, derived from his decentering of history, can be directly rejoined to Lacan's decentering of the subject and Derrida's decentering of the text. In modernity, power is no longer a function of subjects, whether viewed as individuals in authority or as those under their control. Rather, Foucault celebrates the "death of the subject," the next historical stage after Nietzsche's "death of God," as the opening that allows us to recognize clearly the dispersed and subjectless operation of power in modernity. As long as we continue to attribute existing social patterns of domination to the deliberate plans of some group of individuals or believe that "freely acting citizens" can effect meaningful social change, we will have misunderstood and underestimated the real mechanisms by which power operates in the modern world. And just as we must put aside the myth of the subject as the ultimate source

or referent of modern power configurations, so must we discard our habit of viewing texts as authoritative communications between two or more subjects. Rather, cultural texts are themselves fully embedded in the dispersed and heterogeneous functioning of power, open conduits in, through, and around which power continually flows in ever changing configurations. To read a text is not to glimpse the mind of an author at work but to confront a medium by which power is produced, maintained, transformed, and deflected in ever new directions.

6. Foucault's underlying convictions are perhaps best expressed by two slogans of the 1960s: "The personal is the political" and "Our bodies, our selves." While Foucault has often been criticized for not addressing more directly the discourses of modernity concerning women, these two slogans, often cited during the early phases of feminist discourse, are entirely consistent with his overall approach. As to the first, Foucault himself held that the dispersed operations of power in later modernity had succeeded in collapsing the earlier distinction between the public and private spheres, so that all dimensions of our existence had become completely politicized. In later modernity, the principal locus of the political has become the private and personal sphere. It is here that we should seek political resistance, not on the public stage of ideological conflict. More particularly, Foucault locates the operation of power in the personal sphere not in relation to some idealistic subject but to the body itself. It is in the areas that most directly concern the body—pleasure and pain, health and illness, sexuality, hygiene, physical appearance, clothing, diet, and so forth—that the real operations of modern power are felt most acutely and manifest themselves most clearly. And it is in this area that we should most be on our guard for the effects of power. It is this dimension of Foucault's thought, in conjunction with that of Lacan and Derrida, that has been most influential on the next generation of poststructuralist thinkers, which include such feminists as **Luce Irigaray** and **Hélène Cixous** and such post-Marxist/post-Freudian thinkers as **Félix Guattari** and **Gilles Deleuze**.

Postmodern Discourses: Culture and Critique at the End of the Twentieth Century

As already explained in the introduction to this chapter, poststructuralism can be regarded as the opening phase of what has become a much broader postmodernist discussion. A convenient historical reference point for the beginning of the transition to the broader debate are the political events of 1968 in France (and their counterparts elsewhere). This dramatic upsurge of a broad front of political protest and its equally dramatic demise required of almost all intellectuals a confrontation with existing political realities and a reassessment of their positions with regard to basic questions of the nature of contemporary culture and politics, the adequacy of approaches then available for dealing with them, and the very possibility of adopting critical stances toward them. While the poststructuralists had to a great extent directed their efforts toward decentering the Western tradition of metaphysics and its perpetuation in the various modern critical discourses of the twentieth century, postmodern discourses significantly expanded this focus to include discussions of developments that were already under way in the arts, new political configurations and oppositional strategies that emerged from the 1960s, large-scale geopolitical realignments and attendant issues of postcolonial cultures, and fundamental changes in cultural production and reproduction, especially in the media and information technologies, whose spheres of cultural influence seemed to explode in the 1970s and 1980s.

With few exceptions, most major participants in postmodern discussions who are building on the decentering strategies practiced by the poststructuralists take them for granted. In general, rather than developing radically new critical strategies, most postmodern critics seek instead to refine the critical approaches practiced by the poststructuralists, and above all, to extend their application beyond the field of texts to contemporary culture at large. Perhaps, as a gloss, it is fair to say that whereas poststructuralism concentrated more on developing critical strategies than on theorizing concrete developments in contemporary culture, the emphasis of postmodern discourses has been just the opposite. In particular, lying at the heart of much postmodern discussion is the attempt to assess the significance of poststructuralism itself as an element of broader cultural developments in the period following World War II.

While postmodernist discourses lead in widely divergent directions, we can gain an orientation with respect to them by considering several quite different responses to two central and recurrent questions. The first is, What is the nature of the historical break or rupture (if indeed there was one) that makes it possible to distinguish between a modern and a postmodern era, culture, attitude, or style? The second is, What, in terms of its cultural effects, is the significance of the postmodern and what bearing does this have on the contemporary practice of cultural critique? In attempting to answer these questions, we will begin with Jürgen Habermas's defense of the project of modernity, a view that ultimately denies any notable historical break, thus calling the whole postmodernist debate into question. We then will turn to the classical statement of the case for distinguishing between a modern and a postmodern milieu, articulated by Jean-François Lyotard, which affirmatively embraces a postmodern outlook. To this we will contrast the position of Jean Baudrillard, who acknowledges the historical rupture but draws from it quite ominous and pessimistic conclusions. Finally, we will consider Fredric Jameson's post-Marxist attempt to acknowledge the significance of postmodern developments while placing them in a broader historical framework, which he claims is more adequate to continuing the practice of cultural critique.

Habermas on the Incomplete Project of Modernity

In considering postmodernism, it is particularly fitting to begin with the views of Habermas, since he is the most prominent contemporary representative of the

Frankfurt School, a critical discourse that, several decades earlier, had broached many of the issues later taken up by postmodernist discourses. In an address of 1980 entitled "Modernity: An Incomplete Project," Habermas set out to defend the underlying values and aims of modernity while acknowledging, as had the earlier Frankfurt School, that these aims had not yet been fully realized. In the process, he contended that postmodernism must be viewed as legitimately objecting to this incompleteness in fulfillment, although because of its rejection of rational standards for judgment and critique, it could neither constitute a positive moment of historical development nor ground any effective critical practice. In the end, Habermas concluded that the postmodernist stance was a resurgence of irrationalist conservatism.

Habermas began by distinguishing what he called "aesthetic modernity" from the broader "project of modernity" that he meant to defend. The former, associated with avant-garde experimentalism and iconoclasm in the arts of the late nineteenth and early twentieth centuries, was an ideology of the new, a revolt against all traditional norms, values, and conventions. However, once the modernist avant-garde itself became a tradition, it lost its shock-value and was destined merely to repeat its increasingly monotonous and predictable gestures. The project of modernity, by contrast,

> formulated in the eighteenth century by the philosophers of the Enlightenment consisted in their efforts to develop objective science, universal morality and law, and autonomous art according to their inner logic. At the same time, this project intended to release the cognitive potentials of each of these domains from their esoteric forms. The Enlightenment philosophers wanted to utilize this accumulation of specialized culture for the enrichment of everyday life—that is to say, for the rational organization of everyday social life.

Habermas readily admitted that by the twentieth century, this project was beset with a serious problem, namely, that these specialized areas of discourse and practice had become divorced from ordinary understanding and communication, from the "everyday social life" that they were originally intended to enrich. It was this cultural gap between everyday life and the practices and institutions for realizing the ideals of modernity, rather than the ideals themselves, that legitimated the sort of responses characteristic of antimodern and postmodern sensibilities. But, as Habermas asked, "Should we try to hold on to the *intentions* of the Enlightenment, feeble as they may be, or should we declare the entire project of modernity a lost cause?"

In Habermas's view, the postmodern reaction to the project of modernity should be understood not as heralding some new era of history or critique but merely as a repetition of the sort of response characteristic of aesthetic modernism itself. That is, just as the earlier aesthetic modernism of the avant-garde was directed against the incomplete project of modernity defined by the Enlightenment, so postmodernism is yet another recapitulation of the internal logic of modernity itself, an indication, fully circumscribed in the unfolding of modernity, that the intentions of the Enlightenment project have not yet been fully realized. Clearly, for Habermas, nothing was to be gained from yet another "false negation of culture"; rather, the real task was to develop a set of rationally justified norms and strategies that would move us toward bridging the gap between the specialized fields of knowledge and practice deriving from the Enlightenment and the everyday lives of human beings.

In addition to denying that postmodernism marked any novel or significant rupture in the unfolding of modernity, Habermas attempted to undermine any radical or emancipatory claims on its behalf by grouping it with other contemporary cultural trends, all of which he regarded as inherently conservative and regressive. The principal difference between the "young conservatives," among whom he specifically numbered Foucault and Derrida, and the "old conservatives" and "neoconservatives" was the fact that the former "recapitulate the basic experience of aesthetic modernity" while the others either wistfully long for a return to premodern culture or affirm as irrevocable the separation of specialized cultural spheres from everyday life, while pursuing a politics that will contain the effects of that separation as much as possible. For Habermas, there was little motivation to choose among a nostalgia for premodern culture, a politics of containment, and a tired repetition of well-assayed gestures, even if they were dressed up in the complex rhetoric of a Nietzsche or a Heidegger.

To the two questions that we posed at the beginning, then, Habermas responded that postmodernism signified no break at all with the development of modernity and that therefore it had nothing to add to cultural critique that had not been readily available since the nineteenth century. Habermas continues to pursue a sort of critical liberal humanism utilizing strategies borrowed from Marxism as reinterpreted by the Frankfurt School.

Lyotard's "Postmodern Condition": An Affirmative View of Postmodernity

Jean-François Lyotard (b. 1922), long active at the periphery of poststructuralist developments, first emerged as a central figure in postmodernist discussions with the publication of *The Postmodern Condition: A Report on Knowledge* (1979), a study commissioned by the Conseil des Universités of the government of Quebec. While earlier scattered occurrences of the term *postmodern* have been noted, this work brought the word into common usage and set the parameters for subsequent discussion. In this study, Lyotard argued for recognizing the decisive emergence of a new, postmodern configuration of knowledge, legitimation, and critique, casting this development in a positive and affirmative light. If one agrees with his analysis, then Habermas, whose view Lyotard explicitly challenged, appears to have entirely overlooked the significance of the historical developments that Lyotard has charted here, making Habermas himself the "conservative."

Lyotard offers a succinct but highly suggestive definition of *postmodern*: "I define *postmodern* as incredulity toward metanarratives." To unpack this highly condensed statement, we must first understand what Lyotard means by "metanarratives." In the simplest sense, a narrative can be understood as storytelling. According to Lyotard, "Narration is the quintessential form of customary knowledge," the manner in which traditional (that is, non- or prescientific) knowledge is communicated, preserved, and legitimated. In his analysis, a narrative recounts how a protagonist has achieved her or his knowledge or wisdom; employs a rich variety of linguistic devices (including description, evaluation, metaphor, interrogatories, and so forth); presupposes a set of pragmatic rules that specify both the competence of the narrator to speak and the role of the listening audience; and in the act of its recounting, serves to produce its own temporal field, the time of its telling, around itself. Most importantly, however, narratives provide the social bonds that join disparate individuals into groups, allowing them to recognize one another as possessing certain competencies, playing various roles specified by the narratives, and sharing in the bodies of knowledge passed on through the narrative function. For Lyotard, then, culture can be viewed as the dynamic totality of the stories or narratives that circulate in it and among its members.

In their most basic forms in premodern societies, ordinary (nonscientific) experience, and popular culture, narratives are local, multiple, disjunct, and dispersed. However, the rise of science and technology at the beginning of the modern period signaled the onset of new forms of universally valid knowledge detached from and opposed to the traditional narrative function and its varieties of local knowledge. This raised the problem of **legitimation,** of authenticating claims to scientific knowledge outside the traditional channels of local narration. Narrative, however, turned out to be inescapable even for scientific knowledge, and the result was the birth of large-scale **metanarratives** that provided the legitimation and rationale for the project of modern science and its attendant developments in technology and social organization.

According to Lyotard, modernity has unfolded under the banners of two major, and in some respects opposed, metanarratives: the political metanarrative, which sees humankind as the hero of a struggle for enlightenment and liberation from the bonds of superstition, ignorance, dogmatism, and political despotism; and the philosophical metanarrative, which casts humanity as the subject of a great historical process whereby the disparate areas of knowledge produced by the sciences gradually converge in a grand rational synthesis under the aegis of the modern nation-state. Lyotard identifies the first metanarrative with the theory of progress enunciated by such Enlightenment figures as Condorcet and the second with the philosophical system constructions of such figures as Hegel. Clearly, there were significant tensions between the two, since the first legitimized modernity as a process of progressive emancipation of the individual while the second grounded its authority in the gradual rationalization of society.

For Lyotard, the onset of postmodernity, which he tends to date from the late 1950s, involved the rejection of any and all such metanarratives. He cites a number of historical factors contributing to this postmodern rupture with modernity, including the rise of fascism (already well analyzed by the Frankfurt School), the failure of the positivist program to establish any single method by which scientific and nonscientific knowledge could be distinguished, the recognition of paradigm shifts in the sciences themselves, the modernist challenge to the Enlightenment tradition in the arts, and the advent of information technologies. The onset of the postmodern condition occurred as these metanarratives lost their force as legitimations for scientific knowledge as well as for the political institutions and ideologies associated with them. Suspicious of both the alleged emancipatory potential of modern forms of scientific knowledge and the possibility of any unification of the diverse areas of human knowledge under the available forms of political organization, postmodernity is confronted with the task of developing new forms of theory, analysis, critique, and practice adequate to a situation where legitimation is no longer obtainable on the basis of grand metanarratives.

To the question of whether "the postmodern" marks the advent of a newly emergent cultural configuration, Lyotard has responded decisively in the affirmative. Aware, however, of critics like Habermas who have attempted to assimilate postmodernism to the earlier gestures of aesthetic modernism, Lyotard responded that on the contrary, the challenges of the avant-garde to the tradition of modernity must be understood as harbingers and precursors of the postmodern milieu yet to come. Lyotard thus can claim that earlier artistic experiments aimed at challenging the Enlightenment project of modernity share in the "post-" of postmodernism by performing their own local break or rupture with the authority of standards embedded in the metanarratives of modernity. Indeed, for Lyotard, the "gaming" with tradition in the found objects of a Duchamp, the wordplay of a Joyce, and the aleatory sounds of a Cage can serve as effective examples for theoretical and political strategies in a postmodern condition, which can now recognize them as its own.

Baudrillard's Dark Vision of a "Hyperreality of Simulacra"

Jean Baudrillard (b. 1929) began as a Marxist sociologist who, in a way analogous to other of his contemporaries, such as Althusser, attempted to graft onto the Marxian analysis of capitalist production a structuralist theory of the production and circulation of signs. After the events of 1968, however, he gradually abandoned his Marxist-structuralist stance as inadequate for analyzing the fundamental and far-reaching changes evident in contemporary society, and he moved toward an explicitly postmodern outlook, which had consolidated by the early 1980s. Although Baudrillard registered the historical rupture between modernity and postmodernity in terms every bit as decisive as those of Lyotard, the conclusions he drew from this development could hardly be more dramatically opposed to Lyotard's. Lyotard's celebration of the playful opening to diversity of the postmodern condition gave way in Baudrillard to a nightmarish vision of a media-dominated world in which all differences are absorbed in the vertigo of an endless production of images spinning out of control.

In *Symbolic Exchange and Death* (1976) and again in *Simulacra and Simulation* (1981), Baudrillard offered his own distinctive characterization of the historical rupture dividing modernity and postmodernity. In Baudrillard's analysis, the passage from modernity to postmodernity concerns, most fundamentally, a set of historical transformations in the status of what he calls **simulacra**, that is, in the relations between images or representations and the reality that they are taken to mirror or represent. Heavily influenced by Foucault's *The Order of Things*, Baudrillard distinguished between three distinct orders of simulacra. The first order corresponded to early modernity, with its associated forms of early capitalist production, newly emergent from the medieval feudal context. This order was characterized by the replacement of medieval symbols with their corresponding social hierarchies, all based on a divine sanction, with a sign-system oriented toward the imitation of nature, which came to function as a new foundation. In the first order of simulacra, signs were taken to refer to or represent the external reality of nature, which became the criterion for the ascendant bourgeoisie's production of its own, naturalized world. Signs thus proliferated as surrogates or counterfeits for the natural or real world, which they were taken to mirror or represent, and were recognized as such. The second order of simulacra arose during the industrial revolution, which made possible the limitless mechanical production of commodities and corresponding signs, all of which could be exact replicas of one another. While an underlying reality was still presupposed, the mechanically reproduced series of commodities (which Marx, in his doctrine of the "fetishism of commodities," had already equated with signs) came to detach themselves from and conceal this underlying reality, thus constituting a relatively autonomous order of their own. The Marxian and psychoanalytic "hermeneutics of suspicion" of the later nineteenth century, the structuralist revolution of the early twentieth, and the Frankfurt School's recognition of this development in the arts and the media all bore witness to this separation of sign-systems from a still acknowledged, underlying reality. With the third order of simulacra, characteristic of the postmodern milieu, any reference of signs to a reality outside the order of signification disappeared entirely.

Baudrillard contrasted the postmodern era with the one that preceded it as a shift from a society determined by **modes of production** to one organized by **codes of production**. Postmodern society, that is, is no longer structured according to the production of material commodities but according to the structures of the various codes and models produced and operating inside it. Citing developments in computer technology, the information sciences, and the media, Baudrillard declared that the organizing principles of postmodern society are the various models, systems, and simulations that are brought to bear in understanding, directing, and controlling social processes. Again, he highlighted this transformation by distinguishing between a **metallurgic** and a **semiurgic** form of society, that is, one based on the material manufacture of commodities as opposed to one based on the production and circulation of signs in the form of information.

Drawing on the work of media theorist Marshall McLuhan, Baudrillard pointed to an **implosion effect**. In the postmodern situation, where the circulation of signs constitutes its own intersignificational order with no reference to reality at all—where there is no relevant distinction to be drawn between image and reality—images and reality implode and images become reality. Numerous examples of this implosion of image and reality in postmodern culture can be cited: infotainment, infomercials, docudramas, and of course, virtual reality are all by now familiar genres in which the boundaries between image and reality have been obscured or erased. In the same manner, journalism becomes a personality contest governed by the ratings system; politics becomes the province of image experts, spin doctors, and pollsters; work becomes less a matter of production than a sign defining social status; and the media come to define reality instead of merely reflecting it. At no point is it any longer possible to determine, nor does it even make sense to ask, where image ends and reality begins, since the two are now identical.

Baudrillard characterized this third phase of simulation as **hyperreality**. Whereas the simulations of the first phase were **realist** in their mirroring or representation of an autonomous reality, and those of the second **neo-realist** in continuing to refer to a reality that had been detached from the serial production of commodities, the third phase opened the possibility for the production of signs according to models and simulations that would be "more real than reality itself," that is, hyperreal. One of Baudrillard's favorite examples of hyperreality is Disneyland. The tableaux of American architecture, history, and life found at Disneyland are created according to formulae and models from which all the historical, material, and human detritus of the actual sites has been erased, presenting the visitor with a view of small-town America or the American West that is far more vivid, compelling, and seductive than reality itself. As a result, we tend to view the world outside Disneyland in terms of our experiences there, rather than vice versa. But according to Baudrillard—and this is the crucial point—the contrast between Disneyland and the America outside it is merely a ruse concealing the fact that postmodern American society is itself hyperreal, not a real contrast to Disneyland but its extension. Institutions such as Disneyland serve merely to perpetuate the illusion that there is still a relevant difference between image and reality, when in fact no real difference can be located.

In response to Lyotard's celebration of postmodernity as opening the field for a multidimensional affirmation of difference and diversity, Baudrillard countered that this, too, was pure illusion. In Baudrillard's dark view of postmodernity, once images have been detached from any reference to reality, all images become equally interchangeable and of equivalent exchange value, circulating in an endless cycle that issues only in unceasing cultural noise. The postmodern individual becomes merely an exhausted, indifferent, and passive observer of the cultural spectacles to which it is continually subjected, a mere channel through which passes a meaningless bacchanal of the most diverse images and information, which ultimately signify nothing. Postmodern culture's extreme diversity and variety is, at bottom, a monolith of meaningless substitutions of one image for another, a fractal structure where apparent depth is continuously being dissolved by endless repetition, in every cultural domain and at every cultural level, of the same monotonous cycle of substitutions.

Rather than seeing postmodernity as the emergence of a new, dispersed conception of sociality, with its attendant expansion of opportunities for social intervention, Baudrillard viewed it as heralding the "end of the social." In his essay "In the Shadow of the Silent Majorities" (1978), Baudrillard argued that the very category of the social as an identifiable locus of political activism and commitment has, in the society of simulations, imploded into the masses. Undefinable by any previously relevant social categories such as class, race, gender, or political or religious affiliation, which would bind human beings with one another on the basis of common interests, the masses are merely the indifferent units over which various models of simulation range: "They don't express themselves, they are surveyed. They don't reflect on themselves, they are tested. The referendum (and the media are a constant referendum of directed questions and answers) has been substituted for the political referent. Now polls, tests, the referendum, media are devices which no longer belong to a dimension of representations, but to one of simulation."

Any attempt to rehabilitate political activism in the context of a social sphere will necessarily employ categories and strategies appropriate to a historical era that no longer exists. Any such attempts will immediately enter the chain of simulations as just another media event or more information that will be fed back to the indifferent masses as yet more meaningless noise. Of course, with the implosion of the social and the obsolescence of activism comes the end of any need or motivation to develop a critical theory of culture or a practical strategy for intervening in it. For Baudrillard, the postmodern condition is nothing less than the dead end of theory, critique, action, and even discourse.

Jameson's Historical Contextualization of the Postmodern

Fredric Jameson (b. 1934) first published his essay "Postmodernism, or The Cultural Logic of Late Capitalism" in 1984, and it was reprinted in 1991 as the lead essay in a book of the same title. While other Marxists or neo-Marxists such as Habermas have tended to view poststructuralist and postmodernist discourses as jargon-laden games played by fundamentally conservative intellectuals masquerading as radicals, Jameson sees something more substantial and significant in them. Never a doctrinaire Marxist in any sense, Jameson occasionally refers to his own position as **post-Marxism**, a sort of counterpart to the newly emergent cultural formations described in postmodernist discourses and instantiated in postmodern artistic and cultural productions. Jameson acknowledges, with such figures as Lyotard and Baudrillard, that postmodernism does mark a significant historical transition worth noting; unlike them, however, he believes that it can only be understood and theorized in relation to underlying transformations in the nature of the capitalist economic system. As he states the task, we must "make at least some effort to think the cultural evolution of late capitalism dialectically, as catastrophe and progress all together." The title of his essay and subsequent book immediately expresses the same idea: for Jameson, postmodernism is, in fact, nothing other than "the cultural logic of late capitalism." The result of his analysis is a sort of rapprochement between postmodern discourses and more traditional Marxist theory, where each borrows from and stands as a corrective and a supplement to the other.

To begin with, Jameson pointed out that "the various positions that can logically be taken on it [postmodernism], whatever terms they are couched in, can always be shown to articulate visions of history in which the evaluation of the social moment in which we live today is the object of an essentially political affirmation or repudiation." In other words, all the views that we have so far described, and any others as well, presuppose, whether they explicitly acknowledge it or not, both a historical narrative and a political standpoint of evaluation. The question then becomes, What is the most adequate historical framework for describing and theorizing the various changes that the term *postmodern* is designed to mark? In a manner reminiscent of Althusser, Jameson rejects the extreme language of *rupture* or *discontinuity*, preferring to speak instead of the reconfiguration of earlier economic and cultural formations, in which previously subordinate forms come to dominate the cultural and economic spheres. In such a view, postmodernism appears less a complete negation of modernism than the emergence into dominance of certain elements already present but muted in modernism. Nonetheless, Jameson insisted that such reconfigurations, even if there is no decisive rupture, fully warrant the invention of a new term to signify them: "for good or ill, we cannot *not* use [the term *postmodernism*]."

Jameson, drawing in part on earlier views such as those of Baudrillard and Lyotard and in part on his own readings of postmodern cultural productions, provided his own list of significant characteristics of the postmodern. Among them are the following:

1. Postmodernism signals *"the effacement . . . of the older (essentially high-modernist) frontier between high culture and so-called mass or commercial culture."* Postmodern cultural productions often draw on popular images and forms from the mass media, even as they sometimes juxtapose them to other, more traditional representations and themes.

2. Postmodern productions often appear to *lack any sense of historical or social context*. While a hermeneutic approach could be appropriate to the productions of high modernism, the poststructuralists were correct in noting that postmodern cultural productions appear as pure signifiers that do not refer to any historical or social world but only to other signifiers in unending chains.

3. Postmodern works evidence a *lack of "depth,"* that is, a sense that underlying their surface appearance lie deeper strata of meaning or significance that inter-

pretive understanding might disclose. Rather, in postmodern productions, everything turns on the surface play of signifiers; or more precisely, such works seem to
negate the very distinction between surface and depth, so that there is only the
object at hand, precisely as it is portrayed, and nothing more.

4. Postmodern productions also seem *dissociated from any determinant affect* on
the part of the reader or viewer. Where modernist works often tended deliberately
to provoke a sense of existential alienation or anomie, postmodernist productions
are frequently assemblages of various fragments reflecting the nature of the decentered self to which they are addressed. (For these first four characteristics, Jameson
frequently refers the reader to some of Andy Warhol's pop art images.)

5. Postmodernism tends to express itself in terms of *fragmented spaces* rather
than temporal or historical sequences. Many postmodernist works are pastiches
of various images or elements torn from their locations in broader historical narratives and represented in a complicated spatial array. (Postmodern architecture,
which eclectically borrows from many diverse architectural forms and motifs, creating an ambiguous and decentered spatial experience, provides Jameson's primary examples here.)

6. Postmodern cultural productions thus reveal a sort of *crisis in historicity*, pro-
voking in the viewer alternate sensations of nostalgia, schizophrenia, and euphoria,
as decontextualized popular and historical images and forms assault the viewer in
spatial arrays lacking any center or underlying significance. However, Jameson also
notes that the challenge to "relate these differences" may well be giving rise to a new
postmodern aesthetic sensibility on the part of the viewer or reader.

Agreeing in most respects with the other advocates of a distinctively postmodern condition, Jameson parts ways with them in insisting "that postmodernism is
not the cultural dominant of a wholly new social order . . . but only the reflex and
the concomitant of yet another systemic modification of capitalism itself." Drawing on the Marxist economist Ernest Mandel's *Late Capitalism* (1975), Jameson
distinguishes between three historical phases or periods of expansion of the capitalist economic system:

1. Market capitalism, commencing with the machine production of steam-
driven motors, about 1848, which in turn made possible the mass production, on
a national scale, of large quantities of manufactured commodities. The cultural
counterpart and primary mode of expression of this stage of capitalism was real-
ism, represented in literature by such authors as Balzac and Flaubert and in the
visual arts by such artists as Courbet and Millet.

2. Monopoly capitalism, or imperialism, beginning with the machine production of electric and combustion motors in the 1890s, and characterized by the
colonial expansion of the monopolies of the competing industrialized nations in
search of new sources of raw materials and new markets for the increased production of their commodities. The cultural reflection of this stage of capitalism was
modernism, represented by such literary figures as Conrad, Joyce, and Lawrence
and such visual artists as Van Gogh, Picasso, Duchamp, as well as the Futurists.

3. Multinational (sometimes mistakenly called postindustrial) or late consumer capitalism, starting with the machine production of electronic and nuclear-powered apparatuses during the 1940s and characterized by "a new and historically original penetration and colonization of Nature and the Unconscious: that is, the destruction of the precapitalist Third World agriculture by the Green Revolution, and the rise of the media and the advertising industry."

Again following Mandel, Jameson pointed out that this present stage of capitalism is "the purest form of capital yet to have emerged, a prodigious expansion of capital into hitherto uncommodified areas," and it is this that underlies and is registered by the term *postmodern*. The emblem of this stage of capitalism is not the factory, nor such streamlined icons of modernism as the railroad train, but the computer and television—machines not so much of production as of reproduction, information, and mass consumption.

Jameson related the postmodern characteristics cited above to this "new decentered global network of the third stage of capital itself," where nothing, including nature and the unconscious, has escaped commodification and where culture itself is no longer an autonomous sphere but has been fully colonized by multinational capitalist production. In particular, he emphasized: "The conception of postmodernism outlined here is a historical rather than a merely stylistic one. I cannot stress too greatly the radical distinction between a view for which the postmodern is one (optional) style among many others available and one which seeks to grasp it as the cultural dominant of the logic of late capitalism."

From the point of view of cultural critique, the present task is not to pass moral judgment on postmodernism as if it could be chosen or rejected at will, but to "think it dialectically," that is, as our given current condition, which presents its own distinctive problems and potentials for engaging in critical discourse and practical activity.

According to Jameson, the most pressing issue that a critical postmodernist discourse must face is the fact that the global decentered network of multinational capitalism cannot be represented by any of the traditional conceptual or aesthetic forms of representation. Like a person who has landed in the middle of a large, unfamiliar city without a map, the postmodern individual is dislocated and disoriented in the unchartable space of multinational capitalism, something to which the characteristics of postmodern art and theory dramatically attest. Unable to rely on any of the traditional forms of "critical distanciation" in a context that has already been thoroughly colonized by the contemporary economic system, the first imperative of the postmodern critic, according to Jameson, is to undertake a process of **cognitive mapping**. As he put it, "a model of political culture appropriate to our own situation will necessarily have to raise spatial issues as its fundamental organizing concern." This will involve both establishing new models of social relationships in the transnational global space and positioning oneself in relation to them from one's own historical and spatial framework. True to the most fundamental postmodernist convictions, cognitive mapping cannot be some attempt to reestablish a "true" or "point by point" representation of some externally existing reality—no map ever is, and the postmodern global situation is unrepresentable in such form in any event—but rather, an aesthetic as well as theoretical attempt "to grasp our positioning as individual and collective subjects and regain a capacity to act and struggle which is at present neutralized by our spatial as well as our social confusion." Jameson, of course, believes that seeing postmodernism as "the cultural logic of late capitalism" clears the way for an "as yet unimaginable new mode of representing" this global postmodern condition.

Conclusion

While poststructuralist and postmodernist approaches tended to dominate debates about cultural criticism through the 1970s and most of the 1980s and are still influential in certain circles, there were signs, beginning in the mid-1980s, that their heyday had begun to wane. In the case of each of the "metaphysical unities" that poststructuralism had attempted to decenter—subject, text, and history—efforts have appeared to reconstruct them in ways that, while remaining sensitive to poststructuralist critiques, permit new ways of theorizing contemporary culture and actively intervening in it. Such figures as Gilles Deleuze and Felix Guattari perhaps paved the way already in the 1970s in France by decisively rejecting the pantextualism characteristic of structuralism and poststructuralism. In such works as *Anti-Oedipus* (1972), they insisted on the interplay of Freudian desire and Marxian production, neither representable in purely textual terms, as the ultimate basis for any critique of contemporary society. By the mid-1980s, a younger and decidedly more liberal and humanistic generation, sometimes called the "New Philosophers," had arisen in France and had begun to attack the radical posturings of both the poststructuralists and the Marxist tradition stemming from Althusser.

Typical of these new attitudes was *French Philosophy of the Sixties: An Essay on Antihumanism* (1985), by Luc Ferry and Alain Renaut. Relating the "radical French philosophy of the '60s" to the emergence and subsequent failure of the student uprisings of 1968, the work was a scathing critique of the poststructuralists' fascination bordering on obsession with Nietzschean irrationalism and (especially) its extreme mystification in Heidegger, and of certain neo-Marxists with a deterministic and essentially Leninist version of Marx. Pointing to the explicit embrace of an antihumanist stance in both cases, Ferry and Renaut sought a critically chastened return to the subject, one at least adequate to preserving and justifying the democratic and humanistic ideals of the original modern project of the Enlightenment.

Likewise, the radically decentered text of poststructuralism has come under fire from a number of different directions. While few have attempted to reinstate the text as some "transcendent metaphysical unity of meaning," a number of critics have called attention to certain determinate ways in which texts achieve partial unifications by various devices such as narrative structure (Tzvetan Todorov and Gerard Genette), the operations of metaphor and other poetic tropes in texts (Paul Ricoeur), and the reader's own partial constructions of textual meaning (Wolfgang Iser and Reader-Response Criticism).

We have already seen how both Habermas and Jameson insisted on the inevitability of a less decentered notion of history than that typically available in poststructuralist and postmodernist discourses. Both have, in particular, pointed to the necessity of some historical narrative, even if not of the grand philosophical type, on which to base the possibility of meaningful human action and political engagement. The recent New Historicism, associated with such figures as Stephen Greenblatt and Carlo Ginzburg, while owing much to Foucault, also seems more open to charting larger-scale historical trends and continuities than Foucault himself would allow.

Finally, two other trends that have emerged in the wake of the poststructuralist and postmodernist debates deserve mention. The first draws heavily on them but uses their insights to raise issues involving the literary and cultural productions of marginalized groups, which these discussions tended to overlook. Postcolonial cultural studies, as represented by Edward Said's *Orientalism* (1978) and Gayatri Chakravorty Spivak's *The Post-Colonial Critic* (1990), has turned some of the characteristic strategies developed by poststructuralism against its own unrecognized Eurocentric tendencies to assimilate "the Other" to its own cultural frameworks. The second trend involves various attempts to renew more traditional discussions of ethics and interpersonal relationships from a viewpoint that acknowledges the postmodern demand to recognize and respect otherness and difference. Emmanuel Levinas, in particular, has emerged as a major ethical theorist who has attempted a global critique of the Western metaphysical tradition—including poststructuralism in that category—charging that it has covered over and forgotten the fundamentally ethical foundations of human discourse in the face-to-face encounter with the Other, a relation that can never be reduced either to the terms of a metaphysical system or to the play of signs in texts.

Clearly, with the continued proliferation of computer and information technologies and with the further expansion of new configurations of transnational power, especially through the communications media, the issues raised and strategies developed in poststructuralist and postmodernist discourses will continue to be crucial for any future project of cultural critique. However, it is equally clear that these discourses, at least as originally articulated, have come up against certain inherent limitations that a new generation of cultural critics has begun to recognize and move beyond.

Bibliographic Essay

Anyone attempting to read the literature of poststructuralism and postmodernism for the first time should be warned that the primary texts often seem impenetrable and most of the secondary literature not much better. There are a number of reasons for this, including the facts that the twentieth-century French intellectual tradition, which provides so many points of reference for the major figures, is unfamiliar to most English-speaking readers; that the texts' structures and plays on language (often untranslatable into English) not only argue for a deconstruction of the traditional linear or logical modes of exposition but themselves exemplify the self-deconstructing text; and that throughout a discussion that rejects any surface-depth model, style becomes all-important as the author's "signature." In this essay, I will try to direct the reader to the most readable of the available primary and secondary texts, with the caveat that they are not, in every case, the most important in a particular author's oeuvre. While the dates of publication given in the preceding chapter are those of original publication, the dates given here generally refer to the English translations.

By now there are a considerable number of general introductions to poststructuralist and postmodernist discourses. Introductory works on poststructuralism generally divide into those primarily addressed to readers with a philosophical background and interests and those concerned with the study of literature, though there are naturally considerable areas of overlap between the two. One of the earliest and most often cited expositions in English, of interest both to philosophers and literary critics, is John Sturrock, ed., *Structuralism and Since* (Oxford: Oxford University Press, 1979), a collection of essays, each on one of the major figures we have discussed, by authors who would later make their own contributions to the debate. From a more distinctly literary perspective, Jonathan Culler, *The Pursuit of Signs: Semiotics, Literature, Deconstruction* (Ithaca: Cornell University Press, 1981) provides an accessible introduction to some of the major themes, although it relies heavily on Derrida and offers little on Lacan or Foucault. *On Deconstruction: Theory and Criticism after Structuralism* (Ithaca: Cornell University Press, 1982), by the same author, expands the discussion considerably. An interesting philosophical account of poststructuralism, which includes a critical confrontation between the French and British traditions of twentieth-century philosophy, is Christopher Norris, *The Deconstructive Turn: Essays in the Rhetoric of Philosophy* (London: Methuen, 1984). From a decidedly French perspective, Vincent Descombes, *Modern French Philosophy* (Cambridge: Cambridge University Press, 1980) both introduces the major figures of poststructuralism and provides a good deal of necessary background on the French intellectual scene; it is probably the best brief historical overview of the French tradition running from existentialism up to the postmodern debates. Luc Ferry and Alain Renaut, *French Philosophy of the Sixties: An Essay on Antihumanism* (Amherst: University of Massachusetts Press, 1990) presents a helpful exposition and a scathing critique of poststructuralist developments from the point of view of the (French) New Philosophers. In addition to these, there are numerous collections of essays on various figures and topics, from which readers might wish to choose according to their particular interests. For postmodernist discourses, Thomas Docherty, ed., *Postmodernism: A Reader* (New York: Columbia University Press, 1993) is probably the most comprehensive anthology that has appeared to date, containing selections from most of the materials discussed in the postmodernism section of the preceding chapter. Highly recommended for the reader new to this subject matter is Steven Best and Douglas Kellner, *Postmodern Theory: Critical Interrogations* (New York: Guilford, 1991), which presents one of the best available overviews as it develops a thoughtful political critique of postmodern discourses.

Lacan is probably the most difficult poststructuralist figure to access for a reader new to this area. The best places to start are his essays, "The function and field of speech and language in psychoanalysis" and "The agency of the letter in the unconscious or reason since Freud," both in *Écrits: A Selection* (New York: W. W. Norton, 1977). In the same volume, "The mirror stage as formative of the function of the I" is also recommended. Perhaps the most lucid and straightforward presentation of Lacan's views in relation to Freud and semiotics is Kaja Silverman, *The Subject of Semiotics* (New York: Oxford University Press, 1983). Three other works that might be helpful in various ways are: Bice Benvenuto and Roger Kennedy, *The Works of Jacques Lacan: An Introduction* (New York: St. Martin's, 1986); Ellie Ragland-Sullivan, *Jacques Lacan and the Philosophy of Psychoanalysis* (Urbana: University of Illinois Press, 1986); and Mark Bracher et al., eds., *Lacanian Theory of Discourse: Subject, Structure, and Society* (New York: New York University Press, 1994). The latter contains a number of essays "applying" Lacanian theory to various contemporary cultural configurations, quite helpful in accessing Lacan's otherwise complex and abstract ideas.

Probably the best initial access to Derrida's views are three interviews, published as *Positions*, tr. Alan Bass (Chicago: University of Chicago Press, 1981). Beyond this, the reader will eventually want to tackle his *Of Grammatology*, tr. Gayatri Chakravorty Spivak (Baltimore: Johns Hopkins University Press, 1974) and *Writing and Difference*, tr. Alan Bass (London: Routledge and Kegan Paul, 1978). Christopher Norris has been a patient expositor of Derrida to English-speaking audiences; his book *Derrida* (London: Fontana, 1987) provides a good starting point for the uninitiated. Two well-known and often cited works relating Derrida to the history of philosophy are Rodolphe Gasché, *The Tain of the Mirror: Derrida and the Philosophy of Reflection* (Cambridge: Harvard University Press, 1986) and Irene Harvey, *Derrida and the Economy of Différance* (Bloomington: Indiana University Press, 1985). The anthology *Deconstruction and Criticism*, Harold Bloom, ed. (New York: Seabury, 1979), provides a number of interesting perspectives and applications from the viewpoint of literary criticism.

The breadth of Foucault's theoretical and historical writings is well represented in *The Foucault Reader*, ed. Paul Rabinow (New York: Pantheon, 1984). Foucault's *Madness and Civilization*, tr. Richard Howard (New York: Random House, 1965), remains the most often cited example of his archaeological approach to the writing of history. Its theoretical principles are spelled out in *The Archaeology of Knowledge*, tr. A. Sheridan Smith (New York: Pantheon Books, 1972). Appended to this work is his "Discourse on Language" (1970), which marks the transition from his archaeological to his genealogical approach. Crucial also as background to this latter is his "Nietzsche, Genealogy, History" in *Language, Counter-Memory, Practice: Selected Essays and Interviews*, Josué Harari, ed. (Ithaca: Cornell University Press, 1979). *Power/Knowledge: Selected Interviews and Other Writings, 1972–1977*, Colin Gordon, ed. (New York: Pantheon, 1980) and *Politics, Philosophy, Culture: Interviews and Other Writings, 1977–1984*, Lawrence D. Kritzman, ed. (London: Routledge and Kegan Paul, 1988), provide the best introductions to his later thought and his political views. An anthology of expository and critical reflections on his work and its significance is David C. Hoy, ed., *Foucault: A Critical Reader* (Oxford: Basil Blackwell, 1986). Perhaps the best general introduction to his work is Hubert Dreyfus and Paul Rabinow, *Michel Foucault: Beyond Structuralism and Hermeneutics* (Chicago: University of Chicago Press, 1982).

Works discussed in this chapter that are relevant to the postmodern debates are: Jürgen Habermas, "Modernity: An Incomplete Project," in **T.** Docherty, *Postmodernism: A Reader* (cited above, in this bibliographic essay); Jean-François Lyotard, *The Postmodern Condi-*

tion: A Report on Knowledge, tr. Geoff Bennington and Brian Massumi (Minneapolis: University of Minnesota Press, 1984); Jean Baudrillard, "Simulacra and Simulations," in *Jean Baudrillard: Selected Writings,* Mark Poster, ed. (Stanford: Stanford University Press, 1988); and Fredric Jameson, *Postmodernism or, The Cultural Logic of Late Capitalism* (Durham, N.C.: Duke University Press, 1991). In the case of Habermas, a more elaborated version of his views, which engages a number of individual figures whom we have discussed, is *The Philosophical Discourse of Modernity,* tr. Frederick G. Lawrence (Cambridge, Mass.: MIT Press, 1987).

In addition to the above, there are a number of individual works and anthologies tracing the impact of poststructuralist and postmodernist discourses in various fields. Among them are: (in the visual arts) *Deconstruction and the Visual Arts: Art, Media, Architecture,* eds. Peter Brunette and David Wills (Cambridge: Cambridge University Press, 1994), *Art After Modernism: Rethinking Representation,* ed. Brian Wallis (Boston: David Godine, 1984), and Margot Lovejoy, *Postmodern Currents: Art and Artists in the Age of Electronic Media* (Englewood Cliffs, N.J.: Prentice Hall, 1992); (in the information sciences) Mark Poster, *The Mode of Information: Poststructuralism and Social Context* (Chicago: University of Chicago Press, 1990); and (in postcolonial studies) Edward Said, *Orientalism* (London: Routledge and Kegan Paul, 1978) and Gayatri C. Spivak, *In Other Worlds* (New York: Methuen, 1989).

There are also a number of journals devoted to poststructuralist and postmodernist approaches and themes. Among them are *Diacritics, Genre, Critical Inquiry, TriQuarterly, Textual Practice, October,* and *Cultural Critique.* Those readers interested in such issues also should not overlook the various electronic sites on the Internet dealing with general themes and specific figures in poststructuralism and postmodernism.

8
Contemporary
Cultural Studies

Earlier in this volume, we distinguished between cultural studies as a broad characterization of all the various discourses discussed in this book and as a narrower and more recent movement that began in certain British universities in the 1950s. In this chapter, the focus will be on the later and more specific critical discourse and its developments (or sometimes close parallels) in countries beyond the British Isles. Certainly contemporary cultural studies must now be counted as a particular critical discourse, since like earlier discourses we have encountered it has by now developed its own body of foundational texts, a set of distinctive themes and problematics, forums for communicative exchange, and characteristic controversies. However, as a critical discourse, it differs in at least three important ways from most of the critical discourses that preceded it. Considering these differences will help us gain an initial sense of what is involved in this newest sort of critical enterprise.

First, from its very beginning, cultural studies was decisively oriented toward the analysis and critique of *concrete cultural productions and institutions* and their political ramifications. The construction of some general philosophical position or overarching theoretical standpoint was never among its primary aims. This is not to say that cultural studies was purely activist or interventionist and entirely lacking in any theoretical dimension, but only that theory construction remained more a means to various ends rather than an end in itself. Even today, among those involved in the discourse of cultural studies a certain suspicion remains of what is sometimes negatively referred to as *theoreticism,* an emphasis on theoretical discussion that has become too far removed from the actual historical and cultural contexts that it is intended to analyze or critique.

Second, rather than attempting to forge some new theoretical position or methodology, cultural studies has freely and deliberately poached on other existing critical discourses, adapting, joining, and reconfiguring their basic ideas and approaches in whatever fashion seems most adequate to the analysis and critique of the concrete issue or institution under consideration. Certainly it has tended over time to prefer certain concepts, discourses, and configurations over others, but it has rarely undertaken any doctrinaire defense of some preferred methodology or conceptual constellation. Because of this, cultural studies displays a marked diversity in theoretical orientation, which defies any simple or single characterization. Perhaps what its various practitioners most share in common is precisely an openness to methodological alternatives, coupled with an insistence that any use of theory or methodology be justified by its applicability to concrete, and usually contemporary, issues.

Third, cultural studies originated in large part as a critical response to the fact that many of the most important and complex issues in contemporary popular culture tended to fall through the cracks dividing the existing academic disciplines and, to some degree, the available critical discourses. In particular, the explosion of the influence of the mass media following World War II, with its acceleration of the blurring of the traditional lines between high culture and popular culture, seemed to go largely unregistered in academic circles and sometimes in the more traditional discourses as well. Although cultural studies was in spirit more akin to the concerns of the Frankfurt School than any of the other critical discourses, this Continental movement, by the mid-1950s, had arrived at such a generally negative and pessimistic assessment of the recent dramatic changes in culture that it had abandoned any attempt to place the newly emergent forms of popular culture on its agenda. On the other hand, while media studies, originally launched in large part by the earlier Frankfurt School, were beginning to develop at about the same time, particularly in the United States, the earlier figures of the cultural studies movement regarded this emergent discipline as having been coopted by the empirical social sciences, with the result that no genuinely critical stance could be expected to emerge from it. And since the disciplinary academic institutions of the 1950s were ill equipped to take up issues that clearly crossed established disciplinary boundaries and resistant to questioning their traditional commitment to broader liberal humanist concerns, there seemed no alternative but to begin imagining and constituting a new, unabashedly interdisciplinary, eclectic, and practical critical discourse.

One further issue deserves mention at the outset. While cultural studies as a concerted and identifiable movement is generally associated with developments at certain British universities, especially the University of Birmingham, in the 1950s, it would be a mistake to view it simply as a British contribution to contemporary critical discourse for several reasons. First, at quite an early stage, it began to draw on other critical discourses developed on the Continent (and, to a lesser degree, in the United States), especially those of the Frankfurt School, structuralism, and later, postmodernism. Second, many of its characteristic themes and emphases were already emerging independently in other countries such as France, the United States, Australia, and Canada, resulting in a good deal of cross-fertilization. Finally, although cultural studies in each country has retained something of its own characteristic set of emphases and preferred approaches due to the differing cultural configurations characteristic of each national region, the growth of an international economy, the internationalization of the media, and new possibilities for international communication among researchers have resulted in a tendency toward a certain degree of convergence of the various regional discourses of cultural studies.

With these caveats in mind, it is best to begin with a review of the development of cultural studies in Great Britain as our main axis of historical orientation. With this background in place, we will then consider some developments outside the British mainstream that have fed into it at various points. Finally, we will highlight some of the more important theoretical and political controversies that contemporary cultural studies now faces.

The Development of British Cultural Studies: Overview

In its origins, British cultural studies can be viewed as a response to the dramatic changes in the economic, political, and cultural life of Great Britain in the postwar period, especially as reflected in the changing role of British educational institutions. By the end of the eighteenth century, England had become the most industrialized country in Europe, and by the end of the nineteenth, the leading colonial power in the world. However, the general framework of its preindustrial class structure remained to a significant extent intact until World War II. Although Great Britain and the Allies emerged victorious from that upheaval, many of the cultural and political institutions taken for granted before the war had been destabilized. Britain was no longer an unquestioned colonial power nor even a major player in the context of the new world of the cold war, and its basic cultural institutions—its class structure, monarchy, relatively laissez-faire approach to the economy, and elitist educational system—fell increasingly under critical scrutiny. As in other nations, the explosion of the mass media and their propagation of a homogenized popular culture in Britain exacerbated this challenge to traditional cultural institutions. In the arena of British intellectual life and its associated institutions of higher education, this debate unfolded through several relatively distinguishable phases.

Leavisism and the Rise of Culturalism

In the 1930s, the tradition of elitist cultural critique begun by Matthew Arnold in the middle of the nineteenth century (see Chapter 1) was reconsidered, revised, and extended by a number of British cultural critics, the most influential of whom was the literary scholar and critic **F. R. Leavis** (1895–1978). From his position at Cambridge, where he was a sometime lecturer and later fellow, Leavis became, for over 40 years, the principal modern torchbearer of what has been called the **culture-and-civilization movement** in cultural critique.

According to this tradition, best represented in the journal *Scrutiny,* which Leavis edited, literature was the principal mode of expression of a given culture, which in turn was defined in primarily moral and aesthetic terms. The unabashedly evaluative criticism of literature was therefore held to be the preeminent vehicle for a decidedly moralistic critique of contemporary culture. According to Leavis, all genuine or authentic literature emerged as the cultural expression of an **organic community**, by which he meant a (generally) preindustrial and even rural social state, uncorrupted by commercial considerations. Due to the stable and well-defined division of social functions characterizing such communities, "the finest human experience of the past" was conserved and disseminated by a minority cultural elite. In the process, it was assumed that the lower classes would be elevated and civilized by the (alleged) moral and aesthetic standards implicit in this cultural heritage. In stark contrast to this culture of an organic community, Leavis lamented the rise of commercial mass and popular culture (for him identical), which had the opposite effect of leveling all that was best in human experience and culture to a lowest common denominator, a mere pandering to the unruly desires and immorality of the masses.

Although Leavisism, once entrenched as a sort of party line among British academic intellectuals, was deliberately and shamelessly elitist, it nonetheless facilitated the emergence of cultural studies in at least two respects. First, it affirmed, albeit in a nostalgic and mythologized form, the intimate connections between a living culture and its cultural expressions against the attempts, already well under way, to reduce culture and its expressions to the types of economic or social functionality with which the empirical social sciences and certain varieties of materialist thought were enamored. Second, it expanded the formerly much narrower and specialized discourse of literary studies to include expressions of popular culture in its purview, even if (for Leavis) these entered principally as occasions for negative critique and polemic.

The first phase of British cultural studies arose as a direct response to the elitism implicit in the sort of literary studies that the culture-and-civilization viewpoint endorsed and propagated through corresponding academic institutions. Preeminent among these early critics of Leavisism were the literary critics Richard Hoggart and Raymond Williams and the historian E. P. Thompson, whose general approach has sometimes been collectively referred to as **culturalism**.

Richard Hoggart, in his most influential work, *The Uses of Literacy* (1958), offered one of the earliest challenges to the Leavisism prevailing at British educational institutions, even though the extent of this challenge remained somewhat limited and transitional. In the first part of this work, Hoggart, in semiautobiographical fashion, described the cultural milieu of his own working-class origins in Britain of the 1930s. In his account, a vital, life-affirming, and largely self-made communal culture of the working classes was still intact as late as the period between the two world wars, a point that the Leavisites, in their nostalgia for some preindustrial, organic community, had completely failed to consider. However, Hoggart admitted in the second part of his work, paralleling the Leavisites, that in the postwar period, this healthy working-class culture was under severe attack from the combined forces of mass culture, which commercially manufactured a manipulative "candy-floss wonderland" that tended to deaden the formerly affirmative and engaged cultural sensibilities of the working classes.

However, despite certain similarities with the Leavisite position, Hoggart's work suggested two points crucial to the subsequent development of British cultural studies. First, he undermined the Arnoldian and Leavisite notion of culture in industrial society as a privileged possession to be guarded and transmitted "from the top down" by some cultural elite, by insisting on the full legitimacy and "organicity" of recent working-class culture. And second, while he shared with the Leavisites a repugnance for contemporary mass-produced commercial culture, he suggested that the working class itself should not be viewed wholly as its passive dupe. Rather, he maintained that even in the face of the onslaught of mass culture, the working classes still retained the capacity both to create their own popular cultural forms and to assert their autonomous choice with regard to the productions offered them by mass culture. This insistence on the legitimacy and autonomy of working-class cultural production represented a major move away from the cultural elitism of the culture-and-civilization movement of Leavis and his followers.

Raymond Williams (1921–1988), the most influential figure of the culturalist phase of British cultural studies, came, like Hoggart, from a working-class background. He published his first major work, *Culture and Society, 1780–1950,* in the same year as Hoggart's *The Uses of Literacy.* This was followed, in 1961, by *The Long Revolution,* his most important early theoretical statement. While Hoggart leaned heavily toward the anecdotal, Williams began to formulate broad new analytical structures designed to clarify the concept of culture and to place it squarely at the center of a newly emerging critical discourse. In broad terms, it was Williams who first attempted clearly to distinguish between Culture (with a capital C), understood by the Arnoldian and Leavisite tradition in moralistic and aesthetic terms as a sort of storehouse of the best that civilization had to offer, and culture (with a small c), that is, the complex and dynamic set of expressions that human beings employ to make sense of their lived experiences and the historical conditions under which those experiences occur. This "'social' definition of culture," as Williams further explicated it, involves three interrelated claims. First, culture is always a *particular way of life;* second, this way of life is an *expression of "certain meanings and values";* and third, the analysis of culture should aim at *"the clarification of the meanings and values* implicit and explicit in a particular way of life, a particular culture." Williams's theoretical clarification of culture was indispensable for the subsequent development of cultural studies, since it established an autonomous field for inquiry and critique that defied any attempts to reduce it either to an idealized possession of the elite (the Leavisite, and more generally, liberal humanist view) or to some more primitive historical or economic processes (the perspective of more traditional Marxism and certain of the social sciences). This insistence on the theoretical centrality and irreducibility of the concept of culture became the hallmark of the culturalist phase of British cultural studies.

Another important though more controversial theoretical innovation suggested by Williams was his notion of a **structure of feeling**. More overt and explicit than some underlying collective unconscious but less determinate and intellectualizable than an ideology, a structure of feeling is the "particular and characteristic colour" that the ensemble of the values, beliefs, and practices of a given culture imparts to the experiences of its members. In particular, a given culture's structure of feeling will at least influence if not determine the patterns of response of its members in resolving or coping with the dilemmas and contradictions that confront them in their daily lives. For Williams, the principal aim of cultural analysis is to discern and understand this structure of feeling as it manifests itself throughout the entire range of a given culture's expressions.

In line with this, Williams advocated a broad and democratic view of the products, institutions, and practices worthy of serious cultural analysis. From the perspective of the culturalist viewpoint as developed by Williams, the forms of popular culture, such as film, television, music, and sports, were more instructive about culture as experienced and produced in the lives of ordinary people than any collection of the great works of the past. It was to the analysis of the various forms of popular culture that Williams devoted much of his attention in the 1960s and 1970s.

Williams's critics have often pointed out that his cultural theory and critique remained uneasily located between the humanistic orientation often evident in his studies of literature and his practical engagement in and commitment to broadly Marxist and socialist causes. Viewed more affirmatively, and decisive for his influence on the subsequent development of cultural studies, Williams consistently rejected any view that held or implied that cultural activity was merely a product or reflection of forces that lay beyond human control or influence. Rather, culture was that always contested site where historically formed meanings and values were opposed, reconfigured, and sometimes created anew through the continuing process of human cultural activity. Unlike traditional Marxists, Williams believed the revolution would not occur as some economic upheaval at a particular point in time but was already unfolding (hence the title of his work, *The Long Revolution*) and that this gradual movement toward a more democratic and collectivist state was occurring primarily at the level of culture.

Translating the older determinist theory of history into the terms of cultural struggle, Williams asserted that at any point in time, three different types of forces could be seen to be operative in culture: the **dominant**, representing the interests and values of the classes and other groups most empowered at any given point in social development; the **residual**, comprising the values and cultural formations of past (and usually formerly dominant) social configurations, which remain active but subordinate in the present; and the **emergent**, the "new meanings and values, new practices, new significances and experiences, [which] are continually being created" in opposition to the dominant culture and that normally constitute the progressive, future-oriented aspect of culture. Thus, human culture, viewed as a whole, is a dynamic site where these various forces vie with one another for dominance or hegemony, as human agents express their own lived experiences and resist the dominance of others in the cultural realm. As always with Williams, however, the major emphasis remains on the meaning-producing activities of real human agents as they strive to make sense of and express their lived experience in the dynamics of culture.

While Williams was engaged in forging a broad theoretical framework for the analysis and critique of culture that affirmed the role of human agency in its dynamic processes, historian E. P. **Thompson** provided culturalism with a richly detailed but powerful example of how such a view might be applied in the realm of social history. His *The Making of the English Working Class* (1963) opens with the statement: "The working class did not rise like the sun at an appointed time. It was present at its own making." In a way perhaps even more pronounced than in the case of Williams, Thompson's monumental "history from below" adopts a defiantly antiessentialist and historicist stance with respect even to his own most basic theoretical terms. In particular, the concept of class is not some historically constant or theoretically fixed term but "entails the notion of historical relationship." It is a relationship (or, more precisely, a set of relationships) that "must always be embodied in real people and in a real context" and must always be "handled in cultural terms: embodied in traditions, value-systems, ideas, and institutional forms." Strictly speaking, class does not exist, either as a predefinable social grouping or as some ideological consciousness on the part of certain individuals. Rather, "class is defined by men as they live their own history, and, in the end, this is its only definition."

True to the strand of Marxism that insists that history is always a human production, Thompson's work focused principally on the qualitative experiences of those displaced and disenfranchised by the Industrial Revolution and on their efforts to forge new, oppositional cultural forms in which their experiences and aspirations could find expression. Rather than something existing over and above these concrete activities or superimposed on them by the historian or cultural critic, the notion of an English working class was, first and foremost, gradually produced, defined, and revised by its own members in their own cultural activities. Thompson rejected the term *culturalism* to describe his project when used in the sense of a denial of the importance of historically given factors in influencing human cultural production in significant ways; however, his emphasis on the centrality of cultural production and on the importance of human agency operating in this domain, and his careful attention to its popular forms, nonetheless allied his project with the culturalism of Williams and Hoggart.

The Centre for Contemporary Cultural Studies and the 'Paradigm Debate'

In 1960, the National Union of Teachers organized a conference entitled "Popular Culture and Personal Responsibility," which featured, among other speakers, both

Hoggart and Williams as well as Stuart Hall. This event is often cited as the source from which the institutionalized presence of British cultural studies emerged. In direct response to the elitist view of culture endorsed by the then-prevailing Leavisites, the conference's aim was to discuss the possible incorporation of elements of popular culture into the British school system. While no clear consensus emerged from this meeting, it did demonstrate the need for further research and reflection both on the nature of contemporary culture and on appropriate methods for its analysis and critique.

These discussions eventually led to the founding in 1964 of the first, and most influential, institution devoted exclusively to such issues: The **Centre for Contemporary Cultural Studies** (CCCS) at the University of Birmingham. With Hoggart as its first director, the CCCS was primarily concerned with promoting and supporting postgraduate research in cultural studies, maintaining a wary distance from the degree-granting functions of the University of Birmingham itself. Early in its existence, its focus was narrowed somewhat from the broader concern with lived cultures of Hoggart and Williams to the ideological functions of the mass media in contemporary society. Although it was, in one sense, part of a much broader international movement devoted to communication studies, it distinguished itself from the form these took in the United States (and in England) under the influence of the empirical social sciences, as well as from the (by this time) rather convoluted theoreticism and generally negative verdict of the Frankfurt School toward mass and popular culture. Rather, it was principally concerned with the ideological functions of the media in influencing social relations and the power differentials implicit in them.

Stuart Hall, who had served as Hoggart's deputy since 1966, became director of the CCCS in 1969. During the decade of his leadership, the CCCS dramatically expanded in terms of its theoretical base, its research agendas, and its national and international influence. In his essay "Cultural Studies: Two Paradigms," published in 1981 in the indispensable anthology *Culture, Ideology, and Social Process,* Hall reviewed the major theoretical debates that had occupied the CCCS up to that time and provided an admirably balanced perspective on them. The first paradigm, and the one initially adopted by the CCCS, was that of culturalism, especially as developed by Hoggart, Williams, and Thompson. This approach, which views culture as an entire way of life produced out of the experiences of human agents, began to compete, beginning in the mid-1960s, with another, which Hall broadly referred to as "structuralism." The structural paradigm, rather than emphasizing human experience and practical activity as the source of culture, in a sense reversed this view by stressing the structural and ideological features of culture as the ultimate conditions or determinants of human praxis. Rather than makers of culture, human beings (or at least their basic self-conceptions) were depicted as its ideological products.

Although culturalism and structuralism agreed in rejecting the traditional Marxist doctrine of culture as a mere superstructural feature of the economic base or infrastructure and emphasized (to varying degrees) culture's autonomy, Hall noted several crucial respects in which they remained theoretically incommensurable. First, while culturalism viewed the experience of one's historical conditions as the basis of cultural production and of culture as its expression, "structuralism insisted that 'experience' could not, by definition, be the ground of anything, since one could only 'live' and experience one's conditions *in and through* the categories, classifications, and frameworks of the culture." Second, while the culturalists did tend to regard culture as a collective production, the structuralists denied even an important aspect of this claim in maintaining that the structural determinants of culture functioned largely in an unconscious manner, serving to locate individual subjects in particular collectivities, and collectivities in a broader texture of ideology. Culture, for the structuralists, was an expression neither of individuals nor of collectivities; rather, individual subjects or any other consciousnesses of social relations were themselves expressions of largely unconscious, ideological structures. With regard to language, one of the most important of cultural structures, the structuralists maintained that rather than a subject speaking a language, we should say that the speaker is subject to its language, indeed that the very notions of a subject, experience, or consciousness are ideological effects of a given language.

In what remains one of the most balanced assessments of the prospects for cultural studies as a critical discourse, Hall proceeded to outline the relative strengths and weaknesses of these two major poles. In his assessment, the structuralist paradigm has at least three major theoretical advantages over the culturalist one. First, in stressing the "determinate conditions" under which culture is produced, the structuralist approach affirms the fact that human activity, especially under modern capitalism, occurs only in a set of determinate relations, which constitute definite constraints on what can be thought or imagined and what can be accomplished. In this sense, it offsets the tendency of culturalism to see the agency of human beings in the idealized terms of the heroic affirmation of bare individuals. Second, the structural paradigm affirms that the analysis and critique of culture require the introduction of theoretical abstractions into critical discourse in order "to reveal and bring to light," in the otherwise overwhelming and relatively continuous set of cultural practices and institutions, "relationships and structures which cannot be visible to the naive naked eye, and which can neither present nor authenticate themselves." Again, this perspective counterbalances the antitheoretical tendencies of culturalism, which can sometimes be lost in the myriad details of a given cultural complex. Finally, against culturalism's insistence on the total or wholistic nature of culture ultimately based on human agency, structuralism emphasizes the role of differences permeating and constituting the field of culture. Although in structuralism culture must be viewed as a whole, it is a whole that is internally complex, constituted by a structured set of relatively autonomous conflicts and oppositions that are obscured by culturalism's overemphasis on the organicity and fluidity of culture, viewed as the seamless expression of the experiences of human agents.

For Hall, however, this does not signal an unqualified acceptance of the structuralist paradigm, since certain insights of culturalism remain valid and important. Most of all, while the structures that provide conditions and constraints on human action remain always efficacious, cultural production and political transformation require that these largely unconsciously operative structures achieve a certain level of conscious awareness and articulation as individuals form themselves into collectivities and become genuine historical agents. For human beings can, in fact, deliberately intervene in cultural and historical processes and thus can never be adequately viewed as merely inert tokens or markers in an overarching set of impersonal and abstract structural transformations.

Hall concluded his review of the course taken by the major theoretical debate in cultural studies by indicating three theoretical views that he regarded as incompatible with its basic stance. This amounted, in effect, to a negative definition of cultural studies, an attempt to specify what it is by clarifying what it is not. First, the development of structuralism in the hands of psychoanalysis (especially Lacan's version of it) tended to reduce all cultural practice to discourse and all consciousness to a decentered subject defined by largely unconscious discursive practices (see the preceding chapter of this work for a discussion of these concepts). The result of this wedding of structuralism and psychoanalysis was that both the conscious historical agent and the actual historical conditions of its activity were submerged in the ahistorical swamp of a "subject in general" and the universal features of the discourse that determines it. In an opposite though equally abstract direction move positions that attempt to reduce the sphere of cultural production to the economic base. While cultural studies can by no means ignore economic factors, too exclusive a focus on "the logic of capital" tends to obscure "the effect of the cultural and ideological dimension," which requires much more specificity and sensitivity to actual historical and cultural contexts. Finally, having defended a limited version of the structuralist paradigm, Hall criticized certain poststructuralist approaches that had "followed the path of 'difference' through into a radical heterogeneity," singling out that of Foucault (see Chapter 7). While such approaches have respected the specificity and concreteness of particular cultural configurations, which was the hallmark of culturalism, they have tended to insist on such a radical discontinuity between and among various cultural practices that it becomes impossible to reassemble their analyses into a general critique of particular social formations at the level of politics or ideology. As we will see, Hall's attack on the usefulness of poststructuralist approaches in cultural studies later became a matter of heated controversy.

Under Hall's leadership, much of the research conducted under the auspices of the CCCS remained focused on the ideological effects of the media across various signifying systems as these function in various texts (broadly conceived). However, the focus gradually was expanded to include analyses of subcultures (especially those of urban youth and women) that resisted the forces of the dominant culture, and historical and ethnographic studies deriving in various ways from the work of Thompson. During this period, it should be added, the theoretical insights of Gramsci, especially his notion of hegemony (see Chapter 3), became an especially important source for the general orientation of the CCCS's work.

The Theoretical Reorientation of the CCCS: Toward a 'Thematic' and 'Theoretical Pluralism'

In 1979, Richard Johnson succeeded Stuart Hall as director of the CCCS. In his important and still influential essay, "What Is Cultural Studies Anyway?" (1983), Johnson presented a schematic overview together with his own critical perspective of what had by then become a full-blown critical discourse. Methodologically, this essay reflected the growing interest and importance to the CCCS's research of certain poststructuralist approaches about which Hall had earlier expressed skepticism; thematically, it endorsed a rather broad ecumenism as to the various sorts of research projects that might be included under, or at least prove relevant to, cultural studies. In particular, Johnson argued that the complex and multidimensional nature of culture itself dictated that cultural studies must remain interdisciplinary and pluralistic and should resist any tendency to take its place alongside other established disciplines.

Johnson's schematic attempt both to distinguish and to integrate the various dimensions of cultural analysis and critique (see Figure 8.1) remains a very helpful way of locating the diverse methods and thematic emphases of cultural studies. His schema is based on four major assumptions. First, as opposed to the earlier culturalism (and even Hall's limited acceptance of it) as well as to various Marxist and structuralist paradigms, Johnson argued that cultural studies was, in general, principally concerned with the various forms in which **subjectivity** or **consciousness** is produced and reproduced in the dynamics of culture. In his view, both subjectivity and its forms of expression must be taken to include the active process of cultural production as well as the ideological conditions under which this production occurs. Second, Johnson viewed the objective **circuit of capital**, based on a broadly Marxist analysis resembling that developed by the early Frankfurt School, as paralleled by a subjective (in the sense given above) **circuit of culture**. Just as, in capitalism, commodities are produced, established as relatively autonomous, consumed by economic agents, and integrated into their own practical activity, thus reproducing the commodity-form in lived experience; so cultural activity moves through a parallel cycle of production, textualization, reception, and appropriation in lived cultures. Third, Johnson suggested that at every stage, social relations of power must occupy the foreground of analysis and critique. Finally, Johnson was committed to a theoretical pluralism that held that while every stage or moment of this circuit is essential to understanding the dynamics of the whole, each stage, taken as a focus of research, requires its own characteristic methods, offers its own distinctive perspectives on the whole, and dictates different types and degrees of political engagement and intervention. In a

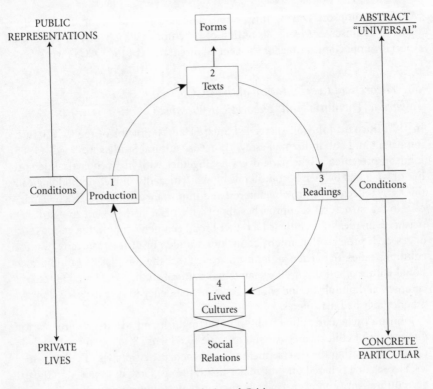

Figure 8.1   Dimensions of Cultural Analysis and Critique

sense, Johnson's schema is a response to the "unity in diversity" of cultural studies to which Hall had already pointed. It should also be added that Johnson's schema strongly implied that the media studies that was characteristic of the period of Hall's directorship was too limited a project to encompass all that cultural studies was, or should be, accomplishing.

1. *Production:* From this perspective, typically the province of sociologists, political economists, social historians, and more recently, certain types of media and literary studies, culture is approached in terms of the economic and social conditions and processes under which various cultural productions originate and first enter into the cycle of cultural circulation. Citing the early Frankfurt School and Gramsci as having provided especially important examples of such studies, Johnson suggested that just as the material forms of commodities are influenced (if not determined) by the material conditions of their production, so the subjective cultural meanings of cultural commodities must be viewed as intimately bound up with the conditions governing their making. To expand on Johnson's discussion with concrete examples, such an approach would include studies of how the mass media are organized to develop, select, and produce certain types of scripts,

how the economic compensation for authors influences their selection of themes and their treatments, and how the fashion industry produces (and reproduces) certain social positions in advertising and marketing their products. However, in presenting this approach, Johnson warns against an overemphasis on the initial phase of material production, which neglects the fact that meanings are also produced in the processes by which various individuals and groups appropriate cultural products.

2. *Text-based studies:* Such approaches begin with cultural products as already made or given, and regarding them (broadly) as texts, provide "more or less definitive 'readings' of them." Such approaches are typical of literary analysis, especially as practiced in the humanities and the arts, which often have borrowed heavily from various forms of structuralism. Most importantly for cultural studies, text-based approaches often aim at delineating and distinguishing both the various forms (in the sense of genres) into which texts can be classified and the various forms (in the sense of signifying structures) that operate in and across texts to produce their meanings. Johnson faulted the usual disciplinary practice of textual analysis as too focused on texts for their own sake without any sense of their broader cultural relevance and functioning; but he saw in them the raw material for an expanded analysis of "the social life of subjective forms" when utilized in the interdisciplinary context of cultural studies. In particular, the various genres of texts and the structures operative in them must be understood as part of a circuit joining their production with their actual and nonspecialized readership.

3. *Readers:* Although cultural texts are produced under concrete cultural conditions utilizing various forms and structures that provide a framework for establishing valid interpretations of their meaning, how various actual (and especially nonspecialist) readers or audiences will understand them is a different question. Further, semiology has emphasized the counterprocess of how encounters with cultural texts bring about the production of subjects, that is, "imply or construct a position or positions from which they are to be read or viewed." While both reception theory in literary studies and research on audiences in media studies represent a fruitful step beyond the pure focus on the text itself, such approaches must not lose sight of the facts that readers not only produce interpretations of texts but are produced as subjects by the texts they read, and that this two-sided process requires the recognition of the importance of contextual elements, including prior readings of other texts.

4. *Lived cultures:* Finally, perhaps the most distinctive contribution of cultural studies to this circuit of cultural production, the process by which texts are produced, structured, and then appropriated by actual readers, culminates in what culturalism had already pointed to as "whole ways of life" or "lived cultures." Just as in reading texts readers at the same time both actively determine textual meanings and are in turn constituted or located as subjects through those textual meanings, so ensembles of variously located subjects sharing complexes of cultural texts can be approached in terms of the lived cultures formed by that shar-

ing of texts. In particular, cultural studies has often focused on the relationships and interactions between the private readings of texts and the public forms in which ensembles of texts become institutionalized. Especially fruitful have been studies highlighting the manner in which products of mass culture have been actively appropriated and transformed to reflect the social positions and needs of various subcultural groups, that is, the actual uses to which they are put. An important result of this approach has been the reaffirmation that cultural production is never a mere passive acceptance of meanings and values produced elsewhere but involves the continual contestation, transformation, and sometimes even reversal of the original intention of the first producers. In such analyses, Johnson argues, the two key questions are, What accounts for the popularity of various cultural forms, leading various groups to prefer the pleasure of one type of form over another; and What are the ultimate outcomes of such selection, in terms of whether they lead to a reproduction of the dominant culture, a contestation of it, or perhaps even to its active transformation?

The CCCS Today: Diversification and Institutionalization

After about a decade under the leadership of Johnson, the directorship of the Centre passed to Jorge Lorrain. Beginning in the late 1980s, the CCCS found it necessary to resist reabsorption into the department of English and has now become a department of cultural studies, offering its own undergraduate degrees. Although the vital and usually collective research agendas that had characterized the CCCS through the 1970s and 1980s have been influenced by the demands of undergraduate teaching, the basic orientation of the CCCS has been widely disseminated elsewhere, so that, especially in the United States, Australia, and Canada, various more or less institutionalized organizations have formed, continuing, with considerable local variation, the thematic orientation and building on the theoretical developments of the original Centre. Such organizations run the gamut from academic departments, through "integrated studies" units, to much looser research consortia, the latter often greatly indebted to forms of national and international communication made possible by the Internet.

Two recent developments in cultural studies as a critical discourse are particularly noteworthy. First, as regards thematics, a number of subfields have emerged under the umbrella of cultural studies, including postcolonial studies, ethnic studies, gender studies, and gay/lesbian/bisexual (queer) studies. Each of these, in turn, has drawn not only on paradigms borrowed from the British tradition of cultural studies but also on other approaches developed elsewhere, considerably expanding both the thematic and theoretical contours of the mainstream movement that we have been discussing. Second, while most of the figures whom we have encountered in British cultural studies have voiced serious reservations about certain of the paradigms offered by various poststructuralist and postmodernist discourses, it is probably fair to say that based on much of the research that has recently appeared, such discourses, under suitable elaboration, have found their place in the broader framework of current cultural studies. There is rarely any question of whether they are compatible with a broadly conceived cultural studies perspective, but only, given their already proven usefulness in cultural analysis, how and in what form they can be integrated into it.

Cultural Studies at Work: Applications

As emphasized earlier, cultural studies has from the beginning been decisively oriented toward concrete analysis and critique, generally letting theoretical issues grow out of and be discussed in relation to such concrete contexts. In order to see how this has occurred, it will be helpful to review a few of the better-known research projects pursued in this critical discourse. The specific projects that will be discussed were selected because they are especially illustrative of the type of theme and approach being employed in cultural studies at a given stage of its development and are ordered in a way paralleling the preceding historical overview. However, they by no means constitute an overview of the entire range of research undertaken to date in cultural studies.

One of the earliest attempts to theorize the area of popular culture and establish it as a legitimate and important area of critical inquiry was *The Popular Arts* (1964), by Stuart Hall and Paddy Whannel. This work grew out of the meeting of the Special Conference of the National Union of Teachers, mentioned earlier, and represented a carefully conceived reaction to the Leavisism that the Teachers' Conference had initially attempted to counter. Although this work expanded the Leavisite focus on high culture to include popular culture as a legitimate area of research and evaluation, its overall approach was not only culturalist, continuing the work of Hoggart and Williams, but remained primarily evaluative and aesthetic, thus maintaining important connections with the Leavisite program. In this work, Hall and Whannel's general thesis is twofold. First, they affirm that from the viewpoint of critical evaluation, the productions of high culture are, generally speaking, superior to those of popular culture. Second, however, they claim that it is possible to develop standards of critical evaluation appropriate to the popular arts, paralleling but necessarily somewhat different from those prevailing in the criticism of high culture. Ultimately, their aim is not so much to level or deny the value of high culture as to rescue popular culture from the prevailing, virtually automatic critical denigration it had traditionally suffered. In their view, popular culture should be judged not as inferior to high culture, but as pursuing different aims and producing different satisfactions. In other words, in the totality of contemporary culture, popular culture plays important and distinctive roles.

In order to promote aesthetic and critical discrimination among the productions of popular culture, Hall and Whannel proposed the novel category of popular art. Harking back to the notion of folk art as the direct expression of an organic community, they acknowledged that while commercialization had to a great extent undermined this type of cultural production, certain instances emerging from popular culture had succeeded in reestablishing a rapport between audience and artist that made them a genuine art "for the people" in ways in which the high arts were not. As they explained the notion, good or successful popular art not only establishes this rapport between artist and audience but it involves "the surprise of art as well as the shock of recognition" and appears as individualized in a shared communal understanding of certain conventions of performance-practice. In contrast to genuine popular art, mass art (which corresponds closely to what the Frankfurt School called kitsch) is repetitive, formulaic, unchallenging, and directed toward a faceless and nondescript mass audience. For instance, in their view a critic might fairly maintain that while the best work of the Beatles may not have the same artistic worth as Bach's cantatas or Stravinsky's *Rite of Spring*, it is certainly superior to anything produced by the Monkees, Beatle clones commercially organized specifically to capitalize on the latter's success.

Although *The Popular Arts* focused primarily on the textual qualities of productions of popular culture and did so in a way that maintained clear ties with its Leavisite aesthetic heritage, it also indicated the need to consider the various types of readers of these texts, and in a tentative way, pointed toward the contexts of lived culture in which popular works function. In these respects, it anticipated several directions that would later be explored in cultural studies.

In the late 1960s and 1970s, mainstream cultural studies shed almost all remnants of the aestheticism still evident in *The Popular Arts* and began moving in several new directions. One strand of this work, clearly influenced by the historical research of E. P. Thompson, is well represented by the anthology, *Popular Culture: Past and Present* (1982, edited by B. Waites, T. Bennett, and G. Martin). Employing different combinations of historical analysis and ethnographic description, these essays focused on various aspects of the development of working-class and more broadly popular culture, especially during the Victorian period and the first half of the twentieth century. Studies focusing on themes such as the role of leisure pursuits—for example, sports, the music hall, and vacationing—as well as the social transformations effected by the rise of electronic mass media continued, in greater detail, the tradition established by Thompson. Here, the concern with popular culture is no longer aesthetic but primarily historical and descriptive, attempting to chart, in various areas, how the popular culture of the working and middle classes came to establish itself in opposition to the previously dominant high culture. Such projects were concerned much less with specific texts and more with the relations among the new forms of production, audiences, and lived cultures established in recent popular culture. The influence of Continental structuralist and poststructuralist theory, although occasionally mentioned, had not yet become conspicuous in such studies. In particular, the ideological formation and location of subjectivities had yet to become an overriding theme.

However, the reception by British cultural studies of Continental theory is clearly and explicitly registered in Dick Hebdige's *Subculture: The Meaning of Style* (1979). The introductory, theoretical essay is a compact and trenchant example of the general orientation and flavor of a good deal of later work in mainstream cultural studies. In presenting his key concepts of culture, hegemony, semiology, and ideology as a preface to his study of youth subcultures in England in the 1950s through the 1970s, Hebdige's book reveals the eclectic theoretical poaching, adapted to the needs of a specific research project, that continues to typify much work in cultural studies.

Reviewing the course that the discussion of culture had taken from the eighteenth century to Hoggart and Williams, Hebdige noted the underlying dependence on a literary sensibility that continued to inform such discussions. According to Hebdige, the idea of **semiology** suggested by Saussure and Barthes provided the first theoretically adequate response to the literary textualism and aestheticism characteristic of the earlier culture-and-society debates. In particular, Barthes's semiology, in insisting that culture be viewed as "the life of signs in society," at once moved critical discourse beyond the narrower scope of literary criticism to include the whole gamut of social interactions and formations; linked specific signifying systems to the dehistoricized and naturalized **mythologies** that function as unreflected rules and conventions underlying specific forms of the production of social meaning; and pursued a rigorous method of analysis that no longer relied on the literary sensibilities of an informed reader. When linked with the Marxist tradition (as Barthes himself did), Barthes's mythologies could be regarded as specific forms of **ideology**, which then becomes the central category of cultural critique.

Ideology, in this approach, performs its work precisely because it is the largely unconscious structural scaffolding of common sense, saturating everyday discourse and all realms of everyday life with concepts and values that seem entirely natural and unquestionable. Citing Althusser, Hebdige went on to claim, against older materialist theory, that ideology is not merely some superstructural feature of a more fundamental economic infrastructure but that even material institutions and social relations are viewed through ideological lenses: "Social relations and processes are then appropriated by individuals only through the forms in which they are represented to those individuals." It is precisely at this intersection, where ideological representations meet concrete reality, that semiology must intervene in order to reveal and "disentangle the codes through which meaning is organized."

However, invoking Gramsci's notion of **hegemony**, Hebdige points out that, in "highly complex societies like ours," we cannot simply speak of a single ideology. Rather, ideologies compete and conflict with one another, though on an unequal basis, since each social class and grouping operates out of its own ideological structures, its own sets of meanings and codes, but under varying degrees of empowerment. Thus, we should speak, rather, of **dominant discourses and ideolo-**

gies, and correspondingly of **marginalized or subordinated discourses and ideologies** that struggle with, contest, and sometimes oppose the former. Hegemony thus consists of the tendency of the discourses and ideologies of certain groups to dominate those of others. However, following Gramsci still further, Hebdige pointed out that hegemony is always a "moving equilibrium," that is, that dominant discourses and ideologies must themselves struggle to maintain their own position of power through commanding the unconscious assent of the dominated majority.

In situations where the ideological consensus breaks down (such as the period following World War II), the hegemony of the dominant ideology will be contested, in the first instance, at the level of signs: It will appear as a struggle over cultural meanings in the arena of **style**. Seemingly superficial and gratuitous stylistic differences in choice of clothing, entertainment, speech patterns, and the like serve both to register the emergence, in the dominant culture, of **subcultures** that resist and oppose its hegemony, and to provide codes and corresponding ideologies in which this resistance can be expressed and promoted. However, since hegemony remains a "moving equilibrium," the researcher must be attentive both to the ways in which styles offer resistance to the dominant culture and to the dynamics by which the dominant culture is, in turn, able to accommodate these stylistic resistances in altered cultural configurations.

Hebdige went on to utilize this theoretical framework in reviewing the sequence of styles in post–World War II Britain—the hipsters, beats, teddy boys, punks, and so forth—employing a broadly semiotic approach to unfolding the specific codes utilized by each subculture, connecting these stylistic codes through the concept of ideology to various shifts in social and class relationships, and finally, considering the implications of this process for the broader dynamics of social hegemony operative in Britain since World War II. While *Subculture* soon found its critics (including, later, Hebdige himself), it nonetheless represented an influential shift in cultural studies away from more narrowly textual analysis and narrative historiography, embracing a more comprehensive semiological theoretical framework and foregrounding the ideological and hegemonic underpinnings of popular lived cultures.

One line of critical response to Hebdige's (as well as others') work on subcultures was developed by Angela McRobbie, perhaps the first and one of the most important advocates for feminist perspectives in cultural studies. In "Settling accounts with subcultures: a feminist critique" (1981), McRobbie leveled three important criticisms against analyses of subcultures such as Hebdige's. The first criticism concerned the framing of the research agenda: McRobbie noted that the roles and experiences of women in the various subcultures discussed were only marginally addressed, if at all. Hebdige's study, for example, was faulted for focusing only on the male construction of subcultures, thus reproducing features of the dominant culture in its own analyses. McRobbie suggested that although this shortcoming could be remedied by another, more appropriately focused study, two other points concerning broader methodological issues must also be considered. First, McRobbie pointed out that "writing about subcultures isn't the same thing as being in one." At issue here is the fact that previous subcultural studies had tacitly relied mainly on public manifestations of subcultural differences, in effect treating their participants as abstractions defined (for example, in Hebdige's case) by adherence to certain styles. A fuller account, however, would recognize that cultural expression "happens as much around the breakfast table and in the bedroom as in the school and the workplace." Second, she suggested that "in order to understand questions about youth culture and politics more fully, it will be necessary to supplement the established conceptual triad of class, sex, and race with three more concepts—**populism, leisure,** and **pleasure.**" This (relatively) early call for the expansion of cultural studies beyond a sort of "critical neo-Marxist structuralism" (outlined by Hall and exemplified by works such as *Subculture*) clearly anticipated a new openness on the part of cultural studies to such postmodern themes as the formation of subjectivities and the differential forms of potentially resistant pleasure associated with them, which in some respects might "transgress" the more public aspects of ideological structures. McRobbie's *Postmodernism and Popular Culture* (1994) contains a number of her essays, the earliest among them written in the mid-1980s, in which the emergence of a distinctively postmodern feminist inflection of cultural studies can be traced. In many of these essays, McRobbie is especially concerned with developing a notion of consumption in relation to the productions of the mass media that would serve as a link between the individual and shared pleasures of the readings of cultural texts and their functioning in various lived cultures (or subcultures).

A related set of concerns underlies Janice Radway's *Reading the Romance: Women, Patriarchy, and Popular Literature* (1987). (This work has the additional distinction of having caught the attention of a number of feminist scholars in the area of literary studies, which had, for reasons already discussed, become somewhat distanced from mainstream work in cultural studies.) Based on an empirical study of a group of female romance readers, Radway explored the circuit by which a certain genre of text was produced, consumed by a specific sort of audience, and finally integrated, though problematically, into the conditions of a lived culture. Radway challenged the receive notion that the contemporary genre of romance is simply a reflection of the need of some women for fantasy or escape. Her analysis is focused on the complex dimensions of the act of reading in relation to the general features that comprise this genre. Drawing on the psychoanalytical work of Nancy Chodorow (see Chapter 4), Radway argues that a woman's act of reading contemporary romances represents a form of regression to the pre-Oedipal state, where, through the relation of the heroine and hero of the novel, she can vicariously experience the emotional fulfillment of the pre-Oedipal, nurturing maternal bond, but in the post-Oedipal form of a relation with a member of the opposite sex. "Ideal" romances will thus provide the vicarious experience of "fatherly protection, motherly care, and passionate adult love." At the center of the act of reading romances is a set of transgressive pleasures derived from several sources: the emotional satisfaction of needs often unfulfilled in everyday life, the sense that reading romances is a sort of special gift that women give themselves in creating their own times and spaces, and a sort of utopian protest against the ordinary roles assigned to women in contemporary culture. Radway concluded from her study that a focus on the act of reading rather than simply on the texts suggests that female readers of popular romances, far from passively reproducing the ideological structures of the dominant culture that commercially produces them for mass consumption, actively select among them and appropriate them as occasions for experiencing forms of pleasure involving self-affirmation and transgression of the limitations of their everyday lives. Radway, of course, does not claim that reading romances is somehow politically efficacious in any direct sense, but she does seek to demonstrate that even with a genre that is widely regarded as a debased form of mass culture when viewed simply in terms of its textual content and structure, a refocusing on the act of reading and its context in lived culture reveals that forms of transgressive pleasure and resistance are at work below the surfaces presented by the text.

Taken together, the works of McRobbie and Radway provide an index of the directions that much current work in cultural studies is taking. Both in terms of theoretical developments and of international events since 1989, several trends in research in cultural studies are notable.

1. Marxist and neo-Marxist orientations have at least in part receded from the theoretical forefront of work in cultural studies.

2. Postmodern orientations and strategies, once regarded with considerable suspicion by those in mainstream cultural studies, have, in many areas, come into their own.

3. Psychoanalysis, especially in its Lacanian and feminist inflections, which previously played little role in mainstream cultural studies, has come to prominence as increasing emphasis has been placed on the ways in which subjectivities are formed and in turn exercise active powers of selection, pleasurable affirmation, and resistance to the structural conditions imposed by the dominant culture.

4. Instead of the earlier emphasis on class, race, and gender as the (more or less) abstract matrix in which research programs in cultural studies were formulated, much more attention is now being devoted not only to more specific combinations of these (for example, the lived cultures of lower-class women of color) but also to the cultural construction of the subjectivities of other groups marginalized by this earlier schema (such as gays/lesbians/bisexuals, postcolonial peoples, and various ethnic subcultures).

5. While the ideological effects of the mass media never ceased to be an important topic in cultural studies, developments in the electronic media themselves, especially on the Internet, have begun to give rise to a new wave of research with a distinctively postmodern orientation.

6. Although the relations between readings, viewed in terms of the formation of subjectivities, and lived cultures, approached as sites of ideological contestation,

remain central to cultural studies, attempts to reintegrate the conditions of production and textual forms into broader research projects have become more prominent than they were in the 1980s. However, the older Marxist approaches to production and the structuralist approaches to texts might no longer be theoretically adequate to contemporary postindustrial production and postmodern cultural texts, thus requiring the development of new theoretical paradigms.

The French Tradition of Cultural Studies: Another Line of Influence

While the Centre for Contemporary Cultural Studies at the University of Birmingham must be regarded as the original conduit for such research as it is pursued today in most English-speaking countries, somewhat parallel movements were developing immediately after World War II in Germany under the auspices of the Frankfurt School (already discussed in Chapter 5) and in France. Although the first attempts of the Frankfurt School to theorize and study popular culture appeared a bit earlier, its mostly negative results made it, generally speaking, less influential on the Anglophone traditions than those that emerged from the work of several (mostly neo-Marxist) French historians and social theorists during the 1950s and 1960s.

Unlike the British tradition of cultural studies, which emerged from the literary disciplines and generally has kept its distance from the empirical social sciences as well as from academic philosophy, the French focus on popular culture emerged principally from two such sources: on the one hand, the field of historiography, and on the other, existentialist philosophy, especially its Marxist-oriented development in Sartre's later works. Further, under the early and crucial influence of structuralism (especially that of Barthes and Althusser), French cultural studies rather naturally came to join cause with certain strands of critical neo-Marxist sociology. While the French influence on Anglophone cultural studies has occurred primarily through the methodological innovations of structuralism and poststructuralism, avenues opened in the French tradition for thematizing popular culture have become more prominent in recent years and show signs of increasing importance abroad.

The Annales School of Historiography

Emerging before World War II and gaining momentum in the immediate postwar period, a movement among French historians arose in opposition to the prevailing positivist orientation of French historiography. This movement, which included such historians as Georges Duby, Le Roy Ladurie, Jacques Le Goff, and Fernand Braudel, was referred to as the New History, or the **Annales School** of historiography (named after the group's first principal journal). Two convictions linked this otherwise quite diverse group of historians: Their rejection both of sequential narrative models for the writing of history and of the closely related idea of history as a sequence of great or influential political, military, and diplomatic events.

In his widely influential synthesis of the theoretical innovations of this work in the preface to *The Mediterranean World* (1949), **Fernand Braudel** suggested that rather than viewing history as a single narrative account of "the feats of the princes and the rich" unfolding in a single time-span, historiographers must acknowledge three different, and in some respects, incommensurable types of time. The first is **geographical time**, which concerns the very long-term relations of human beings to the environment; the second is **social time**, the long-term course of human institutions and attitudes; the third is **individual time**, the short-term experience of individual human beings and groups of their immediate natural, social, and historical environments. In Braudel's view, the events with which conventional history has been concerned are generally only agitations on the surface of the much broader and deeper currents of "long-term," and sometimes, "very long-term" developments.

In the wake of this redefinition of the work of the historian, three concepts emerged in French historiography that were especially significant for the analysis and critique of culture. The first was the notion of **everyday life** as the basic site of the experience of Braudel's "individual time." Focusing on the everyday life of a given historical period implied that although the actions and cultural productions of "the princes and the rich" were not totally irrelevant to historiography, they should be read more as anomalies than as the norm, since these groups constituted only a tiny percentage of the total population—a population whose vast majority was little concerned with and often even ignorant of the doings of the elite. Closely related to this was the notion of **mentalities**, the general "mind sets" of various groups by which their experiences of everyday life were mapped, configured, and given meaning. (This idea seems somewhat analogous to Williams's "structures of feeling" in the British tradition.) These two ideas principally concerned Braudel's "short term," but he nonetheless saw them as intersected in various ways by **ideologies** located more at the level of the "long term," and sometimes, the "very long term." Although the Annales historians, like Braudel, did not deny the importance of ideologies on everyday life and its corresponding mentalities, they did reject the idea that these effects of ideologies were in any way simple, constant, or direct.

Henri Lefebvre and the French New Left

Contemporary popular culture was first theorized in France against the background of this new historiography, joined with semiological methods (especially as applied by Barthes in his *Mythologies*) and other concepts and strategies derived from Marxist-oriented existentialist analyses of "lived experience." Particularly influential for the neo-Marxist orientation was Henri Lefebvre's *Everyday Life in the Modern World* (1967). Lefebvre wrote of "the quotidian"—in his definition, the entire texture of everyday life as it is experienced and lived in modern societies, defined by recurring routines of labor and leisure and characterized, in the final analysis, by what he termed "bureaucratically controlled consumption." Lefebvre's style of writing, alternatively philosophical, literary, and vividly descriptive, evokes a dystopian world in which the ideology of consumerism driving the expansion of mass culture in advanced industrial societies has penetrated so deeply into the quotidian, affecting every aspect of our existence, from human relations to leisure pursuits to urban design, that it has come to seem perfectly natural (a conclusion affirmed as well by Barthes and Althusser). The two most characteristic emphases of Lefebvre, however, are the theoretical necessity to secure everyday life or the quotidian from its assimilation into other broader analytical categories (a tendency of which Marxists, empirical social scientists, and philosophers are equally guilty), and the need to view it as a site not merely of passive compliance and bureaucratic manipulation but equally of a certain degree of autonomy, transgression, and resistance. For example, Lefebvre called attention to a dialectic between the "integrative" and "nonintegrative" or "transgressive" dimensions of leisure activities and popular entertainment, which are based in general on individual satisfaction or pleasure. The make-believe world fostered by the media, when confronted by lived realities in the unstable cauldron of everyday life, can create a sense of contradiction in consumer society between utopian satisfactions and real frustrations. For a "bureaucratic society of controlled consumption," the underlying problem is that the very premise on which it is based, the unlimited human desire for pleasure and satisfaction, by its very nature, can never be completely supplied through programmed bureaucratic (or as Lefebvre sometimes describes them, terroristic) means. Much like Marcuse in the Frankfurt School, Lefebvre ultimately holds that the hyperstimulation of desire in the realm of the quotidian characteristic of consumer society inevitably produces both the degree of erotic energy and the utopian sensibility necessary to found a genuine cultural revolution against "bureaucratic consumer terrorism" in order to resecure the autonomy of the quotidian and its authentic self-generated satisfactions. While Lefebvre developed no new methodology and, like the British, engaged in a good deal of poaching from other quarters, he brought to the forefront of French critical discourse the arena of the quotidian (a close analogue of popular culture) as an area for serious critical analysis.

Michel de Certeau: Everyday Tactics of Resistance

While Lefebvre was quite influential in France, especially as a spokesperson for certain elements of the French New Left in the 1960s, the work of historian and sociologist **Michel de Certeau** has been important not only in France but also in some circles of British and American cultural studies. Certeau's *The Practice of Everyday Life* (1984), the English translation of a selection of his writings based on research conducted in the late 1970s and early 1980s, presents his most influential ideas in the area of cultural studies. Certeau begins from Lefebvre's concentration on consumption as the central problem for critical theory in late capitalist societies, emphasizing a fact that Lefebvre only suggested in a preliminary way—that consumption itself, in the present context, has become a form of production. By this he means that the consumers in a society geared toward and dependent on consumption are not merely passive nodes or moments in the overall circulation of commodities and wealth (as older economic theory, classical and Marxist alike, would have it), but often, and very selectively, take the original mass-produced goods and remake them into vehicles serving their own interests and expressing their own values and aspirations, which may well be opposed to the interests and intentions of the original producers. Straightforward and well-known examples of this at the material level would include the tie-dyed T-shirts of the 1960s counterculture, the deliberately mutilated jeans of the punk and grunge movements, and the low riders of Hispanic groups in the western United States. All of these illustrate the manner in which mass-produced commodities can be transformed into cultural forms that oppose the dominant culture that produced them.

Certeau, however, is even more interested in the parallel interpretive or semiotic level of such processes, where the meanings produced by the dominant ideology are split apart and reconfigured in the process of cultural consumption, thereby actively producing new oppositional meanings from the original semiological materials. Drawing on the work of Wittgenstein and other "ordinary language philosophers," Certeau emphasizes that the practical context of the usage of any linguistic statement—how it is used, by whom, and in what situations—is at least as important a determinant of its meaning as its mere semantic or logical content. Consider, for example, the differences in meaning of the statement, "That's a really bad car," when spoken by a mechanic to a potential buyer of the automobile, by a manufacturer of a competing make of vehicle, and by a black ghetto youth. According to Certeau, all types of signification possess this same context-dependent character and hence provide materials for continual revision, reconfiguration, and opposition to their original, ordinary usages.

To characterize the dynamics of this process more precisely, Certeau introduces a key distinction between strategies and tactics. A **strategy**, as he develops the idea, is the form of action and policy characteristic of a dominant society or culture. It presupposes a type of "political, economic, and scientific rationality" capable of formulating goals to be accomplished in a specific environment that this type of rationality dominates, or intends to dominate. Perhaps the most common occurrence of the word in this sense, outside of its clearly military applications, is in the phrase *marketing strategy,* meaning an ensemble of methods by which a commercial enterprise attempts to achieve a dominant share of a given market. By contrast, a **tactic** cannot count on a given, fixed, or proper space that it plays a crucial role in determining but must function opportunistically, remaining "always on the watch for opportunities that must be seized 'on the wing.'" A tactic thus functions in the space formed by someone else's strategy, utilizing various of its elements in creative but temporary ways that serve its own purposes of the moment. The most important point, Certeau claims, is that "many everyday practices (talking, reading, moving about, shopping, cooking, etc.) are tactical in character." Arguing that advanced consumer societies have created a "marginalized majority"—that is, a numerically superior class of consumers who play no role in the production of the dominant culture—he attempts to erect a new field of study with the goal of determining the logic of these tactical practices that characterize the everyday life of most members of consumer societies.

One of Certeau's favorite examples is that of the modern shopping mall. While shopping malls are planned and developed under the aegis of marketing strategies that dictate that a mall's spatial configuration maximize access to the various shops located in it, the public spaces of the mall often become "tactically appropriated," though sporadically and temporarily, by various groups whose aims are quite different than and even opposed to patronizing the mall's merchants. Various groups of teenagers, for example, often employ the mall as a place to meet, "hang out," and sometimes "stake out their turf." Some groups may even use the mall space as a launching ground for shoplifting sorties into the various stores. While the mall space remains under the general authority of the strategists, the young tacticians become urban guerrillas, temporarily contesting the control of the space and taking pleasure in the small victories available to their socially marginalized groups. In so doing, they manage, albeit sporadically and temporarily, to utilize the space provided by mass consumer culture for satisfying their own aims and creating in it their own opposed meanings.

Certeau and such adherents of his views as John Fiske, in his *Understanding Popular Culture,* have been criticized in Anglophone cultural studies for their overestimation of the political significance of such guerrilla tactics. However, they have unquestionably developed in this idea an important and influential avenue of approach to popular culture and have reaffirmed the need, in its study, to move beyond texts and their interpretations to the contexts or forms of life in which texts and interpretations function in ways often unanticipated by and oppositional to the positions of the producers of the dominant culture.

Pierre Bourdieu and the French Sociological Tradition

The work of French sociologist **Pierre Bourdieu** has developed in ways that sometimes parallel, sometimes intersect, and occasionally oppose the approaches of Lefebvre and Certeau. Bourdieu is at present the most influential figure in French sociology, and his influence in Germany and the Anglophone countries is rapidly growing. While Bourdieu, along with Lefebvre and some of the poststructuralists, exerted an important influence on radical developments in France of the 1960s, the style and focus of his work stand in noticeable contrast to theirs, being more closely allied to the sociological and ethnological tradition of Weber, Durkheim, and Mauss than to the structuralism of Lévi-Strauss and Barthes and the poststructuralist critiques growing out of their work. In his work, Bourdieu employs his own characteristic dialectic between theory-construction and concrete empirical investigation, but the two remain relatively independent and distinguishable—again, more like their development in the traditional social sciences than in the work of Barthes, Derrida, Althusser, or Foucault. In fact, Bourdieu himself regards his work, without apology, as contributing to the social sciences, even while maintaining that the practice of science, especially as applied to social phenomena, must be continuously subjected to rigorous and thoroughgoing critique.

At the heart of Bourdieu's work lie four central theoretical assumptions. First, the primary focus of all his research has been on the social production and reproduction of **structured inequalities**. While this theme is, of course, also present in the work of Bourdieu's French contemporaries, no one has focused on them more directly, concretely, and persistently than Bourdieu. And although he must be regarded as representing a variety of neo-Marxism, he tends, without abandoning the notion entirely, to see class as too coarse a grid through which to view the contemporary forms of social differentiation. Central to the production and reproduction of these structured inequalities is Bourdieu's concept of **agency**. According to Bourdieu, the real focus of sociological analysis (and more broadly, of cultural critique) should be neither individuals (an ideological category) nor subjectivities (a more phenomenological or perhaps psychoanalytical idea), but agency. In Bourdieu's approach, agency consists of dispositions to pursue, in a given sociocultural environment, which he calls a **habitus**, certain **strategies** (in a different sense from Certeau's) by which various forms of social differentiation or **structuration** are accomplished. With this theoretical basis, which parallels in some ways Certeau's notion of tactics, Bourdieu avoids the tendency to think of social action as completely determined by environmental or ideological forces (Althusser comes to mind here) as well as any view that holds that it involves merely the following of culturally predetermined rules (a tendency that can be traced in those influenced by Wittgenstein and his concept of "language games"). Although the habitus does play an important contextualizing role in determining agency, and though the dispositions involved in agency do have determinable structures, Bourdieu believes it wrongheaded to think of agency merely as following rules issuing from elsewhere (usually held to be from ideologies). The strategies with which Bourdieu is concerned cannot be defined by rules or by functional adjustment to the conditions of the environment, but only by the ever shifting possibilities arising as the agent continues to structure and restructure its habitus.

This orientation leads Bourdieu to assert that the proper stance for a critical sociology must be that of **methodological objectivism** in a very specific sense. Precisely because social agents are rarely if ever subjectively conscious of the means and strategies they employ in the process of social structuration, the productive force and results of their actions, which are, in the last analysis, structured inequalities, have a certain objectivity that can be detached from and described independently of questions of subjective intention or conscious rule-following. The task of the critical sociologist, then, is to connect these structured inequalities with the objectively observable and describable strategies producing them, which spontaneously arise in the conditions of the habitus. Unlike Certeau, Bourdieu does not find it necessary to assume either that members of the dominant culture always (or usually) act consciously to maintain their privileged positions or that marginalized groups act in some deliberately oppositional fashion. Nor does either group generally act according to the rules specified by some autonomously existing ideology. Rather, both pursue various informal strategies (in Bourdieu's sense) that produce and reproduce structured inequalities, apart from any overt intentions on the part of either.

Finally, for Bourdieu, the struggles implicit in various opposed strategies are not just over control of material wealth, commodities, or the means of production, but over what he calls **symbolic capital**. Although the inequalities present in capitalist economic systems certainly do involve disparities in the distribution of wealth and the control of the means of production, these distinctions are culturally structured and reinforced by symbolic processes that exclude dominated groups from effective access to the means of economic production. Bourdieu develops this idea in terms of cultural or symbolic capital, the possession of which serves to establish some members of society as culturally competent to the exclusion of others who possess either none or a lesser amount of it.

One important result of Bourdieu's view that economic capital and symbolic capital are two closely connected but partially independent systems is that in modern capitalist societies, the dominant group is itself internally divided between those who control a relatively high amount of economic capital but a low level of symbolic capital (entrepreneurs, bankers, stockholders, and so on) and those who control a large degree of symbolic capital but a relatively low amount of economic capital (teachers, university professors, bureaucrats, persons involved in the arts, journalists, and so forth). The implication is that in certain distinguishable fields of society, various groups not in economically privileged positions nonetheless serve, albeit unintentionally, to reproduce existing structured inequalities by helping to define and control symbolic (or cultural) capital, the possession of which usually serves as a precondition for access to economic capital.

As Bourdieu has pursued this theme of the significance of symbolic capital for reproducing structured inequalities, three areas have figured most prominently in his research. A recurrent theme throughout his work is how educational systems often engage in the (mostly unintentional) process of, on the one hand, holding themselves out as necessities for any successful entry into the economic sphere while, at the same time, operating as filtering and channeling devices by which only certain members of society (those beyond a certain level of economic means, those from certain "preferred families" or prep schools, or those with established levels of test scores) are permitted access to the symbolic capital that educational institutions exclusively offer. Education is closely related to a second of Bourdieu's major themes, that of taste. In the realm of symbolic capital, it is a person's taste, or dispositions to prefer one type of commodity or experience over another, that typically establish her or his relative position in culture. Those who prefer symphonic or operatic performances to rock concerts or television, for instance, are regarded, in the economy of symbolic capital, as culturally superior, thus reproducing, through the distinction between high culture and popular culture, social relations of dominance and marginality. Of course, it hardly needs to be added that one's level of education will play a significant role in determining such preferences as well. Finally, Bourdieu also has traced the way in which language plays a crucial role in such social processes. He might well have pointed to G. B. Shaw's *Pygmalion* (and its reworking as the musical *My Fair Lady*) to illustrate his point that one's linguistic competencies play a central role in establishing distinctions of social class. Again, language cooperates with education and taste in determining the amount of symbolic capital that an individual or group may be regarded as possessing, and this in turn profoundly affects the degree of access of these individuals or groups to economic capital. The upshot is that any critical discourse adequate to address the structured inequalities of contemporary society must be equipped to confront, in the first place, the inequities in the distribution of symbolic capital, which to a great extent regulates access to economic capital.

Bourdieu's outlook understandably has a special appeal today for many who have rejected the economic determinism of classical Marxism but who have been reluctant to embrace the general and often obscurantist critiques of his poststructuralist contemporaries. Further, Bourdieu's work has strenuously contested, through an emphasis on agency, the view that individuals are merely subject positions or subjectivities whose place is predefined by the operation of existing ideologies. Thus, his view holds considerable appeal for those who wish to insist on the active character of individuals and groups as makers of culture in defined contexts rather than merely passive registers of it—a theme that reconnects his work with the tradition of Lefebvre and Certeau, as well as with cultural studies as practiced elsewhere.

Mikhail Bakhtin: The Literary Connection

Another figure, **Mikhail Bakhtin** (1895–1975), although Russian, is probably best discussed under the heading of French cultural studies, since his influence in the West was first felt in France and only later exported to Anglophone countries. Bakhtin occupies a unique position in the development of European (and later Anglo-American cultural studies) for several reasons. First, living and working in the Soviet Union, mostly in obscurity, he developed his ideas independently of the parallel developments going on in Europe, Great Britain, and the United States. Second, his intellectual basis was literature, especially the study of the novel, an orientation that, after Williams, became more the exception than the rule in cultural studies. Finally, while his work covers almost seven decades and went through a number of distinguishable and quite diverse phases, his reputation outside the former Soviet Union rests on only a small, and somewhat unrepresentative, number of these writings. Nonetheless, his influence appears to be increasing and might well continue to do so as more of his works become available in translation. Bakhtin's most important contribution to cultural studies has been to provide paths along which those concerned with more traditional literary criticism can link their projects with themes typical of contemporary cultural studies.

Throughout his life, Bakhtin was deeply skeptical of any preconceived, universalistic explanatory schema, whether in the form of Marxism applied to history, formalism or semiology applied in the field of literary or cultural analysis, or psychoanalytic approaches to individual or social phenomena. Like others in the French tradition already discussed, Bakhtin wished to preserve the uniqueness and plurality as well as the potential for novelty and innovation present in the forms of everyday social life. Instead of striving toward a general and highly theorized "poetics," he focused his attention more on the "prosaic" character of everyday life, which he regarded as best reflected in the modern novel. He employed the term **unfinalizability** to indicate both that the texture of mundane human experience is radically open and full of creative potential and that any explanatory schema will always ultimately confront a residue or surplus of meaning left over after its interpretations have run their course. Finally, the notion of **dialogue** plays a prominent and distinctive role in his thought. Bakhtin believed that the most important truths of human experience and social existence could not adequately be stated monologically, that is, as bare propositions without a definite speaker, audience, or context. Language, in its most authentic usage, is a matter of utterances, of concrete statements made by an actual, concretely located speaker and addressed to another so situated, rather than of logical propositions. Genuine truths relevant to the everyday human condition can only emerge from such two- or multisided conversations between or among actual speakers, not from the monologue of an abstract or idealized "pure consciousness."

Bakhtin believed that the modern novel as a literary genre most closely conformed to and exemplified these convictions and best represented the actual texture of mundane human experience. He sometimes employed the musical term **polyphony**, understood as the weaving together of different voices, perspectives, and forms of experience, to indicate the underlying device by which novels unfold. In this polyphonic unfolding of the novel, Bakhtin called particular attention to "double-voiced words," words that make an assertion and at the same time invite or elicit a response from another, which in turn provokes yet another utterance from the original speaker. On a broader scale, he suggested that all of language must be viewed as comprised of many languages, mapped according to the various and complex social divisions existing in society at any given time, so that various classes, ethnic groups, generations, and even types of leisure activities speak their own distinctive languages. Each language has its own distinctive viewpoint and employs its own characteristic means of describing, interpreting, and evaluating human experience and its social context. Further, any given historical period or social configuration is made up of a complex polyphonic dialogue of various languages, where inevitable conflicts arise as one language is challenged by the perspectives of others. Again, Bakhtin pointed to the modern novel as best exemplifying this dialogic process of **heteroglossia** by placing various languages in dynamic and creative tensions with one another, where no one language is allowed to dominate and where there is always a surplus of meaning remaining as one language attempts the always only partial translation of other languages into its own terms.

Bakhtin's notion of heteroglossia acknowledged that any individual speaks a number of different languages and (employing later terminology) changes her or his subject-place according to the language that she or he is speaking at any given time. In fact, Bakhtin viewed consciousness itself as the "inner speech" or "interior monologue" produced by the polyphonic interplay of the various languages that one has internalized. He therefore rejected Freud's notion of the unconscious with its own more primitive or basic language, viewing the psyche, as did some poststructuralists, as a "play of differences" of various heteroglot languages in the field of consciousness itself. In this sense, human consciousness can be said to be novelistic in its structure. Even from this brief overview, it is easy to see why Bakhtin's ideas met with a very favorable reception in the French milieu, already saturated as it was by semiological and poststructuralist forms of critique.

One particular application of these ideas has been especially influential in the field of cultural studies. In *Rabelais and His World*, written in 1946 and one of the first of his works to be translated into English, Bakhtin introduced the theme of the **carnival** as an especially instructive way of access to the study of popular culture. The carnival, in its more ritualized medieval and early modern forms as well as in parallel social phenomena in the present day, represents an important and characteristic form of social heteroglossia in the realm of the popular: It embodies the conflict between languages of social order and discipline, on the one hand, and those of excessive transgressions associated with otherwise repressed pleasures, on the other. The Rabelaisian carnivalesque involved a temporary suspension of the repressive social norms and conventions imposed by dominant groups through a "world turned upside down," in which marginalized groups parodied the rich and powerful by a ritualized assumption of their roles, airs, and practices. During carnival, thieves could be kings and judges, prostitutes queens and ladies-in-waiting, and pigs bishops and cardinals. While carnivals usually are no longer so ritualized, anyone who has attended Mardi Gras celebrations, circus sideshows, Renaissance fairs, or rock concerts will have some experience of the spirit of the carnivalesque. Bakhtin saw this phenomenon as an important form in which the common and popular asserts its own rights in the cultural domain, employing the devices of parody, laughter, scatology, and physical excess in order to undermine the hegemony of the dominant culture through its internal critique. For Bakhtin, *the idea of transgressing the dominant culture by appropriating and* *then subverting forms borrowed from it* lay at the heart of the spirit of carnival (a theme already encountered in our discussion of cultural studies). His calling particular attention to the bodily excesses of such phenomena, rooted in the liberation of desire from its usually repressed state, has been particularly suggestive for recent work in cultural studies on topics ranging from the reception of Romantic poetry to mass-media sporting events like *American Gladiators* and the multimedia productions of Madonna. Because his discussions have generally been centered on literature, Bakhtin has served as an important vehicle by which literary criticism has been rejoined to more sociological and ethnographic work in cultural studies.

The North American Scene and the Future of Cultural Studies

The emergence of cultural studies as a distinctive critical discourse in North America is relatively recent, dating from about the mid-1980s or a bit later. One marker of its having attained a critical mass here was the publication in 1992 of the massive anthology *Cultural Studies* (eds. L. Grossberg, C. Nelson, P. Treichler), which grew out of an international conference, entitled "Cultural Studies Now and in the Future," held at the University of Illinois at Urbana-Champaign in April 1990. The lengthy list of contributors is instructive about the North American reception of cultural studies, since it provides a profile of the very broad and ecumenical range of approaches and themes that have come to characterize the field here. As one might expect, the majority of participants were North American, many affiliated with academic departments in the field of communications. There also was a significant representation of former or present members of the CCCS at Birmingham, including Stuart Hall, Tony Bennett, and Angela McRobbie. While various Continental approaches to cultural studies were mentioned with some frequency, French and German researchers were conspicuously absent. In addition, a few figures appeared whom one would have ordinarily associated with particular disciplines or "area studies" rather than interdisciplinary cultural studies (as thus far defined), most notably Douglas Crimp (Art History and Criticism), bell hooks (Literature and Afro-American Studies), and Cornel West (Religion and Afro-American Studies). Based on this, one would have to agree with Stuart Hall's comment in his presentation to the conference: "I don't know what to say about American cultural studies. I am completely dumbfounded by it."

Hall went on to clarify this comment, placing American cultural studies in the broader international context. First, he noted that in contrast with his own experience as a marginalized scholar at the University of Birmingham, cultural studies in America had undergone a rapid institutionalization that brought with it the danger of political cooptation. Hall noted the difficulty involved in being both an organic intellectual and an academician and worried that the latter role might overwhelm the former in the American context. Further, he pointed to the theoretical fluency of cultural studies in the United States. Sounding a theme considered earlier in this book, he noted his former suspicion about what he called the "deconstructionist deluge" that had come to dominate "formalist" literary studies in the United States, warning that "if cultural studies gained an equivalent institutionalization in the American context, it would, in rather the same way, formalize out of existence the critical questions of power, history, and politics." While he noted that at present (in 1990), such issues occupied the forefront of American cultural studies, "there is the nagging doubt that this overwhelming textualization of cultural studies' own discourses somehow constitutes power and politics as exclusively matters of language and textuality itself."

While the issues of the institutionalization and textualization of cultural studies remain continuing areas of contention on the North American scene, several other factors complicate even more any general overview or assessment. First, communications (or media studies) was already well established as an academic discipline at many American universities, prior to and independent of the influx into the United States of cultural studies along the lines pioneered at the CCCS. By and large, this discipline typically borrowed theoretical paradigms and research models from the empirical social sciences, and with the exception of occasional influences from the Frankfurt School, did not view itself as having any particular political or critical orientation. Given the importance of the media as an established thematic area for British cultural studies, it was rather natural that this critical approach would find a preexisting academic home in departments of communications. However, the interventionist orientation of cultural studies remains a source of controversy wherever it has been housed in departments of communications, especially as the field of communications has come to focus more heavily on technical issues involved with the emergence of new electronic media.

The relation between cultural studies and academic departments of literature pose problems of a somewhat different kind. As Hall noted, many departments of literature even prior to the influx of cultural studies were divided between more traditional scholars of a broadly humanistic orientation and those who were influenced by various formalist and deconstructionist approaches. Where cultural studies was accommodated in such departments, it was natural that it would side with, and often be viewed as, another variant of European-spawned antihumanism and dealt with accordingly. It went with the territory that those employing the discourse of cultural studies for the most part would have to foreground issues of textuality over more political or sociological questions regarding power, class, and so forth (which might in part explain what Hall was observing in 1990).

Finally, the United States in the 1970s had already witnessed the rise of various area studies programs in academic contexts, including African American, Chicano/Chicana, Native American, Asian, women, and gay/lesbian/bisexual studies. In many cases, it became difficult to see the difference, other than in thematic scope, between research conducted in these areas and cultural studies. Probably the main difference, and a source of some tension, was the fact that cultural studies had generally foregrounded issues of class or at least accorded it equal status with questions of gender, race, and ethnicity. However, the prevailing political interest in diversity in America, together with the often observed American distaste for confronting issues of class, meant that cultural studies, while overlapping such areas at a number of points, would experience points of serious conflict with them as well, even to the point of turf battles and budgetary quarrels.

It is also worth noting that the influx of cultural studies into the United States coincided with the time when most American universities were feeling financial pressures caused by the graduation of the last of the baby boomers. Lacking the political support of any specific diverse constituency, facing a situation where funds were becoming increasingly scarce, and bringing with it a history of political leftism into a post–cold war context where many in positions of power regarded such issues as moot, cultural studies in most places has had to assimilate into existing academic units and (perhaps happily, as some would have it) wage intellectual guerrilla warfare from the bases of the journals, conferences, and associations that it has succeeded in establishing and promoting.

In light of all this, it is interesting to note that in the past few years, there have been signs that the strand of cultural studies heavily influenced by Continental semiotics and poststructuralism has been, to a considerable degree, embraced by those working in the emerging area studies, although the cultural studies perspective had not played a major role in the first wave of area studies that emerged in the 1970s and 1980s. Particularly in the relatively new areas of gay/lesbian/bisexual studies and postcolonial studies, as well as in certain quarters of women studies, the Continental focus on the formation of subjectivities, especially those concerning gender, and of ideologies underwriting newly thematized forms of domination and marginality has been used in forms developed in the broader discourse of cultural studies. That the critical discourse of cultural studies, albeit in a form of which figures like Hall are suspicious, remains fruitful for areas of research that are presently marginal attests to the fact that despite the misgivings of some, cultural studies has remained true to its original commitments and program. Where things will go from here, however, remains to be seen.

Bibliographic Essay

For reasons mentioned in the text, it is often difficult to draw any clear line between writings in the discourse of cultural studies and others that represent closely related, complementary, or overlapping approaches. In this essay, I will focus only on writings that either quite obviously or by their own admission move in its ambit, as this has been presented above. I wish to note, however, that there are many critical discussions growing out of various area studies, communications studies, the more traditional social sciences, and the established humanistic disciplines that might well have been included if the focus were broadened only slightly. I will also generally omit references to works already specifically cited and discussed in the chapter and concentrate on additional resources.

I have found two secondary works especially helpful in formulating this chapter: *An Introductory Guide to Cultural Theory and Popular Culture,* by John Storey (Athens: University of Georgia Press, 1993) and *British Cultural Studies: An Introduction,* by Graeme Turner (New York: Routledge, 1992). While each employs an approach and critical standpoint different from mine, the two read together provide a good triangulation of the current state of this still rapidly developing area. In addition, *Channels of Discourse,* ed. Robert C. Allen (Chapel Hill: University of North Carolina Press, 1987) covers some of the same ground as I have in this chapter but with specific application to television criticism.

Three anthologies that bring together many of the most important, shorter primary essays or selections about issues discussed in this chapter are: *What Is Cultural Studies? A Reader,* ed. John Storey (London: Arnold, 1996); *A Critical and Cultural Theory Reader,* eds. Antony Easthope and Kate McGowan (Toronto: University of Toronto Press, 1992); and *Rethinking Popular Culture: Contemporary Perspectives in Cultural Studies,* eds. Chandra Mukerji and Michael Schudson (Berkeley: University of California Press, 1991). The first concentrates primarily on attempts to define cultural studies in the Anglo-American world and includes the essays discussed above by Stuart Hall and Richard Johnson. The second is much more oriented toward the Continental structuralist and poststructuralist traditions and contains a representative sampling of texts that have proved important for the development of this strand of cultural studies. The third aims to provide a sort of cross-section of state-of-the-art thought and research concerning popular culture, and includes the work of a number of figures with specific area or disciplinary orientations. I wish to note again the anthology that attempts to do the same for more mainstream Anglo-American cultural studies: *Cultural Studies,* eds. Lawrence Grossberg, Cary Nelson, and Paula Treichler (New York: Routledge, 1992).

With regard to the British tradition of cultural studies, beyond the founding works by Hoggart, Williams, Thompson, and Hall and Whannel referred to in the text, one should be aware of the numerous books, anthologies, and research papers sponsored by the Centre for Contemporary Cultural Studies (CCCS) at the University of Birmingham. Unfortunately, a good deal of this material is either no longer in print or was never circulated except in informal, research paper form. Among those that were officially published and may be available in some libraries, several of the more important are: *Culture, Media, Language: Working Papers in Cultural Studies, 1972–1979,* edited under the auspices of the CCCS (London: Routledge, 1980); *Popular Culture: Past and Present,* ed. Bernard Waites, Tony Bennett, and Graham Martin (London: Croom Helm/Open University Press, 1982); and *Culture, Ideology and Social Process: A Reader,* eds. Tony Bennett, Graham Martin, Colin Mercer, and Janet Woolacott (London: Batsford, 1981). Reviewed in the order given here, one can gain a detailed perspective on the work of the CCCS as it broke loose from its culturalist stance and moved through media and more historical and ethnographic studies toward the employment of structuralist approaches in conjunction with the broader theoretical framework provided by Gramscian hegemony and Althusserian ideology theory. A number of recent works have taken up the question of the significance of poststructuralist and postmodern developments for the future course of cultural studies. The most trenchant critique of these developments from the point of view of one of the founders of this discourse is *The Politics of Modernism: Against the New Conformists,* by Raymond Williams (London: Verso, 1989). More sympathetic views, though by no means lacking their own critical edge, can be found in *Postmodernism and Popular Culture,* by Angela McRobbie (London: Routledge, 1994) and *The Postmodern Arts: An Introductory Reader,* ed. Nigel Wheale (London: Routledge, 1995).

There is as yet no good general overview of the French tradition of cultural studies, although certain elements of it are discussed in some detail by John Fiske in his *Understanding Popular Culture* (London: Unwin Hyman, 1989). Two of the key works in this tradition, discussed above, are Henri Lefebvre's *Everyday Life in the Modern World*, tr. Sacha Rabinovitch (New Brunswick, N.J.: Transaction, 1984) and Michel de Certeau's *The Practice of Everyday Life*, tr. Steven Rendall (Berkeley: University of California Press, 1984). Numerous works by Pierre Bourdieu have appeared in English translation in the past few years. The most complete statement of his theoretical principles can be found in *The Logic of Practice*, tr. Richard Nice (Stanford: Stanford University Press, 1990). Other works in English include *Homo Academicus* (Cambridge: Polity, 1988) and *Distinction: A Social Critique of the Judgment of Taste* (London: Routledge, 1984). For a broader overview of contemporary French sociology in which Bourdieu figures prominently, consult the anthology *French Sociology: Rupture and Renewal Since 1968*, ed. Christopher Lemert (New York: Columbia University Press, 1981). Interesting critical discussions of his work can be found in *Bourdieu: Critical Perspectives*, eds. Craig Calhoun, Edward LiPuma, and Moishe Postone (Chicago: University of Chicago Press, 1993). Probably the two best-known works of Mikhail Bakhtin in English are an anthology of four essays entitled *The Dialogic Imagination*, ed. Michael Holquist (Austin: University of Texas Press, 1981) and *Rabelais and His World*, tr. Helene Iswolsky (Bloomington: Indiana University Press, 1984). Much of the critical discussion of his ideas to date has occurred in the field of literary criticism, but their potential for deployment in cultural studies is clearly registered in *The Politics and Poetics of Transgression*, by Peter Stallybrass and Allon White (Ithaca: Cornell University Press, 1986).

Beyond the specific works discussed in the text, a list of relatively recent essays and books that critically employ the discourse of cultural studies would run to many pages. One that seems to have enjoyed some popularity in introductory courses on cultural studies is *Reading the Popular*, by John Fiske (London: Unwin Hyman, 1989), a companion volume to his *Understanding Popular Culture*. Numerous other applications can be found in various journals, including *Cultural Studies, Communication, The Magazine of Cultural Studies, Social Text, Critical Studies in Mass Communication, New Formations*, and *The Journal of Popular Culture*. There are at least as many sites on the Internet devoted to the discussion of cultural studies and its various applications, and their list grows almost daily. Since the Internet changes so rapidly, it is probably best to use one of the standard search engines to find what is currently available under such topics as cultural studies, popular culture, or some more specific area of interest.

Conclusion:
The Future of Critical Discourse

Now that we have surveyed the history and various forms of critical discourse concerning culture over the past several centuries, I want to conclude by assaying several of what I believe to be the more important problems and issues confronting anyone wishing to maintain a critical perspective into the next millennium. Thus far I have generally refrained from introducing my own critical perspectives into the narrative and have remained content to present the criticisms that in fact emerged in or around the various discourses themselves. However, one learns a good deal in carrying out such a project, and it is these insights, and perhaps even prejudices (hopefully in the good sense), that I will now present. Since I believe that the enterprise of cultural critique is inextricably related to its own historical, social, and ideological contexts and that these are in turn described, viewed, and reviewed through the lenses of particular discourses, I will necessarily have to base my discussion on certain assumptions about both the actual contours of the present situation and certain preferences concerning the relative strengths and weaknesses of available discourses. I hope that my presenting these issues mostly in the form of present and future questions to be posed and addressed will underline the fact that critique is, most of all, an ongoing and open-ended task where both an entrenchment in doctrinaire positions and a merely passive waiting to see what comes next are equally out of place. Or, put more positively, it makes sense to undertake the difficult process of cultural critique only if it serves as the initial step of altering conditions for the better that can in fact be altered with sufficient, and above all self-critical, clarity and commitment.

As I noted at the beginning, philosophy as understood in the ancient world was in important ways indistinguishable from cultural critique. This remained largely the case until the beginning of modernity, when philosophy was redirected toward securing the theoretical foundations for the natural sciences, thus elevating logic, epistemology, and metaphysics above questions of moral and political value as the primary concern of the philosopher. Of course, a strong critical strand continued through the Enlightenment, but it unfolded to a great extent outside the increasingly technical discipline of philosophy. The nineteenth century witnessed determined attempts to reunite these divergent traditions, especially in the movements of German idealism and dialectical materialism. Although such attempts were renewed in the twentieth century by phenomenology, existentialism, and the Frankfurt School, the academic discipline of philosophy, as Richard Rorty has often pointed out, has remained largely entrenched in the program laid down in early modernity.

Since my own academic training was in philosophy and cultural history, I am particularly sensitive about relations between philosophy and cultural critique. My general view is that while knowledge of certain major subdivisions of philosophy and of its history provide important and sometimes essential background for cultural critique, the nature of philosophy as it is practiced today in most academic departments is not very conducive to such a project. Probably the most important difference is that philosophy tends to deal with global or universal issues—questions of truth, meaning, validity, the general nature of value, and so forth—while cultural critique is more local and contextual, often intensely so. Generally speaking, the issues most significant for cultural critique tend to fall below the threshold of the philosopher's interest, serving, at most, as intriguing illustrations or test cases of higher-order principles and theories. On the other hand, a background in philosophy can often assist the enterprise of cultural criticism in facilitating an informed understanding of the various critical discourses, in forewarning the critic about conceptual dilemmas and traps that have already been well assayed and have tended historically to recur, and in providing various concepts and materials that might also prove useful outside the limits of the discipline of philosophy.

Nonetheless, philosophy traditionally has been an intensely hegemonic field, regarding itself as dominating all other fields in the most important respects ("Queen of the sciences" is a title that philosophers have commonly conferred on their field). This being the case, the suspicion of many cultural critics about "theoreticism" may be particularly warranted in regard to approaches that are heavily indebted to concepts derived from academic philosophy. So while the cultural critic should remain on friendly terms with the philosopher, she or he should bear in mind that their aims and enterprises remain different in certain crucial respects.

This fact raises a question about the principal way in which many cultural critics have attempted to understand their roles: as organic intellectuals (following Gramsci and Williams) or as *bricoleurs* (as in the French tradition). If one assumes, which I think is fair, that cultural criticism is an undertaking that by its very nature cannot and will not be entirely accommodated by any existing discipline, then it makes sense to regard the critic of culture as somehow functioning at or between the margins of the various recognized disciplines. When Gramsci spoke of the organic intellectual, he had in mind someone whose primary allegiance was to cultural intervention on behalf of progressive forces in society (not to some specific academic discipline) but who was sufficiently conversant with the parts of the various disciplines relevant to cultural critique and intervention to allow her or him to articulate a more global viewpoint connecting disciplinary forms of knowledge and creative activity with transformative social praxis. By contrast, the French notion of *bricolage* refers to the practice of the handyman, who is skilled both in knowing and choosing the proper tools for the job at hand and in employing them effectively. Since no single tool is adequate for the entire range of situations she or he is likely to encounter, and because novel situations sometimes call for unexpected uses for old tools or the creative invention of new ones, the *bricoleur* must remain open to a wide range of possibilities in the execution of her or his tasks.

Though they agree on certain points, there is a tension between these two prevailing models of the cultural critic. Because the organic intellectual must aim at a more coherent or totalizing vision than that available to any specialized intellectual, she or he will tend, as Gramsci did with Marxism, to become an advocate for some preferred manner of theorizing and intervention that may well prove less effective than others under dynamically changing conditions. By contrast, the bricoleur (perhaps best exemplified today by various deconstructionist critics) has tended to become fascinated with the possibilities presented by ever new or creatively reemployed tools, without ever effectively bringing them to bear on the broader job at hand. In important ways, the models of the organic intellectual and the bricoleur are antipodes in a continuum, along which the contemporary cultural critic must place him- or herself; and the self-placement of the critic in this regard should remain an important and continuing issue for self-critique.

These two models of the practice of cultural critique point toward a deeper split in the current context. This can be characterized, in a rough fashion, as the split between types of critique based on materialist (and usually some version of Marxist) assumptions and those based on assumptions that are textualist. Of course, both agree that there are important connections between the material bases of cultural production and the textual artifacts produced under specific material conditions. However, this continuing issue in cultural critique has been complicated by two recent historical developments. On the one hand, the validity of materialist models (of which Marxism has for some time been the principal form) has been called into question by events such as the collapse of the former Soviet Union, the discovery of Stalinist and Maoist atrocities, and research in sociology and economics that has tended to discredit Marxism's theoretical foundations. On the other hand, poststructuralist and postmodernist approaches have now been around long enough to permit critical assessment, and many who were initially drawn to them have come to view them as elitist, self-absorbed, and sometimes downright unintelligible. As a result, there are signs at present that the two major options that have dominated cultural critique for the last thirty years or so have run their course and no longer present viable alternatives.

Although there is certainly something to this, I would offer a caution against the overhasty dismissal of either. Although Marxism, in its traditional or even heavily revised forms, may no longer very well describe or explain the complex divisions in advanced industrialized nations, the global division between such nations or areas of the world and those being exploited by them under increasingly internationalized capitalism remains a major, if often unacknowledged, issue. While Marxist thought tended, through much of its history, to assume, on the international scale, a rift between East and West, which now appears to be on the mend, this is increasingly being translated (roughly speaking) into a split between the Northern and Southern hemispheres, which still demands critical reflection and intervention. Marxist models might ultimately prove inadequate to addressing this development, but the jury is certainly still out on this question. I would thus advise against forgetting Marx just yet.

On the other hand, while poststructuralist and postmodernist approaches seem to have reached the point of unproductively repeating themselves, the mass media's influence, both extensively across the globe and intensively in our everyday lives, continues to grow astronomically. Many, in fact, think that we are now entering an entirely new era, based on developments in linked electronic and computer-based digital communications. Perhaps this new era will call forth new analytical techniques and forms of critique; but for the moment, it seems that certain poststructuralist strategies are the only vehicles adequate to penetrate this new world of floating signifiers, polysemic signs, electronic bodies, multiply-layered informational systems, and new subjectivities arising from their operation. This, I think, will be the next major challenge for cultural critique, and at least on the face of it, poststructuralism has many advantages over older humanistic or hermeneutic models geared more specifically toward older-style literary productions. My general view, perhaps overly optimistic, is that international capitalism, as it increasingly intertwines with emerging developments in the electronic and digital media, will provide a productive meeting ground for materialist approaches, which have already accommodated certain structuralist and poststructuralist strategies, and variants of poststructuralism, which will increasingly require revision and expansion in light of profound changes in the underlying technology for the production of texts.

Intersecting the materialism vs. culturalism debate at various crucial points is a closely related controversy that might be called the conditions vs. subjects debate. This question, posed in various guises including nature vs. nurture, environment vs. organism, and so forth, has a long history and may well be one of those perennial issues that, at least as formulated in such binary terms, resists any final resolution. For the critic of culture, this issue usually hinges on the question of whether subjects or subjectivities should be viewed primarily as products or results of material and (or) significational systems, or whether these latter should be regarded as products of the activities of self-directing or purposive subjects or agents. Most recently, it is this sort of issue that has divided the discourse of cultural studies, pitting the "agency-and-intervention" orientation that emerged from earlier British cultural studies against the "subjectivity-and-ideology" type of discourse stemming from the French tradition, especially as developed by Barthes, Althusser, and Foucault. Some philosophers, following Wittgenstein, have argued that this is another of those intractable philosophical problems that arise only "when language goes on a holiday," that is, that stem from types of discourse or language games that are based on certain misuses of ordinary language. Others, like Bourdieu, have confronted the issue head on, attempting to defeat the appearance of contradiction by a more sophisticated and theoretically alert form of analysis.

Rather than going further into the complexities of this issue or advocating some particular ideological position toward it, I want to point to an important field of research, of relatively recent vintage, that might prove quite significant for such discussions but that has had as yet little impact on cultural critique. I have in mind what has been called cognitive science, a decidedly interdisciplinary field that began emerging in the late 1950s and early 1960s, bringing together researchers from such disparate areas as psychology, neuroscience, computer science, linguistics, and philosophy. Briefly stated, the program of cognitive science, as described by Patrick Gardner, is an "empirically based effort to answer long-standing epistemological questions—particularly those concerned with the nature of knowledge, its components, its sources, its development, and its deployment," by drawing on contemporary theoretical models made available by developments in neuroscience, computer science, linguistics, and philosophy, and validating them through the empirical procedures characteristic of certain types of psychology. (Some parallels with contemporary cultural studies in the field of cultural critique should be evident.) Most importantly, in its overall stance, cognitive science opposes both the formerly prevailing behaviorist and functionalist models on the one hand, and phenomenological, psychoanalytic, and introspectionist standpoints on the other. From the perspective of cultural critique, such a program, in which representations, especially of a linguistic type, play an essential and irreducible role, might suggest certain ways in which the dichotomies mentioned earlier might be reconfigured, if not entirely overcome. If cognitive science manages to produce empirical evidence to the effect, for example, that the human organism (or its brain) is in some sense "hard-wired" to produce certain determinable linguistic (and hence cultural) structures prior to any actual cultural conditioning, or that certain forms of representation have neurological bases, this would have significant implications for how the cultural critic theorizes both the issue of conditions vs. subjectivities and that of the possible constraints on the human production of culture and its possible forms. I am certainly not advocating that at this point cognitive science be embraced wholesale by cultural critique, since its presuppositions and methodologies are still in need of careful criticism; but I am suggesting that as in the earlier case of psychoanalysis, the development of an important new paradigm in psychology, with potentially far-ranging implications for issues germane to cultural critique, should not go unregistered.

Because popular culture will inevitably be altered both materially and conceptually by the historical developments and conceptual reconfigurations noted above, a serious reconsideration of this concept is called for. As we have already seen, the emergence of popular culture as a central theme of modern cultural critique went hand in hand with the development of communications media, starting with printing in early modernity. Because of this, it often has been helpful to distinguish between local and diverse folk cultures and more global and homogenized mass culture, made possible first by mechanical reproduction and later by electronic transmission. To date, the major controversy in the discourse of cultural studies has been over how to characterize and theorize popular culture against the backdrop of the (assumed) relatively clear historical distinction between folk and mass culture on the one hand, and popular culture and high culture on the other.

The major problem, often unremarked in such discussions, is that folk culture takes a variety of forms, some of which (like the early modern carnival) are hegemonically oppositional, while others (like dollmaking or woodcarving) are not. Likewise, while at first blush mass culture would appear to be a clear-cut matter of hegemonic dominance, a more careful analysis might reveal important exceptions to this (for example, the broadcast of some of Brecht's radical plays on German television). Furthermore, while an ideological position favoring high culture at the expense of popular culture might indeed be an affirmation of hegemonic dominance, the actual productions of high culture may themselves be either oppositional or not (as Adorno argued with respect to the modernist avant-garde). The result of this has been an ongoing controversy about the nature and hegemonic status of popular culture. All parties seem agreed that if the phrase *popular culture* means anything, it (1) involves some relevant contrast with high culture and (2) has historically come to have important relations with mass culture. But assuming (1) does not necessarily make it oppositional (for example, the case of kitsch), and assuming (2) does not necessarily exclude its being oppositional. The fact is that despite the tendency of some, like Fiske, to see popular culture as almost exclusively oppositional, it can be either oppositional or not (or more realistically, it might contain a combination of oppositional and nonoppositional elements), depending on who its users or creators are and in what contexts they employ it. The pleasures of popular culture are also not necessarily transgressive, as some critics would have them, nor are the productions of either high or mass culture necessarily vehicles of hegemonic ideology. The tendency of contemporary cultural studies to foreground popular culture in its research should be viewed more in light of the traditional neglect of popular culture rather than as a politically progressive stance in its own right. This is especially true if one sees popular culture as a sort of folk culture for the electronic age, since folk culture itself is ambiguous with regard to its hegemonic status. The point is that the hegemonic status of popular culture is a variable and dynamic phenomenon that cannot be decided by a priori theorizing. We must, then, get beyond the Frankfurt School's complete assimilation of popular culture into mass culture as well as cultural studies' tendency to separate popular culture from mass culture, remembering Gramsci's original warning that hegemony is an ever shifting and dynamic field that calls for continual conceptual and strategic adjustments.

Another problem facing current cultural critique parallels the political challenge facing American society (and others as well, to a greater or lesser extent), a challenge that has been frequently noted in recent times: the problem of accommodating diversity in complex postindustrial societies. Historically speaking, the diversity movements of the past 30 years or so might best be read as a recent stage in the unfolding of the logic of rights first established in the Enlightenment. However, although Enlightenment humanism established the abstract individual, that is, the human being, as the bearer of absolute and inalienable rights, two major problems with this principle gradually came to light. The first, noted by Marx and Engels as well as by J. S. Mill, was that the granting of political rights was a hollow gesture if the question of the material and economic conditions in which it would become possible to meaningfully exercise those rights was not also addressed. The second problem, which became clear only later, was that additional factors defining certain groups in society might continue to serve as bases for their political and economic disenfranchisement by socially dominant groups, even in situations where both legal and economic rights were, in principle, recognized. Particularly in the period after World War II, the tremendously expanding economy in most industrialized nations made the persistence of the structural disenfranchisement of various groups appear all the more irrational and at odds with basic liberal political principles, even though these principles did not, of themselves, recognize group rights. As a result, political history since World War II has witnessed the rise of a new class of rights based on membership in certain formerly (or currently) disenfranchised or exploited groups. Various movements arose to assert such "special" or "group-based" rights (or protections based on them) on behalf of African Americans, Native Americans, Americans of Latin or Hispanic descent, women, and more lately gays, lesbians, and bisexuals. The major problem was that such a development often pitted these various groups in fierce competition against one another over issues of both material and symbolic influence.

This problem was reflected at the level of cultural critique by the founding of various area studies, each a sort of critical discourse in itself, but one usually devoted to furthering the special interests and aspirations of the particular group underwriting it. In the United States, both liberals and conservatives came to decry the fragmentation or ghettoization of American culture, and some, like historian Arthur Schlesinger, prophesied the worst: the American *unum* irrecoverably lost in the *plura* of contending groups. Although cultural critique in a broader sense has been greatly enriched by these more located and regional critiques, it is important to note that each has tended to draw on and replicate, in its critical practice and strategies, the various broader critical discourses that we have discussed in this volume. In other words, these various more localized discourses of critical practice have themselves tended to affirm common languages, conceptual schemes, and strategic interventions, even when employed from the perspective of a particular group. I may be mistaken, but it seems to me that what was only a few years ago sectarian competition is slowly giving way to a recognition of broader structural features of economically advanced societies, which insure that not one but multiple groups will be marginalized by the same structural logic operating in different sectors of society. In other words, the marginalization of one group turns out to be intimately and organically connected to the processes by which others are marginalized as well.

Clearly, the traditional Marxist concept of binary economic classes is not very helpful in describing this situation, which is one reason why Gramsci's more complex notion of hegemony has received so much attention in recent years. However, his emphasis on hegemony as primarily a cultural matter may have obscured the fact that concurrently with the culture wars fought between and among various groups in the past 30 years, the greatest transfer of economic wealth from many to increasingly fewer hands in American history has occurred—which has all too rarely been noted. However, with the expansion of international capitalism during the same period, it has likewise become increasingly difficult to determine who the real winners and losers have been if we look only, as we have been habituated to do, at the national level. It is at this point that the recent emergence of such areas as postcolonial studies seems to me particularly important, since, while the industrialized nations might continue their economic growth or at least hold their own, this is purchased, in postindustrial economies, by the export of their former problems to developing nations. It is no secret that the majority of citizens of postindustrial nations are also beginning to experience the results of these worldwide economic developments; but emphasizing where the real hardships fall is, at present, an important mission that is too easily and conveniently overlooked. My point, then, is that the raising of the sights of cultural critique from its traditionally nation-based concerns to developments on the international stage is especially important for formulating future strategies.

Taking Stock at Century's End

Perhaps the most unsettling thing about a project like the present one, which attempts to identify and present in sequence the history of the various major critical discourses, is that it gives the impression of a sort of smorgasbord from which the reader or student is invited to pick and choose, mix and match. As I indicated in the introduction to this book, it is the ongoing task of any cultural critic to take whatever resources seem useful for a given purpose, and if necessary, reconfigure them into a (hopefully) more coherent and productive complex. In fact, several critical discourses that we have discussed began by doing exactly this. However, I have formed some conclusions of my own in the course of my research and wish to share them with the reader, clearly labeling my comments as one person's view of how someone might go about sorting all this material out. While it is admittedly a bit wooden and an inelegant way of doing it, I will generally follow the order in which we have already discussed the various discourses.

Liberal Humanism

Much ink has been spilled since World War II on the alleged rift between humanistic and antihumanistic approaches to culture. This controversy may be more verbal than substantial, in the very literal sense that it concerns the choice of a certain mode of discourse more than a genuine opposition over basic principles. In what is often cited as one of antihumanism's founding documents, Heidegger's "Letter on Humanism," Heidegger makes clear that the issue is not one between the values implicit in liberal humanism versus some sort of totalitarianism or tyranny, but one regarding the limitations and inadequacy of the traditional humanistic ways of defining and describing man, world, nature, society, value, and so forth. For Heidegger, this discursive complex stands in need of critique, since like any discursive totality it produces its own inherent blindnesses and moves within certain limits. To be antihumanistic in this sense is not to celebrate inhuman historical forces or to condone atrocities against human beings but to begin questioning the limitations of certain historical, and in that sense arbitrary, ways of thinking and speaking about ourselves and the world in which we live. The key word here is *limits,* since there is nothing to prevent us from moving beyond them without discarding all of the basic convictions that they historically circumscribed.

We have achieved a sufficient historical distance from the Enlightenment to be able to realize both its important theoretical advances and its inherent limitations. The salient historical fact is that liberal humanism was the original form assumed by modern cultural critique and was directed at a society still dominated by the ancien régime. But as almost always happens, our shared discourses lag behind the novel historical developments and configurations that they must confront, creating situations where views that were progressive in one era become reactionary in the next. Even so, the discourse of liberal humanism has demonstrated a good deal of potential for revising and repositioning itself to meet dramatic historical changes. For example, it is no accident that procedural democracy, equal rights before the law, and representative government still figure prominently among the demands of the peoples of developing nations. Nonetheless, to frame our current situation solely in terms of legalistically conceived rights the realization of which is typically viewed as an almost exclusively political problem, or to expect general agreement over essentialistic claims regarding man, society, values, or whatever, now seems naive and in some contexts reactionary.

Because of the misunderstandings that the label spawns, few critics of liberal humanism would be comfortable any longer with being called antihumanists, but it would be no better if they were to claim to be humanists in some new and different sense of the term. So to those who in calling themselves humanists wish to reaffirm some alleged set of humanistic values that are presumably being challenged by recent developments in critical discourse, the contemporary cultural critic, realizing that humanism was less a set of specific values than a general critical attitude, should probably resist the either/or tacitly offered by this course. As heirs to the critical spirit of liberal humanism, we are all humanists in a certain sense; on the other hand, refusing to subscribe to the original discourse of liberal humanism does not, by that token, make us antihumanists in the pejorative sense in which the label is usually intended.

Hermeneutic Discourses

The hermeneutic approach to cultural critique arose as an element of the broader aesthetic theory and worldview of Romanticism, which should warn us of its strong bias in favor of the subjective and the mystical or otherworldly and against the objective or scientific and the mundane. When hermeneutic discourse has not declined political commitment altogether in favor of a withdrawal into the internal processes of the subjective imagination, it has tended, as in the case of certain German historians and literary critics of nineteenth-century Prussia, and Heidegger and some of his followers in the twentieth century, to embrace utopian political adventures offering a high level of emotional appeal at the expense of careful, concrete analysis. Realizing this, Gadamer, perhaps hermeneutics' most important contemporary representative, set about rehabilitating the hermeneutic standpoint by claiming (following certain strands of Heidegger's work) that the discourse of hermeneutics represented a universal (philosophical) problematic coextensive with the most fundamental operations of any process of human understanding. While this view of hermeneutics enabled it in a conceptual or methodological sense to trump any other type of discourse (as illustrated, for example, by the exchanges between Gadamer and Habermas mentioned earlier), it also removed hermeneutics, now a purely philosophical position, from the more mundane and contextualized field of critical discourse.

To the degree that any cultural production can be viewed, as hermeneutics insisted early on, as a text requiring a reader's complex processes of understanding for its completion, many of its basic tenets can be readily granted. One could equally well acknowledge that some of its more recent developments in the form of reader-response criticism and reception theory have provided literary criticism, in particular, with some fruitful new insights with which to approach cultural texts at a microanalytical level. However, such subjective interpretive processes are only one aspect of a much broader circuit that includes cultural production, audience formation, and deployment in lived cultures, issues to which such limited analyses have little to contribute. The fact is that hermeneutic discourse, although still fashionable in certain philosophical and literary circles, plays little or no role in contemporary cultural criticism, which now tends to deal with issues that were formerly the more or less exclusive domain of hermeneutics through the more concrete and analytically powerful notions of the formation of subjectivities, ideological effects, and so forth. While a certain romantic nostalgia for the heroic subjective imagination lingers on in some quarters, it seems fair to say that serious contemporary cultural critique has moved beyond such attitudes.

Materialist Discourses

The original force of claiming to adopt a materialist orientation on the part of the cultural critic (as in, for example, Feuerbach's or Marx's materialism) was simultaneously to counter or deny the force of another, relatively well-defined, perspective, that of idealism (in the philosophical sense of the term). Shifts in the conceptual terrain since the middle of the nineteenth century (especially the fact that there are few philosophical idealists on the scene any longer worth opposing) have given this term a somewhat different force. Generally, the relevant opposition now is between methodological materialism (no longer a metaphysical standpoint but a preference for certain assumptions regarding method, field of analysis, and possibly style of exposition) and other ways of proceeding, such as textualism, culturalism, and psychologism, which maintain a certain irreducible and sui generis character and effectivity for something they regard as only inadequately characterizable, if at all, in terms of material processes. Put in these terms, however, such a difference is a relative one concerning not so much what is to be explained but what counts as a proper explanation or analysis.

Certain areas of contemporary ethnography provide a fair bellwether for such debates—for example, where the avowed cultural materialism of Calvin Hall is pitted against the explicitly hermeneutic culturalism of Clifford Geertz. Neither Hall nor Geertz believes that any firm or final line, like that between classical Marxism's infrastructure and superstructure, can be drawn between material determinants of culture, such as economic production systems, climate and soil, patterns of human reproduction, and so forth, and their representations in the context of meaning-making systems. The real question concerns only the amount of theoretical weight to be accorded one or the other. Likewise, the history of Marxism to date generally has moved in the direction of gradually denying the basic terms of the classical distinction by increasingly emphasizing the importance of the cultural sphere as itself an element of production, circulation, and reproduction. Finally, further complicating this entire scenario is the ambiguous status, with respect to the difference between material and cultural or textual factors, of the emerging digital media. The distinction between hardware and software or channel and program just doesn't parse very well into the material vs. cultural (or textual) distinction, since its basic term, information, can be viewed as including both or neither, depending on how a given discussion is framed.

What remains vital from the materialist tradition of cultural critique, then, is primarily an insistence that whatever sort of analytical theory one endorses or employs, it ultimately concern itself not merely with concepts, ideas, methodologies, or styles but with the concrete realities, including but not limited to economic forces, which determine the everyday lives of human beings living in actual societies. And it affirms the famous statement of the young Marx that the point is not merely to understand these conditions but to intervene in and change them. It is this contextualist and interventionist attitude toward theory that remains the major legacy of materialist cultural critique, even in the face of the historical slippage in meaning of its original terms.

Psychoanalytic Discourses

Few types of discourse have been so vehemently attacked and equally vigorously defended as has psychoanalysis. At the moment, one can only say that the jury is still out on this matter. Freud's work in laying the foundations for this science, which originally was envisioned not as a large-scale critical discourse but rather as a theoretical basis for certain novel clinical practices, soon filled a lacuna in an intellectual world divided along the lines of the Cartesian dualism between body (the province of biology and medicine) and mind (the realm of the representational, ideational, moral, and aesthetic). Psychoanalysis represented a bold attempt to explore the crucial area of their interface by simultaneously showing that our biological makeup (particularly in the arena of sexuality) influences our psychic processes in critical ways and that our psychic representations play a crucial role in reconfiguring the conditions under which our biological impulses exert their forces.

Freud introduced, as a cardinal tenet of this discourse, the notion of the unconscious as the principal mediator between what had previously been severed into the physical and the mental. Despite all the other more peripheral controversies that have arisen surrounding psychoanalysis, which has in fact proved relatively adaptable in response to such criticisms, the notion of the unconscious has remained theoretically both the major advantage as well as the Achilles' heel of this discourse. Freud's own treatment of the unconscious as a relatively independent psychic system or set of processes tended to insulate it from any direct influence by cultural factors, even as he claimed that it lay at their basis. While many figures, especially Marxists and existentialists, tended to dismiss the unconscious as a theoretical mystification, it was Lacan, more than anyone else, who succeeded in demystifying this notion by firmly implanting linguistic (and hence cultural) structures at its heart. As a result of the work of Lacan and his followers, a heavily revised version of psychoanalysis has become a major element of contemporary cultural critique. Especially when wedded with such views as Althusser's notion of ideology, it now functions as a major vehicle for understanding the processes by which subjectivities are formed and by which they in turn reproduce cultural forms in which they are reflected. This development has been especially appealing in light of the opacity to most materialist forms of analysis of the actual operation of cultural reproduction at the level of the individual subject or of groups falling below the threshold of larger social or economic classes.

Still, for the cultural critic, the nagging question remains as to whether Lacanian analysis, even when wedded with theories of ideology, produces results that continue to reinforce the deterministic outlook of Freud's original form of psychoanalysis. While such a view may go far in accounting for the reciprocal formation of subjectivities and their cultural conditions, it has much less to say about the processes by which this circuit might be interrupted or altered. For theories of social intervention and transformation, the cultural critic will likely have to look elsewhere, even though this discourse may have a good deal to offer regarding the parameters in which these developments can take place.

The Frankfurt School of Critical Theory

An eclectic mixture of ideas derived primarily from the earlier materialist and psychoanalytic traditions, early Frankfurt School criticism was most effective as a critique of culture when it focused critical attention on the role of the emerging electronic media in transforming modern society and culture and the inadequacies of existing discourses to address these changes, and least persuasive when it strayed into more abstruse areas concerning overarching philosophical issues of rationality, agency, and social justice. Somewhat later, during the 1950s, the Frankfurt School became seriously divided between those like Adorno and Horkheimer who despaired of the leveling effect of mass culture, and those like Marcuse who somewhat naively touted the liberational potential of the aesthetic experiments emerging in popular culture. The major problem was that having opened the Pandora's box of modern cultural developments to critical scrutiny, the earlier Frankfurt School failed to produce any coherent theory about its concrete functioning. Its heir, the later neocritical school led by Habermas, has tended to abandon the cultural field entirely, preferring to position itself as a sort of messenger or go-between operating at the interface of philosophy, the social sciences, and abstract social theory.

The Frankfurt School does deserve credit for having thematized some of the main areas of concern for contemporary cultural critique, and its early attempts in this direction merit some reconsideration. However, its methodological grid in dealing with them must inevitably impress a contemporary cultural critic as being too coarse-grained to be very helpful. On the other hand, while the methodologies of the current neocritical school are anything but coarse-grained, they have been trained on themes arising at levels rather far removed from concrete cultural processes, attempting to formulate more global or comprehensive theories whose concrete applications remain unclear.

Structuralisms

There can be little doubt that the contributions of structuralism to twentieth-century cultural critique have been profound and far-ranging. More than anything else, structuralism (and its immediate descendant, semiotics) staked out a level of analysis and critique that fell below the threshold of more abstract philosophical reflection but above that of the merely subjective processes of cultural production and interpretation. By insisting that communicable meaning can be produced only in the more or less determinate totality of a system of signs, not just through the romantic heroics of a hermeneutic consciousness, and maintaining that culture is a complex product of the intersections of these various differential systems, structuralism demonstrated that cultural analysis and critique could proceed on a basis that was neither purely subjective and arbitrary nor exclusively political, economic, and institutional.

The limitations of structuralism, however, were already apparent in its self-confessed preference for the synchronic over the diachronic, since any shift toward the historical change and transformation of meaning-systems would render its basic methodological premises unstable and questionable. Accordingly, the problem with structuralism has always been that the more one focuses on the interactions among and corresponding alterations in various systems, the more questionable structural analysis appears to be.

Generally speaking, while structural analysis is often an effective starting point for concrete cultural critique, providing an initial definition of a field and a set of interrelated distinctions for approaching it, it is somewhat like a ladder that one must climb and then kick down when one has reached the last rung. As in the case of Barthes's *Mythologies,* structural analyses accomplish little until they are harnessed to a more comprehensive critical enterprise that connects them with some broader conception of ideology, subjectivity-formation, or historical transformation, such as Barthes offers in the second part of this work. However, such a stance, like Barthes's endorsement of a vaguely neo-Marxist orientation, neither directly follows from purely structuralist assumptions nor necessarily requires them. Structuralist analysis, then, certainly calls attention to interrelations of various complex aspects of culture that otherwise would be easily overlooked, but it is at best an important tool in the contemporary critical workshop, which accomplishes nothing until it is employed in the context of a broader task.

Poststructuralisms and Postmodernisms

There is currently a great deal of debate over how exactly to characterize the relation of the various developments in critical discourse as well as in concrete cultural production during the period following the heyday of structuralism. Besides poststructuralism and postmodernism, various terms such as deconstructivism, neostructuralism, late structuralism, neomodernism, and even neo–avant-garde have been proposed. Underlying all these discussions seem to be two convictions shared by all: first, that structuralism and modernism (in some ways the former's aesthetic counterpart) represented a characteristic and crucial phase or stage in the development of twentieth-century culture, and second, that beginning in the 1960s, their rather sophisticated and complex theoretical scaffolding and its aesthetic and practical consequences began to be dismantled, though without jettisoning the remaining pieces entirely. The differences in preferred terminology mostly reflect differing assessments regarding either the degree to which these critical reactions against structuralism and modernism actually represent a novel and (relatively) independent enterprise or the validity of the criticisms of the structural paradigm offered by them.

In the context of such debates, two things should be kept in mind. In the first place, such terms as poststructuralism and postmodernism would have little meaning without presupposing some foil against which they represent reactions. Or as has often been observed on a somewhat different level, deconstruction must first assume a (more or less) determinate structure that requires dismantling. In general, then, such post-movements must be classed with other essentially skeptical moments of intellectual history that are aimed at challenging various dominant assumptions without falling into the trap of themselves affirming yet another position requiring its own skeptical critique. Secondly, however, although poststructuralism and postmodernism for the most part have resisted establishing themselves as an affirmative option in the sense of producing yet another theoretical totality to replace the former one, they have, at a less expansive level of analysis and critique, developed a number of critical strategies that, though something less than a coherently worked-out methodology, must nonetheless now be counted as important and perhaps even indispensable tools in the current critical arsenal.

Viewed in this way, poststructuralism and postmodernism represent more a loose collection of certain ways of framing issues and strategies for approaching them rather than affirmative positions in their own rights. Certainly attempts have been made, both by their practitioners and their critics, to formulate them in such a manner, but such discussions are primarily philosophical in nature and add little to the utility and effectiveness of poststructural and postmodern strategies in the context of cultural critique. It should also be noted that as in the case of semiotics, such strategies and stylistic gestures can accomplish little unless deployed in the context of a broader critical discourse that addresses notions of power, ideology, hegemony, and their effects on the formation of subjectivities and lived cultures.

Cultural Studies

Cultural studies as originally developed and pursued in Great Britain, especially at the Birmingham Centre, represented a relatively well-defined set of positions and research programs. However, its character has rather dramatically changed with its export to other countries with different institutional and political configurations, especially those prevailing in North America; its assimilation of structuralist and poststructuralist strategies from the Continent; its usually only partial rapprochement with empirically based communication studies; and, most recently, its encounter with the partially overlapping projects of various area studies engendered by movements on behalf of cultural diversity. As a result, its currently paradoxical situation, as noted by the former director of the Birmingham Centre, Stuart Hall, is that on the one hand, cultural studies has enjoyed levels of support and a corresponding expansion unimagined by its originators, but on the other, it has lost a good deal of its original focus and definition and now runs the risk of being coopted by its new institutional status.

The major advantage of contemporary cultural studies is that it has continued to focus attention on popular culture and everyday lived experience, while remaining open to developments of critical strategies that may assist in their analysis and critique, and insisting that beyond these, broader issues concerning power configurations and political commitments to intervention remain on the agenda. The major question now facing cultural studies, however, is whether or not it will ultimately be absorbed into some combination of more traditional literary studies, communications theory and research, and various area studies. With Marxist and more generally leftist positions now on the wane (at least temporarily), cultural studies remains the only cultural discourse with a tradition of broaching, in a substantial way, the issue of increasing economic and class disparities both in and among existing nations and of mapping them onto the other types of social differences highlighted by the various area studies. Although its earlier allegiance to analysis and critique based on concepts of class as this category functions in various national socioeconomic configurations might seem dated in the more complex postmodern context of international capitalism, as Jameson among others suggests, such issues will not go away simply because they fail to fit the paradigms of the various discourses of diversity. If the discourse of cultural studies is to have a viable future, it must not lose its general orientation toward theoretical openness and practical critique and intervention trained on existing socioeconomic differences as they are reflected in the everyday lives of contemporary human beings. And it must not fail to address these issues in light of the recent and dramatic socioeconomic changes on a global scale and of the new communications technologies supporting them. If it responds in this way, it will have much to offer the cultural critic of the new millennium; if it does not, we are likely to see the emergence of a new critical discourse that will do so in its stead.

Index